THE TOWNSHIPS
map on page 122
FURTHER AFIELD
map on page 184
THE GARDEN ROUTE
map on page 208
SOUTHERN SUBURBS
map on page 128
Robben Island
0 10 km
0 10 miles
Robben Island
Bloubergstrand
Table View
Milnerton
Table Bay
Cape Town
Clifton Bay
Camps Bay
Koeël Bay
Table Mtn 1073
Robben Island
Breakwater
East Pier
Victoria Basin
Elbow
South Arm
Duncan Dock
Eastern Mole
Mole
Main Quay
Tanker Basin
Jackson Wharf
Repair Quay
Ben Schoeman Dock
Elliot Basin
Small Craft Harbour
Sturrock Dock
Ocean
Container Depot
PAARDEN
Auckland St
Neptune
Street
Calcutta St
Section St
Cape Town International Convention Centre
Duncan Road
Artscape Theatre
Malan House
Airways Terminal
Civic Centre
Cape Town Railway Station
Hertzog Blvd
Heerengracht
Coen Steytler Ave
D. Pirow St
Table Bay Boulevard
FORESHORE
Esplanade
Beach
Lwr Church St
Tide St
Rd
The Castle of Good Hope
New Market Street
Sir Lowry Rd
Francis St
Woodstock
Strand St
Salt River
Voortrekker Road
Albert Road
Victoria Road
Foundry Rd
Kent St
Malta Road
Hanover
Chapel St
Keizergracht
Tennant St
Cape Technikon
ZONNEBLOEM
Eastern Boulevard
TRAFALGAR PARK
Barton St
Woodstock Hospital
Plein St
Essex St
Devon St
Salt River
Hopkins St
Durham Ave
Burns Rd
Cecil Rd
Tower Main
Liesbeek
LIESBEEK PARK
Justisie Street
Constitution Street
De Waal Cres
Lever St
Salisbury St
Chamberlain St
The Ave
Victoria Road
Queens Pk
Heere St
Perth
Park Rd
Chester St
Palmerston Rd
Cambridge St
Premier Rd
QUEENS PARK
Eastern Boulevard
Selbourne Rd
Rhodes Ave
De Waal Crescent
DEVIL'S PEAK ESTATE
Gardenia Ave
Nazareth House
Derry
St James St
Street Road
Browning Rd
MOSLEM CEMETERY
Groote Schuur Hospital
Main Road
Station Rd
Trill
Main Rd
Nuttall Rd
Florence Ave
Observatory
Willow
Stuttens Road
Dane Street
Settlers Way
Mowbray
MOWBRAY
Prince of Wales Blockhouse
Queen's Blockhouse
Tafelberg Road
Table Mountain National Park
Mount Prospect
Minor Peak 855
King's Blockhouse
Rhodes Memorial
Mostert's Mill
Avenue Rd
Drive
Rhodes Ave
St Peters Rd
Liesbeek Pkwy
Cecil Rd
Road
ROSEBANK
Woolsack Drive
Main
Lower Nursery
Rosebank
Devil's Peak 986
GROOTE SCHUUR ESTATE
Rhodes
Walk
NEWLANDS FOREST
University of Cape Town
Stanley Rd
Belmont
Rondebosch
RONDEBOSCH
Kirstenbosch National Botanical Garden
Mountain
Eastern Table

INSIGHT GUIDES

CAPE TOWN

APA PUBLICATIONS
Part of the Langenscheidt Publishing Group

How to Use This Book

This book is carefully structured both to convey an understanding of the city and its culture and to guide readers through its attractions and activities:

◆ The Best Of section at the front of the book helps you to prioritize. The first spread contains all the Top Sights, while the Editor's Choice details unique experiences, the best buys or other recommendations.

◆ To understand Cape Town, you need to know something of its past. The city's history and culture are described in authoritative essays written by specialists in their fields who have lived in and documented the city for many years.

◆ The Places section details all the attractions worth seeing. The main places of interest are coordinated by number with the maps.

◆ Each chapter includes lists of recommended shops, restaurants, bars and cafés.

◆ Photographs throughout the book are chosen not only to illustrate geography and buildings, but also to convey the moods of the city and the life of its people.

◆ The Travel Tips section includes all the practical information you will need, divided into four key sections: transport, accommodation, activities (including nightlife, events, tours and sports), and an A–Z of practical tips. Information may be located quickly by using the index on the back cover flap of the book.

◆ A detailed street atlas is included at the back of the book, with all restaurants, bars, cafés and hotels plotted for your convenience.

Places and Sights

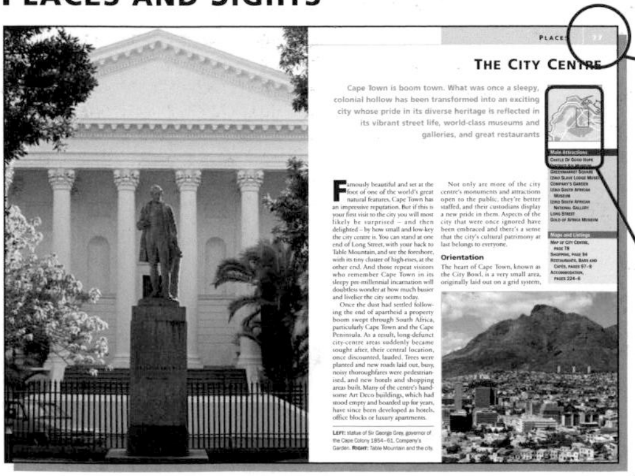

Chapters are **colour-coded** for ease of use. Each neighbourhood has a designated colour corresponding to the orientation map on the inside front cover.

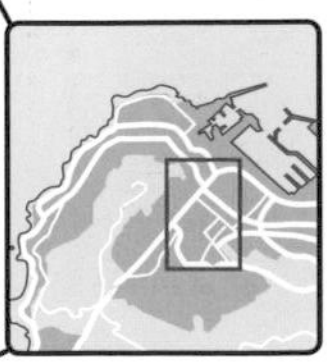

A locator map pinpoints the specific area covered in each chapter.

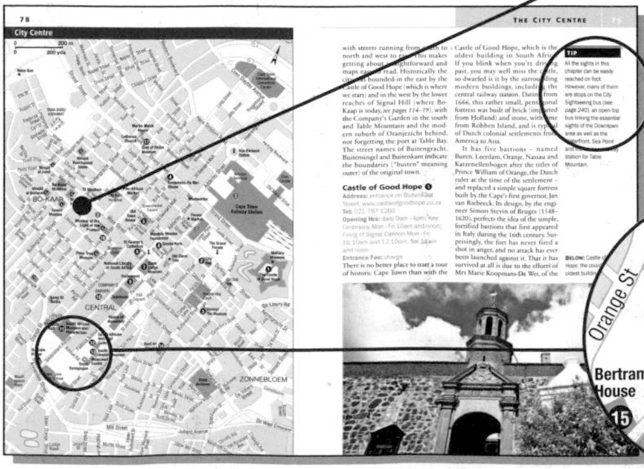

Margin tips provide extra snippets of information, whether it's a practical tip, a whimsical quote, an historical fact or advice on shopping and eating.

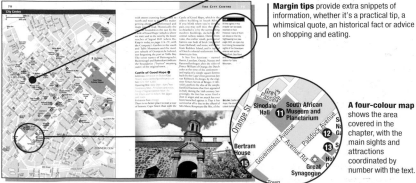

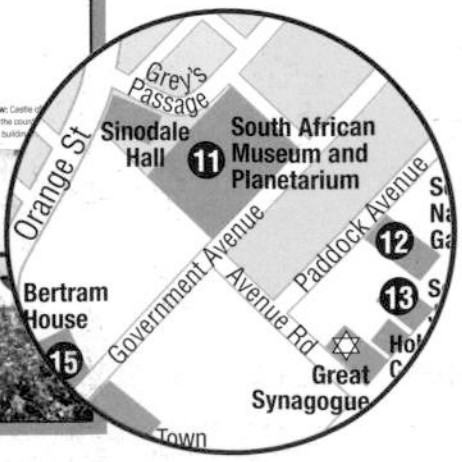

A four-colour map shows the area covered in the chapter, with the main sights and attractions coordinated by number with the text.

PHOTO FEATURES

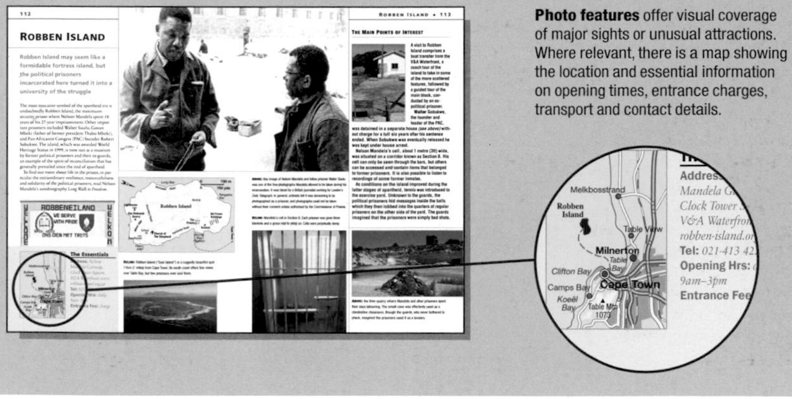

Photo features offer visual coverage of major sights or unusual attractions. Where relevant, there is a map showing the location and essential information on opening times, entrance charges, transport and contact details.

SHOPPING AND RESTAURANT LISTINGS

Lookout Deck
Lookout Beach. Tel: 044-533 1379. www.lookout.co.za
Open: L & D daily. **$–$$**
This superb beachfront restaurant offers great sea views, and there is a good chance of spotting dol-phins frolicking in the

Shopping listings provide details of the best shops in each area. **Restaurant listings** give the establishment's contact details, opening times and price category, followed by a useful review. Bars and cafés are also covered here. The coloured dot and grid reference refers to the atlas section at the back of the book.

TRAVEL TIPS

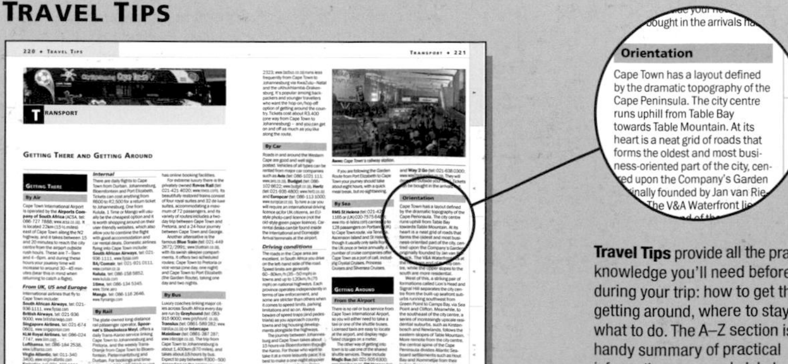

Travel Tips provide all the practical knowledge you'll need before and during your trip: how to get there, getting around, where to stay and what to do. The A–Z section is a handy summary of practical information, arranged alphabetically.

Contents

Introduction

The Best of Cape Town 6
The Mother City 17
Cape Communities 19

History

Decisive Dates 26
The Making of Cape Town 31
From Apartheid to Democracy 39

Features

Cooking up a Feast 55
Creative Cape Town 61

Insights

MINI FEATURES

Architecture 67
What's Happening on the Waterfront? 106
Conserving Table Mountain National Park 150

PHOTO FEATURES

Sport Mad, Sport Crazy 52
Robben Island 112
The Cape in Bloom 156
Cape Wine 202

Places

Introduction 73
The City Centre 77
The Victoria & Alfred Waterfront 101
Bo-Kaap 114
The Townships 121
The Southern Suburbs 127
Table Mountain National Park 147
The Cape Peninsula 159
Further Afield 183
The Garden Route 206

LEFT: Camps Bay.

Travel Tips

TRANSPORT

Getting There **220**
- By Air **220**
- By Rail **220**
- By Bus **220**
- By Car **221**
- By Sea **221**

Getting Around **221**
- From the Airport **221**
- Orientation **221**
- By Bus **222**
- By Car **222**
- By Train **222**
- By Taxi **222**
- Cycling **222**
- Motorbike Hire **222**

ACCOMMODATION

Choosing a Hotel **223**
City Centre and the City Bowl **224**
Victoria & Alfred Waterfront **226**
Southern Suburbs **228**
Atlantic Seaboard **229**
False Bay **230**
Further Afield **231**
The Garden Route **233**

ACTIVITIES

Festivals **234**
The Arts **235**
Nightlife **237**
Sightseeing Tours **239**
Sports **240**
Children's Activities **241**

A–Z

Admission Charges **242**
Budgeting for Your Trip **242**
Children **243**
Climate **243**
Crime and Safety **243**
Customs Regulations **244**
Disabled Travellers **244**
Electricity **244**
Embassies/Consulates **244**
Emergencies **245**
Gay and Lesbian **244**
Health and Medical Care **245**
Internet **246**
Lost Property **246**
Media **246**
Money **246**
Opening Hours **247**
Postal Services **247**
Public Holidays **247**
Religious Services **247**
Student Travellers **247**
Tax **248**
Telephones **248**
Time Zone **248**
Toilets **248**
Tour Operators **248**
Tourist Information **249**
Visas and Passports **249**
What to Bring **249**
Women Travellers **249**

FURTHER READING

History and Biography **250**
Culture **250**
Fiction **250**
Natural History **250**
Food and Wine **250**
Special Interest **250**
Other Insight Guides **250**

Maps

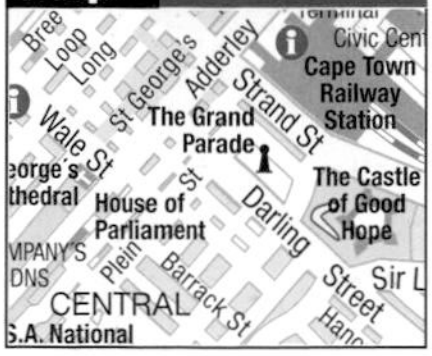

Cape Town **74–5**
City Centre **78**
Victoria & Alfred Waterfront **104**
Robben Island **112**
Bo-Kaap **116**
The Townships **122**
Southern Suburbs **128**
Kirstenbosch National Botanical Gardens **137**
Constantia Valley **139**
Table Mountain National Park **148**
Cape Peninsula **160**
Simon's Town **172**
Further Afield **184**
Stellenbosch **186**
The Garden Route **208**
Map Legend **251**
Street Atlas **252–62**

Inside front cover: Cape Town Orientation Map.
Inside back cover: Table Mountain.

THE BEST OF CAPE TOWN: TOP SIGHTS

At a glance, the Cape Town attractions you can't afford to miss, from Table Mountain to Cape Point and Long Street to the V&A Waterfront, as well as surrounding highlights

△ **Long Street** Funky, bohemian and just a touch insalubrious, Long Street is the heart of Cape Town's backpacker and night-owl scenes, lined with pubs, restaurants, craft shops and alternative boutiques that combine a cosmopolitan outlook with a distinctly African flair. *See page 93.*

△ **Cape of Good Hope** The southern third of the Peninsula, now part of Table Mountain National Park, terminates at spectacular Cape Point, with its historic lighthouse overlooking the windswept crags and wave-battered beaches below. *See page 168.*

▷ **Victoria & Alfred Waterfront** It's a shopper's paradise, for sure, with literally hundreds of boutiques, supermarkets, bookstores and craft stalls to explore, but the Waterfront is also a great spot for a relaxed harbourside drink or seafood meal. *See page 101.*

△ **Robben Island** South Africa's Alcatraz was a place of incarceration from 1658 to the 1980s, when activists such as Nelson Mandela were exiled there. Guided tours by former inmates invoke the racial divisions of the apartheid era. *See page 112.*

△ **Table Mountain** Cape Town's crowning glory, rising a kilometre above Table Bay, this omnipresent mountain provides a spectacular backdrop to the city centre and a sensational vantage point for views all over the peninsula. *See page 147.*

▽ **Kirstenbosch Botanical Garden** Set on the eastern slopes of Table Mountain, this peaceful suburban retreat, criss-crossed with walking trails, is studded with salmon-pink proteas and other fynbos plants unique to the Cape Floral Kingdom. *See page 135.*

△ **Two Oceans Aquarium** This superb central aquarium is home to more than 3,000 marine creatures, ranging from sharks and rays to seals, penguins and the rare black oyster-catcher. *See page 104.*

▽ **Camps Bay** The trendiest beach in Cape Town, nestled below the striking Twelve Apostles formation, sandy Camps Bay has a lovely Atlantic seafront lined with chic street cafés and seafood restaurants. *See page 163.*

△ **Groot Constantia** The Cape viniculture industry started at this pretty estate in the southern suburbs – notable today for its fine Cape Dutch architecture, fascinating museum, and a selection of award-winning wines to match any produced in the country. *See page 139.*

▽ **Stellenbosch**
South Africa's second-oldest town, Stellenbosch, retains an architectural integrity lacking in its older sibling, and it is also the hub of the Cape wine industry, surrounded by historic estates and the ancient pinnacles of the Cape Fold Mountains. *See page 185.*

THE BEST OF CAPE TOWN: EDITOR'S CHOICE

Setting priorities, saving money, unique attractions... here, at a glance, are our recommendations, plus some tips and tricks even the locals won't always know

BEST MUSEUMS

- **District Six Museum** Memorabilia, documents, personal accounts and recreations of homes and businesses evoke the flavour and culture of this characterful area, famously destroyed by apartheid's Group Areas Act. *See page 81.*
- **Iziko Koopmans De Wet Museum** This elegantly furnished 18th-century town house conveys a vivid sense of the comfortable lifestyle of wealthy early European settlers. *See page 83.*
- **Iziko Bo-Kaap Museum** Also in a fine period town house, this museum documents the Muslim contribution to the development of the city. *See page 117.*
- **Irma Stern Museum** Visit this museum in the Southern Suburbs for an almost private view of the painter's home and studio. *See page 129.*
- **Gold of Africa Museum** A dazzling display of traditional gold jewellery and ceremonial objects from West and South Africa. *See page 95.*
- **Iziko South African Museum** Come here to learn more about the San, the original bushmen of the area, in particular their mysterious rock art. *See page 89.*

ABOVE: Chapman's Peak Drive offers stunning coastal views.

BEST VIEWS

- **Bloubergstrand** A short drive north of the city centre, this is the place from where to take a definitive shot of Table Mountain towering above the bay. *See page 197.*
- **Chapman's Peak Drive** For truly scenic motoring, drive to Noordhoek via the Atlantic Seaboard and Hout Bay. The best views unfold as you enter Chapman's Peak Drive. The road soars up the cliff face, defying the vertiginous drop to the sea below. *See page 167.*
- **Signal Hill** Another fantastic drive, this runs from Kloof Nek below Lion's Head past a succession of viewpoints facing the city bowl below Table Mountain and the harbour. It is best at dusk when the city is lit up. *See page 148.*
- **Best hotel views** For a room with a great view, book into the Cape Grace on the Waterfront, or the Twelve Apostles on Victoria Road between Bakoven and Llandudno. *See pages 226 and 229.*

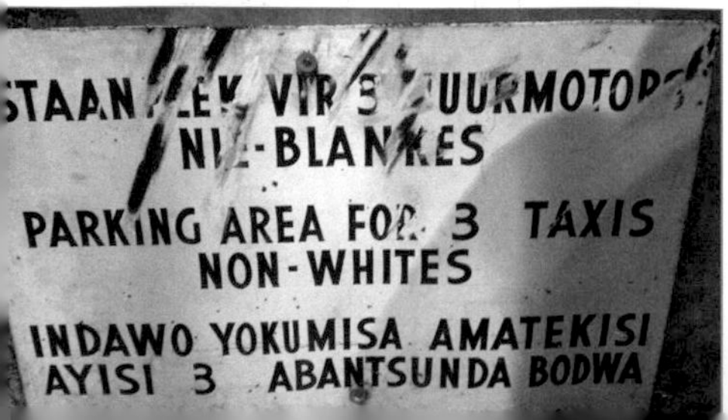
PARKING AREA FOR 3 TAXIS
NON-WHITES
INDAWO YOKUMISA AMATEKISI
AYISI 3 ABANTSUNDA BODWA

LEFT: an apartheid-era sign on display in the District Six Museum.

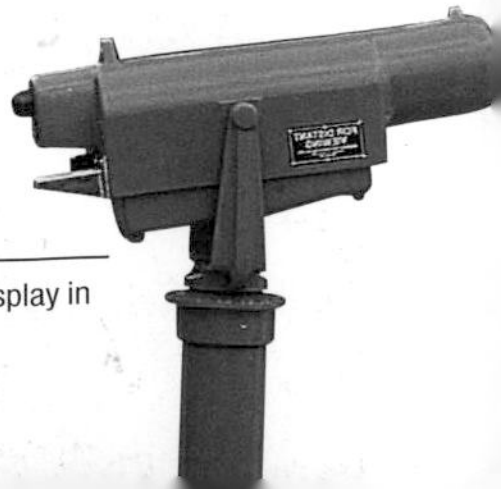

CAPE TOWN FOR FAMILIES

These attractions are popular with children, though not all will suit every age group.

- **Predator-feeding time, Two Oceans Aquarium** Make sure you're here at 3pm, feeding time for the seals, sharks and other marine predators. *See page 104.*
- **Table Mountain Cableway** For most children, being whisked up Table Mountain in a revolving pod beats a sweaty hike up any day. *See page 149.*
- **World Of Birds** A profusion of colourful indigenous and exotic birds is housed in the walk-in aviaries here, and kids also love the semi-tame monkeys and meerkats. *See page 166.*
- **Market Square, V&A Waterfront** Mime artists, musicians, clowns... there's almost always something child-friendly going on at the Waterfront's main square. *See page 103.*
- **Scratch Patch** Children (and adults) can learn more about South Africa's glittering gemstones at Scratch Patch on the Waterfront and in Simon's Town. *See pages 105 and 174.*

For more information, see Children's Activities, page 241.

ABOVE RIGHT: performers at Market Square, V&A Waterfront.
BELOW: take a boat to Seal Island to see Cape fur seals.

FUN FESTIVALS AND EVENTS

- **New Year** The year kicks off with the Cape Town Minstrel Festival. *See page 234.*
- **Cape Town Jazz Festival** A dazzling annual international jazz festival. *See page 234.*
- **Stellenbosch Wine Festival** Held over five days in July, this offers the opportunity to taste the produce of 140 leading Cape Estates. *See page 187.*
- **Cape Town Comedy Festival** Local and international stand-up comedians keep Cape Town chuckling throughout September. *See page 234.*
- **Kite Festival** Catch the Cape's south-easter at Muizenberg in September or October. *See page 234.*

BEST WILDLIFE

- **Whale-watching** Hermanus is the best place for land-based whale-watching in season (May–Nov), but False Bay can also be good. *See page 194.*
- **Seal Island** Regular 45-minute boat trips run from Hout Bay to Seal Island, which supports 75,000 Cape fur seals, as well as marine birds. *See page 207.*
- **Cape of Good Hope** This vast tract of fynbos on the southern peninsula is home to endemics such as Cape mountain zebra, bontebok and the lovely orange-breasted sunbird. *See page 168.*
- **Aquila Private Reserve** Set in the dry scrub of the Hex River Mountains, an upmarket camp serves what is the closest "Big Five" reserve to Cape Town. *See page 194.*
- **Boulders Beach** Few wildlife encounters are quite so endearing as meeting the strutting penguins that breed here. *See page 169.*

Best Beaches

- **Clifton** Clifton's four beaches, backed by the Twelve Apostles, are the most beautiful and also good for people-watching. *See page 162.*
- **Muizenberg** The best beach for swimming is not Clifton, but Muizenberg, on the False Bay coast, where the water temperatures are warmer. *See page 176.*
- **Llandudno** on the Atlantic Seaboard is considered one of the best places for experienced surfers. *See page 164.*
- **Beaches in Cape of Good Hope** Several superb places for a remote picnic here – wild scenery, no buildings, few people, and a chance of antelope wandering on the beach or whales out at sea. *See page 168.*
- **St James** Strong currents make swimming inadvisable on many beaches, but there are tidal pools where children can splash about safely. St James, renowned for its colourful beach huts, is one of the best places for tidal pools. *See page 176.*

Best Walks

- **Lion's Head** For a short but dramatic walk, follow the path spiralling up to the summit of Lion's Head. It offers a 360° panorama of the ocean, mountain and city. *See page 151.*
- **Platteklip Gorge** For a sense of achievement, ascend Table Mountain on foot via this fairly simple zig-zag route of 3km (2 miles). *See page 151.*
- **Kirstenbosch** As well as offering botanical trails, Kirstenbosch is a springboard for hikes into the Table Mountain National Park. Skeleton Gorge is one of the most popular. *See page 135.*
- **Noordhoek** For a long bracing walk on the beach it is hard to beat Noordhoek, but take care here because it is also one of the Peninsula's remotest spots. *See page 167.*
- **Hoerikwaggo Trail** For serious hikers, this five-day organised hike, designed by the Table Mountain National Park, runs from the city to Cape Point. Accommodation is available en route. *See page 152.*

Above Left: the peninsula's stunning coastline. **Above Right:** Kirstenbosch National Botanical Garden. **Below:** St James.

Best Wine Estates

- **Vergelegen** Founded in 1700, this premier estate boasts some fine period architecture and superb award-winning wines. *See page 189.*
- **Boschendal** First planted with vines in 1685, this great all-rounder near Franschhoek has a lovely setting, a period-furnished manor house dating to 1812, and yummy French-style 'Pique Niques' on the lawns. *See page 191.*
- **Cabrière** This small estate outside Franschhoek produces world-class sparkling wines, opened at wine-tasting sessions with a sword! *See page 190.*
- **Laborie** Home to the renowned KWV collective, this vineyard in suburban Paarl dates to 1691 and has a matching old-world ambience. *See page 191.*
- **Spier Estate** Though it lacks the gracious ambience of the above, this populist estate south of Stellenbosch, with its varied facilities and activities, is tailor-made for family outings. *See page 189.*

Best Architectural Highlights

- **The Castle of Good Hope** The oldest building in Cape Town and arguably where the modern history of South Africa began. *See page 79.*
- **Cape Town Stadium** Future generations may raise a brow or three, but for now all eyes are on this spanking new stadium, built for the 2010 FIFA World Cup. *See page 109.*
- **Manor House, Groot Constantia** This Cape Dutch gem was built by Simon van der Stel, one of the first governors of the Cape Colony. *See page 139.*
- **Village Museum, Stellenbosch** This museum comprises a trio of early Cape houses, all fully restored and open to the public. *See page 186.*
- **Church Street, Tulbagh** Lined with National Monuments, this street houses South Africa's largest concentration of Cape Dutch buildings. *See page 192.*

Left: the Vergelegen wine estate. **Above:** Castle of Good Hope.

Money-Saving Tips

Cape Town Pass Despite intermittent talk of creating a two-tier system with higher admission fees for foreign visitors, at present entry to museums and other attractions is low compared with major European and American cities.

However, organised tours to the Winelands and along the Cape Peninsula, although plentiful, are fairly expensive. An alternative, if you don't have your own transport, is to buy the 6-day Cape Town Pass for R750 (you can also get cheaper 1-day, 2-day and 3-day passes), which offers free entrance to over 50 of the best attractions, a tour of the Winelands and a day exploring the Peninsula.

Some activities are included too, such as horse riding on the beach, sand-boarding and a harbour cruise. If you order online before you go, (www.capetownpass.co.za), you can have the pass delivered directly to your hotel and will also be given a mobile phone to use for the duration of your stay.

Getting Around Sedan taxis are relatively expensive, but due to the skeletal public transport system essential for anyone without their own vehicle. If you take a taxi to somewhere such as Table Mountain or Kirstenbosch, you can ask the taxi driver to wait, though there is now a charge for this, so it would be cheaper to take the driver's phone number and call when you are ready.

If you want to explore the False Bay coast of the Cape Peninsula, consider going by train (a direct service runs from Cape Town Railway Station), but for safety reasons be sure to travel in the restaurant car.

A very affordable way of getting around is the City Sightseeing bus *(see page 240)*, a red roofless double-decker that connects 17 top sights in the city bowl and on the northern peninsula, with departures every 20 minutes. Full details are available on the website, which also has online booking facilities.

122
120

THE MOTHER CITY

Once a magnet for all manner of European migrants, from fortune-hunters to political refugees, Cape Town is now South Africa's most popular tourist focus, attracting 80 percent of the country's visitors

Called the Mother City, Cape Town is South Africa's oldest European settlement, strategically situated on a deep sheltered bay at the south-western tip of the continent. An irresistible draw to its founders was the iconic Table Mountain, which formed an important beacon to early mariners, and was known to the local Xhosa as *Umlindi Welingizunu*, "Watcher of the South". To this day, in spite of the hustle and bustle of modern city living, the majestic presence of Table Mountain impinges on the visitor's consciousness as a South African emblem more potent than wine, gold, wildlife or rugby.

Come to Cape Town to see its mountain, beaches, wine estates and unique flora, and to experience life in the townships, which embody such a rich chunk of South Africa's cultural, historical and political identity. But come too to eat in its array of superb and affordable restaurants, to explore the colourful traditional Muslim quarter of Bo-Kaap, and to see the gracious Cape Dutch architectural heritage that is best represented in nearby Stellenbosch.

Cape Town is rich in interesting diversions provided by its creative and entrepreneurial inhabitants. It has first-class bookshops and antique shops, vintage clothing stores and many excellent and stylish hotels and guest-houses run with pride and care. Churches, mosques and synagogues reflect the city's varied cultural heritage, while a full calendar of festivals celebrates everything from food, wine, art and music to antiques, cars and flowers.

Further afield, hire a car to explore the scenic West Coast National Park or the Overberg (for whale-watching), or follow the famous Garden Route through a stunning landscape of coastal lagoons, fynbos and rainforest. ❑

PRECEDING PAGES: the rainbow houses of Chiappini Street in the Bo-Kaap area; Camps Bay. **LEFT:** performer at Cape Town Festival. **ABOVE LEFT:** proteas at the flower market at Trafalgar Place. **ABOVE RIGHT:** the brooding bulk of Table Mountain at dusk dominates Cape Town.

CAPE COMMUNITIES

Cape Town has one of South Africa's most diverse populations. And in spite of their differences, the majority of its 3.5 million inhabitants wouldn't want to live anywhere else on Earth

At first sight, Cape Town seems very much a tale of two cities: one in which affluent whites enjoy a leisurely, luxurious lifestyle, with access to good health care and education, and another in which the overwhelming majority of blacks live on next to nothing in the shacks of the Cape Flats, visible on any journey to and from the airport. The city centre itself seems to fall into two halves: the eastern side, around the Castle of Good Hope, run-down and black, the western side prosperous and white. The two halves meet at Adderley Street, which, like much of the city centre, now has a racially integrated look and feel.

But spend more time here, visit the different areas and start to understand the many strands in Cape Town's history through its museums and culture, and you will notice that it is not two cities, but many cities. There is perhaps no city that is more of a melting pot of different groups and communities. The historical background to this diversity is often tragic, one of imported slaves, refugees, economic migrants and displaced peoples through the centuries. As the so-called Mother City, from which settlers spread north, it has also become the Mother City of Africa, to which many groups from elsewhere on the continent come in search of a living. It is a vibrant, cosmopolitan city shaped by an amazing range of communities.

A good place to go to see genuine racial integration is Observatory in the Southern Suburbs, a young and funky area close to the University where a liberal attitude prevails.

Local politics

Historically Cape Town has had a liberal political tradition, shaped by its strong English-speaking community, who enjoy poking fun at the Afrikaners' gung-ho chauvinism. The seat of parliament, and packed with Victorian public buildings, the city still has an unmistakably

LEFT: Huguenot Memorial Museum in Franschhoek.
RIGHT: inside a shebeen (African bar) in the Knysna township, where cultural tours take place.

European feel, which is somewhat scorned by Johannesburg but loved by visitors and home-grown liberals. But the Western Cape to which Cape Town belongs is strongly Afrikaans and tied traditionally to the National Party.

As a legacy of slavery, the Cape also has a large coloured population, either of Asian or mixed descent, who in the first democratic election of 1994 voted overwhelmingly for the National Party, fearful of losing their relative privileges under the ANC. It wasn't until the 2004 elections that the ANC won the Western Cape. And they lost it again in 2009, when the provincial vote went to the Democratic Alliance, led by Cape Town's outspoken mayor Helen Zille, and the Western Cape became the only one of South Africa's nine provinces not to fall under ANC control.

The affluent white community

Cape Town is widely perceived as being a white, English-speaking city. It certainly isn't in terms of numbers *(see box, below)*, but it is easy for visitors to get that impression while exploring Kirstenbosch or Groot Schuur in the Southern Suburbs, soaking up the sun at Camps Bay, hiking on Table Mountain or dining alfresco on the Waterfront. All these are traditional stomping grounds for English-speaking whites and represent a comfortable lifestyle that is easy to like and link into even if you're only visiting for a short while. What other major city offers up a virtually traffic jam-free daily journey to and from work and the possibility of being able to sit on the beach at five minutes past five on a Friday afternoon?

Vital Statistics

The last census, held in 2001, revealed the following statistics concerning the racial composition of Cape Town:
Black Africans 31.68 percent
Coloureds 48.13 percent
Whites 18.75 percent
Indian/Asian 1.43 percent
The average annual income of working adults was:
Black Africans $2,025
Coloureds $3,459
Indians/Asians $6,648
Whites $10,579
Some 29.5 percent of people were officially unemployed.

The Southern Suburbs, with their oak-lined roads of spacious family homes, excellent private schools such as Bishops and Rondebosch Boys,' Anglican churches and sedate but upmarket shopping centres such as Dean Street Mall, are prosperous in an established, old-moneyed way. A little further out is Constantia, one of the wealthiest suburbs of Cape Town, with a mix of Edwardian and modern homes set in leafy grounds behind big walls, maintained by gardeners, cooks and maids. Social cliques are based on snobbish clubs and old school ties.

Equally expensive, but brasher and more youthful, Camps Bay, with its restaurant-covered pavements and stunning mountain backdrop, contains some of the most expensive real estate in South Africa. Here the Capetonians' preoccupation with the body beautiful reaches new heights. The atmosphere is superficially relaxed and easy, and staff in the café-bars won't give a hoot if you are wearing a bathing costume, but you'll need to make sure it's a good one, that your shorts are the right length and your body's toned and trim. If you can't own up to one, or all, of these, you may not get a seat at all.

In general, English-speaking Capetonians prospered under Afrikaner-inspired apartheid. When the new South Africa dawned, many of those who could afford it dusted down their

British passports and connections and left the country altogether. Those who remained are keen to retain their advantages but, having done so for the first decade of democracy, are also willing to invest in the country's future, if only by paying their taxes and parking fines in a responsible way.

Afrikaners in the Northern Suburbs

For Capetonians, the so-called "Boerewors Curtain" begins as you head out along the evocatively named Settlers Way or Voortrekker Road towards the Northern Suburbs with their predominantly white Afrikaner population. Many people here are descendants of farming families who moved to the cities after World War II. Suburbs such as Parow and Goodwood, where people are poorer and less educated, are perceived as right-wing, but even these are gradually accepting the change to the status quo and attitudes are softening.

Left: inhabitant of Knysna township. **Above:** browsing at the flea market in Long Street, Cape Town. Long Street buzzes with shoppers during the day, while its bars and clubs are a focal point for nightlife.

More affluent suburbs, such as Plattekloof, Tygervalley and Welgemoed, off the N1 freeway, are modern and bristling with new property developments, including upmarket shopping malls such as the Tygervalley Centre and Canal Walk at Century City, set to rival the Waterfront as Cape Town's premier leisure complex, making it unnecessary for locals to venture into the centre of Cape Town at all.

> *A high profile convert to the New South Africa, Melanie Verwoerd – granddaughter of apartheid architect Hendrik Verwoerd – joined the ANC in 1991 and later became the youngest woman to serve in the South African parliament.*

The Northern Suburbs are widely regarded as the territory of the traditional Afrikaner, of *braais*, beer and rugby and right-wing politics, but "nuwe Afrikaners" or progressive freethinkers are found everywhere from Durbanville to Stellenbosch University to the Boland. This reformation is rooted in a history of dissident

Afrikaans literature from the 1960s "Sestigers" movement, characterised by André Brink's *Kennis van die Aand* ("Knowledge of the Night"), a sensitive attempt to explore the colour bar and a book that was banned for many years.

Many younger white Afrikaners have engaged deeply and radically with the transition process and are highly committed to creating a strong and successful society for all. Desmond Tutu has remarked on how Afrikaners who were once bitterly opposed to the ANC have generally been more ready to embrace the new South Africa than English-speaking liberals. He puts this down to Afrikaners having no liberal tradition and therefore no interest in a middle ground.

Township living

In spite of the ending of apartheid, most blacks in Cape Town continue to live in the townships

The Huguenots of Franschhoek

The Huguenots were French Protestants and members of the Reformed Church established in 1550 by John Calvin. Persecuted for their religious beliefs by Louis IX, many left France for England, America or Holland. Organised emigration of Huguenots to the Cape occurred in 1688–9, following the example of individual Huguenots who had already made the journey, such as François Villion (1671) and the brothers François and Guillaume du Toit (1686).

By 1692 a total of 201 French Huguenots had arrived at the Cape. Most of them settled around the town of Franschhoek ("French Corner"), some 70km (43 miles) outside Cape Town *(see page 190)*, where many farms still bear their original French names (such as La Motte, Bien Donné and Grande Provence). The skills of the Huguenots – many of whom had left vineyards behind in France – contributed to the development of the local winemaking industry.

Simon van der Stel, the Dutch commander of the Cape at the time, insisted that the immigrants use Dutch rather than French for instruction and worship, and so spoken French disappeared within a century. But many old Afrikaner families have French first names such as Etienne, Jean, André, Marie, Jacques, Pierre and Louis, and French surnames such as Du Toit, Le Roux, De Villiers, Labuschagne *(pronounced La-boo-skag-nee)* and Marais are also common.

in which they were confined by the Group Areas Act of 1950. This is largely due to economic necessity, but also because for the time being most township-dwellers prefer to stick to their own people, in spite of the inconveniences of township life. This is much less the case in Johannesburg, a much larger, more dynamic city, where a burgeoning black middle class has left Soweto and moved to the city's prosperous northern suburbs. Cape Town's black middle class is smaller and less confident, often complaining of having no suitable place to go.

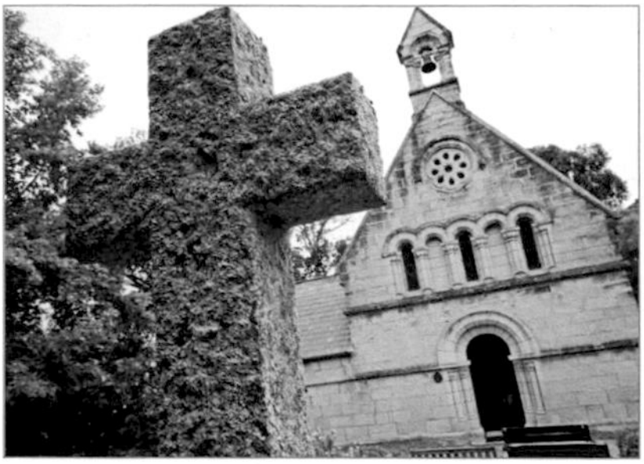

Far Left: discover Huguenots' origins. **Left:** Huguenots building homesteads after immigrating to South Africa. **Top:** township along the Meiringspoort Pass, Little Karoo region. **Above:** replica Norman church, Belvidere.

The biggest advantage of life in a township is the strong sense of community and the vibrant outdoor life. Basic services and facilities have improved dramatically since 1994, with electricity, telephones and water supplies (at least in the form of a stand pipe) reaching more and more homes each year.

Unemployment, however, remains very high. Most township dwellers rely on the informal economy – selling merchandise on the pavement – to make a living, and with no state benefits to fall back on, vast numbers of people are perpetually on the bread line. Initiatives to open up the townships to outsiders and create wealth include township tours for tourists and craft initiatives. But crime and violence are still rife. In some areas rival gangs hold sway and rough justice is meted out by vigilante groups.

Perhaps because of this, religion has become an important focus in many people's lives. Popular are the (various) African Indigenous

Churches (AIC), which broke away from the mainstream denominations in the 1880s and still operate independently from them today. Key features of their faith include a belief in prayer healing and baptism by total immersion, along with a general prohibition on tobacco, alcohol, medication and pork. Many elements of traditional African religion inform the AIC belief system. Healing and religion are closely interrelated and there is a strong belief in faith-healers. The biggest churches have several faith-healers, with constantly overcrowded consulting rooms, who sell their own range of herbal treatments.

The Cape Coloured community

"Coloured", originally pejorative but now used widely and no longer regarded as offensive, is the official term for South Africans of mixed descent. The Cape Coloureds population group is the third-largest population group in the country and today numbers just over three million. Coloureds (as they are usually called) live primarily in and around the Western Cape with subcultures existing within the broad grouping: Cape Coloureds, Griquas and Cape Malays.

The coloured community has diverse origins. Dutch colonials in the Cape began importing slaves from as early as 1658. The slaves came from elsewhere in Africa (the coasts of East and West Africa) and from islands in the Indian and Atlantic oceans (Cape Verde, Guinea Bissau, Mauritius and Madagascar). Forebears were also local to the Cape: Khoi, San, Xhosa and white Europeans, especially Dutch, German and English along with Spanish and Portuguese sailors. The Cape Malay has Indian, Arab, Malagasy, Chinese and Malay blood. The Griquas, who have a strong sense of identity, come from the Northern Cape. They are descended from Khoikhoi and white ancestors who lived about 200 years ago.

Coloured workers were traditionally fishermen, farm labourers and servants. Today, many are farm labourers working on farms across the Boland and Western Cape. Gradually more and more people from the coloured community are taking their rightful places in politics, commerce, industry, education and the arts. Coloured folklore and music have become an integral part of the cultural scene in South Africa.

After being forced out of District Six and older Cape Malay settlements in Newlands, Claremont and Simon's Town, coloured populations were relocated to the Cape Flats, Mitchells Plain, Bonteheuwel, Elsies River and Lavender Hill. Most coloured workers in Cape Town still live on the Cape Flats.

The living idiomatic heart of Afrikaans is coloured and not white, owing something to the work of coloured writer Adam Small *(Kitaar my Kruis* and *Kanna Hy Ko Hystoe)* and District Sixer Richard Rive, whose 1986 novel *Buckingham Palace District Six* has been assigned as a set work in schools in the Western Cape.

Gay Cape Town

South Africa's constitution ensures the protection of gay civil rights and Cape Town is fast rivalling Sydney as a "pink" destination of choice, with a large number of gay-friendly clubs, restaurants and guesthouses.

In the 2003 film *Proteus*, Cape Town film-maker Jack Lewis and Canadian film-maker John Greyson trace Cape Town's gay credentials to the start of the colonial era. They tell the story of an affair between a young Khoi man, Claas Blank, and Rijkhaart Jacobsz, a sailor from Amsterdam, who were imprisoned on Robben Island in 1735. The affair rocked the society of that time but passed into urban folklore.

For generations, cross-dressing and transgendered men from the Cape Coloured community have been known as "moffies", and the Cape boasts one of the most famous transsexuals of Victorian times, Dr James Barry, who reformed medical practice in the Cape, fought duels over a local beauty, and was discovered on his deathbed to be a woman. Known for its beautifully restored historical cottages, pretty tree-lined streets and vibrant village atmosphere, De Waterkant Village is the official gay village of Cape Town.

Left: working together in a local store. **Above Left:** music lover in Greenmarket Square. **Above:** Bronx, the bar and club in Green Point, is popular with the gay crowd.

The Jewish community

The first significant immigration of Jews to the Cape, mostly from Lithuania, came with the diamond and gold boom of the late 19th century. Jews continued to arrive during the 20th century in spite of discrimination during the early years. Eastern European Jews formed the second-largest immigrant group after Western Europeans. Poor families settled in Woodstock, District Six or Salt River, moving later to Gardens, Tamboerskloof, Oranjezicht or Sea Point. They retained many of their cultural traditions, the strength of which was evident in the establishment of a Yiddish theatre, press and three Hebrew bookshops.

Many Jewish activists and lawyers participated in the struggle against apartheid, among them Progressive MP Helen Suzman (for many years the only dissenting voice in parliament), Albie Sachs, Arthur Chaskalson and Gill Marcus. ❑

DECISIVE DATES

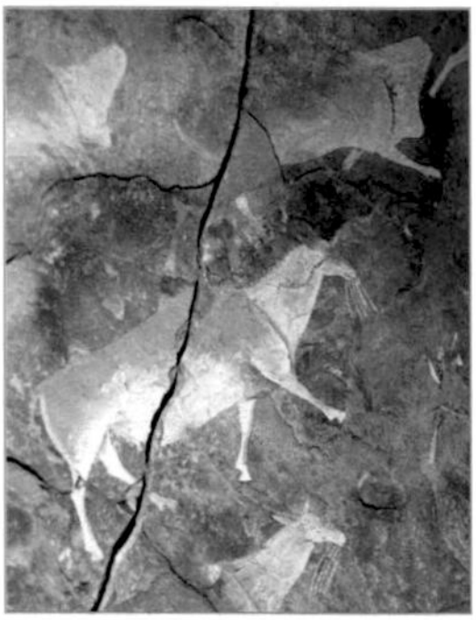

30,000 BC
San hunter-gatherers, probably descendants of a Late Stone-Age people, live in the South Africa region.

AD 300
Emergence of Khoikhoi tribespeople, closely related to the San.

900
Iron-Age Bantu-speaking tribes, probably ancestors of the Xhosa, settle in the coastal grasslands in the far east of the Western Cape region.

1487
Portuguese explorer Bartolomeu Dias rounds the Cape, which is named the Cape of Good Hope.

1498
Vasco da Gama completes the route to India via the Cape.

1503
Antonio de Saldahna anchors at Table Bay and encounters the Khoisan inhabitants.

1580
Francis Drake reaches the Cape.

1647
The Dutch vessel *Haerlem* is wrecked in Table Bay. Survivors bring back glowing reports of the region.

1652
The Dutch East India Company sends Jan van Riebeeck to the Cape to establish a supply station.

1657
The station becomes a permanent settlement when company servants are granted their own farms.

1658
The first major group of slaves arrives from the Dutch East Indies.

1659
The first wine from Cape grapes is pressed.

1679
Simon van der Stel is appointed commander of the Cape settlement.

1688
Arrival of 200 French Huguenots.

1713
First smallpox epidemic hits the Khoisans.

1755
Second smallpox epidemic all but wipes out the Khoisan.

1795–1803
British occupy Cape Town.

1779
Skirmishes between the settlers and Xhosas.

1803
The colony reverts to the Dutch.

1814–15
Cape Colony is formally ceded to the British by the Congress of Vienna.

1820
British settlers arrive in Eastern Cape.

1834
Cape slaves are emancipated.

1834–40
The Great Trek sees large numbers of Boers (Dutch-speaking farmers) emigrate from the Cape up into what would later become the Transvaal and the Free State.

1854
The Cape establishes its own representative parliament.

1870
Diamonds are discovered in Griqualand West; Alfred Dock opens.

FAR LEFT TOP: rock carving in Iziko South African Museum. LEFT: van Riebeeck landing at the Cape of Good Hope in 1652. ABOVE: Cecil John Rhodes. ABOVE RIGHT: General Cronje's principal commanders after surrendering in the Boer War, 1900. RIGHT: statue of Jan Smuts.

1880-1
The Transvaal declares itself a republic. The first Anglo-Boer War.

1886
Gold is discovered in the Transvaal and the mining town of Johannesburg is founded.

1890
Cecil John Rhodes becomes prime minister of the Cape Colony.

1895
Rhodes resigns after instigating the abortive Jameson Raid on the Transvaal goldfields.

1899–1902
The second Anglo-Boer War, in which the Boers are beaten and their settlements destroyed, leads to Free State and Transvaal becoming British colonies.

1910
Crown colonies of Cape, Natal, Transvaal and Free State amalgamate as Union of South Africa, creating the country we know today. Cape Town becomes the legislative capital.

1912
A black civil rights movement, the South African National Congress, is formed, known after 1923 as the African National Congress (ANC).

1913
The Native Land Act is passed, limiting land ownership for blacks.

1936
Black voters are disenfranchised.

1939
World War II breaks out. South Africa, led by President Jan Smuts, joins the Allies.

1948
National Party voted into power by white-dominated electorate on apartheid (segregated development) platform.

1950–3
Apartheid is entrenched still further with the Group Areas Act, and the forced removal of communities.

1956
Cape Coloureds lose voting rights.

1960
ANC and PAC march against pass laws. Protestors killed at Langa and Nyanga townships. Warrants issued to arrest ANC leaders.

1961
Union of South Africa leaves the Commonwealth to become Republic of South Africa in response to pressure to liberalise apartheid laws.

1963
ANC leader Nelson Mandela is sentenced to life imprisonment.

1966
60,000 residents of Cape Town's District Six are forcibly removed. Prime minister Verwoerd is assassinated.

1976
Soweto schoolchildren protest against measures to make Afrikaans the language used in all black schools.

1983
Constitution gives coloureds and Asians limited rights. Anti-apartheid United Democratic Front is founded.

1984
Anglican Archbishop Desmond Tutu is awarded the Nobel Peace Prize. Various "petty apartheid" acts are abolished, including the official ban on mixed marriages.

1986
A state of emergency declared.

1989
F. W. de Klerk becomes president.

1990
Nelson Mandela is released after 27 years in prison.

1991
Apartheid is officially dissolved.

1993
Mandela and F. W. de Klerk jointly receive the Nobel Peace Price.

1994
The first democratic general election results in a landslide victory for the ANC. Nelson Mandela is elected president.

1995
South Africa hosts and wins rugby's World Cup. The Springboks team includes one black South African.

1996
Robben Island prison opens to the public as a museum.

1997
South Africa's new Constitution comes into effect.

1998
Truth and Reconciliation Commission hearings get under way as South Africa comes to terms with its past.

1999
Nelson Mandela retires. His deputy Thabo Mbeki becomes president following ANC general election victory. Robben Island is declared a Unesco World Heritage Site.

2004
South Africa's third democratic election is held. Mbeki and the ANC win a 70 percent majority. South Africa wins the bid to host the 2010 World Cup.

2005
Thabo Mbeki sacks Deputy President Jacob Zuma over corruption scandal in June. Zuma is charged with corruption in October and with rape in December.

2006
A bushfire on Table Mountain destroys large areas of indigenous fynbos. Zuma is found not guilty in the rape trial. South Africa becomes the first African country to legalise same-sex marriage, and is selected as a non-permanent member of the United Nations Security Council. Helen Zille becomes the mayor of Cape Town after the Democratic Alliance (DA) beats the ANC in municipal elections.

2007
Jacob Zuma replaces Mbeki as ANC chairman. South Africa wins 2007 Rugby World Cup. Reggae singer Lucky Dube shot dead in a burglary in Johannesburg.

2008
Corruption charges against Zuma are controversially dismissed. Mbeki resigns as President of South Africa and deputy leader Kgalema Motlanthe takes over as Acting President. Cape Town's Helen Zille voted World Mayor of the Year.

2009
ANC wins fourth successive election with convincing majority in eight of nine provinces. Zuma made President, while Zille becomes premier of Western Cape following DA victory in that one province.

2010
FIFA World Cup held in South Africa over June and July.

FAR LEFT TOP: ANC President Albert Luthuli (right) receives the 1960 Nobel Peace Prize. LEFT MIDDLE: de Klerk and Mandela. LEFT BOTTOM: Nelson Mandela leaves prison. ABOVE: the Springboks win the rugby World Cup. RIGHT: the now infamous vuvuzela, used at football matches.

THE MAKING OF CAPE TOWN

The Dutch founded Cape Town as a refreshment station for European ships en route to the Indian Ocean and Asia. By the early 19th century, however, it was a cosmopolitan port marked by political conflict between Dutch settlers and British colonists, a rivalry that culminated in the Anglo-Boer War of 1899–1902

The history of Cape Town is first of all a history of the singular mix of people who shaped the city, their conflicts and their struggle to live together. It is also the history of an extraordinary place, of prime strategic value, with its narrow peninsula, two oceans and distinctive flat-topped mountain.

Stone-Age hunter-gatherers

The earliest evidence of man on the Cape is of Early Stone-Age hunter-gatherers, who inhabited the area around 1.4 million years ago. Tools belonging to such people have been found on Table Bay and near the Cape of Good Hope. More widespread are finds from the Middle Stone-Age period (200,000–40, 000 years) and of the Late Stone Age (from around 21,000 years ago). The San, or Bushmen as they are also known, were hunter-gatherers who arrived in the area about 30,000 years ago, and lived in caves around the Cape Peninsula and foraged on the beaches. Their rock paintings have been found in caves and overhangs throughout the Cape and elsewhere in South Africa, comprising the largest collection of Stone-Age art in the world.

About 2,000 years ago the San were joined and to some extent displaced by the pastoralist Khoikhoi (Khoi), who migrated to the Cape from the north, along with their trademark fat-tailed sheep. It was the Khoi whom the Europeans encountered when they sailed into Table Bay in the 15th century. As the colony developed and settlement fanned northwards, they also encountered the San.

LEFT: the Dutch East India ship *Noordt Nieuwlandt* sailing into Table Bay in 1762. **RIGHT:** San Hunters, from a painting by Samuell Daniell (1830).

Early exploration

The first Europeans to reach the Cape were the Portuguese, who had spent much of the 15th century trying to establish a maritime route between Europe and India via Africa, culminating in Bartolomeu Dias' perilous 1488 expedition as far as Mossel Bay (some 500km east of Cape Town). Dias christened the site of present-day Cape Town "Cape of Storms", on account of the fierce weather he encountered there, but King João II of Portugal, on hearing Dias relate

the story of his voyage, renamed it the Cape of Good Hope, believing that its successful navigation would bring the riches of India within Portugal's reach at last.

But it was a full 10 years after Dias' historic journey that Vasco da Gama became the first explorer to land on Indian soil via the Cape. From then on Table Mountain became an important landmark for mariners, a place where they could shelter their vessels, get fresh water and barter meat from the local Khoi people.

Van Riebeeck's brief in 1652 was to establish a "fort and a garden". Both can be seen today as the Castle on the Foreshore and the Company's Garden above Adderley Street.

Although the Portuguese soon established a strong presence on the coasts of present-day Mozambique, Tanzania and Kenya, they made no effort to settle the Cape. This is partly because the Cape was notorious among mariners for its stormy weather, but also because of a series of violent clashes with the Khoi. In 1510, for example, a viceroy of the Portuguese Indies attacked the Khoi, whose retaliation forced the Portuguese back to the shore, where 50 sailors were killed. But English and Dutch ships regularly put into Table Bay to trade and get fresh water.

Dutch settlement

By 1590 the Dutch controlled the trade route to India, largely through the Dutch East India Company (Vereenigde Oost-Indische Compagnie or VOC).

From 1610, the English used Robben Island as a penal colony and, in 1620, the Dutch threw mutineers overboard in Table Bay. The English briefly considered annexing the Cape at this time, but its reputation as a "Cape of Storms" discouraged them. Then, in 1647, the Dutch ship *Haarlem* ran aground in Table Bay, leaving

some of the crew stranded for a year. The shipwrecked crew found the local Khoi friendly and helpful and they recommended permanent Dutch settlement to the VOC directors.

In 1652 the VOC, under the command of Jan van Riebeeck, occupied the Cape to set up a permanent refreshment stop for the fleets of the Dutch East India Company. This event was later romanticised by Afrikaner nationalists, with re-enactments of the landing presented as pageants in 1938 and 1952, but as attempts at colonisation go, it was somewhat tentative.

The directors in Amsterdam saw the Cape settlement as having a dual role: to establish a defensive fort that would protect Dutch interests against both the local Khoi and any antagonistic foreign powers, and to ensure a supply of fresh vegetables and meat for Dutch sailors.

But the soils of the peninsula are notoriously poor – one reason for the uniqueness of the Cape vegetation known as fynbos that thrives in such conditions – and until the Dutch began to explore beyond the bay, there was little in the way of food crops. And aside from the increasingly hostile Khoi, exploration was a hazardous affair. Lions roamed the bay and anyone wandering outside the fort was vulnerable to attack. In the early years the settlement was dependent on food supplies from Amsterdam and could produce very little fresh produce itself.

ABOVE LEFT: an early view of Table Bay. **LEFT:** map of the Cape of Good Hope, 1581. **ABOVE:** Saartjie Baartman, popularly known as the Hottentot Venus. **ABOVE RIGHT:** Charles Bell's 1850 painting of Van Riebeeck's landing.

From 1657 freeholders were granted land along the Liesbeeck River on the southerly side of the mountain and colonisation began in earnest. These early burghers followed the practice of the Dutch in the East Indies and began to import slaves. Slavery was to be the key labour practice of the Cape for 200 years.

Khoi resistance

For centuries the Khoi pastoralists had followed transhumance grazing routes around the Cape mountains and valleys. They fiercely resented the intrusive settlement of the Dutch whom they had previously seen as simply passing through. Because the Dutch had seen no permanent settlement on arrival they had assumed that the Cape was largely unoccupied, which was not the case.

In 1659–60, open war broke out between the Dutch and the Khoi. Cape Town was settled by conquest and not negotiation, an ominous precedent for the future of South Africa, and

Khoi leaders asked angrily: "Who should give way, the rightful owner or the foreign intruder?" Van Riebeeck marked out the settler territory with palisades and ditches, ordering that a hedge of bitter almonds be planted along the southern boundary. Part of this hedge can still be seen today in Kirstenbosch Botanical Garden *(see page 135)*.

The Cape's slaves brought Islamic and cultural traditions from countries bordering the Indian Ocean. Their cuisine and artisanship contributed much to the ambience of Cape Town.

The appearance of the Cape changed quickly as hedges and enclosures for sheep were erected and forested areas chopped down for shipbuilding timber.

Encouraged by the premiums paid by the Company, Dutch soldiers decimated the local lion and leopard populations, and killed seals for oil. Beyond the Cape lay the fabled lands of Monomatapa and Prester John, guarded by the Mountains of Africa (today's Hottentots-Holland). Dutch expeditions were mounted in search of gold, but returned with the carcasses of antelope and eland. Most activities, though, centred on the Cape settlement itself.

Slave labour

By 1648 more than half the recorded population of the settlement were chattel slaves, brought from Guinea, Angola, Mozambique and Madagascar. They worked as farm labourers and domestic servants, following the usage prevalent in Dutch Batavia. Many of these slaves fled across the mountains of Africa under the illusion they could find their way back home to East and West Africa.

Fears of a slave insurrection troubled the colonists almost as much as the Khoi incursions. Slaves were sorted into a crude hierarchy: the first were the mansoors born in the Slave Lodge *(see page 85)*, skilled and trusted with the distribution of food and clothing, then skilled artisans brought from Dutch East Indian colonies and finally the labourers captured on slave raids to Madagascar or Mozambique. But the slaves' resistance to their owners took many forms: running away, arson, poisoning, physical attacks and riots. Even after the legal emancipation of slaves in 1834, many farms across the Cape Colony continued to buy and sell slaves.

Slave resistance was organised to counter another form of oppression: the political exile

of leading Muslim clerics such as Sufi scholar Sheik Yusuf, deported from the East to the distant Cape. The public practice of Islam was outlawed until the end of the 18th century and so developed a quality of resistance under such conditions.

Newcomers

Gradually Cape Town came to resemble a pleasant Dutch colonial town, with low whitewashed houses and market gardens set out on a strict grid of streets running down from the mountain to the bay; they were arranged to accommodate mountain streams channelled into watercourses from the Company Gardens down the Heerengracht.

As efforts were made by the free burghers to establish a cleaner, more respectable town, the Cape began to acquire its less savoury reputation as the "tavern of the seas", with pubs (the *taphuis*), cheap lodging houses, gambling dens and brothels plying trade alongside the premises of butchers, blacksmiths, tanners, shoemakers and bakers. Sailors boasted of the excellent food (spiced in the Malay tradition with curries and *bredies*) and cheap liquor.

Along with increased trade there came German mercenaries and French influences, a new European influx of deserters from the strife in the Low Countries and gold-diggers in search of new opportunities.

But in 1795 a British fleet of warships sailed into False Bay. Britain seized the Cape

ABOVE LEFT: 1719 image of a Khoi funeral. **LEFT:** Cecil John Rhodes, diamond magnate, arch-colonialist and national builder. **ABOVE:** a view of St George's church in 1845. It became a cathedral two years later.

THE HOTTENTOT VENUS

Saartjie Baartman was born in 1789 into the Griqua tribe of the eastern Cape, a subgroup of the Khoisan. A local doctor examined her and was fascinated by her steatopygia – enlarged buttocks – and unusually elongated labia, and persuaded her to go to London as a subject of anthropological research. At first, she was put under anatomical scrutiny by scientists, but in 1814, after spending four years being paraded around London, she was taken to Paris and handed to a "showman of wild animals" in a travelling circus. After her death her body was exhibited in the Musee de l'Homme. Eventually South African protests led to the return of her body for burial in 2002.

to prevent its use by France, which was then allied to Holland. The colony was returned to the Dutch in 1803 but was again occupied by the British in 1806. The 1814–15 Congress of Vienna ceded the colony to the British on a permanent basis.

> *In 1863 the Confederate raider* The Alabama *put into Table Bay, arousing huge controversy from the population of ex-slaves. Many* ghommaliedjies *or folk songs such as* Die Alabama *date from this time.*

Prosperity came with the English, as did intermarriage between "English officers and Dutch vrouws". Many of the Cape Dutch homesteads date from this period. World trade was expanding and wheat and wines from the Cape were much in demand. Demographics were changing too: the 1820 settlers arrived in the Eastern Cape and many would move to the Cape Town area to avoid the violence of the skirmishes with the Xhosa on the eastern frontier.

Britain introduced a number of reforms. In 1828, the Khoi people were given the explicit protection of the law, including the right to own land, while in 1834 the colony's slaves were emancipated, leading to the establishment of the colourful Bo-Kaap district on the eastern slopes of Signal Hill. But although Britain was responsible for ridding the Cape of slavery, its new labour laws laid the basis for an exploitative system barely more liberal than the system it had abolished. Pass laws prevented thousands of dispossessed blacks from acquiring work in the colony. And the "multiracial" constituency of a parliament established in the Cape in 1854 excluded the vast majority of non-whites who could not meet the financial criteria of suffrage.

Nevertheless, the liberalising tendencies of the British and the emancipation of slaves were anathema to the descendants of the first (mostly Dutch) settlers, who referred to themselves as Afrikaners or Boers (farmers). As a result, some 12,000 Boers signalled their disapproval by abandoning the Cape Colony in the late 1830s, a mass northward migration known as the Great Trek. These so-called Voortrekkers established the first European

Above: two rickshaw-pullers in Durban at the turn of the 20th century. **Right:** Voortrekkers (Boer farmers) on the Great Trek northwards from the Cape Colony to the Transvaal, in the 1830s,

settlements in the present-day South African provinces of KwaZulu-Natal, Free State, Gauteng, Mpumalanga and Limpopo, and established several Boer Republics, the most significant of which were the Transvaal and Free State, whose respective capitals were Pretoria and Bloemfontein.

A Victorian city

Cape Town now took on the characteristics of Victorian cities everywhere: churches were built (Anglican, Methodist and Presbyterian), as was Government House in the Company's Garden; gentlemen's clubs and the Freemasons were established. There were trams, hansom cabs and railways reaching as far as the military camp at Wynberg. In the 1860s a South African museum of scientific, botanical and historical curiosities was created, the South African library was built, and the Observatory enlarged. The Dutch-style buildings of Adderley Street were replaced by Victorian shop fronts and hotels. Architects such as Sir Herbert Baker drew on the simple and beautiful Cape Dutch architecture and combined it with Arts and Crafts influences to create the likes of Groote Schuur, which was commissioned by the legendary British businessman and politician Cecil John Rhodes, who served as prime minister of the Cape colony from 1890–6. The Diamond Jubilee of Queen Victoria in 1897 was a glittering occasion in the city.

Capetonians were proud of their city and initially they displayed little interest in the "Boer Republics" that were established further north in the aftermath of the Great Trek. That all changed, however, with the discovery of the world's largest diamond vein at Kimberley in 1867, followed by an even wealthier mass of gold deposits in the southern Transvaal (around present-day Johannesburg) in 1888. Soon, the regional balance of economic power shifted northward to the Transvaal and Free State, as *uitlanders* (foreigners) streamed through Cape Town on their way to the goldfields and diamond mines. This scenario provided further fuel to the colonial aspirations of Rhodes, who had effectively secured Rhodesia (now Zimbabwe) as his own colony in the 1890s. As a new century dawned, the former insularity of the Cape gave way to the shadow of war with its mineral-rich northern neighbours. ❑

FROM APARTHEID TO DEMOCRACY

The Anglo-Boer War planted a militant Afrikaner nationalism in South Africa, ushering in an apartheid government whose draconian and divisive policies dominated the country for more than 40 years

The 20th century began inauspiciously with the Anglo-Boer War – sometimes referred to as the South African War – which would last from 1899 until 1902. It was not only a war waged by the British Empire against the rebellious landlocked republics of the Transvaal and Orange Free State, but a civil war in which the Cape Colony was fiercely divided, with English-speakers and Afrikaners at loggerheads as to which side the Colony supported. Black civilians were summarily forced to support their employers' choices – many unarmed black men were killed playing a supportive role in combat. English troops poured into the Cape, from where they made their way north.

The Cape Colony's relative isolation, in part already altered by the late 19th-century scramble by foreigners for gold and diamond resources around Kimberley and the Transvaal, was ending as refugees and Boer prisoners arrived in the city. Prisoner-of-war camps and camps for women and children were established in crowded tents on Greenpoint Common and in Wynberg. It was a hard-fought war and it left a residual legacy of bitterness that would give impetus to a militant Afrikaner nationalism which would bring in an apartheid government after World War II.

The Boer War cost the British more than £200 million and more than 22,000 British lives were lost. The Boers lost over 34,000 people, mostly women and children. More than 15,000 black people were killed.

LEFT: F. W. de Klerk and Thabo Mbeki stand alongside Nelson Mandela at his inauguration in 1994. **RIGHT:** the South African Light Horse regiment parades down Adderley Street in the Anglo-Boer War.

But the immediate result of British victory in the Anglo-Boer War was to unite South Africa politically and economically, so that in 1910, the Union of South Africa was created out of the Cape, Natal, Transvaal and Free State. It was essentially a white union in terms of political rights and powers.

Rail and road

Cape Town and the peninsula and Boland had long been separated from the interior by mountain ranges. The passes built by Thomas Bain, a geologist and roadbuilder known as "the man with theodolite eyes", were the only routes out. In addition to these mountain pass roads, which still stand as a testament to stonewalling techniques, the first railway from the Cape had reached the ramshackle mining town of Johannesburg in 1892. By 1894 there was a Cape road to Rhodesia (present-day Zimbabwe) via Mafeking. In 1897 crowds gathered in Pretoria to admire a small Benz Voiturette with wire-spoked wheels, the first motor vehicle to reach South Africa. With the discovery of the enormous Cullinan diamond – intact at 3,106 carats — on the Rand, the South African economy began to shift from agriculture towards industry.

The widespread hope of a prosperous united Union of South Africa was dampened by World War I. South African Prime Minister Louis Botha launched an attack on German-held South West Africa (now Namibia), a wildly unpopular move, especially amongst Afrikaners who remembered Germany's support for their Boer commandos in the Anglo-Boer War. English-speaking young South African men were gradually drawn into the European conflict and more than 2,000 South African soldiers died in the Battle of Delville Wood alone. Far worse casualties were sustained when the Spanish influenza swept across continents in 1918 just after Armistice Day.

Black Inspiration

Black protest found inspiration in a number of prominent black figures in the late 19th and early 20th centuries. These included the mission-educated writer Sol Plaatje, who as well as writing the first novel in Setswana, *Mhudi*, an account of black history not defined by white and Western understanding, was part of two delegations to Britain to protest against the Land Act of 1913. Also influential was Clements Kadalie, the first black trade unionist, who was born in Nyasaland in 1896. He formed the Industrial and Commercial Workers' Union in the Cape in 1919; for a brief period the ICU was the most powerful political force outside parliament.

Early black protest

Invisible for so long, the history of black consciousness and liberation is now a matter of public record and no longer an afterthought to Western events and the ambitions of white South Africans. Along with the American civil rights struggles, many nascent black movements emerged out of independent churches, land movements and a growing urban discontent.

Black opposition was inevitable. Organised political activity among Africans started with the establishment of the South African National Congress (later to become the African National Congress or ANC), in 1912 in Bloemfontein in the Free State.

In 1921, the Communist Party came into being at a time of heightened militancy, not yet fully multiracial but connecting South African workers to international political struggles. Yet, in the face of a groundswell of opposition to racially defined government, the Natives Land Act was legislated in 1913. This defined the remnants of black ancestral lands for African occupation. The "homelands", as they were subsequently called, eventually comprised about 13 percent of South Africa's land. More discriminatory legislation – particularly relating to job reservation favouring whites and the disenfranchisement of coloured voters in the Cape – was enacted. Meanwhile, Afrikaner nationalism, fuelled by job losses arising from worldwide recession, was on the march.

LEFT: memories of the pioneering spirit of the Great Trek of the 1830s inspired Afrikaner nationalism in the 20th century. **ABOVE:** in 1919 Sol Plaatje (bottom right) led a group to England to protest against the 1913 Land Act.

Conflict and depression

Almost without warning conflict broke out in 1922 with a miners' strike (predominantly white miners) on the Rand. It was violently suppressed by the government. Prime Minister Jan Smuts used martial law to brutally suppress the strike and, in killing more than 200 miners, lost himself the next election. Afrikaner nationalism was growing, even in the more sedate Cape, fuelled by a determination that the brutal tactics of the Anglo-Boer War and the execution of pro-German sympathiser Jopie Fourie

> *The powerful Dutch Reformed Church produced a biblical defence of apartheid and kept churches, schools and graveyards segregated.*

in World War I would not happen again. With the Depression and a disastrous drought of 1933, the Cape, together with the rest of South Africa, struggled with soup kitchens and relief programmes.

In 1937 Afrikaners re-enacted the Great Trek, an emotive and charged event, the significance of which was missed in the dramatic build-up to the outbreak of World War II. Here again, South African support for the Allies was ambivalent. Many Afrikaners joined a pro-German Fascist organisation named the Ossawa Brandwag. Black servicemen were conscripted to lend support or even to bear arms in the battle raging against Rommel in North Africa and in Italy.

The winds of change

After World War II colonialism was ending for the British Empire, but in 1948, ironically following on from a highly successful royal visit to the country during which Princess Elizabeth broadcast from a small stinkwood table in Government House on her 21st birthday, a new government came into power in South Africa, shocking the more liberal Cape. Field-marshal Jan Smuts, an internationally reputed peacemaker and statesman who had worked with the League of Nations as well as the Allies, lost the election to Dr D. F. Malan of the Nationalist Party, which was supported by the predominantly Afrikaner white population. The Nationalists stood for racial segregation and the creation of Afrikaner wealth to oppose the economic power of English businesses and the mining houses.

These experiences would lead many black soldiers from Kenya, West and East Africa to begin the struggle for independence from colonial powers. As Ghana, Zambia and Kenya

The Pan Africanist Congress

The Pan Africanist Congress (PAC) was established in 1959 by ANC dissidents who opposed that group's multiracial orientation and advocated black liberation within an exclusively black nationalist context. The party was founded in the townships of Orlando and Soweto, outside Johannesburg, although support was also found in Cape townships. The government declared the PAC an unlawful organisation in 1960. Like the ANC, it was recognised by the United Nations (UN) and by the Organisation of African Unity (OAU) as an official South African liberation movement. It was legalised on 2 February 1990. The PAC's senior leaders included Robert Sobukwe.

moved towards independence, the situation in South Africa became more anomalous. In 1963, ending the Federation of Rhodesia and Nyasaland, the British prime minister Harold Macmillan would stand up in the Cape parliament to declare that "The winds of change are sweeping across Africa."

Apartheid rules

Malan's first speech to the House of Assembly was an ominous foretelling of what was to come. "The principle of apartheid," said Malan, "is that we have two separate spheres, not territorial spheres, but with separate rights." Despite the protests of many white Cape citizens belonging to multiracial organisations such as the Torch Commando, black and coloured people were systematically stripped of any political rights. Leaders emerged from the racially integrated District Six: Dr Abdurahman and his daughter Cissie Gool were to lead protests and civil disobedience campaigns for many years. The South African Communist Party moved from protecting the interests of white workers to a multiracial position, only to be banned as the Cold War intensified in the 1950s.

Peaceful protest achieved nothing as ever more degrading and dehumanising legislation was passed, making relationships across the colour bar illegal (the Mixed Marriages Act, 1949), demanding that all black people carry passes if they entered "white areas", enforcing the eviction of black and coloured people from land declared white-owned. Whenever illegal black shanty towns mushroomed on the sandy plains to the east of Cape Town, they would quickly be flattened by government bulldozers, their occupants dragged away and dumped in the homelands. Within weeks the shanties would rise again.

The Cape Coloureds could not be granted a homeland, so the western half of the Cape province was declared a "coloured preference area" in which no black person could be employed

LEFT: Boer soldiers in the Anglo-Boer War. **ABOVE LEFT:** South African prisoners of World War II. **ABOVE:** the paths of two domestic workers on their way to Crossroads, a camp on the outskirts of Cape Town, cross with a student from the prestigious Bishops school, 1986.

Cape Town's District Six

District Six was so named in 1867 as it was the sixth municipal district of Cape Town. Originally established as a mixed community of freed slaves, merchants, artisans, labourers and immigrants, it took on a polyglot bohemian and tolerant character, vibrant and unconventional, with close links to the city and the port. By the beginning of the 20th century, however, the history of removals and marginalisation had begun.The first to be "resettled" were black (mostly Xhosa) South Africans, forcibly displaced from the District in 1901. As the more prosperous inhabitants, including German and European immigrants, moved away to the suburbs, the area became the neglected ward of Cape Town. In 1966, District Six was declared a white area under the Group Areas Act of 1950, and by 1982, the life of the community was over. Some 60,000 people were forcibly removed to barren outlying areas aptly known as the Cape Flats, and their houses in District Six were flattened by bulldozers.

Restitution attempts began in 2004 for descendants of original Cape Coloured families wishing to return. The District Six Museum, which opened at 25 Buitenkant Street in December 1994, documents the lives of the original inhabitants and the trauma of their resettlement. It is well worth a visit *(see page 80)*.

unless it could be proved that there was no suitable coloured person for the job.

"Petty apartheid" meant that black people could not travel on trains or buses in the same coaches with whites, could not enter shops or post offices, could not be born in the same hospital wards as whites, could not lie dead in the same morgues. Examples of the infamous "Non-Europeans only" and "Whites Only" signs dating back 40 years can be seen on display in the District Six Museum *(see page 81)*.

The Defiance Campaign of the early 1950s carried mass mobilisation to new heights under the banner of non-violent resistance to the pass laws. In 1955, a Freedom Charter was drawn up at the Congress of the People in Soweto. The Charter enunciated the principles of the struggle, binding the movement to a culture of human rights and non-racialism.

Sharpeville and its aftermath

In 1960 an anti-pass march by the Pan Africanist Congress under the leadership of Robert Sobukwe in Sharpeville, near Vereeniging, led to unprecedented state violence. Armoured cars, fighter jets and soldiers armed with sten guns killed 67 unarmed black marchers, including women and children. Riots took place the

following day in Cape Town's Langa township, and a 23-year-old university student and PAC member named Philip Kgosana led a crowd of 30,000 protesters from Langa up over De Waal Drive to Caledon Square Police Station. Thanks to the prescience and diplomacy of a police colonel there, the marchers were persuaded to return home and no force was used.

The inevitability of armed resistance to apartheid had moved a step closer. As international protest about the Sharpeville massacre mounted, local arrests made it clear that the struggle against apartheid would be multi-racial: arrested along with Sobukwe, Nelson Mandela and Walter Sisulu was Helen Joseph, the president of the South African Federation of Women.

In 1961 South Africa became a Republic and thereafter began the social and political isolation that would characterise it as a pariah state for more than 30 years. In 1963 the Rivonia trials sent Nelson Mandela and seven other members of the African National Congress to prison on Robben Island. The armed struggle had begun.

LEFT: the aftermath of the Sharpeville massacre, where unarmed black marchers were killed by armed members of the Pan Africanist Congress. **ABOVE:** the funeral of Steve Biko in 1977.

The good life for some

Throughout the 1960s and '70s prosperous white Cape Town was largely oblivious of the impact of apartheid on black people living in townships and ghettos around the peninsula. (It was against the law for unauthorised whites to enter black locations or settlements.) The average white lifestyle resembled that of southern California, with household servants, gardeners, nannies and chauffeurs ensuring relative leisure and luxury.

But southern African politics were shifting. The unilateral declaration of independence by Ian Smith in Rhodesia was supported by South Africa: white Rhodesia, like South Africa, would "go it alone" against international sanctions and disapproval. South African prime minister Hendrik Verwoerd, a leading architect of apartheid, was stabbed to death in the Cape parliament in 1966 by a parliamentary messenger, Demetri Tsafendas. This assassination was presented as

the act of a madman and only much later did the extent of Tsafendas's political hatred of apartheid emerge.

The spirit of resistance was confined to universities – University of Cape Town students faced tear gas and baton charges in St George's cathedral in 1974 – and to clandestine organisations including the militant wing of the ANC, Umkhonto we Sizwe or "Spear of the Nation", which developed in the historically black universities such as the University of the Western Cape and the black communities.

Two episodes served as important catalysts to change, provoking black outrage and attracting international condemnation. In June 1976, the black township of Soweto, near Johannesburg, exploded into violence as black schoolchildren marching in protest at a new requirement for all lessons to be taught in Afrikaans, the language of the oppressor, were killed by police. Riots followed countrywide, but were suppressed. Media censorship was extensive.

The following year, Black Consciousness leader Steve Biko, an activist from the Eastern Cape, was murdered in police detention *(see panel, left)*. The then Minister of Police Jimmy Kruger announced in public that Biko's death "leaves me cold".

With the independence of Zimbabwe in 1980, South Africa became isolated from the rest of southern Africa. The final decade of apartheid was the most brutal, with South African forces leading incursions and bombing raids into Zambia and Lesotho as well as black townships. State of emergency legislation was

Death in Police Custody

Steve Biko, a co-founder of the Black Peoples Convention (BPC), which united some 70 Black Consciousness groups, was interrogated four times between August 1975 and September 1977 under apartheid anti-terrorism legislation. On 21 August 1977 he was detained by the Eastern Cape security police and taken to security police headquarters where, on 7 September, he sustained a head injury during interrogation. Biko was then taken to Pretoria – a 12-hour journey which he made lying naked in the back of a Land Rover. A few hours later, on 12 September, alone and still naked, on the floor of a cell in the Pretoria Central Prison, Biko died from brain damage.

passed to deal with anyone opposing the Pretoria government. Hundreds were detained in prison without trial, died after torture or were sentenced to death.

Church leaders led protests, with leaders such as Anglican archbishop Desmond Tutu calling apartheid a heresy. Police brutality was deplored internationally and economic sanctions and disinvestments led to many international companies withdrawing from South Africa. As organisations were banned (the United Democratic Front had been formed in 1983), the Mass Democratic Movement emerged and organised several vast marches through Cape Town calling for political change.

On one of the last mass protest marches in Cape Town, police sprayed marchers with purple dye so that they could be identified and charged with illegal protest. Marchers raised hastily scribbled placards that read, "The purple shall govern"

LEFT: in 2004 a ceremony was held to mark the return of former residents to District Six. **ABOVE:** Biko on the cover of *Drum* magazine, 1977. **RIGHT:** former President Thabo Mbeki in Cape Town.

From prisoner to president

Apartheid's grip on South Africa began to give way when F. W. de Klerk replaced P. W. Botha as president in 1989. De Klerk, who belonged to a new generation of Afrikaners, was elected on a platform of unspecified reform. He removed the ban on the ANC, and released its leader, Nelson Mandela, in 1990, after 27 years of imprisonment. The Inkatha Freedom Party, a black opposition group led by Mangosuthu Buthelezi, which was seen as collaborating with the apartheid system, frequently clashed with the ANC during this period.

As media reports commented, it was evident that civil disobedience had become a way of life, that change was not only inevitable but unstoppable. In 1991, a multiracial forum led by de Klerk and Mandela, the Convention for a Democratic South Africa (CODESA), began working on a new constitution. In 1993, an interim constitution was passed, which dismantled apartheid and provided for a multiracial democracy with majority rule.

The peaceful transition of South Africa from one of the world's most repressive societies into a democracy is one of the 20th century's most remarkable stories. Mandela and de Klerk were jointly awarded the Nobel peace prize in 1993.

The 1994 election, the country's first multiracial one, resulted in a massive victory for Mandela and the ANC. The new government included six ministers from the National Party and three from the Inkatha Freedom Party. A new constitution was adopted in May 1996.

In 1997 the Truth and Reconciliation Commission, chaired by Archbishop Desmond Tutu, began hearings regarding human rights violations between 1960 and 1993. The commission promised amnesty to those who confessed their crimes under the apartheid system. In 1998, F. W. de Klerk, P. W. Botha, and leaders of the ANC appeared before the commission, and the nation continued to grapple with the enlightened but painful process of national recovery. Rightwing Afrikaner groups threatened to disrupt the peace process, but failed to do so.

Passing on the torch

Mandela retired in 1999, after one presidential term, cementing his reputation as a far-sighted and gracious statesman. His chosen successor Thabo Mbeki led the ANC to landslide victories in 1999 and 2004, and turned around an ailing economy to achieve an average annual economic growth of 4.5 percent over his two terms. However, posterity will most likely associate Mbeki's name with his inept handling of the country's unprecedented Aids crisis. About 5 million South Africans, more than 10 percent of the total population, are estimated to be HIV-positive, a greater number than in any other country in the world. Mbeki's tendency to underplay the direct link between HIV and Aids, and to emphasise the role of poverty and poor nutrition in the disease's progression, thwarted the fight against this epidemic. This

GOD BLESS AFRICA

At midnight on 26 April 1994, *Die Stem van Suid-Afrika* (the Call of South Africa), the old Afrikaans national anthem, was sung and South Africa's old flag was lowered. A new rainbow flag was raised and the new anthem, *Nkosi Sikele iAfrika* (God Bless Africa), composed by a Methodist mission teacher in 1897 and the anthem of the ANC since 1925, rang out. Under apartheid, people had been jailed for singing this beautiful, stirring hymn, as it was considered an act of defiance. Today's national anthem combines *Sikele iAfrika* and *Die Stem*, though the two halves are not always sung with equal fervour.

hands-off policy, which drew condemnation from the international community, health activists, and the likes of Nelson Mandela and Desmond Tutu, was reversed in 2003, but earlier action might have saved hundreds of thousands of lives, and the government's commitment towards combating the epidemic remains ambivalent.

Since 2004, South Africa's politics has been dominated by infighting within the ANC, much of it linked to a culture of corruption and inefficiency that permeates all tiers of local and national government, often at the expense of service delivery to the poorest and neediest sectors of society.

The most prominent figure of the period has been Jacob Zuma, who was fired as Deputy President in 2005 in response to strongly substantiated allegations of corruption. Despite this setback, Zuma emerged from the charges of corruption (which were controversially dropped) and a rape trial (verdict: not guilty) to assume leadership of the ANC in 2007 and lead the party to its fourth successive electoral landslide in 2009. Zuma's presidency has been undermined by his controversial personal life (an open polygamist, he has three wives and 20 children, most born out of wedlock) and the public rift between himself and his former protégé, the ANC Youth League leader Julius Malema – a spat that has the potential to dominate the immediate future of South African politics just as did the rivalry between Mbeki and Zuma from 2005–8.

LEFT: Treatment Action Campaign demands access to life-saving drugs for all HIV-positive people. ABOVE: Lekota, a founding member of COPE. RIGHT: ANC campaign bus. FOLLOWING PAGES: Imizamo Yethu township, Hout Bay.

Cape Town and the Western Cape have bucked the national trend, with ANC support having declined in favour of the Democratic Alliance (DA), formed in 2000 from the ashes of various smaller parties. DA support has grown strongly under the leadership of Helen Zille, a former political journalist, anti-apartheid activist and Member of Parliament who was elected Mayor of Cape Town in March 2006 (and won the "World Mayor of the Year" award two years later). In the 2009 election, Zille led the DA to a provincial victory that means she currently serves both as Premier of the Western Cape and, with the DA holding 67 seats in the national assembly, as leader of the opposition on a national level. The build-up to the 2009 election also saw the emergence of the Congress of the People (COPE), an ANC splinter that took 30 seats in the national assembly. Post-2009, the DA, COPE and various other minority parties have made public noises about strength in coalition, but with the ANC currently holding 264 of 400 seats, meaningful opposition still seems a long way off. ❑

SIYAKHULA
SPAZA SH

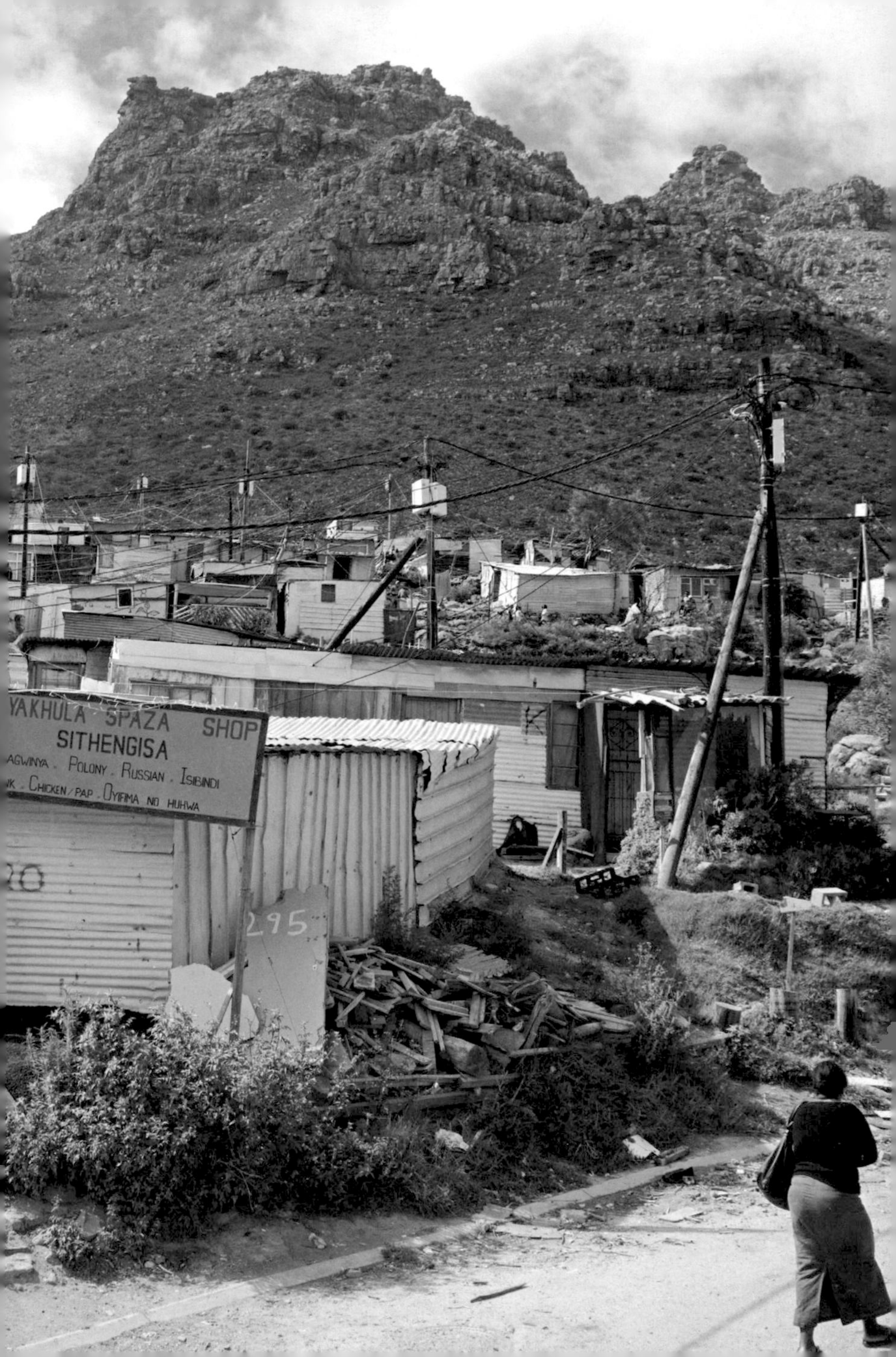
YAKHULA SPAZA SHOP
SITHENGISA
AGWINYA . POLONY . RUSSIAN . ISIBINDI
K . CHICKEN/PAP . OYIFIMA NO HUHWA
295

SPORT MAD, SPORT CRAZY

South Africans are fanatical about sport, and none more so than Capetonians, for whom it is a year-round preoccupation

ABOVE: two-time winner of the Rugby World Cup, South Africa is known for the physicality of its game, a trait that is equally pronounced at provincial level in the Super 15 and Currie Cup competitions.

With two oceans to the fore and the Table Mountain National Park to the rear, and a year-round sunny climate, Cape Town is the perfect environment for sport and outdoor pursuits. The city is the focus for a host of national and international tournaments, rugby and cricket events in particular. But the competitive and body-conscious Capetonians don't just watch sport, they do it, whether it be adventurous sports such as rock climbing, abseiling and surfing or more sedate forms such as golf.

During apartheid, South Africa was boycotted by many international teams and barred from the Olympics. Since then, South Africa has been welcomed back into the international sporting fold, where it has met with considerable success. The international rugby side, known as the Springboks, won two of the subsequent four Rugby World Cups, the first at home in 1995 and the most recent in 2007.

The national cricket side, the Proteas, has been ranked among the world's top test and One Day International-playing nations since readmission, and individual South Africans have also excelled in golf, athletics and swimming. The football side Bafana Bafana won the Africa Nations Cup in 1996 and made the final of the same event two years later, since when form and results have slumped.

LEFT: two South African fans watch the visiting West Indies take on South Africa at the Newlands Cricket Ground.

RIGHT: the sheer rocky sides of Table Mountain offer spectacular abseiling.

RIGHT: kitesurfing is a popular pastime at Muizenberg Beach, also one of the best surfing sites on the Cape Peninsula.

BELOW: the annual Cape Argus Cycle Tour is a 105km (65-mile) race around the Cape Peninsula, beginning on Herzog Boulevard and ending at Green Point.

WORLD CUP FEVER

In June 2010, South Africa became the first African country to host the FIFA World Cup, an event greeted with such anticipation locally that some newspapers started a day-by-day countdown more than three years in advance. New stadiums were built in Cape Town and other major cities especially for the event, and hotels doubled or tripled their rates to cash in on the associated tourist boom.

Despite advance misgivings about security in the international media, the event was universally judged to be a huge success. One disappointment for home fans, however, was the poor showing of the six African nations that contested it. South Africa never made it past the group stage, despite scoring a victory against France and a draw with Mexico in their three matches. Indeed, the only African team that did make the final 16 was Ghana, who beat the USA en route to the quarter-final before being knocked out by Uruguay.

ABOVE: Spain celebrates the 1-0 victory over the Netherlands that secured its first World Cup Title in 2010.

RIGHT: the international success of black cricketers such as fast bowler Makhaya Ntini has inspired fresh interest in the sport among township youngsters.

PERDIX
PERDIX

Cooking up a Feast

A sophisticated food culture has emerged in South Africa, and Cape Town is leading the way. But its chefs aren't simply following international trends. They are rediscovering traditional regional cuisine and earning a place in the global kitchen

Foodie culture has developed exponentially in Cape Town in the last few years. The city is filled with interesting cafés and restaurants, and has many well-known chefs and caterers. Popular food and wine fairs such as the Cape Gourmet Festival in May include tastings of all kinds of locally produced food and drink. Local lifestyle magazines feature recipes matching locally sourced food and wine.

Food shops and supermarkets have been quick to embrace this new trend and stock virtually anything you might need for a whole gamut of recipes, from Asian to North African, European to Japanese. And the variety of restaurants expands all the time; you're as likely to find good Chinese food as you are Cajun, Pacific Rim or Italian.

Global influences

World trends in food are as common in Cape Town as elsewhere. What you eat and drink in New York or Sydney you might well find in Cape Town's Southern Suburbs or in a trendy downtown eatery – the city has a window on the world and is proud of it. But what is also evident, as South Africans grow increasingly confident of their roots, is a renewed interest in their own unique cuisine. And chefs are not just dishing up old favourites. Instead, South African cuisine is being re-formed, re-tested and freshly presented in ways that acknowledge world trends and tastes without compromising unique characteristics. Old European favourites are also being rediscovered and presented in new and exciting ways.

Left: a street trader cooking chicken *sosaties* (skewers).
Right: continental European dishes are easy to find.

Culinary traditions

But what is South African cuisine? In this "rainbow nation", with its rich cultural heritage and varied colonial past, there are plenty of culinary traditions to draw on. Diverse ingredients and flavours have enriched the cooking pot, from the first Dutch settlers and their slaves and the artisans from Sri Lanka and Indonesia who arrived with the Dutch East India Company in the 17th century to the French Huguenot refugees of the 18th century, the German traders and missionaries and the colonising English,

not to mention Indian indentured labourers brought to Natal in the 19th century.

African cuisine from rural peasant traditions has been slower to catch on. Although many city restaurants offer a few token dishes, some South African, others from across the continent, you have to visit a restaurant or shebeen in a township to taste the real thing: slow-cooked dishes, such as wild spinach or morog, tripe and pumpkins. Samp, for example, a mash of maize and beans, is best home-made.

Eastern flavours

But it's the cuisine of the Cape that is making an impact at an international level. Real Cape cooking is characterised by spiced, curried or sweetened dishes that originated as European meat, game, fish and dessert recipes, influenced by East Indian and Asian flavourings and preservatives. The most original dishes – and certainly those that all Capetonians know – are those that are either Dutch or Malay or a blend of both, like the *bredies*, *sosaties*, *boboties*

EATING OUT IN CAPE TOWN

The biggest concentration of restaurants is in the city centre and along its edges in Kloof Street, the Waterfront, and in the Gardens and Green Point districts. These are Cape Town's older neighbourhoods, and some of their restaurants have a venerable vintage. There are first-class restaurants in most of the top hotels – the Mount Nelson, the Cape Grace and the Table Bay among them.

Capetonians of the older generation like to eat early, though this fashion is changing. However, eating at 8.30pm is considered very late, even by fashionable standards, and it's not unheard of for restaurant kitchens to close at 10pm. Some restaurants operate a first sitting at 7–7.30pm with a second sitting at 9pm. Don't forget to make a reservation; Capetonians love to eat out, and they often make bookings weeks in advance, particularly during the Christmas holidays.

Service has traditionally been poor, but it is improving, not least because waiting staff depend on their tips (expect to tip 10 percent on top of the bill). City venues have been criticised for refusing to serve tap water or for charging for it (it should be freely available). Smoking is illegal in restaurants, although some have dedicated smoking sections. You should always check with the waiter before lighting up.

Also popular are home-baked breads, *melkterts* (milk tarts), cheesecakes and *koeksisters* (very syrupy and moist plaited pastries), no doubt responsible for the large girth of many countryfolk. Afrikaans farmhouse cooking is enjoying a revival right now, aided by the publication of new editions of *Leipoldt's Cape Cookery* by Louis Leipoldt. Doctor, writer and gourmet, in the 1930s and '40s Leipoldt collected traditional recipes, embellishing or editing them as he saw fit, producing in the process a foundation for a Cape style of cooking.

and *breyanis*. *Bredies* are slow-cooked stews of meat, vegetables and spices. Most characteristic is *waterblommetjie bredie*, made from an indigenous pond plant layered with Karoo mutton. There are also potato, tomato, green-bean and spinach *bredies*. *Sosaties* are skewers of marinated chicken breast or cubed lamb, grilled and served with rice and spicy cooked fruit. But *bobotie* is best-known: ground meat, turmeric, cumin, pepper, fresh lemon leaves and a host of other spices are mixed together and baked, then topped with a savoury custard and served with yellow rice. Lastly, there are the ever-popular *samoosas*, deep-fried triangles of pastry filled with spicy meat or vegetables.

Country cooking

Much of the country cooking of the *boere*, the farmers, evolved in a climate of making do in a harsh living environment. *Potjiekos* is a meat or fish stew cooked in a characteristic three-legged iron cooking pot, while biltong – the local answer to beef jerky – comprises dried strips of beef, ostrich or game meat cured with lashings of coriander seeds and pepper. Salted, spiced and hung up to dry, biltong evolved at a time when it was the only way to preserve meat, particularly when travelling the new lands on ox-wagon, and it is still the snack of choice for many South Africans. You will also find *droewors* (dried sausage), which evolved in a similar manner, and various preserves and chutneys.

Great game

Many of Leipoldt's recipes centre on game and most of the best city restaurants will have a least one game dish on the menu. Venison in South Africa includes kudu, various antelope, warthog and even giraffe. South Africans love their meat – the rarer the better – and one thing you can be sure of is that any menu will almost certainly include a first-class steak. If you are a keen carnivore, try the Famous Butcher's Grill, which has branches in the Park Inn Hotel on Greenmarket Square and the Cape Town Lodge Hotel on Buitengracht Street.

New twists

Nowadays, of course, you may well find various combinations of any of the above. Ginja, on New Church Street, for example, a trendy city

LEFT: city-centre restaurant Ginja specialises in international fusion cuisine. **ABOVE:** organic bread can be found at markets. **RIGHT:** find huge pots of mussels being cooked on the beach.

restaurant famous for delectable combinations of African and Asian flavours and ingredients, might serve Karoo lamb with a Thai green curry. The Signal Restaurant in the Cape Grace Hotel and Cape Malay Restaurant in the suburban Cellars-Hohenort serve superb traditional Cape dishes with a modern twist. Other places, such as Biesmiellah, a wonderfully down-to-earth Cape Malay eatery in a private house in the Malay quarter of Bo-Kaap, remain unremittingly ethnic in their menu choices. Its speciality is tamarind lamb – *denningvleis* – and it doesn't need to be adapted: it's mouth-watering just as it is. Their crayfish *salomie* is a trademark.

Other restaurants present dishes not so much ethnic as simply locale-inspired. What about the marinated eland steak at Khaya Nama (Loop Street), or the pan-seared loin of springbok and warthog at Emily's at the Clock Tower on the Waterfront? This is contemporary South African food and it's delicious.

Cape Town's chefs are leading this change. People such as Garth Stroebel, owner of the South African Chefs Academy, a culinary school for aspiring chefs, is a leading light in this regard, promoting a new food-and-wine culture that integrates South African traditions with exotic new flavours and influences from abroad.

Barbecues are best

South Africans love their *braai* (barbecues) and alfresco eating is a way of life. Perhaps a legacy from the days when outdoor cooking was the only option out in the veld, cooking outdoors, like being able to throw off your shoes and walk around barefoot, is one of the luxuries of living in a hot, sunny climate. *Braai* happen anytime, although late Sunday lunches are a favourite for which *boerewors* (a chunky spiced sausage) and lamb chops or snoek (a barracuda-like fish) basted with apricot jam are a favourite.

Other ingredients that cook beautifully over the hot coals are spatch-cocked chicken or lamb, and firm line-fish such as kingklip or red roman. Everyone gathers round, and there's much drinking of ice-cold local beers and chilled white wine.

Good ingredients

In addition to all this, South Africans are lucky to live in a fecund land where food production gets better and better. Mediterranean-style cuisines fit perfectly here. Olive oil from the Western Cape has won many international awards, while local cheese-making has gone from strength to strength. The annual cheese festival at Franschhoek is known for the varieties of local and unusual cheeses that the organisers have hunted down on remote country farms. Boerenkaas, "farmers' cheese", is a staple in many homes. Even the big supermarket chains such as Pick 'n' Pay, Woolworths, Spar and Checkers have exciting cheese counters where once they might have sold only a rubber-like orange cheddar.

And then there's the fruit, which is delectable. In season you can buy boxes of ripe grapes, melons, peaches, apricots and plums from roadside vendors – refreshing bounty that adds to the pleasure of motoring in the Western Cape.

Cape Town is also one of the best places in South Africa to eat fish and seafood. Indeed, much of it is sent abroad and to Johannesburg. Fish to look out for are snoek, though it can be very bony, kabeljou (great grilled and served with lemon and garlic), galjoen (best baked), kingklip (a firm-fleshed fish that is delicious simply grilled), oysters, mussels and very occasionally perlemoen (local abalone), which is increasingly rare due to a variety of poaching catastrophes. There is also some excellent sushi – for the best in town go to Willoughby's in Victoria Wharf on the Victoria and Alfred Waterfront or Wakame at Mouille Point. ❑

Even the smallest museum usually has a café. Try the Company's Garden (daily specials), the Anglo-Gold Museum (good wines) and the District Six Museum (home-made cakes).

LEFT: Caveau wine bar and deli allows visitors to sample wines from all along the Cape wine route.
ABOVE LEFT: fresh from the *braai* – *boerewors* and *sosaties*.
ABOVE RIGHT: fish market at Kalk Bay.

• *Restaurant recommendations are listed at the end of each chapter in the Places section.*

Creative Cape Town

Cape Town has experienced an explosion in the arts scene in the past decade, in spite of cuts in funding. The city is buzzing with new ideas from plays to literatureand fine arts to jazz

The end of apartheid and the emergence of a democratic South Africa in 1994 created an entirely new social environment based on a constitution that guarantees freedom of speech and expression, with a clause in the Bill of Rights – the only one of its kind in the world – that specifically gives artistic expression greater latitude. Both practitioners and consumers of art are now multiracial, multilingual and cross-cultural.

The fundamental question for South African artists post 1994 was where to go once protest against apartheid was no longer the overriding imperative. Over subsequent years, the ideological preoccupations of most contemporary art forms under apartheid has been set aside, and performers and audiences alike have emerged to produce work that is more individualistic, playful and personal. Artists have eagerly taken to what is the natural province of the arts – a world where our preconceptions of the past, of good and evil, of true and false, are proven far from trustworthy.

The film U-Carmen eKhayelitsha, *which was set in the township of Khayelitsha and based on Georges Bizet's* Carmen, *with a libretto translated into Xhosa, won the Golden Bear at the 2005 Berlin Film Festival.*

Left: contestant at Body Spectra – CityVarsity's annual body-painting event. **Right:** Abdullah Ibrahim, writer of *Manenberg*, the unofficial anti-apartheid anthem.

Nevertheless, as might be expected of a country in cultural transition, one characterised by high levels of poverty and unemployment, much contemporary art focuses on social issues. These include the subversion of traditional values through urbanisation (often idealising rural life) and generational conflict. HIV and Aids, domestic violence and the position of women, unemployment, crime and alcoholism are the new arenas of artistic activism. Black artists have started to unlock themes previously taboo, such as homosexuality, black xenophobia, witches and violence against women in a deeply patriarchal society.

There was always a strong historical association between the arts and the anti-apartheid

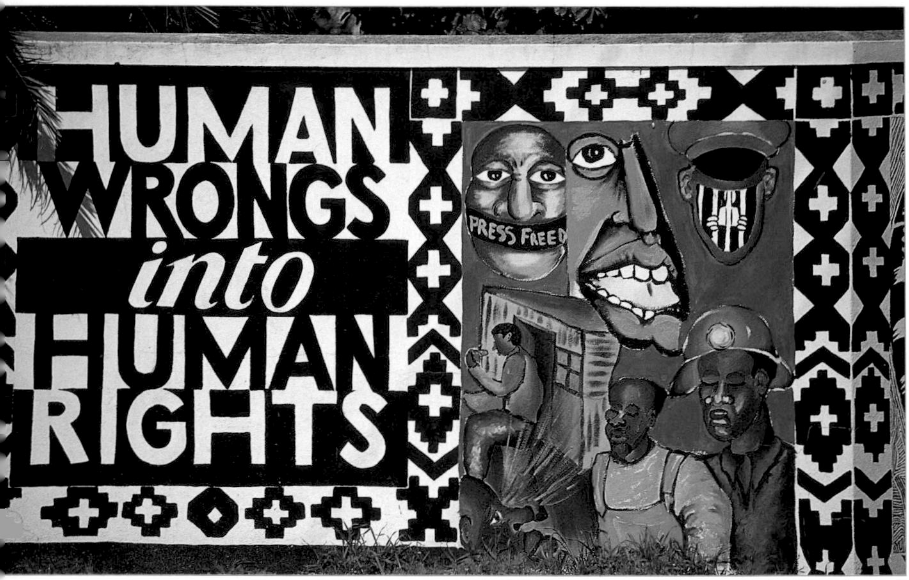

movement, and white artists have generally embraced non-racialism with a positivity not always displayed in other fields. Nevertheless, European culture is still dominant in disciplines such as drama, and it is sometimes difficult for whites to understand the realities faced by their black compatriots – even something as simple as how an out-of-work black actor will struggle to get to auditions in the city centre.

But even this is changing. Artistic cross-pollination between different cultural groups is increasingly a hallmark of the local art scene, often enriched by broader pan-African influences from which both black and white South Africans were formerly isolated. The result is an arts renaissance with an extremely diverse cultural landscape, both in form and content.

Literature

Although literature does exist in all the 11 official languages, most is in English, with a very strong, especially poetic tradition in Afrikaans.

FUNDING THE ARTS

Even though South Africa has many needs, today's democratic government is far more enlightened about art than the apartheid regime, and has grasped the important role that culture plays, not least in reconciliation. The ANC government abolished the monolithic provincial arts councils and created the National Arts Council of South Africa (www.nac.org.za) to which all artists can now apply. The organisation was created in 1997 as part of the Department of Arts and Culture, and provides financial support in creative fields such as literature, fine art, choreography and theatre.

Although this is a far more progressive approach, its bureaucratic application has frequently been incompetent. The collegiate benefits of repertory theatre companies have been lost, while orchestras, opera and ballet companies are no longer secure. Through its funding agencies, government is promoting work that celebrates diversity and highlights social ills, although this agenda is sometimes pursued to a fault by zealous functionaries.

An interesting legacy of apartheid is that there are still no effective trade unions for South African artists, and there is unhappiness surrounding remuneration and working conditions. Black women are especially under-represented in theatre, film, fine art and publishing.

Many black writers, such as Zakes Mda, have returned from exile, and the luminary Wally Serote became adviser on heritage to the president. The 2004 Nobel Prize for Literature was awarded to former Capetonian J. M. Coetzee, whose books *The Life & Times of Michael K* and *Disgrace* won the Man Booker Prize in 1983 and 1999 respectively. The Nobel Prize was also awarded to Nadine Gordimer back in 1991, though internationally the most well-known Cape Town writer is probably the bestselling author Wilbur Smith.

The dominance of English, the perceived precariousness of Afrikaans, and related issues such as elitism and a Eurocentric hegemony are matters of great cultural sensitivity in modern-day South Africa.

The best-selling Afrikaans writer Andre Brink is a Professor of English at the University of Cape Town, and his work has been translated into every major language. Also living in Cape Town is Damon Galgut, whose critically acclaimed *The Good Doctor* was short-listed for the Man Booker Prize in 2004.

Theatre

The sheer number of productions makes Cape Town the theatre capital of South Africa. It is also the seat of an emerging "Coloured" folk theatre, such as Oscar Petersen and David Isaacs's Joe Barber series, and the internationally acclaimed musicals of David Kramer.

Drama reached a low point in the mid-1990s, but traditional plays have since made a comeback. Playwrights are abandoning the "workshop" method of creation and returning to solid scripts such as John Kani's *Nothing but the Truth*.

Great works by black playwrights were denied platforms under apartheid. Many black writers (like Lesego Rampolokeng and Mbongeni Ngema) continue with overtly ideological themes, but the new protest theatre has moved on from simply blaming colonialism.

White English-language dramatists, including South Africa's most famous playwright internationally, Athol Fugard, have concentrated on reconciliation and the difficult reforging of relationships in the emergent "Rainbow Nation".

Although European formats – with proscenium arches and reticent audiences – still dominate, practitioners of community and educational theatre are eagerly importing African story-telling techniques, music and dance. Director Brett Bailey uses traditional healers and ceremonies, and has created a unique new form of theatre.

Theatre-maker extraordinaire Marthinus Basson cracked open the Pandora's box of Afrikaans theatre with his postmodern collaborations with poet Breyten Breytenbach in the 1990s. English plays by Afrikaners like Reza de Wet are well worth attending, and often concentrate on the reinterpretation of cultural symbols.

The classical arts

Cape Town takes pleasure in and feels uncomfortable about its reputation as a more Eurocentric city than most in Africa. This trait finds expression in a strong tradition of symphony concerts, operas and ballet galas, which have been around since the slave orchestras of the Dutch colonists in the 1600s.

LEFT: a striking township mural. **RIGHT:** the hugely popular Cape Town International Jazz Festival attracts fans from all over the world.

Although the Cape Philharmonic Orchestra (formed in 1914) remains mostly white, unlike for instance the KwaZulu-Natal Philharmonic Orchestra in Durban, it has played a strong role in broader development across racial groups, resulting in the creation of the Cape Philharmonic Youth Orchestra in 2004. It's an orchestra with an enormous repertoire, playing its own symphony season and accompanying Cape Town City Ballet and the Cape Town Opera, which puts on grand full-scale operas by Verdi, Puccini and Bizet.

Cape Town Opera was for many years under the stewardship of Angelo Gobbato, and today is 85 percent black. More often than not the singing is world-class, with local leads performing alongside visiting international divas.

The Cape Town City Ballet pursues an increasingly varied repertoire. Evergreen favourites from Tchaikovsky are always on the programme, but new works by talented young choreographers attract a younger following.

Modern dance

Out of all the performing arts in South Africa, dance has always enjoyed the greatest audiences, from packed theatres to public events. The blend of both a strong formal European choreographic tradition and a rich African heritage has created a new wave of exciting work that is gaining international recognition.

> *A recent explosion of stand-up satire was pioneered by the internationally acclaimed Pieter Dirk Uys, creator of the Evita se Perron theatre in Darling. Other comedians include Marc Lottering, David Kau and Loyiso Gola.*

Jazzart's annual Danscape fundraiser is a showcase of the best emerging work. The La Rosa Spanish Dance Theatre in Mowbray is making waves with its seamless blend of flamenco and such African styles as pantsula. The Remix Dance Company creates remarkable pieces using able-bodied and disabled – often wheelchair-bound – dancers. Jikeleza, based in Hout Bay, under the guidance of Edmund Thwaites, takes children living on the streets, puts them in foster homes, sees that they get an education, and develops them as professional dancers and tutors.

The fine arts

While Johannesburg is the powerhouse for South African fine art, Cape Town is home to the South African National Gallery, many resident artists and more commercial galleries than any other city in the country.

South African artists, though hardly registering at home, are making big waves internationally. No longer following trends from overseas and applying them to local subject matter, and no longer voicing tortured protests against State oppression, they are finding their own creative language, both introspective and turning a critical eye on the world around them within and beyond the borders of South Africa. William Kentridge, with his powerful drawings and animated films, is world-famous.

Neglected by the establishment under apartheid, most black artists were excluded from the benefits of formal education and the support of patrons and galleries, and so they developed a strong tradition in cheaper materials, such as lino and woodcuts. That situation has now changed, and the contemporary scene looks forward to a new burst of creative energy, fuelled by acclaimed artists such as the late Gerard Sekoto and George Pemba, and younger artists such as Mgcineni "Pro" Sobopha and Colbert Mashile. An important focus is Greatmore Studios in Woodstock, a base for a constantly changing coterie of emerging artists.

The permanent collection of the South African National Gallery offers a good overview of South African art, and several rooms are devoted to special exhibitions, often photography.

Crafts

Traditional crafts are now recognised as a vibrant part of the country's cultural life, with colourful markets everywhere. The government actively supports craft initiatives, seeing them as an opportunity for stimulating new jobs and businesses in rural areas. The variety is overwhelming. A whole new aesthetic has emerged, using recyclables such as tins, plastic and metal

Fine Art Showcase

The best place to get the pulse of South African fine art is Michael Stevenson Contemporary, a custom-designed white-cube space in Green Point. It has an active exhibition schedule and curates shows across the spectrum of media. Many of the brightest and best are represented by the gallery including Berni Searle, Wim Botha, Guy Tillim, Sabelo Mlangeni and Zanele Muholi. They also have a stock of select but pricey late 19th-century African art. All exhibitions come with published catalogues or books, a rarity in South Africa, back copies of which are available and make a valuable resource for anybody interested in South African art.

LEFT: *Poet and Prophetess*, a collaboration by Sweden's Norrland's Opera and Cape Town Opera. **ABOVE:** at Jazzart Dance Theatre. **RIGHT:** painting in the Ndebele style.

bottle tops, wire, multicoloured telephone flex and mass-produced beads. Craft markets and entrepreneurs abound, and the Fair Trade accredited collective Streetwires in Shortmarket Street has engaged top designers from Europe to help generate ideas.

All that jazz

Just as the penny-whistle playing *kwela* defines Johannesburg internationally, so the strains of Cape Jazz are identified with Cape Town.

> *The eponymous Irma Stern Museum in the Southern Suburbs houses the work of one of Cape Town's greatest artists, and also has excellent contemporary shows in the gallery upstairs.*

Developed by musicians such as Basil Coetzee, Robbie Jansen and Hotep Idris Galeta, it's an infectious musical style brought to its apotheosis by the legendary Abdullah Ibrahim (formerly known as Dollar Brand), who created the unofficial anti-apartheid anthem *Manenberg*, and founded the city's M7 Music Academy. Cape Town abounds in good places to enjoy jazz, and big names like Hugh Masekela and Judith Sephuma regularly perform.

Gospel, choirs and church music have a strong African following. Imported and hybridised versions of reggae, hip-hop and rap are all present, though the major musical and cultural force since the 1990s is *kwaito*, the voice of the black youth who make up almost 50 percent of the population.

Film

A whole industry around film has sprung up in the past decade in Cape Town, and there is a continuous stream of visiting Hollywood stars. Locally made feature films are at last receiving recognition. In 2005 *U-Carmen eKhayelitsha* won the Golden Bear for Best Picture in Berlin and *Yesterday* received an Oscar nomination for the Academy's Best Foreign Film. In 2006, the relatively unfancied South African gangster flick *Tsotsi* stole the show at the Academy Awards ceremony, winning the Oscar for the Best Foreign Language Film, while two films set in South Africa, *Invictus* and *District 9*, featured among the nominees in the 2010 Oscars.

The Out in Africa Gay and Lesbian Film Festival is one of the biggest film festivals in Africa. ❑

Architecture

A singular architectural legacy is the Cape Dutch style, which originated in the 17th century. The works of Sir Herbert Baker are also internationally recognised

The so-called Cape Dutch style is characteristically gabled, low and whitewashed. It's a local adaptation of imported styles, in this case Baroque and neoclassical, and unique to the Cape. It is shaped by the materials most readily to hand and the limited availability of inspired, well-trained craftsmen. All over Cape Town, the Winelands and further afield are wonderful examples of Cape Dutch buildings, from farmsteads, barns and outbuildings to churches and civic buildings.

In the city centre, there are still some surviving buildings from the time of the first British Occupation in the 18th century, and masses of buildings both public and domestic from the second. The late Victorian era is particularly well represented, with streets and streets of villas, some in terraces, with ornate facades decorated with intricate wrought-iron fretwork.

In the 19th and early 20th centuries Sir Herbert Baker drew inspiration from this "indigenous" style of architecture. His interest began when Cecil Rhodes invited him to remodel his Cape Town mansion, Groote Schuur in Rosebank, in the Cape Dutch style and tradition. This contributed to a wide-scale revival of interest in Cape Dutch. More accessible works include the central St George's Cathedral and the Rhodes Memorial on the eastern slopes of Table Mountain. He designed many suburban houses but most are closed to the public.

Art Deco is another defining feature of the city: houses and apartment blocks in Vredehoek and Sea Point, and commercial buildings in the city centre *(see page 81)*. The 1930s, '40s and '50s contributed mansions and bungalows to the suburbs, though it's not these that add to the city's resonance.

Increasingly visible is the new wave of modern domestic architecture. This includes sleek homes by architects such as Stefan Antoni on the Atlantic Seaboard (in particular Camps Bay and Llandudno), and others by Van der Merwe Mysewski, who specialises in buildings that make the most of the city's extravagant views and panoramas, and the brilliant husband and wife duo Gwen and Gawie Fagan, with their preference for more intimate scale, searching for styles that respond to changing light, topography and the vernacular of

the surroundings. In that sense, they're as important to Cape Town and as unique as the traditional Cape Dutch style.

There are many architects today doing magnificent things in the city and elsewhere in South Africa. In this huge open country there's plenty of space to build, and domestic architecture in particular has benefited. Easy, laid-back lifestyles require a certain type of space in which to live. The evidence is all over the wealthier areas of Cape Town. ❑

LEFT: documentary film *The Choir* shows music uniting South African inmates. **RIGHT:** Long Street.

K
DTC
3587B
KB34A

PLACES

A detailed guide to Cape Town and the Cape Peninsula, with excursions to the winelands and along the Garden Route. Principal sites are numbered and clearly cross-referenced to maps

Laid out on a grid west of the Castle of Good Hope, central Cape Town is easy to navigate, with landmarks such as the ABSA tower block dominating the northern (ocean) end and Table Mountain the other. Running between these two are Adderley Street and Long Street, the former lined with grandiose Victorian civic buildings and bank headquarters, the latter with a wonderfully eclectic mix of junk shops, second-hand bookstores, backpacker hostels, bars and galleries. A short walk away are the African craft stalls of Greenmarket Square.

Detached from the centre by a multi-lane highway, the V&A Waterfront is a thriving redeveloped harbour with malls, hotels and a host of entertainment options, from jazz bars to pleasure cruises. It is a great spot for an afternoon of shopping or an evening stroll, followed by an alfresco dinner.

Cape Town is as much about its suburbs as its centre or waterfront. The Southern Suburbs sweep around the base of Table Mountain, enfolding great 19th-century estates such as Groot Constantia and Kirstenbosch, the latter now one of the world's great botanical gardens. Just a stone's throw away, over Lion's Head, are fashionable Clifton and Camps Bay, from where the Atlantic seaboard sweeps down to Cape Point via a string of stunning beaches and the little fishing town of Hout Bay.

South African cities, including Cape Town, have a reputation for crime. In order to change this, and as part of a general attempt to revitalise the CBD in the post-apartheid era, the city's tourism authority has worked alongside local businesses and government agencies to improve security. Surveillance cameras and mounted guards are abundant, both day and night, particularly around the ATM of major banks. As a result, crime is no longer a major cause for concern in areas regularly frequented by tourists, though wandering around the city centre late at night remains inadvisable. ❑

PRECEDING PAGES: the Table Mountain backdrop; fishing at Kalk Bay. **LEFT:** St James beach. **ABOVE LEFT:** Simon's Town. **ABOVE RIGHT:** view from Chapman's Peak Drive.

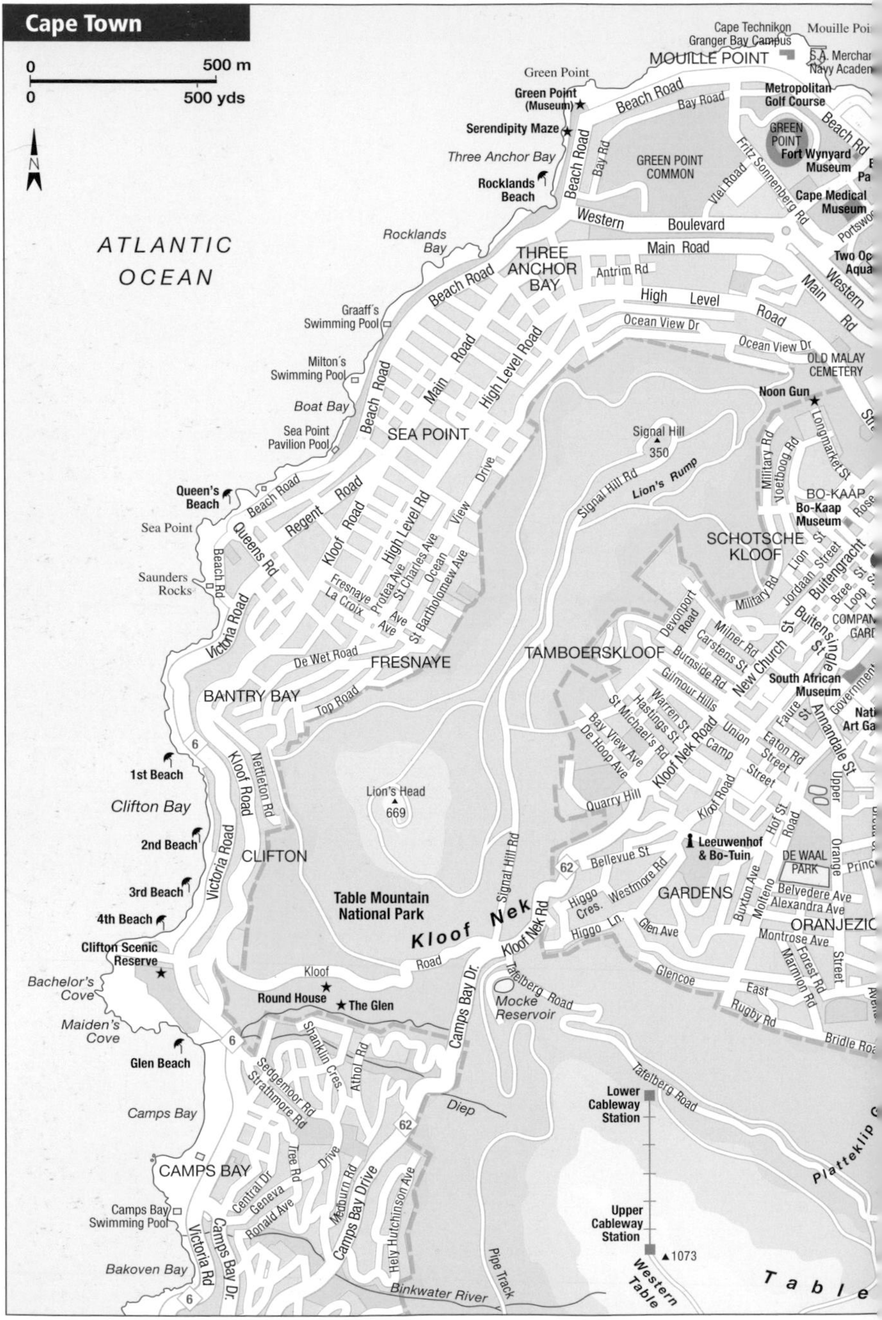
Cape Town
0
500 m
0
500 yds
N
ATLANTIC
OCEAN
Cape Technikon
Granger Bay Campus
Mouille Poi
MOUILLE POINT
S.A. Merchar
Navy Academ
Green Point
Green Point
(Museum)
Serendipity Maze
Three Anchor Bay
Rocklands
Beach
Rocklands
Bay
Beach Road
Bay Road
Bay Rd
Metropolitan
Golf Course
GREEN
POINT
Fort Wynyard
Museum
GREEN POINT
COMMON
Fritz Sonnenberg Rd
Vlei Road
Cape Medical
Museum
Western
Boulevard
Main Road
Two Oc
Aqua
THREE
ANCHOR
BAY
Antrim Rd
High Level Road
Ocean View Dr
Ocean View Dr
OLD MALAY
CEMETERY
Graaff's
Swimming Pool
Milton's
Swimming Pool
Boat Bay
Sea Point
Pavilion Pool
Main Road
High Level Road
SEA POINT
Noon Gun
Signal Hill
350
Signal Hill Rd
Lion's Rump
Longmarket St
Military Rd
Voetboog Rd
BO-KAAP
Bo-Kaap
Museum
Queen's
Beach
Sea Point
Saunders
Rocks
Beach Rd
Queens Rd
Regent Road
Kloof Road
High Level Rd
St Charles Ave
Ocean View Drive
St Bartholomew Ave
Protea Ave
Fresnaye Ave
La Croix Ave
SCHOTSCHE
KLOOF
Lion St
Jordaan Street
Buitengracht
Bree St
Loop St
Military Rd
Victoria Road
De Wet Road
FRESNAYE
TAMBOERSKLOOF
Devonport Road
Milner Rd
Carstens St
Burnside Rd
Gilmour Hills
New Church St
Buitensingle St
COMPAN
GARD
South African
Museum
BANTRY BAY
Top Road
Warren St
Hastings St
St Michael's Rd
Bay View Ave
De Hoop Ave
Kloof Nek Road
Union
Camp Street
Eaton Rd
Faure St
Annandale St
Nati
Art Ga
Kloof Road
Nettleton Rd
1st Beach
Clifton Bay
Lion's Head
669
Quarry Hill
Kloof Road
Hof St
Upper Orange
2nd Beach
Victoria Road
CLIFTON
Signal Hill Rd
Leeuwenhof
& Bo-Tuin
Bellevue St
Westmore Rd
DE WAAL
PARK
3rd Beach
Table Mountain
National Park
Higgo
Cres.
GARDENS
Buxton Ave
Molteno
Belvedere Ave
Alexandra Ave
4th Beach
Kloof Nek
Kloof Nek Rd
Higgo Ln.
Glen Ave
ORANJEZIC
Montrose Ave
Clifton Scenic
Reserve
Bachelor's
Cove
Kloof
Road
Camps Bay Dr.
Tafelberg Road
Mocke
Reservoir
Glencoe
East
Forest Rd
Marmion Rd
Street
Round House
The Glen
Rugby Rd
Maiden's
Cove
Bridle Roa
Glen Beach
Shanklin Cres.
Athol Rd
Sedgemoor Rd
Strathmore Rd
Diep
Tafelberg Road
Lower
Cableway
Station
Camps Bay
Tree Rd
Drive
Platteklip
CAMPS BAY
Central Dr.
Geneva
Ronald Ave
Medburn Rd
Camps Bay Drive
Hely Hutchinson Ave
Upper
Cableway
Station
Camps Bay
Swimming Pool
Victoria Rd
Camps Bay Dr.
Pipe Track
1073
Bakoven Bay
Binkwater River
Western
Table
Table
6
62

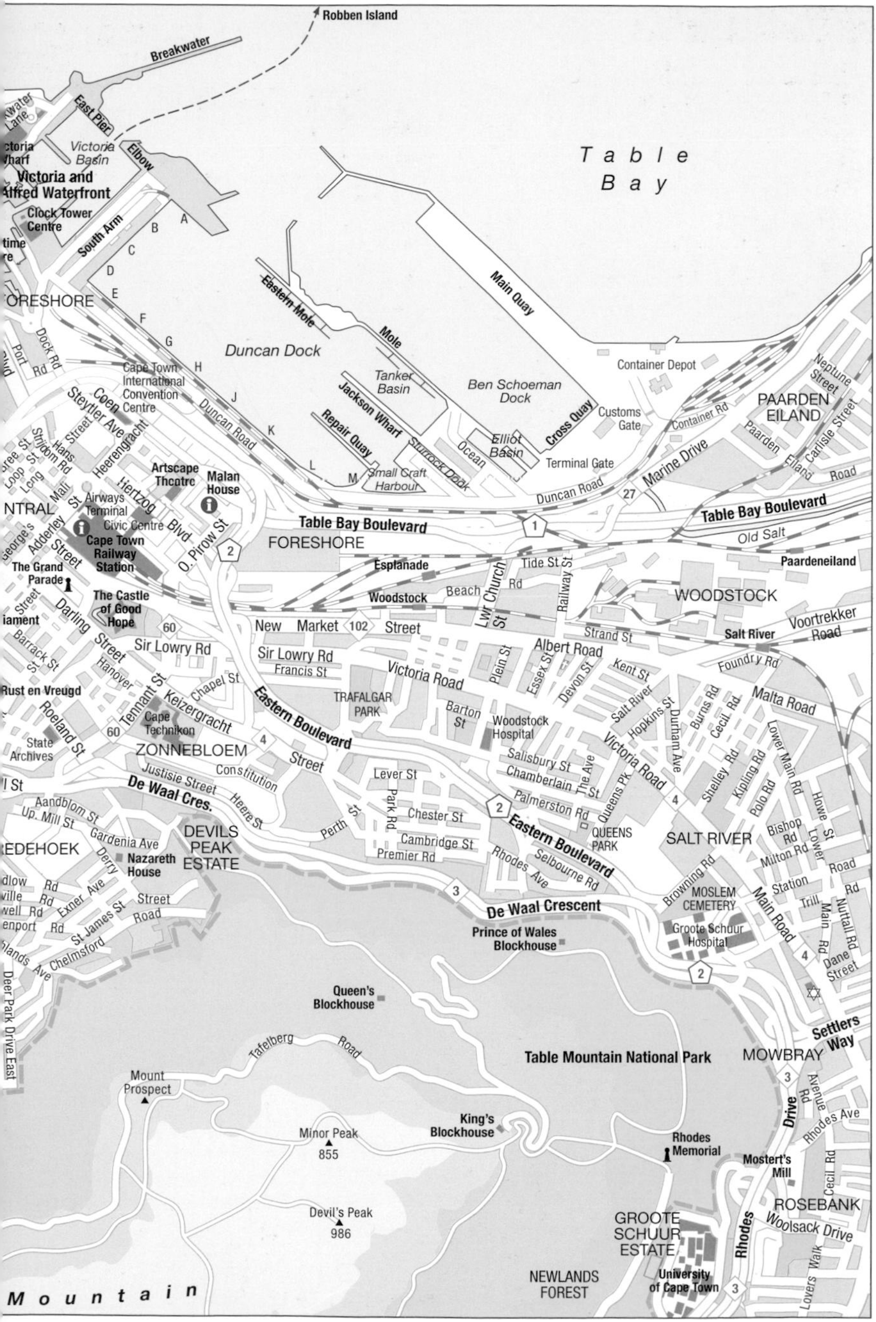

Robben Island
Breakwater
Table Bay
East Pier
Victoria Basin
Elbow
Victoria and Alfred Waterfront
Clock Tower Centre
South Arm
FORESHORE
Duncan Dock
Eastern Mole
Mole
Main Quay
Tanker Basin
Ben Schoeman Dock
Container Depot
Jackson Wharf
Repair Quay
Sturrock Dock
Small Craft Harbour
Elliot Basin
Cross Quay
Ocean
Customs Gate
Terminal Gate
Container Rd
Neptune Street
PAARDEN EILAND
Carlisle Street
Paarden Eiland Road
Marine Drive
Duncan Road
Dock Rd
Port Rd
Cape Town International Convention Centre
Duncan Road
Coen Steytler Ave
Heerengracht
Hans Strijdom Rd
Artscape Theatre
Malan House
Hertzog Blvd
Airways Terminal
Civic Centre
Cape Town Railway Station
Adderley St
Street
O. Pirow St
Table Bay Boulevard
FORESHORE
Old Salt
Paardeneiland
Esplanade
Woodstock
Tide St
Railway St
Beach Rd
Lwr Church St
WOODSTOCK
The Grand Parade
The Castle of Good Hope
Darling Street
New Market Street
Strand St
Salt River
Voortrekker Road
Sir Lowry Rd
Francis St
Albert Road
Foundry Rd
Kent St
Victoria Road
Plein St
Essex St
Devon St
Malta Road
TRAFALGAR PARK
Barton St
Woodstock Hospital
Salt River
Hopkins St
Durham Ave
Burns Rd
Cecil Rd
Lower Main Rd
Hanover
Tennant St
Keizergracht
Chapel St
Eastern Boulevard
Cape Technikon
ZONNEBLOEM
Constitution Street
Rust en Vreugd
Roeland St
State Archives
Barrack St
Salisbury St
Chamberlain St
The Ave
Queens Pk
Victoria Road
Shelley Rd
Kipling Rd
Polo Rd
Howe St
Justisie Street
De Waal Cres.
Heere St
Lever St
Park Rd
Perth St
Chester St
Cambridge St
Premier Rd
Palmerston Rd
QUEENS PARK
Eastern Boulevard
Selbourne Rd
Rhodes Ave
SALT RIVER
Bishop Rd
Milton Rd
Lower Road
Aandblom St
Up. Mill St
Gardenia Ave
DEVILS PEAK ESTATE
Derry
Nazareth House
Exner Ave
St James St
Street Road
Chelmsford
Deer Park Drive East
De Waal Crescent
Browning Rd
MOSLEM CEMETERY
Main Road
Station Rd
Trill
Main Rd
Nuttall Rd
Groote Schuur Hospital
Dane Street
Prince of Wales Blockhouse
Queen's Blockhouse
Tafelberg Road
Table Mountain National Park
MOWBRAY
Settlers Way
Avenue Rd
Drive
Rhodes Ave
Mount Prospect
Minor Peak
855
King's Blockhouse
Rhodes Memorial
Mostert's Mill
Cecil Rd
Devil's Peak
986
GROOTE SCHUUR ESTATE
ROSEBANK
Woolsack Drive
Rhodes
Lovers Walk
NEWLANDS FOREST
University of Cape Town
Mountain

SIR GEORGE GREY, K.C.B.
GOVERNOR
1854 — 1861

THE CITY CENTRE

Cape Town is boom town. What was once a sleepy, colonial hollow has been transformed into an exciting city whose pride in its diverse heritage is reflected in its vibrant street life, world-class museums and galleries, and great restaurants

Main Attractions

CASTLE OF GOOD HOPE
DISTRICT SIX MUSEUM
GREENMARKET SQUARE
IZIKO SLAVE LODGE MUSEUM
COMPANY'S GARDEN
IZIKO SOUTH AFRICAN MUSEUM
IZIKO SOUTH AFRICAN NATIONAL GALLERY
LONG STREET
GOLD OF AFRICA MUSEUM

Maps and Listings

MAP OF CITY CENTRE, PAGE 78
SHOPPING, PAGE 94
RESTAURANTS, BARS AND CAFÉS, PAGES 97–9
ACCOMMODATION, PAGES 224–6

Famously beautiful and set at the foot of one of the world's great natural features, Cape Town has an impressive reputation. But if this is your first visit to the city you will most likely be surprised – and then delighted – by how small and low-key the city centre is. You can stand at one end of Long Street, with your back to Table Mountain, and see the foreshore, with its tiny cluster of high-rises, at the other end. And those repeat visitors who remember Cape Town in its sleepy pre-millennial incarnation will doubtless wonder at how much busier and livelier the city seems today.

Once the dust had settled following the end of apartheid a property boom swept through South Africa, particularly Cape Town and the Cape Peninsula. As a result, long-defunct city-centre areas suddenly became sought after, their central location, once discounted, lauded. Trees were planted and new roads laid out, busy, noisy thoroughfares were pedestrianised, and new hotels and shopping areas built. Many of the centre's handsome Art Deco buildings, which had stood empty and boarded up for years, have since been developed as hotels, office blocks or luxury apartments.

Not only are more of the city centre's monuments and attractions open to the public, they're better staffed, and their custodians display a new pride in them. Aspects of the city that were once ignored have been embraced and there's a sense that the city's cultural patrimony at last belongs to everyone.

Orientation

The heart of Cape Town, known as the City Bowl, is a very small area, originally laid out on a grid system,

LEFT: statue of Sir George Grey, governor of the Cape Colony 1854–61, Company's Garden. **RIGHT:** Table Mountain and the city.

City Centre

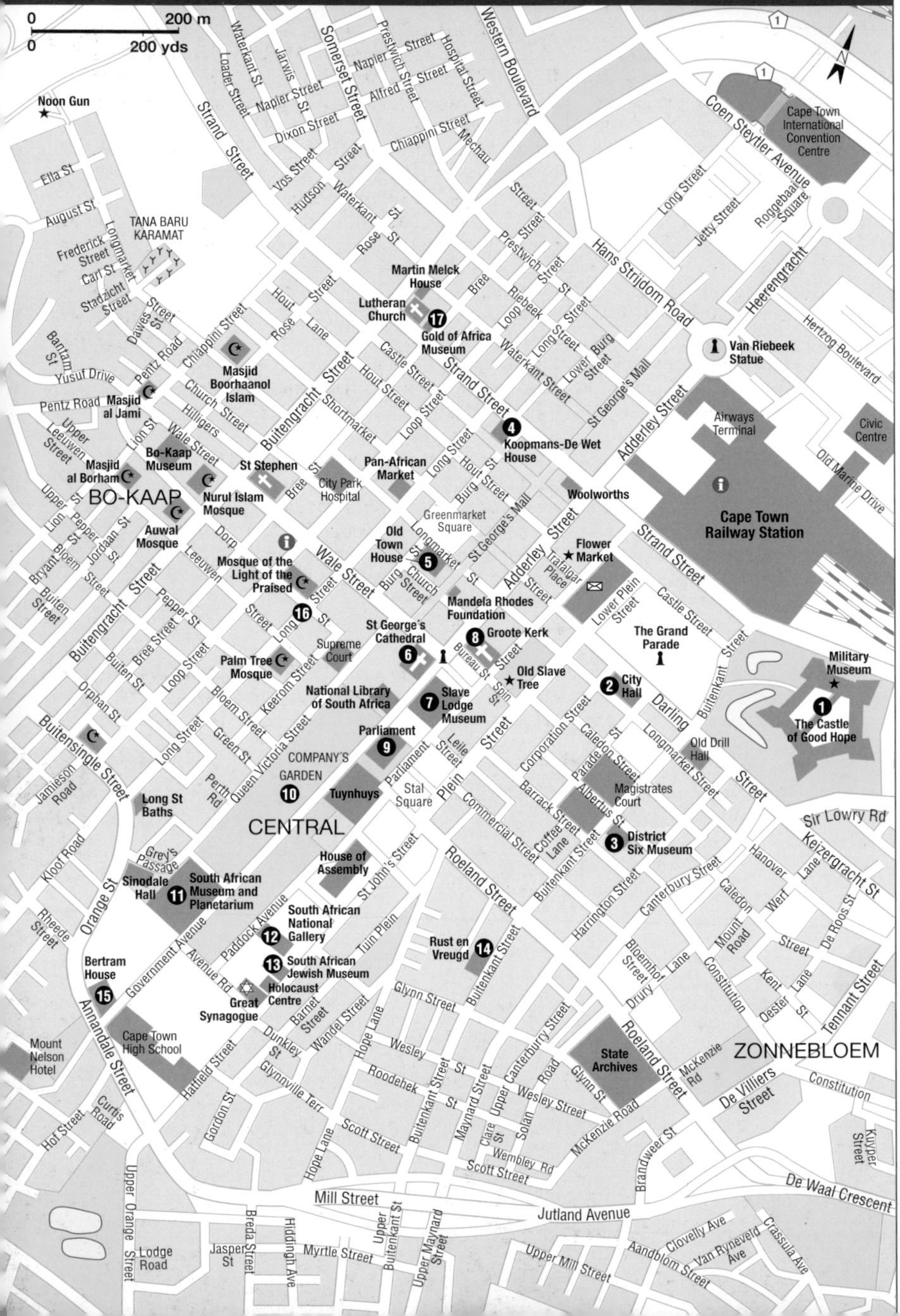
0
200 m
0
200 yds
Noon Gun
Ella St
August St
Frederick Street
Carl St
Stadzicht Street
Longmarket Street
TANA BARU KARAMAT
Dawes St
Bantam St
Yusuf Drive
Pentz Road
Pentz Road
Masjid al Jami
Upper Leeuwen Street
Masjid al Borham
Lion St
Wale Street
Bo-Kaap Museum
BO-KAAP
Upper Lion St
Pepper St
Bryant St
Bloem Street
Jordaan St
Buiten Street
Auwal Mosque
Dorp St
Nurul Islam Mosque
Chiappini Street
Church Street
Hilligers St
Masjid Boorhaanol Islam
Strand Street
Loader Street
Waterkant St
Jarvis St
Napier Street
Somerset Street
Prestwich Street
Napier Street
Alfred Street
Hospital Street
Dixon Street
Chiappini Street
Mechau Street
Western Boulevard
Vos Street
Hudson Street
Waterkant St
Rose St
Hout Lane
Rose Street
Buitengracht Street
Shortmarket Street
St Stephen
Bree St
City Park Hospital
Martin Melck House
Lutheran Church
17
Gold of Africa Museum
Castle Street
Hout Street
Loop Street
Strand Street
Bree Street
Prestwich Street
Riebeek St
Loop Street
Long Street
Lower Burg Street
Waterkant Street
4
Koopmans-De Wet House
Pan-African Market
Long Street
Hout St
Burg Street
Greenmarket Square
Old Town House
5
Longmarket St
Church Street
Burg Street
St George's Mall
Adderley Street
Trafalgar Place
Flower Market
Woolworths
Mosque of the Light of the Praised
Wale Street
16
Long St
Leeuwen Street
Pepper St
Buitengracht Street
Bree Street
Buiten St
Loop Street
Palm Tree Mosque
Keerom Street
Supreme Court
St George's Cathedral
6
Mandela Rhodes Foundation
8
Groote Kerk
Bureau St
Spin St
Old Slave Tree
National Library of South Africa
7
Slave Lodge Museum
Orphan St
Bloem Street
Long Street
Green St
Queen Victoria Street
Buitensingle Street
Jamieson Road
Perth Rd
Parliament
9
COMPANY'S GARDEN
10
Long St Baths
Tuynhuys
Parliament St
Leile Street
Stal Square
Plein Street
CENTRAL
Kloof Road
Grey's Passage
Sinodale Hall
11
South African Museum and Planetarium
House of Assembly
St John's Street
Orange St
Rheede Street
Government Avenue
Avenue Rd
Paddock Avenue
12
South African National Gallery
Tuin Plein
13
South African Jewish Museum
Holocaust Centre
Great Synagogue
Bertram House
15
Annandale Street
Cape Town High School
Mount Nelson Hotel
Hatfield Street
Barnet Street
Wandel Street
Dunkley St
Glynnville Terr
Rust en Vreugd
14
Buitenkant Street
Glynn Street
Hope Lane
Wesley St
Roodehek St
Buitenkant Street
Maynard Street
Upper Canterbury Street
Solan Road
Clare St
Wesley Street
Wembley Rd
Scott Street
Scott Street
Hope Lane
Curtis Road
Hof Street
Gordon St
Mill Street
Jutland Avenue
Upper Orange Street
Lodge Road
Jasper St
Breda Street
Hiddingh Ave
Myrtle Street
Upper Buitenkant St
Upper Maynard Street
Upper Mill Street
Aandblom Street
Clovelly Ave
Van Ryneveld Ave
Crassula Ave
De Waal Crescent
Brandweer St
McKenzie Road
Glynn St
State Archives
Roeland Street
McKenzie Rd
De Villiers Street
ZONNEBLOEM
Constitution
Kuyper Street
Coen Steytler Avenue
Cape Town International Convention Centre
1
Long Street
Jetty Street
Roggebaai Square
Hans Strijdom Road
Heerengracht
Hertzog Boulevard
Van Riebeek Statue
St George's Mall
Adderley Street
Airways Terminal
Civic Centre
Old Marine Drive
Cape Town Railway Station
Strand Street
Castle Street
Lower Plein Street
The Grand Parade
Buitenkant Street
Military Museum
1
The Castle of Good Hope
2
City Hall
Darling Street
Old Drill Hall
Corporation Street
Caledon Street
Parade St
Longmarket Street
Magistrates Court
Albertus St
Barrack Street
Commercial Street
Coffee Lane
Buitenkant Street
3
District Six Museum
Roeland Street
Sir Lowry Rd
Keizergracht St
Hanover Street
Lane
Canterbury Street
Harrington Street
Caledon Street
Werf Street
De Roos St
Mount Road
Bloemhof Street
Drury Lane
Constitution Street
Kent St
Lane
Oester St
Tennant Street

with streets running from south to north and west to east. This makes getting about straightforward and maps easy to read. Historically the city was bounded in the east by the Castle of Good Hope (which is where we start) and in the west by the lower reaches of Signal Hill (where Bo-Kaap is today, *see pages 114–19*), with the Company's Garden in the south and Table Mountain and the modern suburb of Oranjezicht behind, not forgetting the port at Table Bay. The street names of Buitengracht, Buitensingel and Buitenkant indicate the boundaries ("buiten" meaning outer) of the original town.

Castle of Good Hope ❶

Address: entrance on Buitenkant Street, www.castleofgoodhope.co.za
Tel: 021-787 1260
Opening Hrs: daily 9am–4pm; Key Ceremony Mon–Fri 10am and noon; Firing of Signal Cannon Mon–Fri 10.10am and 12.10pm, Sat 11am and noon
Entrance Fee: charge

There is no better place to start a tour of historic Cape Town than with the Castle of Good Hope, which is the oldest building in South Africa. If you blink when you're driving past, you may well miss the castle, so dwarfed is it by the surrounding modern buildings, including the central railway station. Dating from 1666, this rather small, pentagonal fortress was built of brick (imported from Holland) and stone, with lime from Robben Island, and is typical of Dutch colonial settlements from America to Asia.

It has five bastions – named Buren, Leerdam, Oranje, Nassau and Katzenellenbogen after the titles of Prince William of Orange, the Dutch ruler at the time of the settlement – and replaced a simple square fortress built by the Cape's first governor, Jan van Riebeeck. Its design, by the engineer Simon Stevin of Bruges (1548–1620), perfects the idea of the simple, fortified bastions that first appeared in Italy during the 16th century. Surprisingly, the fort has never fired a shot in anger, and no attack has ever been launched against it. That it has survived at all is due to the efforts of Mrs Marie Koopmans-De Wet, of the

TIP

All the sights in this chapter can be easily reached on foot. However, many of them are stops on the City Sightseeing bus *(see page 240)*, an open-top bus linking the essential sights of the Downtown area as well as the Waterfront, Sea Point and the lower cableway station for Table Mountain.

BELOW: Castle of Good Hope, the country's oldest building.

Koopmans-De Wet House *(see page 83)*, who fought its proposed demolition in the 19th century.

For the first 150 years of colonial rule the Castle of Good Hope was the centre of government. It housed the governor and the military, and had dungeons built below sea level. Although there is still a military presence at the castle, it is minimal (you may occasionally see a soldier crossing the yard), and the complex now functions mainly as a museum and as a venue for exhibitions and other cultural activities.

Visitors enter through a handsome gate, topped by a 17th-century bell tower, on the castle's northwest side. This replaced the original sea-facing entrance, which was vulnerable to high tides. As you enter, look up at the gateway to see the VOC monograms of the East India Company and the characteristic broken pediment containing a crowned lion. Commissioner Van Rheede van Oudtshoorn was responsible for building the Kat, a 12-metre (40-ft) -high building slicing across the open courtyard. The Kat balcony is almost certainly the work of Anton Anreith (1785–91), the Dutch East India Company's master sculptor. Most famously it houses the bulk of the **William Fehr Collection** (www.iziko.org.za; 9.30am–4pm; charge) of Africana – oil paintings, furniture, silverware, glass, carpets and porcelain relating to the Cape's earliest colonial period. Of particular interest are the oil paintings depicting life in the Cape between the 17th and mid-19th centuries.

Diagonally opposite the Kat wall, between the Katzenellenbogen and Buren towers, is the **Military Museum**, displaying regimental costumes, weaponry and military artefacts, and documenting colonial expansion. There is a particularly interesting section on the Boer War.

ABOVE: exhibit in the castle's Military Museum. **RIGHT:** street signs from a vanished neighbourhood, District Six Museum. **BELOW:** the restaurant at the Castle of Good Hope.

Grand Parade and City Hall

From the castle cross Buitenkant Street, turn left and then right into Darling Street for City Hall and the Grand Parade.

Completed in 1906, the massive **City Hall** ❷ replaced the Old Town House *(see page 84)*, which by the end of the 19th century had become

Noor Ebrahim, a co-founder of the District Six Museum and guide to visiting groups, grew up in District Six. His book Noor's Story, My Life in District Six *is an engaging account of his family and community.*

far too small. Built of sandstone in a grandiose style, it is typical of the town halls that populated the British Empire. It became known internationally when Nelson Mandela addressed a 70,000-strong crowd from its main balcony following his release from prison in 1990, the first time he had been seen in public for 27 years. As well as housing municipal offices and the public library, City Hall has a handsome concert hall that is home to the Cape Philharmonic Orchestra *(see page 235)*. The exterior was restored in the 1990s as part of a project to regenerate the eastern side of the city' the interior is also set to receive a makeover.

The **Grand Parade** was once a military parade ground. Nowadays it is home to a large flea market and a daytime car park for office workers in the neighbourhood. Vegetables, fruit and traditional medicines are for sale here too.

From the City Hall, head back the way you came, down Darling Street, and turn right into Buitenkant Street. A few blocks along on the other side of the road is the District Six Museum.

District Six Museum ❸

Address: 25A Buitenkant Street, www.districtsix.co.za
Tel: 021-466 7200
Opening Hrs: Mon 9am–1.30pm, Tue–Sat 9am–4pm
Entrance Fee: charge; book in advance for guided tours

Established in 1994, this important heritage museum should ideally be located in the district it commemorates, which was named as the sixth municipal district of Cape Town in 1867. In some respects, though, it is fitting that the museum is some distance removed.

Like Bo-Kaap *(see page 114)*, District Six was originally a lively, colourful neighbourhood populated by the descendants of freed slaves, artisans, tailors, merchants, labourers and immigrants. Its population grew dramatically in the 1780s and the beginning of the 19th century as a result of a general rise in the population of the city. It was a mainly poor area, but its

ABOVE: the Art Deco-style Old Mutual Building, which dates from 1939.

Cape Town's Art Deco

Art Deco was the favoured architectural style in Cape Town during the 1930s. It marked a distinctive break in the way South Africans viewed themselves. No longer looking towards Britain and the colonial tradition (Victorian or neoclassical styles), South Africa's first giant corporations built towering new office blocks inspired by America, and new functions, like cinema, demanded new styles. Construction boomed as the country emerged from the Great Depression, and the price of gold rose when the gold standard was abandoned in 1932. As elsewhere in the world, Art Deco adapted to suit local tastes.

A good place for visitors to start is **Greenmarket Square**, three-quarters of which is 1930s. Close by is the 1932 **Waalburg** building (28 Wale Street) whose facade features some interesting reliefs. On the sumptuous **Old Mutual Building** (Darling Street), built in 1939, you'll find the only Deco proteas, and baboon and elephant heads in the world and a stone frieze depicting the history of South Africa. On Parliament Street there are massive stone figures representing African tribesmen. A map plotting Cape Town's Art Deco buildings can be obtained from the Tourism Visitor Centre on Burg Street.

TIP

Just around the corner from the Koopmans-De Wet House, on the corner of Burg and Castle streets, is the downtown Tourism Visitor Centre (closed Sat and Sun afternoons). As well as providing maps and leaflets, it's the starting point for several specialist walking tours.

inhabitants had lived there for many generations and kinship networks and other relationships were intricate and solid.

In 1966, under the Group Areas Act it was declared a White Group Area, and for the next 15 years a policy of systematic forced removal of the inhabitants and the destruction of their homes and workshops was pursued until there was virtually nothing left.

The museum commemorates the community and illustrates the resulting devastation of the lives and livelihoods of its inhabitants. There are historic maps, personal photographs and poignant reminders – street signs and so on – of the character of a neighbourhood that is sadly gone. A room in a typical home of the neighbourhood has been re-created, along with a school house, a barber's shop and other original settings, all enlivened with evocative recordings of District Six inhabitants relating their stories. The museum also has an interesting bookshop and a cosy café selling good coffee and home-made cakes.

On the hill where the neighbourhood stood, a once scarred landscape has been partially restored to its original owners. On 11 February 2004, 38 years to the day after the area was re-zoned, Nelson Mandela handed over the keys of newly-built houses to the first returning residents Ebrahim Murat and Dan Ndzabela, both in their 80s. It was hoped that another 1,600 families would be settled there by 2007, but

RIGHT: flower stall on Trafalgar Place. **BELOW:** Adderley Street.

this process has been delayed by disagreements between the District Six Beneficiary Trust and Cape Town Municipality.

Adderley Street

From the museum, retrace your steps along Darling Street to **Adderley Street**, which is generally regarded to be the city's main thoroughfare. It is named after the 19th-century British politician Charles Adderley, and while its original name Heerengracht (Gentlemen's Street) indicates its early refinement, the road is not particularly inspiring today. It is, however, flanked by a variety of fine 19th- and 20th-century commercial buildings, including some superb examples of Art Deco architecture *(see page 81)*. Look out for the splendid Standard Bank, distinguished by the statue of Britannia which sits on the dome of the building, and the First National Bank. Adding a splash of colour to Adderley Street is the **Trafalgar Place Flower Market**, where a number of women (and, increasingly, men) from Bo-Kaap sell their floral wares. Not far away is **Woolworths**, a popular department store (along the lines of Marks & Spencer in the UK), whose excellent food hall is a good place to assemble the ingredients for a picnic.

A block northwest of Adderley Street, **St George's Mall** can be enjoyable to explore. Lined with interesting little shops, the pedestrianised mall attracts a lively cast of musicians, performers and street traders who lay out their goods on the pavement. This part of town is undergoing steady transformation, as buildings that once housed offices are being turned into downtown lofts and apartments, heralding a boom in cafés, restaurants, hotels and gyms.

ABOVE: Koopmans-De Wet House. **BELOW LEFT:** the Old Town House, displaying the Michaelis Collection of oil paintings. **BELOW RIGHT:** mounted police.

Iziko Koopmans-De Wet House ❹

Address: 35 Strand Street, www.iziko.org.za
Tel: 021-481 3935
Opening Hrs: Tue–Thur 10am–4pm
Entrance Fee: charge

From St George's Mall, turn north into **Strand Street** and follow it uphill to this small but beautiful

ABOVE: Old Town House. **BELOW LEFT AND RIGHT:** Greenmarket Square flea market.

two-storey 18th-century town house, which stands on the left-hand side of the road, wedged between two modern tower blocks. A relic of the time when downtown streets were lined with elegant homes, it is a perfect example of neoclassical Cape architecture, with mullioned windows, pilasters, a classical pediment, a magnificent fanlight, and interior murals depicting architectural details such as dados, door cases and plinths.

The house was acquired by the De Wet family in 1806, and at the beginning of the 20th century was inhabited by Mrs Marie Koopmans-De Wet (1834–1906) and her sister. When they died it became the property of the city. The core of the collection of antiques in the house is the Koopmans-De Wet family's inheritance, and it would have been furnished as a fashionable town house at the beginning of the 19th century. It has a first-class collection of early Cape furniture, arranged traditionally, Dutch Delft ceramics, fine porcelain, glass and silverware.

Greenmarket Square

Turn right out of Koopmans-De Wet House, walk down Strand Street, take the first right into Burg Street and continue for a couple of short blocks to cobbled **Greenmarket Square**, another relic of old Cape Town. Established as Burgher Watch Square in 1696, it was used as a slave market after 1710, and later became a vegetable market, before being converted to a parking lot in the 1950s. Today, its cobbled stones support one of the city's best flea markets (Mon–Sat 9am–4pm), with stalls specializing carvings, jewellery and fabrics, while others stock second-hand books and bohemian-style clothing. At the top of the square is the Famous Butcher's Grill restaurant *(see page 99)*, an offshoot of the original Butcher's Grill on Buitengracht Street.

Old Town House ❺

Address: Greenmarket Square, www.iziko.org.za
Tel: 021-481 3933
Opening Hrs: Mon–Fri 10am–5pm, Sat 10am–4pm
Entrance Fee: voluntary donation

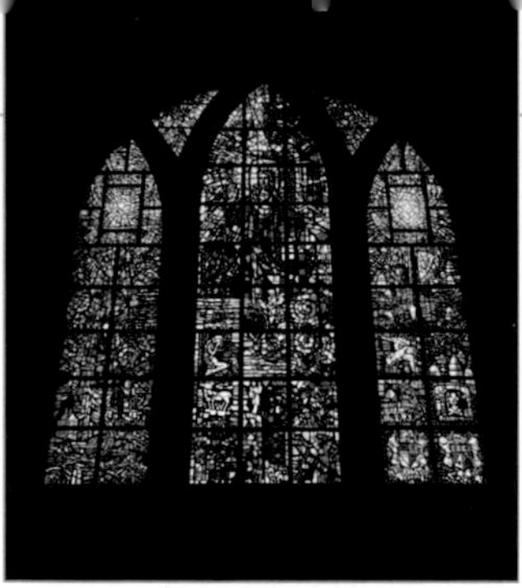

Although Greenmarket Square's surrounds have changed greatly since the days when it was a vegetable market, one surviving landmark still links it to colonial times. This is the old Burgher Watch House, also known as the Old Town House, a very fine survivor in a city bereft of many of its historic buildings. The extant Watch House was constructed in 1761 on the site of an older thatched dwelling, and is thought to have been one of the first two-storey buildings in Cape Town. It originally housed the Burgher Council, which over the years altered and aggrandised it, then, in the 19th century, it became the magistrate's court. In 1840, when Cape Town became a municipality, the building was chosen to become the Town Hall.

It was in 1917 that the Old Town House first became an art gallery, and at the same time its interior was remodelled to have the look of a 17th-century Dutch guildhall. The interior is extremely handsome, but it's quite unlike anything you would have found in the Cape at the time. It is, in fact, a rather good example of the English Arts and Crafts movement of the late 19th century. The Dutch appearance was subsequently considered to be an appropriate setting for the **Iziko Michaelis Collection**, a large collection of 17th-century Dutch and Flemish paintings amassed and donated by Sir Max Michaelis in 1914. The works include still-lifes, portraits and landscapes.

St George's Cathedral ❻

Address: Wale Street, www.stgeorgescathedral.com
Tel: 021-424 7360
Opening Hrs: Mon–Fri 8.30am–4.30pm
Entrance Fee: free

From Greenmarket Square, continue

St George's Cathedral became famous during the apartheid era when Desmond Tutu was the Anglican Archbishop of Cape Town from 1986–95. The Archbishop, who was branded a dangerous communist by the government, ran his anti-apartheid campaign from here. In order to operate in this downtown area, the Archbishop was required to carry a pass.

ABOVE LEFT: stained-glass window in St George's Cathedral.
BELOW LEFT: a plaque on Church Square marks the site where slaves were sold.

Life in the Slave Lodge

The slaves living at the Slave Lodge worked for the Dutch East India Company (VOC), in its farms, fisheries, quarries and the Company's Garden. Some worked as bricklayers, bakers, blacksmiths, potters, carpenters or in other trades. Mulatto slaves of part-European descent were generally given the better jobs, as well as better conditions.

Slaves could buy their freedom or were entitled to request their freedom after 30 years' good service (less in the case of mulattos), providing they were confirmed in the Dutch Reformed Church, spoke Dutch and had the means to support themselves outside the lodge. However, few attained the 30 years, as the death rate from disease and insanitary conditions was high (20–30 percent in some years). Others were too institutionalised to survive in the world outside.

Slaves who were born in the lodge were baptised and could not be sold to private individuals. They also received an education (in Dutch) up to the age of 12, something that few children living in the town received. They were taught by fellow slaves or freed slaves who received a salary.

TIP

Also worth seeing in connection with the slave trade is the Bo-Kaap area, still inhabited by the descendants of freed slaves *(see pages 114–9)*.

down Burg Street until you reach Wale Street. Just to the left you'll see St George's Cathedral, which was designed by Herbert Baker and built in 1901 to replace a lovely Greek Revival building that sat alongside it until 1954. King George V, while still the Duke of Cornwall and York, laid the foundation stone. The cathedral contains some fine stained glass, including *Christ in Triumph over Darkness and Evil* in the Great West Window, commemorating Lord Louis Mountbatten, who spent a lot of time in Cape Town during the latter stages of his life.

The building is not considered one of Herbert Baker's best works, and is more interesting, perhaps, for its political role during the last years of apartheid when Anglican Archbishop Desmond Tutu *(see margin note, page 85)* preached anti-apartheid sermons from its pulpit. A modest but illuminating display evokes the church's role in the 1980s anti-apartheid struggle. A newer addition, which opened in 2004, is a courtyard labyrinth replicating the one laid in the floor of Chartres Cathedral *c.*1220.

RIGHT: the National Library of South Africa.

Next door to the church is the white stucco 19th-century building that houses the National Library of South Africa, and beyond that the Company's Garden *(see page 88)*.

Iziko Slave Lodge Museum ❼

Address: 49 Adderley Street, on the junction with Wale Street, www.iziko.org.za
Tel: 021-460 8242
Opening Hrs: Mon–Sat 10am–5pm
Entrance Fee: charge, audio tours available

Diagonally opposite St George's Cathedral, this museum is housed in Cape Town's second-oldest building, constructed by the Dutch East India Company in 1679 as a shelter for slaves shipped to Cape Town from India, Madagascar, Ceylon, Malaya and Indonesia. At one point during the 18th century there were more slaves than free citizens at the Cape, and the lodge held an average of 500 slaves during this period, rising to 1,000 at its peak, whilst also housing the colony's mental patients. In 1803 Louis Michel Thibault, the Inspector of Public Buildings, described the insanitary, disease-ridden state of the lodge, which had no proper ventilation or provision for natural light. Following the abolition of slavery in 1834, the building became the city's

Cape Town as Legislative Capital

South Africa is unusual in having three capitals: Pretoria, the administrative capital and seat of government; Bloemfontein, the judicial capital; and Cape Town, the legislative capital. This arrangement dates from the foundation of the Union of South Africa in 1910 when agreement could not be reached on which of the four provinces, Cape, Natal, Transvaal or the Free State, should contain the national capital.

Following independence in 1961, the government maintained the status quo that had prevailed previously, with non-whites excluded from national elections. Over the following years increased participation was given to coloured and Indian citizens, and in 1984 a three-chambered parliament was established consisting of one house for whites, one for coloureds and one for Indians, though whites were given greater power. Blacks were excluded from national politics until the country's first democratic elections in 1994, when Nelson Mandela and the ANC were swept to power. Today, the inconvenience of having three capitals sometimes leads to calls for power to be centralised in Pretoria, a move fiercely resisted by Western Cape.

first post office, then the library and then the supreme court.

Seeing the beautifully restored building from the outside, its insalubrious past is hard to imagine. But inside, the focus is firmly on the building's history as a slave lodge, and the broader history of slavery in the Cape and further afield. The audio tour available at the entrance is highly recommended, as it explains the original purpose of each room and describes the horrifying conditions endured by the slaves.

This is an important site, since slavery had such a huge impact on the culture of South Africa and has directly affected its language, customs, cuisine, labour laws, religion and architecture. Today the Slave Lodge Museum is an important leg on the International Slave Route Project established by Unesco.

Just outside the building, in nearby Spin Street, a plaque marks the site of the Old Slave Tree where slaves were auctioned.

Groote Kerk 8

Address: Church Square, Spin Street, www.grootekerk.co.za
Tel: 021-461 7044
Opening Hrs: Mon–Fri 10am–2pm
Entrance Fee: free

Around the corner from the Slave Lodge Museum, the Groote Kerk – literally 'Big Church' – is, as its name suggests, the most important Dutch Reformed edifice in the country, and the oldest in Cape Town. It was built in 1704, and is famous today for the magnificent Baroque pulpit (1789) made by master sculptor and woodcarver Anton Anreith and cabinet-maker Jan Graaf. Before the church was built, services were held in the castle, until Governor Willem Adriaan van der Stel decided that a new, permanent place of worship was needed.

The Anreith pulpit is still in use today, and is one of Cape Town's most treasured possessions. The lions supporting it symbolise the power of faith, the anchor is for hope and the urn on the canopy for mortality. Over the years the building was altered, and in 1841 was remodelled entirely. Now, only its steeple, which you can barely see, is original. The facades front and back are a strange mixture of Gothic and neoclassical style.

ABOVE: statue of General Louis Botha, South Africa's first prime minister, in front of Parliament.
BELOW: detail on the Baroque pulpit in the Groote Kerk.

Houses of Parliament 9

Address: Parliament Street, www.parliament.gov.za
Tel: 021-403 2262/3683
Opening Hrs: guided tours only, by advance arrangement
Entrance Fee: free

Once the bastion of white supremacy, the Houses of Parliament, though technically accessible from a northern extension of Adderley Street, are better viewed from the Parliament Street side. The massive building of red brick and tall white pilasters was completed in 1864 using mostly imported materials. Presided over by

EAT

The Company's Garden has a good little tearoom with a shady terrace, where you can get inexpensive hot and cold meals, cakes, cool beers and other refeshments, including daily specials.

ABOVE: the statue of Cecil John Rhodes is a focal point in Company's Garden. **BELOW:** the beautiful rose garden in Company's Garden.

a statue of Queen Victoria, it owes nothing to its African setting, but it's worth a visit to see how Parliament works. Ask to see the art collection and the interesting collection of early maps of the African continent.

Further up Government Avenue, just behind the Houses of Parliament, is the office of the State President, the **Tuynhuys**, once called Government House. At the Treaty of Amiens, which ratified the British occupation of the Cape, this mid-18th-century residence of the Governor of the Cape was Georgianised by Lord Charles Somerset. It was restored in the late 1960s by Gawie Fagan, who attempted to revive its earlier Dutch appearance, visible through the railings from the Avenue. Behind you now is the entrance to the Company's Garden.

Company's Garden ⑩

Address: Queen Victoria Street, at the north end of Adderley Street
Opening Hrs: daily 8am–6pm
Entrance Fee: free

Right at the heart of the city, the 6-hectare (15-acre) **Company's Garden** is all that survives of the original 18-hectare (44-acre) vegetable garden laid out by the Dutch East India Company and developed as a source of fresh fruit and vegetables for their ships as they passed by on their way between Europe and the East. Its origin dates back to 1648, when the crew of the shipwrecked Dutch vessel *Haarlem* *(see page 32)* sowed vegetable seeds near a stream of fresh water coming down from Table Mountain. In 1652, the settlement's master gardener, Hendrik Boom, prepared the first beds.

Over time, as farming was established on the Cape, the Company's

Garden became a botanical garden. Oaks were planted by Governor Simon van der Stel, whose master gardener laid out an elaborate system of canals that were fed by mountain springs. Pines were introduced, and so were roses, herbs and medicinal plants. In 1751 Jan Andries Auge became Superintendent of the Gardens, and was responsible for adding many indigenous species that he had collected on his trips around the Cape.

There are some very interesting specimens here, if only because of their great age. There's a Saffraan pear, which is thought to have come from Holland in the time of van Riebeeck, making it one of the first trees to have been cultivated in South Africa. There's also an Outeniqua yellowwood, thought to have been planted in the late 1700s, and a 17-metre (56ft) tree aloe, believed to be the tallest in the country. There's also a black mulberry, said to have grown from a seedling from one of the original mulberry trees planted by van Riebeeck in an attempt to establish a silk industry in the Cape (the venture failed because van Riebeeck ordered the wrong kind of mulberry trees).

There are now more than 8,000 species of trees and plants here, plus a fernery, a palm grove, a herb garden, a fuchsia house and a conservatory. The abundant grey squirrels were introduced from America by Cecil John Rhodes.

Until 1803 the upper part of the Gardens was used as a zoo, and at the top of the Avenue is the so-called Lioness Gateway, with stucco animals by Anton Anreith *(see page 87)*, that once led into the Menagerie. On the left-hand side was the bird and antelope park, and to the right, the beast of prey park. The Lioness Gateway now leads into the aviary. There are enough of these old structures left to give an idea of Louis Michel Thibault's plans to turn the area into a handsome public park (Thibault was Inspector of Public Building in the early 19th century).

The garden is hemmed in by Queen Victoria Street on the west side and the Avenue on the east. To the north it's overlooked by the National Library and to the south, beyond a more formal area of rose gardens, water gardens and fountains, is the Iziko South African Museum and the South African National Gallery.

ABOVE: Iziko South African Museum.

BELOW: whale skeleton within the Museum.

Iziko South African Museum ⓫

Address: 25 Queen Victoria Street, www.iziko.org.za

Tel: 021-481 3800

Opening Hrs: daily 10am–5pm

Entrance Fee: charge

Founded in 1825 and relocated to its present site at the south end of the Company's Garden in 1897, the South African Museum houses permanent collections on both the natural and the human sciences.

ABOVE: Iziko South African National Gallery.

Oddly, San artefacts are exhibited alongside fossils (come here before you go fossil-hunting in the Karoo), rocks and minerals, and skeletons of animals and whales, and there's a magnificent collection of South African beadwork and other cultural items from the country's indigenous people. Among the highlights is the mysterious rock art of the San *(see box)*. This indigenous people, who were wiped off the map of South Africa but survive in the Kalahari in Namibia, are represented in life-size dioramas of their everyday life.

Also look out for the coelacanth, a prehistoric fish found in the 20th century still to be living off the coast at East London, and the Lydenburg Heads, seven ceremonial terracotta heads dating from 500 BC.

The South African sky at night is remarkable, and one of the best places to view it is the Karoo, in Sutherland. However, city-bound stargazers have the superb **Planetarium** (tel: 021-481 3900; several shows daily; charge), an extension of the Iziko South African Museum recognisable by its domed roof. It has a "theatre of the stars" projected onto the interior of the dome, and a programme of events including "star finder" astronomy courses, changing exhibitions (some designed for children) and field trips to the country to explore the night skies.

The Rock Art of the San

The most interesting exhibits in the Iziko South African Museum relate to the rock art of the hunter-gatherer people (known to outsiders as "San" or "Bushmen") who lived in southern Africa until the end of the 19th century and still live in neighbouring Namibia. The examples here are perhaps no more than 200 years old, but they are of considerable interest. In particular, look out for the Linton panel, removed from a cave on a farm in the Eastern Cape in 1918. About 2 metres (6ft) long, it depicts eland, a swift and powerful animal, and a supine human form with cloven hooves. It is thought that the painting represents a spritual experience attained through trance, during which the shaman (medicine man) is at one with the animal and acquires supernatural healing powers. The museum shows a short film of a trance dance performed by the San of today.

To learn more about the rock art read *The Mind in the Cave* by David Lewis-Williams, the leading anthropologist in this field. Lewis-Williams has found links between the rock art of the San and that of ancient European people, such as the cave paintings at Lascaux in the Dordogne in France.

Iziko South African National Gallery (12)

Address: Paddock Avenue, entrance via the Company's Garden, www.iziko.org.za
Tel: 021-467 4660
Opening Hrs: Tue–Sun 10am–5pm
Entrance Fee: charge

Situated amongst the old oak trees between the Company's Garden and Parliament, this national gallery is one of the top showcases of South African art, and it also has an eclectic collection of European works, including British, French, Dutch and Flemish art. Ultimately, though, it's the local paintings, sculpture, ceramics, beadwork and textiles that people come here to see, and for changing exhibitions.

South African Jewish Museum (13)

Address: 88 Hatfield Street, www.sajewishmuseum.co.za
Tel: 021-465 1546
Opening Hrs: Sun–Thur 10am–5pm, Fri 10am–2pm
Entrance Fee: charge

Set alongside the National Gallery in a modernistic building whose inauguration in 2000 was attended by Nelson Mandela and Helen Suzman, this museum presents a compelling account of the Jewish community in Cape Town, and stages some of the liveliest temporary exhibitions in town. South Africa has a large Jewish community, mostly descended from the contingent of European Jews drawn by the discovery of diamonds in the 1860s, and a second influx of refugees from the pogroms in Russia 20 years later. The museum incorporates the **Old Synagogue**, which is recognisable by its classical temple front, and is South Africa's oldest such edifice built in 1862. Next door is the **Great Synagogue**, built in 1904.

Cape Town Holocaust Centre

Address: 88 Hatfield Street, www.ctholocaust.co.za
Tel: 021-462 5553
Opening Hrs: Sun–Thur 10am–5pm, Fri 10am–1pm
Entrance Fee: free

ABOVE: Iziko Rust en Vreugd. **BELOW LEFT:** newspaper cuttings in the South African Jewish Museum. **BELOW RIGHT:** inside the Great Synagogue, with its huge copper-clad dome.

TIP

After visiting Bertram House you can take afternoon tea on the veranda of the Mount Nelson Hotel *(see page 224)*. This venerable establishment, which has hosted royalty and international statesmen, remains one of Cape Town's top hotels. Its buffet breakfast (before 11am) is good, too.

Situated on the first floor of the Albow Centre in the same compound as the Jewish Museum, this is the only centre of its type in Africa. Its main focus is the European holocaust associated with World War II, but it also places these events in the context of racism in South Africa. With changing exhibits, archival documents and films, tableaux and survivor testimonies, it is a place of remembrance and learning which documents the disastrous consequences of unchecked racial discrimination.

Iziko Rust en Vreugd ⓮

Address: 78 Buitenkant Street, www.iziko.org.za
Tel: 021-464 3280
Opening Hrs: Tue–Thur 10am–4pm
Entrance Fee: voluntary donation

The old houses of Cape Town once had wonderful gardens, few of which survive. However, this fine Cape Dutch mansion, built in 1777, has had its garden restored in period style. It's slightly out on a limb but it is well worth coming to see, not only for the garden, but also for the William Fehr Collection of Africana – part of the bigger collection housed in the Castle of Good Hope *(see page 79)*. Drawings, etchings, watercolours and other works depict views and scenes of life in early Cape Town, historical events, and notable people and buildings.

Rust en Vreugd is a lovely and peaceful spot. Remember to look up at the facade of the building, with its attractive period fanlights and handsome architraves. The carved teak doors are almost certainly by Anton Anreith, and are the finest rococo ornament in the Cape.

RIGHT: *boerewors* take-away on Long Street.

BELOW: facade of Mama Africa restaurant, Long Street.

Iziko Bertram House ⑮

Address: Hiddingh Campus, pedestrian entrance on Annadale Street, www.iziko.org.za
Tel: 021-481 3940
Opening Hrs: Mon and Fri 10am–5pm
Entrance Fee: voluntary donation

Another old home worth visiting in this area of town is this small and little-known museum housing the Winifred Ann Lidderdale Bequest – a collection of English porcelain, silver and 19th-century furniture. The late Georgian, red-brick building stands at the top of the Avenue, shaded by the oaks on the university's Hiddingh Campus and facing the magnificent columned entrance to the sumptuous **Mount Nelson Hotel**, a landmark for discerning travellers since it opened in 1899. Past guests at the hotel have included Lord Kitchener, the young Winston Churchill and the Prince of Wales (later the Duke of Windsor), for whom the hotel's grand entrance, the Prince of Wales Gate, was commissioned in 1925.

From Mount Nelson Hotel, head back towards the centre of town along Kloof Road, which eventually leads into Long Street. Kloof Road is an interesting area for upmarket groceries and delis, with some good cafés along the way.

Diverse attractions

Running a block west of the Company's Garden, **Long Street** ⑯ is the longest, liveliest and most famous – some would say infamous – street in Cape Town. It links mountain and sea, and you can stand with your back towards the mountain at one end and see ships berthed in the dock at the other. Table Bay and the coast at Bloubergstrand can be seen away in the distance.

For a long time it represented the heart and soul of this maritime city, and today it has many faces. Anything – and everything – happens here. There are delis, cafés, restaurants, all-day bars and nightclubs; churches and two mosques; vintage- clothing shops, bookshops, antiques and bric-a-brac shops, markets and pharmacies; banks, pawn shops and porn shops; apartment blocks, hotels, backpacker lodges and offices.

It's a street of seemingly endless possibilities. A man once bought some 18th-century English silver by Paul Storr in a junk shop on Long Street, and it's now in the Metropolitan Museum in New York. Less fortunate men have met beautiful women in dodgy bars here, then accompanied them home only to discover that they're not women at all, but a singular brand of South African cross-dresser commonly known as a "moffie".

It's safer by far to stick to the shopping – perhaps invest in a limited edition book with rare views of early Cape Town – or dine out on Asian or African food, have an old-fashioned

ABOVE: one of a host of eateries on Long Street.

BELOW: statue of Queen Victoria, whose reign (1837–1901) oversaw the Boer Wars.

Shopping

The Long Street area is the main focal point for shopping in the city centre, with the emphasis on smaller and quirkier shops than you'd associate with the V&A Waterfront and the other malls that characterise suburban Cape Town. Second-hand bookstores and trendy clothes boutiques are plentiful, but the area also boasts some superb galleries and the city's best specialist African music store.

Books

Book Lounge
71 Roeland St. Tel: 021-462 2425. www.booklounge.co.za p256, B3
Voted South Africa's best bookshop in 2009, this attractively decorated bibliophile's haven has passionate staff, a dedicated reading room and coffee bar, and an up-to-date stock of new books.

Clarke's Bookshop
211 Long St. Tel: 021-423 5739. www.clarkesbooks.co.za p256, A2
Established in 1956, this excellent second-hand bookshop is highly rated by serious collectors for its specialist collections of Africana and tomes about South African art.

Clothing

Mali South Clothing
90 Long St. Tel: 021-426 1519. www.malisouthclothing.co.za p256, A2
Malian designer Maiga Abdoulaye uses the colourful cloths traditional to West Africa as the basis for an innovative range of men's, women's and children's clothing – it's a great place to buy your first Madiba shirt.

Misfit
287 Long St. Tel: 021-422 5646. www.misfit.co.za p256, A2
This hip boutique is the main walk-in outlet for Saskia Koerner, whose trendsetting designs combine a classical and vintage feel with a contemporary rock 'n' roll edge and elements of batik.

Crafts

Greenmarket Square Flea Market
Corner of Shortmarket and Burg streets. p256, B2
This is probably the city's best one-stop for African crafts, and the vendors here are as varied in African origin as their wares. Beware of pickpockets, however, as they are rife in this touristy area.

Pan-African Market
76 Long St. Tel: 021-426 4478. p256, A2
Sprawling across three floors, this is a wonderful place to dig around for carvings, textiles, beadwork, ceramics, tableware, clothes, shoes, baskets, jewellery and CDs from all over Africa.

Tribal Trends
72–4 Long St. Tel: 021-423 8008. p256, A2
This owner-managed store has the finest selection of African crafts, artworks and antiques you're likely to encounter anywhere, all laid out with a genuine enthusiast's flair. Prices are high but the quality is superb.

Food

Melissa's
94 Kloof St. Tel: 021-424 5540. www.melissas.co.za p255, E4
A Tamboerskloof institution, this superb deli specialises in preservative- and additive-free wares, from yummy homemade goodies to wholefoods and fresh produce.

Jewellery

African Women's Trading Market
112 Long St. Tel: 021-424 5356. www.affricanheritage.co.za p256, A2
The inexpensive jewellery here is made entirely from natural African materials, ranging from semi-precious stones and pebbles to bones, leaves, leather, beads, porcupine quills, feathers – even lengths of old telephone wire.

Afrogem
181 Buitengracht St. Tel: 021-424 0848. www.afrogem.co.za p256, A2
For the serious buyer, this stocks a vast selection of ready-to-buy tanzanite, diamonds and other jewellery, as well as unset stones that can made into custom-made artefacts within 36 hours.

Music

African Music Store
134 Long St. Tel: 021-426 0857. p256, A2
This is the best specialist African CD shop on the continent, with knowledgeable staff and racks stacked with everything from local *kwaito* to the latest sounds from Mali, Congo and Ethiopia.

Wines

Caroline's Fine Wine Cellar
62 Strand St. Tel: 021-419 8984. www.carolineswine.com p256, B2
Run by the same owner-manager for over 20 years, this place stocks an excellent range of local and international wines, and hosts regular wine tastings.

Wine Concepts
50 Kloof St. Tel: 021-426 4401. www.wineconcepts.co.za p255, E3
After 15 years in the business, this boutique store remains an enthusiastic showcase for lesser-known wines that are well priced and easy drinking, as well as finer bottles for special occasions.

shave with a cut-throat razor, or lie around in a hot, steamy Turkish bath.

Architectural melting pot

The tone of Long Street ranges from smart to seedy to downright sleazy, and these contrasts are its very essence. The buildings that line the street are similarly diverse, forming a veritable textbook of the architectural styles that have come and gone in Cape Town. The buildings span every century, from the earliest days of the colony to the present. At No. 206 is Cape Town's most exuberant High Victorian building, awash with ornate metalwork, turrets and fancy gables. At No. 185 is the **Palm Tree Mosque** (not open to non-Muslims), converted from a house on the site early in the 19th century. The palm tree is still at the door in what was once the garden.

At the mountain end of Long Street on the corner of Orange Street, **Long Street Baths** (tel: 021-400 3302; daily 7am–7pm; charge) have been a city institution since they opened in 1908. The complex includes a heated swimming pool, steam and dry-heat rooms and a massage parlour.

But the most interesting sights on Long Street are generally the transient ones. Shops come and go, but there are some that are well established and worth looking out for. The **Pan-African Market** *(see opposite)*, halfway along the street, is filled with artefacts and curios from all over Africa, including carvings, textiles, beadwork, ceramics, tableware, clothes, shoes, baskets, jewellery and music CDs and cassettes. Also on an African theme is the **African Music Store** *(see opposite)*, selling a wide and wonderful range of music from all over the continent.

Gold of Africa Museum ⓱

Address: 96 Strand Street, www.goldofafrica.com
Tel: 021-405 1540
Opening Hrs: Mon–Sat 9.30am–5pm
Entrance Fee: charge, audio guide available

This is the city's newest museum and well worth a visit. Established by Anglo-Gold, the world's largest gold mining company, and based on a collection originally displayed

LEFT: heated swimming pool at Long Street Baths. **ABOVE:** Art Deco architecture on Long Street. **BELOW:** sign for the Gold of Africa Museum.

in the Barbier-Mueller Museum in Geneva, it houses a stunning collection of gold jewellery and cultural artefacts from around the African continent. West Africa, particularly the Akan kingdoms, gets a good showing – there are examples from Mali, Senegal and Ghana – but there are items from Zimbabwe and South Africa as well, from ceremonial objects used by royalty to smaller amulets carried by traders and warriors. Pieces are beautifully displayed, with good background information on the cultural and symbolic importance of gold in African cultures. Early maps illustrate gold and other trade routes.

The museum is housed in the 18th-century Martin Melck House, a fine original town house dating from 1788. There is a delightful courtyard café that serves coffee and cakes, and an excellent selection of wine and light meals. At night this becomes the excellent Gold Restaurant *(see opposite)*, which serves a leisurely pan-African set menu over several courses, accompanied by West African drumming, and masked and stilted dancing influenced by the Dogon people of Mali.

The Lutheran Church

Next door to the museum is the **Lutheran Church**. In 1780 the Lutheran congregation was still worshipping in an old barn in Strand Street, given to them by Martin Melck, a wealthy Lutheran merchant. In 1791 the congregation commissioned Anton Anreith to transform the barn into a church. The bulk of the facade is almost certainly his design, but in the 19th century the top half was altered and the bell tower built. It's the only known facade by Anreith.

The interior is filled with late 18th-century and early 19th-century decorative art. Like the Groote Kerk *(see page 87)* it has an Anreith-designed pulpit, but is rococo rather than Baroque, and a lectern also designed by Anreith. The interior of the Lutheran Church is finer than that of the Groote Kerk. With the flanking period houses – No. 96 (the Gold of Africa Museum, *see page 95*) and No. 100 – it is part of a unique surviving 18th-century street frontage. ❑

ABOVE: detail in the Lutheran Church.
BELOW: Lutheran Church's exterior.

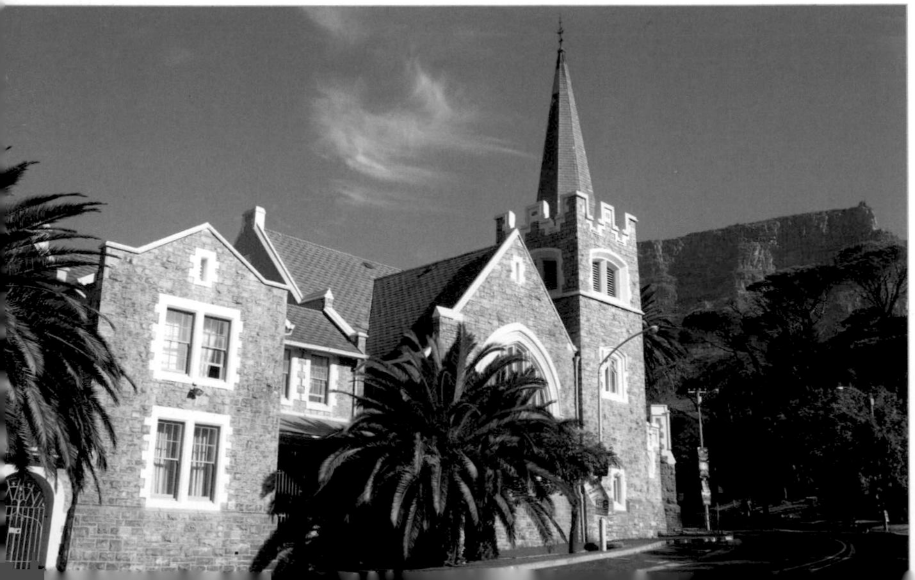

BEST RESTAURANTS, BARS AND CAFÉS

Restaurants

In addition to the CBD delineated by Buitengracht, Buitensingel and Buitenkant, it is worth trying the area known as De Waterkant on the north side of Buitengracht. Popular with the gay community, it is a lively area with plenty of bars, cafés and restaurants.

African

Gold Restaurant
96 Strand St. Tel: 021-421 4653. www.goldrestaurant.co.za Open: D Mon–Sat. **$$$** 1 p256, A1
Part of the Gold of Africa Museum *(see page 95)*, this is a great place to sample cuisine from all over Africa, and the multiple-course set menu is complemented by a fine wine list, vibrant drumming, and Dogon masked dancers. It's worth booking a place on the interactive drumming session that precedes dinner.

Asian

Chef Pon's Asian Kitchen
12 Mill St. Tel: 021-465 5846. www.chefponsasiankitchen.co.za Open: D Mon–Sat. **$** 2 p256, A4
Everybody knows Chef Pon's Asian Kitchen, with its eclectic selection of spicy dishes from Vietnam, Mongolia, Japan, Thailand, China and elsewhere, not least of which are the aromatic crispy duck and the tom yum soup. It is busy and noisy, the wine is affordable and the Asian beers are a treat.

Haiku
33 Church St. Tel: 021-424 7000. Open: L & D Mon–Fri, D Sat. **$$–$$$** 3 p256, A2
A hotspot new-age Asian tapas venue in sexy surroundings. The varied menu includes five-spice calamari, translucent steamed dumplings filled with spinach and cream cheese, and their famous Peking duck. Pricey but well worth every cent.

Prices for a three-course dinner per person with a half-bottle of house wine:
$ = under R200
$$ = R200–350
$$$ = more than R350

Ethiopian

Addis In Cape
41 Church St. Tel: 021-424 5722. www.addisincape.co.za L & D Mon–Sat. **$**
4 p256, A2
Situated just off Long Street, this welcome addition to Cape Town's culinary scene is the ideal place to try Ethiopia's little-known but delicious cuisine, which comprises fiery *wat* stews accompanied by pancake-like *injera*. Vegetarians are well catered for, but there is also a good selection of meat dishes, all at what are rock bottom prices for Cape Town.

Bars and Cafés

In many of the aforementioned restaurants food is optional, the dividing line between bar and restaurant being fairly indistinct in many Cape Town establishments. In addition, De Waterkant, Long Street and Kloof Road are full of all kinds of bars.

For pre-dinner cocktails, try the **Planet Champagne and Cocktail Bar** (Mount Nelson Hotel, 76 Orange St; tel: 021-483 1737; www.mountnelson.co.za 1 p255, E3/4), where you can expect to find a mix of young and mature, locals and tourists, maybe even an international star or two, all sipping on champagne cocktails and tapping their feet to the funky music. At the other end of the scale, **Rafiki's** (13 Kloof Nek Rd; tel: 021-426 4731; www.rafikis.co.za 2 p255, E3), which is Swahili for *friend's*, attracts a mixed bunch of locals and young foreigners. Its balcony bar is always heaving, and you can also play pool.

There's plenty of choice on Long Street - indeed you could pub crawl all night without ever leaving this road - but none more vibey than **Cape to Cuba** (227 Long St; tel: 021-424 2330; www.capetocuba.com 3 p256, A3), whose a relaxed mood, Cuban-style decor, and indoor or balcony seating, make it ideal for a mellow evening sipping cocktails, or a late-night malt whisky and cigar.

For a more historic setting, there is nowhere better than the **Fireman's Arms** (corner of Buitengracht and Mechau streets; tel: 021-419 1513; www.firemansarms.co.za 4 p256, B1), which is the city's oldest pub, dating back to 1864. It offers a good choice of draught beer and pub grub, with homely decor complemented by large-screen TVs for sports events and a good sound system.

For coffees and light lunches, there are several cafés not far from Long Street. Try **Frieda's on Bree** (15 Bree St; tel: 021-421 2404; www.friedasonbree.co.za 5 p256, B1) for a quick snack or a long lazy breakfast on a Saturday morning. Unfussy and kitted out in retro kitchen equipment, it is popular with a youngish crowd who pop in here after trawling the vintage clothing stores on Long Street. A Tamboerskloof institution, **Melissa's Food Shop** (94 Kloof St; tel: 021-425 5540; www.melissas.co.za 6 p255, E4) doubles as a deli and café, with the emphasis on hearty nutritious whole foods. It's a great spot for an affordable but tasty breakfast, light lunch or early dinner.

Fusion

Aubergine Restaurant
39 Barnet St. Tel: 021-465 4909. www.aubergine.co.za Open: L Wed–Fri, D Mon–Sat. **$$$** ❺ p256, A4
Situated in a restored 19th-century mansion, this classy restaurant has received numerous accolades for its innovative cuisine, which fuses elements of South African, French and Asian cooking to sublime effect.

Bowl Restaurant
Adderley Hotel, 31 Adderley St. Tel: 021-469 1900. Open: B, L & D daily. **$$** ❻ p256, B2
Sit overlooking buzzing Adderley Street on the balcony or inside a lofty indoor space. Think simple, Euro-Asian style food served in white bowls, filled with creative combinations.

Ginja
70 New Church St. Tel: 021-426 2368. Open: D daily, except Sun in winter. **$$$** ❼ p256, E3
Fusion-style food with some good South African-inspired dishes. The food is delicious, the wine list extensive and the venue has a boho chic ambience that attracts a sophisticated crowd. After dinner head upstairs to the venue's Shoga bar.

Indian

Bukhara
33 Church St. Tel: 021-424 0000. www.bukhara.com Open: L & D Mon–Sat, D Sun. **$$$** ❽ p256, A2
Possibly the best curry restaurant in town, Bukhara is noisy and busy, so be sure to make a reservation. The food is authentic and delicious – the butter chicken is the all-time favourite. Helpful and informative staff.

International

Beluga
The Foundry, Prestwich St. Tel: 021-418 2948. www.beluga.co.za Open: B, L & D daily. **$$–$$$** ❾ p253, D4
This is a busy, high-profile American-style venue for smart, young professionals. The menu varies from steaks, ostrich and game to freshly caught fish and big seasonal salads. The emphasis of the main menu is South African specialities and shellfish, and there's a separate Pacific Rim menu.

Five Flies
14–16 Keerom St. Tel: 021-424 4442. www.fiveflies.co.za Open: L Mon–Fri. D daily. **$$** ❿ p256, A2
An historic building gives this smart, roomy restaurant huge appeal. Always busy, it attracts lawyers from the nearby courts at lunchtime and a mixed bag of regulars in the evenings. The somewhat complicated menu offers wonderful fish-and-sauce combinations, and there's a fine selection of wines.

Italian

95 Keerom Street
95 Keerom St. Tel: 021-422 0765. www.95keerom.com. Open: L Thur–Fri, D Mon–Sat. **$$$** ⓫ p256, A3
This is Milan meets Cape Town. Set in a restored 17th-century stable, it is smart, cool and fashionable, attracting high-profile editors, film stars and bankers, alongside rich Italians. The food is swankily simple, with dishes such as fresh line-fish with mashed potato, butternut and ricotta ravioli with burnt butter and sage sauce. It is owner-run, so the service is personal.

Col'Cacchio
2 Spearhead Building, 42 Hans Strijdom Ave. Tel: 021-419 4848. www.colcacchio.co.za Open: L Mon–Fri, D daily. **$** ⓬ p256, B1
This is just outside the CBD, at the junction of Hans Strijdom Avenue and Loop Street. Proper pizzas are the order of the day, and the toppings are generous and varied. There are also pastas and salads. A big barn of a place popular at lunchtime with office workers.

Kurdish

Mesopotamia
Corner of Long and Church streets. Tel: 021-424 4664. www.mesopotamia.co.za Open: D only daily. **$–$$** ⓭ p256, A1
The only Kurdish restaurant in South Africa. Recline on floor cushions to eat authentic Kurdish food (the *iskender* – oven-roasted diced lamb with bread, garlic yoghurt and tomato sauce – and the *beyti* – minced-chicken kebab rolled in nan bread with garlic yoghurt – are delicious). There's tons of atmosphere, with hookah pipes, kelims on the floor and belly dancers to entertain. It's always busy, mostly with a young crowd.

Portuguese

Toni's Portuguese Restaurant
88 Kloof St. Tel: 021-423 6717. Open: L & D daily. **$** ⓮ p255, E4
With prices geared more to local wallets than tourists, this quiet and affable Mozambican-style eatery with indoor and outdoor seating a short walk north of Long Street is excellent value, and the food is fantastic – try the trademark Mozambican chicken peri-peri or grilled prawns.

South African

The Cape Colony
Mount Nelson Hotel, 76 Orange St. Tel: 021-483 1948. www.mountnelson.co.za Open: D daily. **$$$** ⓯ p254, E3/4
Smart dining at its finest, in Cape Town's favourite old colonial-style hotel, situated just outside the CBD. The global glitterati, if they're in town, will be here too, dining under a huge mural depicting the city 200 years ago. Dress up and enjoy chic Afro cuisine – with a strong emphasis on seafood and game meat.

Jardine
185 Bree St. Tel: 021-424 5640. www.jardineonbree.co.za Open: L Wed–Fri & D Mon–Sat. **$$$** ⓰ p256, A2
Offers an exceptional fine dining experience. Sit and

watch chef George Jardine at work in his open-plan kitchen, preparing specials that include a beetroot tart, delicate crayfish risotto or seared sirloin with Béarnaise sauce. Optional wine pairing with each course. Finish off with a shot of grappa.

Mama Africa Restaurant and Bar
178 Long St. Tel: 021-426 1017. www.mamaafricarest.net L Tue–Fri, D Mon–Sat. **$$** ⓱ p256, A2
This energetic, funky restaurant serves a good selection of South African dishes, including Malay-style curries and venison grills, and there's marimba music live every night from 8pm until late.

Nyoni's Kraal
98 Long St. Tel: 021-422 0529. www.nyoniskraal.co.za Open: B, L & D daily. **$$** ⓲ p256, A2
A traditional South African dining experience in funky surroundings. Try its signature pap and meat towers made from steamed corn discs layered with tender steak, spinach, creamed butternut, whole kernel sweet corn and smothered in beef gravy.

Savoy Cabbage
101 Hout St. Tel: 021-424 2626. www.savoycabbage.co.za Open: L Mon–Fri, D Mon–Sat. **$$$** ⓳ p256, A2
Founded in 1998, this is one of the oldest fine dining venues in Cape Town, with modern warehouse-style decor in an historic setting. The emphasis is on fresh local ingredients, so the menu sometimes reflects seasonal availability, and it's unusual for the Cape in that game and other red meats take precedence over seafood. Try the signature tomato tart followed by rare warthog shank or kudu steak. An excellent wine list matches the food.

Prices for a three-course dinner per person with a half-bottle of house wine:
$ = under R200
$$ = R200–350
$$$ = more than R350

Steakhouse

Famous Butcher's Grill
Cape Town Lodge, 101 Buitengracht St. Tel: 021-422 0880. Open: L & D daily. **$$** ⓴ p256, A2
If you want a good-quality steak, cooked to perfection, then this is the place for you – it's a carnivore's delight. And they go a step further – they will match the wine to what you're eating. There is another branch on Greenmarket Square.

Tapas

Fork
84 Long St. Tel: 021-424 6334. www.fork-restaurants.co.za Open: L & D Mon–Sat. **$$** ㉑ p256, A2
Think contemporary tapas-style food in a laid-back bistro setting. Exposed brick walls, low-hanging lights and tea-towel napkins. Try the delicious tender lamb cutlets with cumin and coriander sauce, chorizo served with a cheese fondue or the diced tuna loin on a cannellini bean salad. Excellent local wine list.

Wine Bar-Restaurant

Caveau Wine Bar and Deli
92 Bree St, Heritage Square. Tel: 021-422 1367. www.caveau.co.za Open: L & D Mon–Sat. **$$** ㉒ p256, A2
Situated off Heritage Square, Caveau has quickly established a reputation. Sample an impressive local wine list, tasty tapas, hearty main dishes for the hungry, or choose deli favourites such as home-grown charcuterie and cheeses to nibble on. Festive atmosphere and excellent service.

Chenin Restaurant and Wine Bar
Cape Quarter, Dixon St. Tel: 021-425 2200. www.cheninrestaurant.co.za Open: L & D daily. **$$** ㉓ p253, D4
Situated in the heart of this trendy area, this restaurant is a good option for sitting with friends over a glass or three of quality wine (with 40 different options available by the glass, and tasting courses held on Monday nights). The food is pretty good too, but it's mostly about the wine, the location and the friendly, helpful staff.

RIGHT: the bar at Jardine restaurant.

THE VICTORIA AND ALFRED WATERFRONT

The regeneration of Cape Town's historic harbour has been a huge success. Capetonians of all ages and races, as well as tourists, come here to socialise, shop and hang out

Known locally simply as the Waterfront, the revitalised harbour of Cape Town, historically one of the world's busiest ports, is a model example of how to breathe life back into a dying area without losing its original function or sacrificing its character. It is still a working harbour with a thriving ship repair business, but it has a range of other uses, among which shopping, dining and entertainment are prominent.

The V&A Waterfront is home to hotels, restaurants and cafés, museums, an aquarium and craft workshops. It has a buzzing street life, and there are buskers, trees to sit under, benches overlooking the water, and covered shopping areas (most shops here remain open until 9pm) selling everything from the latest Italian fashions to fresh fish. You could come here simply for an evening stroll along the quays. Alternatively, you can test-drive the latest BMW, listen to music, meet your friends, watch films, taste local wines, read the works of South Africa's new and upcoming authors, sail your yacht or catch a helicopter for a trip around the Cape Peninsula.

Amid all this, the V&A Waterfront retains its role as a harbour; passenger ships dock while you sip cappuccino on the quay, and it is still home to the city's colourful fishing fleet. This is also the place to come for all kinds of boat trips, including those to Robben Island *(see pages 107)*. Serious yachts are berthed here, in the Marina Basin behind the Cape Grace Hotel, and some of the world's finest yachtsmen and women arrive in Cape Town to participate in various prestigious

Main attractions

- VICTORIA WHARF MALL
- RED SHED CRAFT WORKSHOP
- TWO OCEANS AQUARIUM
- SCRATCH PATCH
- ROBBEN ISLAND

Maps and Listings

- MAP OF THE V&A WATERFRONT, PAGE 104
- MAP OF ROBBEN ISLAND, PAGE 112
- SHOPPING, PAGE 108
- RESTAURANTS, BARS AND CAFÉS, PAGES 110–11
- ACCOMMODATION, PAGES 226–7

LEFT: a ship's figurehead outside the African Trading Post store on the waterfront.
RIGHT: Victoria & Alfred Waterfront.

ABOVE: serene view of the V&A waterfront as night falls. **BELOW RIGHT:** elephant sculpture on the waterfront.

TIP

The Victoria and Alfred Waterfront is cut off from downtown Cape Town by the Foreshore and its tangle of busy roads. It is a 15- to 20-minute walk from, say, Adderley Street, but the route is well signposted. The journey by taxi costs about R50. Motorists will find plenty of parking behind Victoria Wharf. To get back to the city centre after an evening out, take a taxi from the taxi rank off St Alfred's Mall or behind Victoria Wharf.

yachting events, such as the Volvo Ocean Race Global Challenge.

History of the harbour

What began as a tiny staging post for ships putting in at the Cape to restock their supplies on the long and often gruelling journey between Europe and the East had, by the beginning of the 20th century, become an industrialised port serving the considerable demands of its imperial owners.

The Anglo-Boer War had the most dramatic effect on its development. Between 1881 and 1899, shipping in Cape Town trebled and the docks could hardly cope. New jetties were constructed, cranes purchased and warehouses were built. The early buildings that have survived today date from this period. They centre on the two harbour basins commemorating Queen Victoria and her son Alfred, built between 1860 and 1920.

In 1980 Cape Town architect Gawie Fagan proposed regenerating the basins, which, too small for modern container vessels, had fallen into disrepair by the 1960s. In 1988 Fagan's brainchild became a reality, when the port authority was privatised and the Victoria and Alfred Waterfront Company came into being. The project had wide implications for the identity of the city as a whole, as old buildings were restored or adapted for new uses. The North Quay became a hotel and a small shopping mall, while Victoria Wharf was turned into a much larger mall with cinemas, restaurants and another hotel. Since then, several other cities around the world have copied the Cape Town model and revived their own degenerating docklands.

The BMW Pavilion

There are two reasons for visiting the **BMW Pavilion** ❶ (tel: 021-419 5850; daily 9am–10pm; free). First, you can see the very latest BMW cars and motorbikes before they're available to the public, and browse among the BMW accessories at their Lifestyle Store; secondly, the pavilion complex also houses a restaurant, conference centre, auditorium and theatre, hosting a varied programme of exhibitions, concerts and theatrical productions.

Consumer choice

One of the largest and smartest shopping malls in the country, **Victoria**

Wharf ❷ (tel: 021-408 7600; daily 9am–9pm) is a magnet for locals and tourists alike. There's plenty of parking in a subterranean garage, and there are lifts and escalators to the main floors. If all you have is one day for shopping in Cape Town, then this is the best place to head. There are chic boutiques and chain stores selling all the trendiest local and international fashion labels, along with some excellent craft and curio emporiums – African Curiosity, Out of Africa and Out of the World are among the best. People also pick up their weekly groceries here, at branches of the South African stalwarts Woolworths and Pick 'n' Pay, as well as fine wines and specialist deli items *(see page 108)*.

Exclusive Books *(see page 108)*, Wordsworth Books and CNA have a wide range of local and internationally published books, magazines and newspapers. There are plenty of restaurants for all purses, inexpensive fast-food joints, fish-and-chip takeaways and numerous busy cafés and bars *(see page 110)*. There are also two cinema complexes, with one – the Cinema Nouveau *(see page 235)* – specialising in art-house movies.

At the east end of the shopping mall is one of Cape Town's most luxurious places to stay, the **Table Bay Hotel.** The hotel also has direct links to Quay 6 and Jetty 2 where luxury cruise liners dock.

Creative crafts

In Dock Road, but more easily accessed from Victoria Wharf shopping Mall, the **Red Shed Craft Workshop ❸** (daily 9am–9pm; free) is a showcase for all kinds of crafts. There are fabric printers, furniture makers, jewellers and ceramicists, as well as people telling fortunes, offering tattoos or selling snacks. It's worth having a wander around, and you just might find something a bit more unusual than the pan-African goods on sale at the enormous African Trading Store on the Pierhead.

Linking Victoria Wharf with Alfred Mall, **Market Square ❹** is an open space for exhibitions and fairs in season. To one side is the **Amphitheatre**, a venue for concerts, festival

LEFT: Victoria Wharf shopping mall. **ABOVE:** Table Bay Hotel, one of several luxurious places to stay on the Waterfront.

Rock Pool Riches

More than 2,000 marine invertebrate and vertebrate species have been identified along the southern African coastline from Namibia to Mozambique, and as many as 33 percent of them occur on the Cape Peninsula, which makes up only 3 percent of this coastline. All 24 species of fish that you find in the little rock pools of the Cape are endemic to southern Africa, and the large number of seaweed species found along the southern African coast reaches its highest density around the Cape.

The Cape's west coast is characterised by dense kelp beds, particularly sea bamboo and split-fan kelp, sheltering sea urchins, mussels, abalone (perlemoen) and rock lobster. And this is where you find rich troves of hake, pilchards and anchovy. The greater diversity of the east coast makes it even richer, with Indo-Pacific fish, including sharks, coming down even as far as False Bay.

Learn more about the marine life of the Cape at the Two Oceans Aquarium *(see page 104)* and explore it close up for yourself in the rock pools of the peninsula, the best of which are at Sea Point and St James near Muizenberg.

ABOVE: statue of Nelson Mandela on Nobel Square.

events *(see page 106)* and street theatre, and a popular meeting point.

Just below the Amphitheatre, along Quay 5, you can pick up one of a variety of boat trips (these are particularly magical around sunset) and also enquire about booking a helicopter ride over Cape Town and the Peninsula.

Alfred Mall and Nobel Square

On North Quay and just to the west of Pierhead is **Alfred Mall**. It has a variety of little shops and cafés and is directly linked to the **Victoria & Alfred Hotel** *(see page 226)*, fashioned from the historic 1904 North Quay Warehouse. Situated right in the heart of the docks, it is another great place to stay. From the hotel windows you can see, hear and smell the passing boat traffic and watch the seals playing in the water, while all the amenities of the Waterfront are just a stone's throw away.

On the west side of Alfred Mall, **Nobel Square** is adorned with slightly larger-than-life (and not madly faithful) statues of South Africa's four Nobel Peace Price laureates: joint winners Nelson Mandela and F. W. de Klerk (1993), Desmond Tutu (1984) and the late ANC president Albert Lithuli (1960).

Two Oceans Aquarium ❺

Address: Dock Road, around the corner from Nobel Square, www.aquarium.co.za
Tel: 021-418 3823
Opening Hrs: daily 9.30am–6pm
Entrance Fee: charge

Celebrating the meeting point of two very different oceans, this imaginatively designed building contains more than 3,000 fish, invertebrates, mammals, birds, reptiles and plants, from sharks to seals, penguins to plankton, and turtles to clown fish. Check out the Predators Tank for ragged-tooth sharks and stingrays;

The Victoria and Alfred Waterfront

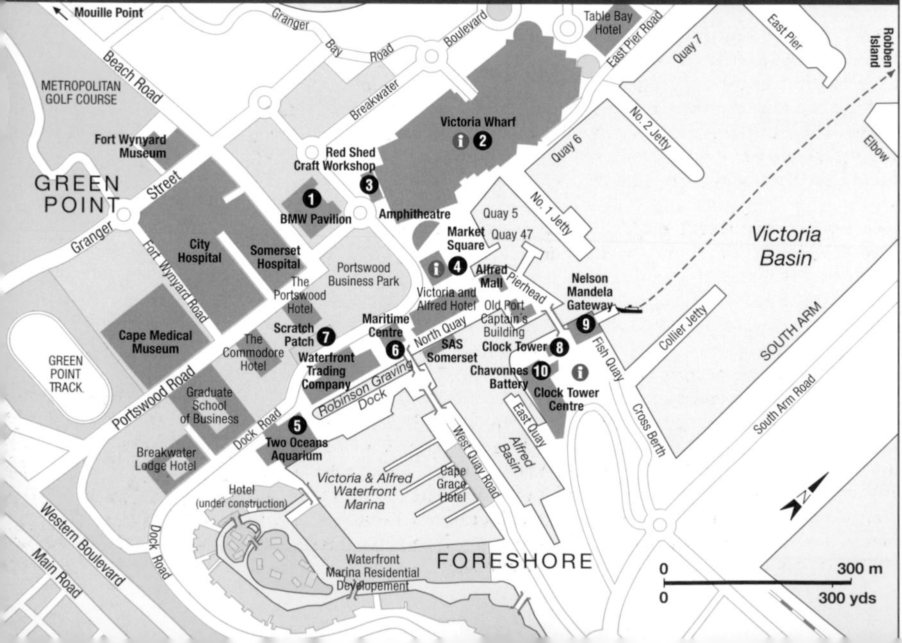

the mesmerising Kelp Forest, a habitat found off South Africa's west coast; and the Cape seals, which can be viewed at basement level.

There are opportunities to don a wet suit and dive with the sharks (you must be an experienced diver), or you can feed the fish, touch a variety of sea creatures in shallow tanks, and, with the help of the very friendly staff, study the tiniest form of aquatic life under a microscope. Children of all ages will love the Aquarium, as will any adult with fond memories of delving in rock pools as a child.

Iziko Maritime Centre ❻

Address: Union Castle House, Dock Road, www.iziko.org.za
Tel: 021-405 2880
Opening Hrs: daily 10am–5pm
Entrance Fee: free

Although rather traditional in its presentation, this is an essential venue if you want to make sense of Cape Town as a maritime city. It illuminates the long history of shipping in this part of the world. There's a large collection of model ships, a history of Table Bay Harbour and a display documenting the shipwrecks that litter the coastline, many of which can be seen on walks along the beaches and coastal paths of the Peninsula.

Housed within the Maritime Centre is the John H. Marsh Maritime Research Centre, whose core resource is the library of its namesake, who amassed a collection of several hundred shipping reference books going back to the 1800s prior to his death in 1996. The centre also holds negatives and photographs of more than 9,000 ships that called at Cape Town, most taken by Marsh between 1921 and 1953.

Scratch Patch ❼

Address: Dock Road, opposite the Maritime Centre, www.scratchpatch.co.za
Tel: 021-419 9429
Opening Hrs: daily 9am–6pm
Entrance Fee: free, but you are required to spend a minimum of R14

The inspiration behind this place was the amazing variety of minerals in South Africa. You can have fun picking out your favourite stones from colourful heaps scattered about, have them weighed, then take them home and keep them in deep bowls

ABOVE: giant stingray and ragged-tooth shark in the Predator Exhibit at Two Oceans Aquarium. **BELOW:** a red stumpnose, whose numbers have been reduced by overfishing.

What's Happening on the Waterfront?

There is always something going on at the Waterfront, from buskers to festivals and other annual events, many of them free. Here are some of the highlights

JANUARY

Sounds of Summer, a series of free concerts including big bands and classics, held in the amphitheatre in early January.

FEBRUARY

V&A Waterfront Amateur Dance Championships, usually starts in late January, with finals in early March.

APRIL

Club Crew World Championship Dragon Boating, one of the leading events on the International Dragon Boats calendar. Held at Jetty 2 and Victoria Basin in mid-April.

Freedom Day Sing-a-thon (27 April), presented by the Cape Town Opera and the V&A Waterfront, this is seven hours of popular opera, held at the amphitheatre. Free.

MAY

The V&A Waterfront Wine Affair, meet the winemakers in Market Square and taste wine from over 100 of the Cape's top estates. Early May; charge.

AUGUST

National Women's Day (9 August), tribute to women all over the world featuring some of Cape Town's top female performers.

V&A Waterfront Winter Food Fair, sample tasty local cuisine and wine in Market Square in mid-August. Free.

SEPTEMBER

International Comedy Festival, leading local and international comics perform for the first three weeks of the month. Charge.

Simon's Town Penguin Festival, a firm fixture on the conservation calendar in mid-September, raising funds for the penguin community. Free.

Blessing of the Fishing Fleet, the Portuguese Welfare Association blesses fishing boats for a safe and plentiful season. Traditional folk dancing, music and food, mid–late September. Free.

OCTOBER

Oktoberfest, Bavarian cuisine and beer at the Paulaner Bräuhaus in the Clock Tower Precinct from mid to late October. Free.

International Oriental Dance Festival, this two-day festival in the Craft Centre attracts performers from all around the globe. Charge.

NOVEMBER

V&A Waterfront Schools Performing Arts Showcase, competitive event involving school choirs, bands and amateur drama from around Cape Town.

DECEMBER

Festive Season Choir Festival, held in the amphitheatre in mid-December, this event features some of the city's best-known choirs.

Sunsetter Music Festival, a series of very popular free sunset concerts at the amphitheatre during the last week of December.

Aqua Opera, the Cape Philharmonic, a mass choir and the city's best new voices perform at North Wharf and the V&A Marina in mid-December. Free.

New Year's Eve, music and fireworks on the water's edge. Free. ❑

LEFT: entertaining the crowds.

on the coffee table. Or you might like to choose a more serious gem from the **Mineral World** "factory shop", including rare and unusual specimens, some of which have been turned into a wide range of products, from jewellery to keyrings and executive desktop games.

Gleaned from across Southern Africa, the stones here are an indication of the extraordinary wealth lying beneath the surface of this part of the world. Children also enjoy Scratch Patch, and another, bigger and better branch can be found on Dido Valley Road in Simon's Town *(see page 170)*.

Clock Tower Centre

Head back past Alfred Mall, follow the line of the quay to the Pier Head and cross the swing bridge (which regularly opens to admit the passage of large vessels between Victoria and Alfred basins) to reach the distinctive **Clock Tower** ❽, which may well have been your starting point for a tour of the Waterfront if you approached it on foot from the city centre. The Victorian tower is a famous city landmark. Built as the Port Captain's office in 1883, it overlooks Victoria Basin and marks the original entrance to the docks. With its pointed windows and little pinnacled belfry, it has a distinctly Gothic look. The tower now forms part of Emily's, an upmarket restaurant (the balcony makes a fine, if rather conspicuous, dining spot), but even if you are not intending to eat here you are welcome to take a peek inside the tower to view its ornate interior.

There are benches in the sun, cafés and places to eat around the tower, and the **Clock Tower Centre** has a small number of boutiques for clothing, sunglasses and so on, as well as the **Tourism Cape Town Information Centre** (tel: 021-405 4500). This centre is open later than the downtown branch, and is a good place to pick up information about tours and activities in and around Cape Town.

ABOVE: ferry to Robben Island. **BELOW:** the Victorian Clock Tower.

Nelson Mandela Gateway to Robben Island ❾

Address: Clock Tower Square, www.robben-island.org.za
Tel: 021-413 4220
Opening Hrs: daily 9am–3pm
Entrance Fee: charge

Adjacent to Fish Quay where the fishing boats dock, Nelson Mandela Gateway is the sole point of departure (and the place to make bookings) for trips to Robben Island, Cape Town's "Alcatraz". Famous for holding Nelson Mandela for some 18 years of his 27-year imprisonment, it also held a host of other black and coloured anti-apartheid activists (whites were held elsewhere); the former maximum security prison *(see pages 112–3 for more details)* is now a Unesco World Heritage Site of immense importance. A penal colony from the earliest colonial days, it's now celebrated as a symbol of reconciliation.

ABOVE: Robben Island penal colony.

Tours depart four times daily (9am, 11am, 1pm and 3pm), weather permitting, and last for 3½ hours, including the 30-minute boat ride in either direction, a coach tour of the island, and a walking tour of the prison, guided by an ex-prisoner. It is highly advisable to book your trip in advance, as this is one of the most popular excursions in the city, and if you just turn up you may well be disappointed.

Chavonnes Cannon Battery Museum ⑩

Address: Clock Tower Square, underneath the BoE/Nedcor building, www.chavonnesmuseum.co.za
Tel: 021-416 6230
Opening Hrs: Wed–Sun 9am–4pm
Entrance Fee: charge (includes guided tour)

This museum is housed in the remains of an 18th-century military installation built by the Dutch East India Company to protect the Cape. It was discovered when the nearby Clock Tower Centre was under construction in 1999. The Chavonnes Battery was an intrinsic part of the Cape's formidable original fortifications, and is thought to be one of the oldest surviving European structures in South Africa. It most probably remained in

SHOPPING

The V&A Waterfront is one of the most popular shopping venues in Cape Town, with most shops open until 9pm. However, the high rents mean that it is dominated by countrywide chain stores rather than individual boutiques, and prices are often geared to tourists rather than locals. The range of shops here is daunting, but a few favourites follow.

Books

Exclusive Books
Victoria Wharf. Tel: 021-419 0905. www.exclus1ves.co.za p253, E2
The largest Cape Town branch of this countrywide chain, this bookshop stocks an immense selection of current fiction and is also strong on books dedicated to all things South African. There is also a great coffee shop where you can read while you sip.

Clothing and Outdoor Gear

Cape Union Mart
Quay Four. Tel: 021-425 4559. www.capeunionmart.co.za p253, E2
Left your hiking boots or safari outfit at home? Cape Union Mart is the place to stock up on everything from hardy outdoor clothing to water bottles, compasses and GPS devices.

Crafts

Craft Market and Wellness Centre
Dock Rd, near Nobel Sq. Tel: 021-408 7842. p253, E4
Not to be confused with the Red Shed Craft Workshop, this covered market is not only good for curio shopping, but it's also home to the city's biggest concentration of stalls dedicated to alternative health treatments and holistic wellness products.

Gifts

Carrol Boyes Shop
Victoria Wharf. Tel: 021-418 0595. www.carrolboyes.com p253, E2
Best known for the curvaceously abstract homeware designed by its South African namesake, this shop also stocks interesting ceramics and beaded artefacts supplied by Monkeybiz.

Jewellery

Charles Grieg Jewellers
Victoria Wharf. Tel: 021-418 4515. www.charlesgreig.co.za p253, E2
The Cape Town branch of one of South Africa's best and most established jewellers sells a world-class range of classy diamond, gold and tanzanite products, along with brand name watches and other swanky accessories.

Music

Musica Megastore
Dock Rd, off Nobel Sq. Tel: 021-425 6300. www.musica.co.za p253, E4
Though it lacks the specialist range of the African Music Store on Long Street (see page 94), this vast double storey warehouse is brimful with CDs and DVDs, and the African selection is very extensive.

Wine

Vaughan Johnson's Wine Shop
Market Sq. Tel: 021-419 2121. p253, E3
The eponymous owner-manager of this long-serving emporium is one of the country's leading wine experts, and his shop is a good place to sample and stock up on Cape wines, which can be shipped anywhere in the world.

use under British rule during the 19th century, and was finally taken out of commission in 1861.

Mouille Point

The V&A Waterfront is a self-contained area, cut off from the rest of the city centre by major roads and the ocean, so most visitors do not venture further around the shoreline to **Mouille Point**, even though the Cape Town Explorer links the two and operates a regular "hop on, hop off" open-top bus service. Until recently this was the last stretch of undeveloped coastline in the heart of the city, but Mouille Point is now cloaked in new upmarket apartment blocks and other luxury developments, their sweeping sea views helping to push their prices sky-high.

The area gets its name from a mole (*moilje* in Dutch) that formed part of Cape Town's harbour in the 18th century. This is long gone, but if you come up here on a stormy day you'll see the kind of tremendous waves that swept innumerable ships on to the rocks at this point. The remains of one such casualty can still be seen.

Green Point

To the southwest of Mouille Point is **Green Point**, only a small stretch of which fronts the sea. **Green Point Common**, a protected area that was originally common pastureland for local farmers, is the site of the new 69,070-seat Cape Town Stadium, which was custom built for the 2010 FIFA World Cup and hosted eight games in the tournament, including the first-round clash between England and Algeria, and the semi-final between the Netherlands and Uruguay.

The Green Point Lighthouse, the oldest in South Africa, was constructed in 1824, and still acts as a beacon for ships entering and leaving the harbour. Its handsome red-and-white-striped bulk is today practically dwarfed by the new apartment blocks behind. The popular Green Point Flea Market (www.greenpoint-fleamarket.co.za; tel: 021-439 4805; Sun and public holidays 8.30am-5pm) takes place in the main car park of Cape Town Stadium.

Green Point stretches over the Common and up onto the flank of Signal Hill. It is a lovely neighbourhood characterised by 19th-century terraced houses and steep old streets. To the north of Green Point lies Sea Point, a rather less affluent district *(see page 160)*. ❑

TIP

Call 021-430 7300 to find out about inexpensive guided tours of Cape Town Stadium. These leave every Tue, Thur and Sat at 10am, noon and 2pm, and incorporate visits to the stands, the players' changing rooms, the VIP/hospitality area and the "prison cell".

ABOVE: Pinotage on sale at Vaughan Johnson's Wine Shop.
BELOW: Cape Town Stadium.

BEST RESTAURANTS, BARS AND CAFÉS

Restaurants

The V&A Waterfront is an extremely popular place to come to eat, not just for tourists who like its safe environment, but for locals too. This listing also includes a few restaurants at Green Point and Mouille Point, a little further along Beach Road.

V&A Waterfront

The Atlantic Restaurant
The Table Bay Hotel. Tel: 021-406 5918. Open: B & D daily. **$$$** 24 p253, E2
The decor and ambience are rather overbearing in this smart hotel restaurant. The food, however, is worth coming for, particularly on a special occasion. It's fine dining with silver service, but expect interesting twists on old favourites.

Baia
Upper Level, Victoria Wharf. Tel: 021-421 0935. www.baiarestaurant.co.za Open: L & D daily. **$$$$** 25 p253, E2
A tourist-crowded venue where the food and drink will cost you an arm and a leg. However, the choice of seafood here is legendary, most of it caught locally, with a wine list to match.

Balducci's
Lower Level, Victoria Wharf. Tel: 021-421 6002. www.balduccis.co.za Open: B, L & D daily. **$$** 26 p253, E2
Popular café-bar-restaurant with a great terrace for people watching. There is a wide range of options, from South African game to Thai green curry or sushi. There's also great coffee and a popular wine list. Meet friends here after shopping or for a drink before a film.

Belthazar Restaurant and Wine Bar
Shop 153, Victoria Wharf. Tel: 021-421 3753. www.belthazar.co.za
Open: L & D daily. **$$–$$$** 27 p253, E2
Popular with wine-lovers – it claims to have the world's biggest selection of wine by the glass – this place has also won several awards, including Steakhouse of the Year on two occasions, for the simple but excellent food. Steaks, obviously, are the speciality, but there's good seafood too. The attached shop sells chefs' knives, glassware and T-shirts as well as beef and sauces.

City Grill
Shop 155, Victoria Wharf. Tel: 021-421 9820. www.citygrill.co.za Open: L & D daily. **$$** 28 p253, E2
Fresh seafood and a wide range of venison are the speciality of this relaxed restaurant, which overlooks the harbour, and whose proprietor has a track record dating back to 1966, when he opened Johannesburg's first steakhouse.

Den Anker Bar and Restaurant
The Pierhead. Tel: 021-419 0249. www.denanker.co.za Open: L & D daily. **$$$** 29 p253, E3
Prominently situated on the Pierhead, Den Anker has great views of the passing scene, including the comings and goings of the fishing boats and yachts. It is a large, bustling place, serving Belgian food such as marrow on toast and bowls of mussels and fries.

Emily's
202 Clock Tower. Tel: 021-421 1133. Open: L Mon–Sat, D daily. **$$** 30 p253, E3
Occupying the famous Victorian Clock Tower near the Pierhead, this famous Cape Town establishment serves inventive South African dishes that impress and amaze. Classics have been updated and typical South African dishes have been borrowed from the kitchen table and smartened up.

Greek Fisherman
Shop 157, Victoria Wharf Tel: 021-418 5411. www.greekfisherman.co.za Open: L & D daily. **$$$** 31 p253, E2
Next door to the City Grill *(see left)* and under the same management, this award-winning Waterfront stalwart specialises in Greek and other Mediterranean cuisine – try great grilled seafood, or get a group together and work though the meze menu.

LEFT: the Green Dolphin.

The Green Dolphin
Alfred Mall. Tel: 021-421 7471. Open: L & D daily. **$$$** 32 p253, E3
For dinner with good live jazz, this is a great place to come. Dinner is compulsory in the restaurant (advisable to book), which overlooks the performance area, but there is also a small bar without views.

Signal Restaurant
Cape Grace Hotel. Tel: 021-410 7080. www.capegrace.co.za Open: B, L & D daily. **$$–$$$** 33 p253, E3
This is one of the nicest hotel dining rooms in the city, with excellent service and very reasonable prices by Waterfront standards. The decor has an African theme and this is extended to the food. It also does a fabulous tasting menu with a different wine to match every course. After dinner visit Bascule, the hotel bar *(see right)*.

Willoughby & Co
Lower Level, Victoria Wharf. Tel: 021-418 6115. Open: L & D daily. **$$** 34 p253, E2
Situated deep inside Victoria Wharf Mall, with no ocean views, this serves some of the best fish in town and is always packed. Impeccably prepared dishes range from sushi to English-style fish and chips. You can't book, so just turn up and wait your turn.

Prices for a three-course dinner per person with a half-bottle of house wine:
$ = under R200
$$ = R200–350
$$$ = more than R350

Green Point/ Mouille Point

Anatoli Turkish Restaurant
24 Napier St. Tel: 021-419 2501. www.anatoli.co.za. Open: D Mon–Sat. **$$** 35 p253, D4
The dining here is mostly about meze. Countless tasty morsels are brought to your table on vast trays, accompanied by chunks of hot bread for dunking into various Middle Eastern dips. The restaurant is built around a tiny internal courtyard.

Bravo
121 Beach Rd. Tel: 021-439 5260. Open: B, L & D daily. **$** 36 p252, B2
On the ground floor of the upmarket Splendido apartment block, Bravo is a stylish Italian-inspired restaurant with a relaxed terrace. A great spot to watch the sun set. Good antipasti, pasta and main-course fare, as well as pizzas.

Il Leone
22 Cobern St. Tel: 021-421 0071. Open: L & D Tue–Sun. **$$** 37 p253, D4
A classic bistro-style Italian eatery situated inside a bright and breezy heritage building. Enjoy traditional classics like escalopes of veal with fresh porcini or a generous bowl of handmade pasta in a light tomato-based sauce.

Wakame
Corner of Beach Rd and Surrey Pl. Tel: 021-433 2377. Open: L & D daily. **$$** 38 p252, C2
This is a busy seaside restaurant and sushi bar with a fantastic terrace overlooking the ocean. Expect Pacific Rim food with Asian-style dishes and a sprinkling of classic European and American fare. There's also good sushi on the menu. It attracts a fashionable crowd, sometimes just for a drink.

Bars and Cafés

Many of the restaurants listed above also operate as bars, including **Balducci's** and **Wakame**, two fashionable but relaxed venues.

One of the best bars on the Waterfront, overlooking the marina, is the **Bascule Whisky Bar and Wine Cellar** (Cape Grace Hotel; tel: 021-410 7100. 7 p253, E3) which offers more than 400 whiskies, an extensive wine list, plush leather sofas, breathtaking views of Table Mountain and tasty nibbles. Although you might break the bank with a single glass of icy Sauvignon Blanc, this place really buzzes on a Friday evening, when people spill out onto the marina.

For a more affordable and down-to-earth night out, visit **Ferryman's Tavern** (East Pier Rd facing Market Sq; tel: 021-419 7748; www.ferrymans.co.za 8 p253, E2), which has graced the V&A Waterfront since 1989 and has cosy indoor seating, a beer garden, and a good selection of local beers and inexpensive pub grub. Right next door is **Mitchell's** (tel: 021-425 9462; www.mitchellsseafront.co.za 9 p253, E2) which serves a range of ales and beers from in its own Knysna-based brewery.

At the other end of the waterfront, near the Clock Tower, the **Paulaner Brauhaus** (tel: 021-418 9999; www.paulaner.co.za 10 p253, E3) is an authentic German *brauhaus* that brews the best beer in town and also has a comprehensive German menu.

Mouille Point is a lovely spot for enjoying a sundowner (if it isn't too windy). If you prefer to be indoors, try the **Buena Vista Social Café** (81 Main Rd; tel: 021-433 0611; www.buenavista.co.za 11 p253, D3), which is the closest you'll get to a hot Havana night in Cape Town – mojitas, cigars, revolutionary images on the walls, and a friendly atmosphere that happily unites the bar-restaurant-lounge areas.

A great spot for coffee, smoothies or a five-star gourmet sandwich is the **Sundance Gourmet Coffee Company** (Surrey Place, 18 Bay Rd; tel: 021-439 4572; www.sundancecoffeeco.com 12 p252, C2), a modern, seaside space, part of a city chain owned by Cape-Town-based Michelin-starred chef Conrad Gallagher. It's a visual feast with hundreds of chocolates and other treats on display in giant candy jars.

ROBBEN ISLAND

Robben Island may seem like a formidable fortress island, but the political prisoners incarcerated here turned it into a university of the struggle

The most evocative symbol of the apartheid era is undoubtedly Robben Island, the maximum-security prison where Nelson Mandela spent 18 years of his 27-year imprisonment. Other important prisoners included Walter Sisulu, Govan Mbeki (father of former president Thabo Mbeki), and Pan-Africanist Congess (PAC) founder Robert Sobukwe. The island, which was awarded World Heritage Status in 1999, is now run as a museum by former political prisoners and their ex-guards, an example of the spirit of reconciliation that has generally prevailed since the end of apartheid.

To find out more about life in the prison, in particular the extraordinary resilience, resourcefulness and solidarity of the political prisoners, read Nelson Mandela's autobiography *Long Walk to Freedom*.

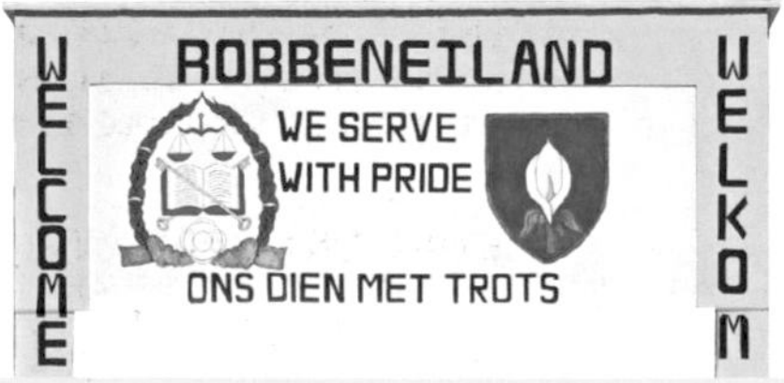

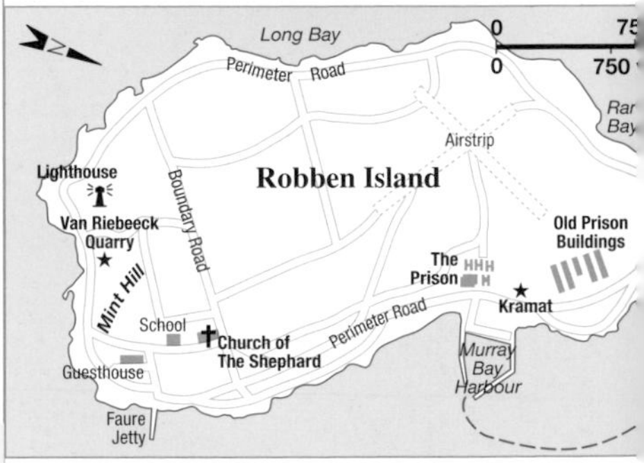

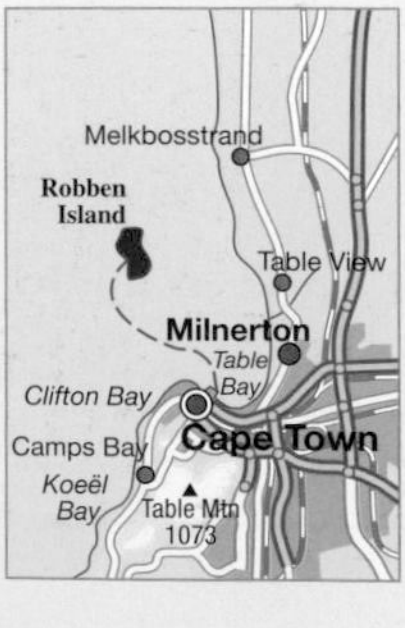

The Essentials

Address: *Nelson Mandela Gateway, Clock Tower Square, V&A Waterfront, www.robben-island.org.za*
Tel: *021-413 4220*
Opening Hrs: *daily 9am–3pm*
Entrance Fee: *charge*

BELOW: Robben Island ("Seal Island") is a ruggedly beautiful spot 11km (7 miles) from Cape Town. Its south coast offers fine views over Table Bay, but few prisoners ever saw them.

ABOVE: this image of Nelson Mandela and fellow prisoner Walter Sisulu was one of the few photographs Mandela allowed to be taken during his incarceration. It was taken by a British journalist working for London's *Daily Telegraph*. In general, activists felt it was demeaning to be photographed as a prisoner, and photographs could not be taken without their consent unless authorised by the Commissioner of Prisons.

BELOW: Mandela's cell in Section B. Each prisoner was given three blankets and a grass mat to sleep on. Cells were perpetually damp.

THE MAIN POINTS OF INTEREST

A visit to Robben Island comprises a boat transfer from the V&A Waterfront, a coach tour of the island to take in some of the more scattered features, followed by a guided tour of the main block, conducted by an ex-political prisoner.

Walter Sobukwe, the founder and leader of the PAC, was detained in a separate house *(see above)* without charge for a full six years after his sentence ended. When Sobukwe was eventually released he was kept under house arrest.

Nelson Mandela's cell, about 1 metre (3ft) wide, was situated on a corridor known as Section B. His cell can only be seen through the bars, but others can be accessed and contain items that belonged to former prisoners. It is also possible to listen to recordings of some former inmates.

As conditions on the island improved during the latter stages of apartheid, tennis was introduced to the exercise yard. Unknown to the guards, the political prisoners hid messages inside the balls which they then lobbed into the quarters of regular prisoners on the other side of the yard. The guards imagined that the prisoners were simply bad shots.

ABOVE: the lime quarry where Mandela and other prisoners spent their days labouring. The small cave was effectively used as a clandestine classroom, though the guards, who never bothered to check, imagined the prisoners used it as a lavatory.

BO-KAAP

On the slopes of Signal Hill, Bo-Kaap is traditionally populated by the descendants of Cape Town's slaves, brought here from Asia by the East India Company. Their legacy is apparent in the area's attractive architecture and tasty cuisine, known as Cape Malay

Main Attractions

IZIKO BO-KAAP MUSEUM
AUWAL MOSQUE
NURAL ISLAM MOSQUE
NOON GUN TEAROOM
BIESMIELLAH'S RESTAURANT

Maps and Listings

MAP OF BO-KAAP, PAGE 116
RESTAURANTS, PAGE 119

The old Bo-Kaap district of Cape Town is also sometimes known as Schotschekloof, taking that name from a pre-existing farm whose homestead survives much altered in Upper Dorp Street. It's a vibrant district on the slopes of Signal Hill, and, now that District Six has vanished, it is the place to find the real flavour of old Cape Town. Also sometimes known as the Old Malay Quarter, it is bounded by Wale, Rose and Waterkant streets, and to the north by Signal Hill. "Bo-Kaap" means "above Cape Town".

Uniquely in Cape Town, you can walk the streets in this lovely neighbourhood and see people sitting on their high *stoep* (veranda). They watch you pass by, neighbours chat over the wall, and children play ball on the cobbled streets. It's not a big district, but it is densely packed, and its flavour is not unlike what you might find in an Arabic city somewhere in the eastern Mediterranean, or perhaps in the old quarter of a city in Sicily. Spicy cooking smells waft up from the kitchens, Muslim women cover their heads as you pass, and you can hear muted conversations and muffled radio sounds from deep within the labyrinth of buildings.

There are bakeries, shops selling spices, ad hoc cafés set up in people's houses, butchers, tailors, and artisans fixing cars and bikes. There are many mosques in the district; indeed, a characteristic sound of the area is the muezzin's daily calls to prayer.

Highlights of the area

Visitors come to Bo-Kaap to see its attractive early Cape Dutch and Cape Georgian houses, to visit the little Bo-Kaap Museum and to absorb the atmosphere of the neighbourhood

LEFT: Signal Hill rises to the north of the Bo-Kaap district. **RIGHT:** Shafee Mosque on the corner of Chiappini Street.

streets. The area is credited with having been the birthplace of Islam in South Africa, and it is also the location of the origin of the Afrikaans language – which, surprisingly to many foreigners, is the main language spoken by Bo-Kaap's Muslim residents today.

Today Bo-Kaap has an insular feel, and you may feel as though you're intruding. But that's not true, particularly if you meet the residents on a guided walk of the district.

Architectural gems

Bo-Kaap was originally an area of *huurhuisies*, little houses for rent, put up by the landowner Jan de Waal on his property Walendorp in the 1780s. Wale Street, today a major city artery running from east to west and up the slopes of Signal Hill, was named after it. It was during this period that the architectural character of the district emerged: rows of flat-roofed houses with two rooms at the front facing the street and a narrow passage up the middle. Many have a little roofless *stoep* in front of them, and a courtyard at the back where inhabitants can cool off in summer. Originally roofs were made of a mixture of whale oil and molasses, and were hidden behind a curved parapet. The perfect example of this is the Bo-Kaap Museum building *(see page 117)*, once a *huurhuisie*, dating from around 1763.

ABOVE: vibrantly coloured buildings in Bo-Kaap, also known as the Cape Malay quarter.

TIP

To get the most out of a visit to Bo-Kaap, it is a good idea to take a guided tour. Tana Baru Tours specialises in walking tours of the area. Their tour (duration two hours) includes the Bo-Kaap Museum, notable mosques and architecture, shrines at the Tana Baru burial ground, and tea and Malay cakes. Tel: 021-424 0719 or email: tanabarutours@webmail.co.za

Many homes have their original sash windows – and original glazing (rare in an inner-city district, but possibly only because people were too poor to alter it).

Bo-Kaap proper, and the adjacent streets, make up Cape Town's largest concentration of architecture predating 1850. Some are still lived in by descendants of the original owners. Many have been restored and are painted in distinctive bright colours.

The people of Bo-Kaap

Bo-Kaap was also a district of artisans brought in to assist with the development of a quickly growing town. As the town developed, the Europeans who lived here tended to move on to places like Woodstock and Mowbray, and the Muslim population moved in, particularly after 1834, when slaves were liberated. They moved into the better houses of the district, including many of the places you see here today.

The area is mostly associated with the Muslims who arrived in the Cape from 1658 onwards, as slaves, political exiles and convicts from East Africa and Southeast Asia. The political exiles tended to be people of high rank and culture, and from the beginning they bonded through their religion. They were known as Cape Malays – a misleading term since the majority of Bo-Kaap's residents are not of Malaysian descent.

ABOVE AND BELOW: the colourful buildings of Bo-Kaap. **RIGHT:** Bo-Kaap resident.

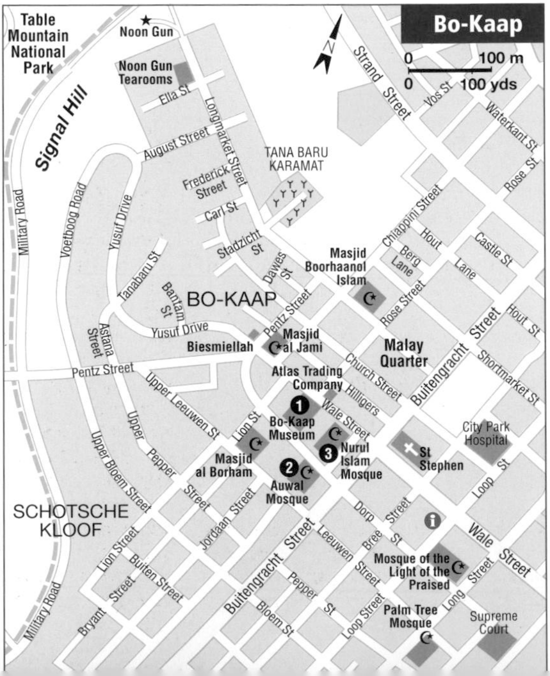

Many of today's residents are the descendants of skilled craftsmen, silversmiths, shoemakers, tailors, fishermen and cooks.

Cape Town still has a reputation for good-quality cabinet-making, fine plastering and other building trades, and Cape Malay cuisine is uniquely South African, with its combination of Asian, Arabian and European influences. Dishes such as *bobotie* (spiced patties of ground lamb) were created when slave women and their masters' wives worked together in the kitchen. The hands of slave artisans are evident in the Cape Dutch architecture they built.

Today this is not a wealthy area by any means, and attempts to gentrify Bo-Kaap have met with fierce resistance. If you join an organised tour you'll hear passionate defence of the area, whose history reflects the political machinations of South Africa. Under the Group Areas Act it was declared a residential area strictly for Muslims, and if you didn't fit the bill you had to leave. At the time, coloured Muslims in Cape Town were encouraged by the divide-and-rule government to see themselves as ethnically distinct from the rest of the non-White population.

Ironically, Bo-Kaap is one of the few working-class areas left in today's South Africa that is situated right on the edge of a city centre. All the others were cleared under the Slum Clearance Act. Today Bo-Kaap has a renewed lease of life as it enters a new phase in its unique development.

Iziko Bo-Kaap Museum ❶

Address: 71 Wale Street, www.iziko.co.za
Tel: 021-481 3939
Opening Hrs: Mon–Sat 10am–5pm
Entrance Fee: charge

On the left-hand side of Wale Street as you ascend from Buitengracht) the **Iziko Bo-Kaap Museum** is where any visit to the district should begin. It has a "wavy" parapet above the facade which is a unique survival of a type of building common to the city in the third quarter of the 18th century. All the early woodwork survives, including the original teak windows, teak shutters, the doors and the lovely fanlight above the front door.

Inside, it's been restored to resemble the home of a Muslim household

ABOVE: celebrating Tweede Nuwe Jaar, Bo-Kaap's principal festival.

New Year Celebration

New Year's Eve in Bo-Kaap is a lively affair. The area, including many of the surrounding streets, throngs with banjo-playing minstrels, dressed in flamboyant suits, who dance through the streets in commemoration of Tweede Nuwe Jaar (Second New Year). The festival, known as the Kaapse Klopse or Cape Carnival, first took place in 1862 and was traditionally confined to 2 January, the only day in the calendar when slaves were allowed to down tools and enjoy a holiday.

Traditional Malay choirs are an important element of the festival. Only men and boys take part, singing a mixture of *ghommaliedjies* (folk songs), hymns, funeral dirges and the gypsy violinist's wistful songs of homelessness. The different troupes of singers are in fierce competition with each other. The celebrations culminate at Green Point *(see page 109)*, with the announcement of the winning troupe.

With its long history, Tweede Nuwe Jaar is a hugely important annual holiday, and the coloured population, including Muslims, take it very seriously. The carnival is now somewhat controversial; it has come close to being called off several times, and only five minstrel troupes were permitted to perform at the 2010 event.

ABOVE: younger inhabitants of Bo-Kaap. **BELOW:** the Auwal Mosque on Dorp Street.

of the 19th century. Most of the furniture is either English or Dutch, and of a type found in such a house at the time. The kitchen is more 18th than 19th century, with a floor of original Robben Island slate.

The museum contains photographs and pictures depicting the lifestyle of the community as well as interesting relics of daily life such as a fish-seller's horn, once typical of the door-to-door fish hawkers who frequented the city's streets. There is also memorabilia of the religious leader Abubakr Effendi, who was brought to the Cape from Turkey in 1862 to help the British administration mediate between the city's feuding Muslim factions.

Upstairs, the museum tells the story of the local community in its sociopolitical and cultural contexts, with an extensive picture gallery. In particular, it portrays the devastating effects that apartheid and the Group Areas Act had on the community.

There is no longer a courtyard café at the museum, but you can pop over to the grocery shop directly opposite.

Auwal Mosque

Bo-Kaap still has some of its mosques, burial grounds and shrines, known as *kramats* (there are three in Bo-Kaap and two more on Signal Hill behind the district). The **Auwal Mosque** ❷ in Dorp Street, one block south of the museum, is the oldest mosque in South Africa. Founded in 1798 during the first British Occupation of the Cape, it is a Shafee mosque (conforming to the doctrines of Muslims of Indonesian origin), and was founded by Tuan Guru, Imam Abdullah Kadi Abdus Salaam. The mosque was the main Muslim religious institution in the first half of the 19th century.

Tuan Guru was its first imam. A prince from Tidore in the Ternate Islands, he was brought to the Cape by the Dutch government as a prisoner. He was incarcerated on Robben Island, and while there wrote a treatise on Islamic law and wrote down the Holy Qur'an from memory. His handwritten works became the main reference for Cape Muslims, and over the years had a tremendous influence on Islam here. He established the first organised school where the Qur'an was taught to slaves and free black

TIP

If you admire the African beadwork on sale in many gift shops in Cape Town, visit Monkeybiz at 43 Rose Street, Bo-Kaap (tel: 021-426 0145; www.monkeybiz. co.za). It sells a gorgeous array of beaded dolls, animals and bags made by women living in the townships. Monkeybiz, which celebrated its tenth anniversary in 2010, has proved an astounding success and you will find its products in cities all over the world.

children – in fact his name, Tuan Guru, means "teacher". It is thought that Afrikaans first emerged at the Auwal Mosque.

Tuan Guru is buried in the Tana Baru Karamat. This can be seen at the top of Longmarket Street, on the slopes of Signal Hill. This important burial ground also contains the graves of other holy men banished to the Cape from the East, Abubakr Effendi and Tuan Sayed Alawie among them. The latter came from the Yemen, and was known for his work in the Slave Lodge. He served a prison sentence of 11 years and, after his release, became the first official imam of the Cape Muslims.

Nurul Islam Mosque

There are other mosques in Bo-Kaap. The **Nurul Islam Mosque** ❸ is in a lane off Buitengracht Street. The city's third oldest (the second oldest is the Palm Tree Mosque in Long Street – *see page 95*), it was founded by Imam Abdul Rauf, the youngest of Tuan Guru's sons, in 1844. At 62 Chiappini Street is the **Masjid al Jami**, and further on the **Masjid al Borhan** which had the first minaret in Cape Town. The **Masjid Boorhaanol Islam**, in Longmarket Street, is fairly large and has remained unaltered since it was built in 1886. There are others, all of them still in use.

Cape Malay cuisine

A fitting end to a tour of Bo-Kaap would be a meal at Biesmiellah's or the Noon Gun Tearoom *(see below)*, set in a Bo-Kaap home on Longmarket Street.

The **Noon Gun** is located at the top of vertiginous Longmarket Street (for direct access by road, follow the signpost up Carisbrook and Military streets from Buitengracht). Following a long tradition dating from colonial times, when the gun signalled the arrival of an important ship, as happened in other colonial outposts such as Hong Kong, a cannon shot is fired every day at noon. Though it is loaded by hand, it is fired automatically after receiving an electronic signal from Cape Town Observatory *(see page 129)*. There is not that much to see, but it is worth walking up for the magnificent views of the ocean and Table Mountain. ❑

ABOVE LEFT: Boorhaanol Mosque, Longmarket Street.
ABOVE RIGHT: halal menu at a local restaurant.

RESTAURANTS

Biesmiellah
Corner of Wale and Pentz streets. Tel: 021-423 0850. www.biesmiellah.co.za
Open: L & D Mon–Sat. **$**
㊴ p256, A2
This restaurant is a must. In fact it's a private house, and you come here to eat well-prepared and authentic Cape Malay cooking, including chicken or mutton *breyani*, *bredies* (stews), and an array of curries. All dishes are halal and alcoholic drinks are not permitted.

Noon Gun Tearoom
273 Longmarket St. Tel: 021-424 0529. www.noonguntearoom.co.za Open: L & D Mon–Sat. **$**
㊵ p256, A1
Also specialising in Cape Malay cooking, the Noon Gun Tearoom at the top of Longmarket Street serves tasty set lunches and dinners and teas. Desserts include syrupy *koeksisters* and delicious *melkterts*. Alcohol not served.

Prices are for a three-course dinner per person with a half-bottle of house wine.
$ = under R200
$$ = R200–350
$$$ = more than R350

GUGA
S'THEBE

THE TOWNSHIPS

No trip to Cape Town is complete unless you've paid a visit to the townships. Once you've seen the beaches, climbed Table Mountain and sampled the good life of the Cape, it's time to visit South Africa's monuments to social engineering, the flip side of the coin

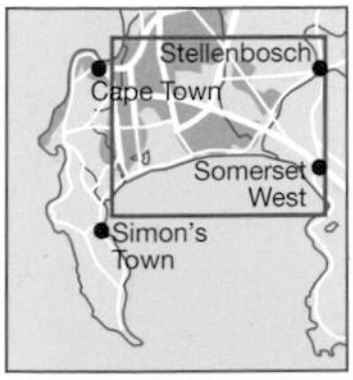

Main Attractions

GUGA S'THEBE ARTS AND CULTURAL CENTRE
GUGULETHU
LANGA-SHARPEVILLE MASSACRE MEMORIAL
KHAYELITSHA CRAFT MARKET
LWANDLE MIGRANT LABOUR MUSEUM
IMIZAMO YETHU

Maps and Listings

MAP OF THE TOWNSHIPS, PAGE 122

Most visitors get their first glimpse of the city's townships on their drive from the airport. The worst of them butt up to the busy N2 highway as it sweeps into the city from the southern Cape, crossing the infamous Cape Flats, the windy, dusty flatlands prone to flooding that lie between the wealthy Southern Suburbs and and the Hottentots Holland Mountains. This is where the majority of Cape Town's population live.

The townships include Langa ("Sun"), Gugulethu ("Our Pride"), Nyanga ("Moon"), Khayelitsha ("New Place"), Crossroads, Bonteheuwel, Hanover Park (named after District Six's main street) and Bishop Lavis Town. They are the areas in which non-whites were forced to live during apartheid. Blacks, coloureds and Indians were separated into their own areas.

Several of the black townships have evolved from what were essentially labour camps, where male-only hostels for migrant workers from the Transkei (an apartheid era "independent homeland" now integrated into Eastern Cape province) and elsewhere were set up to meet the needs of the nearby city. If a man lost his job or grew too old or ill to work, he lost his right to live in proximity to the city and was required to return to his designated tribal homeland.

The townships today

In spite of the ending of apartheid, mostly for economic reasons the status quo generally survives, and people continue to live in the townships in which they were born. But the inhabitants also stay for social reasons.

LEFT: mosaic work at a the Guga S'Thebe cultural centre in Langa. **RIGHT:** former workers' hostel, Langa township.

TIP

If you want to immerse yourself in genuine, modern-day African culture, consider an overnight stay in a township B&B. Chances are it will be one of the highlights of your visit to Cape Town. *(For recommendations, see page 224 of Travel Tips.)*

Extensive communities of families and friends have evolved, many of whom have lived together for nearly half a century. These networks are difficult to leave. In Johannesburg some prosperous residents have chosen to invest in magnificent new homes in the townships rather than move to former white areas.

That said, some affluent black, and more particularly coloured and Indian Capetonians have started moving into white suburbs. It is virtually unknown, however, for poor whites to move into the townships.

Since the ending of apartheid, facilities in the townships have improved dramatically. The provision of basic services such as electricity and water was a priority of the new government in 1994, initially under Joe Slovo, Nelson Mandela's first Minister of Housing. But massive and continuing migration from the former homelands outstrips provision.

Visiting a township

During apartheid, crime and violence escalated in the townships, and the legacy of this, perpetuated by the extreme poverty, is still evident today. It is therefore inadvisable for strangers to enter a township independently. Roads are badly signposted and maintained, and there is a slight but real risk of ending up in a threatening situation. The only safe way to visit a township is to join an organised tour with people who know the locals and know precisely where to go.

A trip to a township is less about seeing the sights than it is about the opportunity to experience a living culture – to meet the locals in township taverns, jazz clubs and restaurants, browse among roadside stalls where you can buy anything from a sheep's head to hair oil, have your car repaired or your hair cut.

In the face of often grinding poverty, visitors are encouraged to support local artists and community

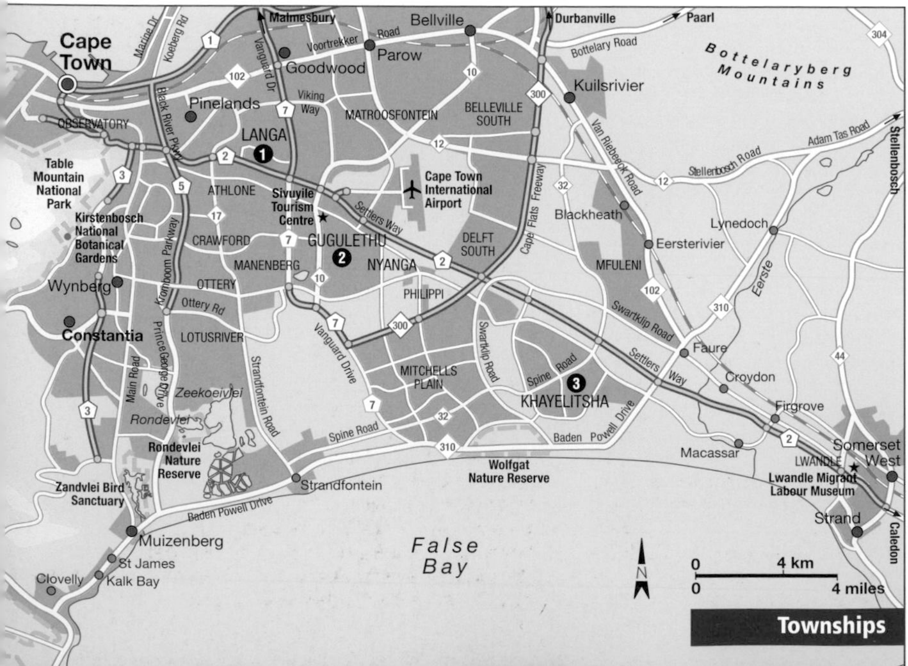

Townships

Christianity is an important influence in the lives of many black South Africans. For decades missionary schools were the only means by which black children could receive an education beyond primary level. Today, a huge number of pentecostal Christian sects are active in the townships.

projects, and buy the produce and merchandise on sale. They can even spend a night in a township. Conditions will be simple, and almost certainly mean sharing a bathroom with a stranger, but this is about looking at the way township people do things and, more importantly, it's about joining them. It is a relevant cultural exchange with people who rarely, if ever, get the chance to meet foreigners. This way the locals and visitors are exposed to other viewpoints, other languages and cultures. Strangely, it's something white Capetonians rarely do.

The economic advantages of the tours, too, are enormous. They help residents earn a living in a place where only about 30 percent of them are formally employed. People are taught to be guides, to wait at table, cook or pour the wine in township restaurants. There are opportunities to sell visitors home-made goods such as rugs, baskets and all kinds of decorative items from beaded dolls to papier-mâché bowls. If someone has a skill, he or she can use it to put food on the table. And there are more direct benefits to be had: whole containers have arrived from foreign parts filled with books, bicycles, even school furniture, sent by interested visitors.

The three most visited townships in the Cape Town area are Langa, Gugulethu and Khayelitsha.

LANGA

Cape Town's oldest township, dating from 1927, **Langa** ❶, a few kilometres east of Mowbray, is currently being transformed into a modern suburb complete with schools, clinics and sports facilities. Perhaps it was here that township life as we now know it came into existence. The enforced

LEFT: hairdresser's in the Imizamo Yethu township.

Township Tours

It is estimated that 5–10 percent of all visitors to Cape Town take a township tour. Recommended operators include:

Around the Cape Tours (www.aroundthecape.co.za; tel: 021-788 2739) offer full- and half-day tours, as well as a wide range of other tours in and around Cape Town.

Cape Capers (www.tourcapers.co.za; tel: 021-448 3117). A varied programme, including a Trail of Two Cities on the Cape Care Route *(see Tip, page 124)*.

Ezizwe Travel and Tours (www.touringcapetown.com; tel: 021-697 0068). Offers informative and diverse tours, taking in Langa, Gugulethu and Khayelitsha townships, run by the ebullient Thabang Titoti.

Hylton Ross Exclusive Touring (www.hyltonross.co.za; tel: 021-511 1784). Includes Bonteheuwel, Nyanga and Crossroads in addition to the more usual townships.

Nomvuyo's Tours (www.nomvuyos-tours.co.za; tel: 083-371 9131). Organises tours to Khayelitsha, including overnight stays.

Zibonele Tours (www.ziboneletours.com; tel: 021-975 2010). A varied range of packages including daily township tours.

TIP

One of the most interesting tourism initiatives in recent years is the Cape Care Route, focusing on self-help projects both in the townships and elsewhere that have community or ecological benefits. Cape Capers *(see page 123)* are among the tour operators offering the option in their programme.

RIGHT: DJ at Mzoli's bar, Gugulethu. **BELOW:** Gugas Thebe Arts and Cultural Centre.

intimacy of the residents, living in cramped conditions, meant that neighbours ate together, socialised and helped one another more than usual. The Church was, and remains, an important institution which helped keep society together. Langa today is at the opposite end of the scale from Khayelitsha; the former is more organised and suburban with homes of bricks and mortar, the latter is utterly impoverished, made up of little more than shacks.

Plenty of operators *(see page 123)* will take you on a walking tour of Langa, visiting the vibrant **Gugas Thebe Arts and Cultural Centre**, a hub of many and varied activities from dance classes to arts-and-crafts workshops, as well as a *shebeen* (tavern), and an informal settlement of adjoining shacks, often home to three generations of a single family. Langa's citizens grow their own food at **Tsoga Environmental Centre**, where they are also educated about the environment, an outcome of which is a successful community-run waste-recycling centre.

A tour may also include lunch in a private house or in a neighbourhood restaurant, a visit to the men's hostels, where migrant workers lived for years without their families, and an encounter with a traditional healer, who would still be visited by many township dwellers in preference to a trained Western doctor. You may also visit the **Langa-Sharpeville Massacre Memorial**, unveiled on 20 March 2010 close to the site of the tragic incident in which some 50,000 people, led by the PAC leader Philip Kgosana, protested against the pass laws and were fired upon by police exactly 50 years earlier.

GUGULETHU

A tour of **Gugulethu** ❷, 20km (12 miles) southeast of Cape Town, is likely to include visits to several struggle sites, where important and often tragic events during the fight against apartheid are commemorated. They will include monuments dedicated to the Gugulethu Seven, seven young men who were shot in the head after driving into a police trap in 1986, and Amy Biehl, a 26-year-old American Fulbright scholar stoned and stabbed to death in 1993. A white anti-apartheid activist, she had been giving friends a lift home when she was seized by young Pan Africanist Congress supporters responding to the call "one settler, one bullet".

Also on the itinerary will be the **Sivuyile Tourism Centre,** an offshoot of Cape Town Tourism, based at Sivuyile Technical College, a centre for about 80 artists, making pottery, painting fabrics and so on.

KHAYELITSHA

The second-largest township in South Africa (after Soweto near Johannesburg), **Khayelitsha** ❸ features in all the programmes offered by the township tour operators. Covering an area of about 28 sq. km (11 sq. miles) 35 km (22 miles) east of Cape Town along the N2 to Somerset West, it comprises a mix of formal and informal dwellings, the latter constantly growing as more and more people flow in from the countryside.

A visit to Khayelitsha normally begins with an overview of the township from **Lookout Hill**. It will also include the **Khayelitsha Craft Market**, set up in 1997 as a self-help organisation. There are all sorts of good-quality crafts on sale, some of them made for export to the US and Europe. You may also visit the **Abalimi Bezekhaya Peace Park and Community Garden** (www.abalimi.org.za), set up as a means of bringing peace to communities in conflict and now operating as a successful market garden.

Imizamo Yethu

The older townships mostly lie to the east of Cape Town, but there are others around the peninsula. The best known is **Imizamo Yethu** (literally "Through Collective Struggle"), which supports 35,000 people at the foot of Table Mountain above Hout Bay. Established in the 1990s, it was originally a shack settlement with no formal infrastructure, but several hundred proper houses have now been built by an Irish volunteer programme established by the millionaire philanthropist Niall Mellon. It is a more relaxed setup than the larger townships of the Cape Flats, and tours can be arranged with private guides – contact the Hout Bay Tourist Office for recommendations (tel: 021-790-1194; www.houtbaytourism.com).

ABOVE: roadside grill, Khayelitsha.

Another success story is Golden Nongawuza, a Khayelitsha man who makes flowers out of cut-up tin cans. Formerly destitute, Nongawuza was reputedly inspired to start his business by a recurring dream. You can join him painting his spectacular tin blooms.

One of the best ways of experiencing Khayelitsha is to attend a cultural event at **Oliver Tambo Hall** (the big white sports hall by the Mew Way turn-off from the N2).

Migrant Labour Museum

Further from Khayelitsha, on the N2 outside Somerset West, is the **Lwandle Migrant Labour Museum** (www.lwandle.com; tel: 021-845 6119; Mon–Fri 9.30am–4pm; charge). Housed in a former hostel, it preserves life as it was for the migrant labourers and documents the rules by which they lived. The hostels were notorious institutions, designed for men only (who were fined if their wives stayed over), but towards the end of apartheid inhabited by whole families, each member allotted a single bed.

While the other hostels in Lwandle have now been converted into decent family homes, with innovative solar heating, Hostel 33 is a poignant reminder of how life was in Lwandle and many other townships just a few years ago. ❑

EAT

In Langa, ask the tour driver to stop quickly at **Mzoli's**, a popular and easygoing bar that might rank as the most integrated venue in greater Cape Town. *Braais* (barbecued meat) are the culinary speciality, and there's usually some lively local music on the speakers and plenty of beer flowing.

THE SOUTHERN SUBURBS

Follow De Waal Drive around the base of Devil's Peak and you will enter the Southern Suburbs, a salubrious residential area containing several grand estates from the colonial era, including Groote Schuur and Groot Constantia

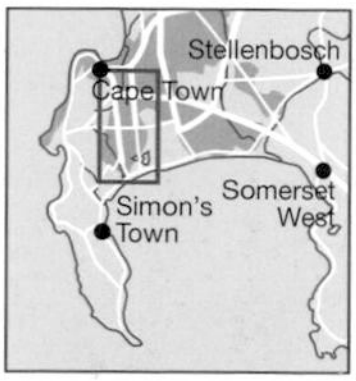

Main Attractions

IRMA STERN MUSEUM
RHODES MEMORIAL
KIRSTENBOSCH NATIONAL BOTANICAL GARDEN
GROOT CONSTANTIA
STEENBERG ESTATE

Maps and Listings

MAP OF THE SOUTHERN SUBURBS, PAGE 128
MAP OF KIRSTENBOSCH NATIONAL BOTANICAL GARDENS, PAGE 137
MAP OF CONSTANTIA VALLEY, PAGE 139
RESTAURANTS, BARS AND CAFÉS, PAGE 142–3
ACCOMMODATION, PAGE 228

The string of old villages running along the southeast flank of Table Mountain below Devil's Peak, collectively known as the Southern Suburbs, forms the oldest part of the suburban sprawl that continues all the way to the coast of False Bay. Established along the road to Muizenberg in the 18th century, these villages became very fashionable with well-heeled Capetonians following the opening of the railway line to Simon's Town in the 1860s, and by the early 20th century they had merged into one more-or-less contiguous band of leafy suburbia.

The Southern Suburbs are traditionally regarded as the most affluent part of Cape Town (a title now vied for by the likes of Clifton and Camps Bay on the Atlantic Seaboard), and the area remains conspicuously wealthy by comparison to the bordering townships and dormitory suburbs of the more easterly Cape Flats, whence the victims of the Group Areas Act were banished in the 1960s and 1970s.

The landscape

There are some exceptional monuments out here, but above all it is a place of great natural beauty, dotted with wine farms, restaurants and viewing points, and much more lush and green than the peninsula's rocky coastal landscape, particularly along the upper fringes of Newlands in the Newlands Forest, and Bishopscourt, where Kirstenbosch links it with Constantia. There's every chance it might be raining here when the sun is shining over the Atlantic coast; not for nothing was this area developed as gardens soon after the colony was settled. It was practically guaranteed that the land would yield sufficient

LEFT: Kirstenbosch. **RIGHT:** George Frederick Watts's statue *Energy* at the Rhodes Memorial.

produce to supply the ships passing by on their way to and from Europe and the East.

Woodstock and Observatory

This chapter roughly follows the M3 out of the city centre, accessible from the mountain end of Long Street. Between the city and the Southern Suburbs is **Woodstock**, the oldest of Cape Town's suburbs, established at the beginning of the 19th century, and today regarded as one of its poorer areas. Its old houses are ramshackle and its streets are ghetto-like. But it has lots of character, with little squares and streets of Victorian terraces. If you want to get an idea of how District Six might once have looked *(see page 44)*, have a stroll around Woodstock. However, things are changing here as people looking for inexpensive housing cash in on the district's proximity to the city centre, creating an observable trend towards gentrification.

Next to Woodstock, **Salt River**, built near marshy ground surrounding the eponymous lagoon, is a busy, industrial area of factories and workshops. In spite of this, like Woodstock,

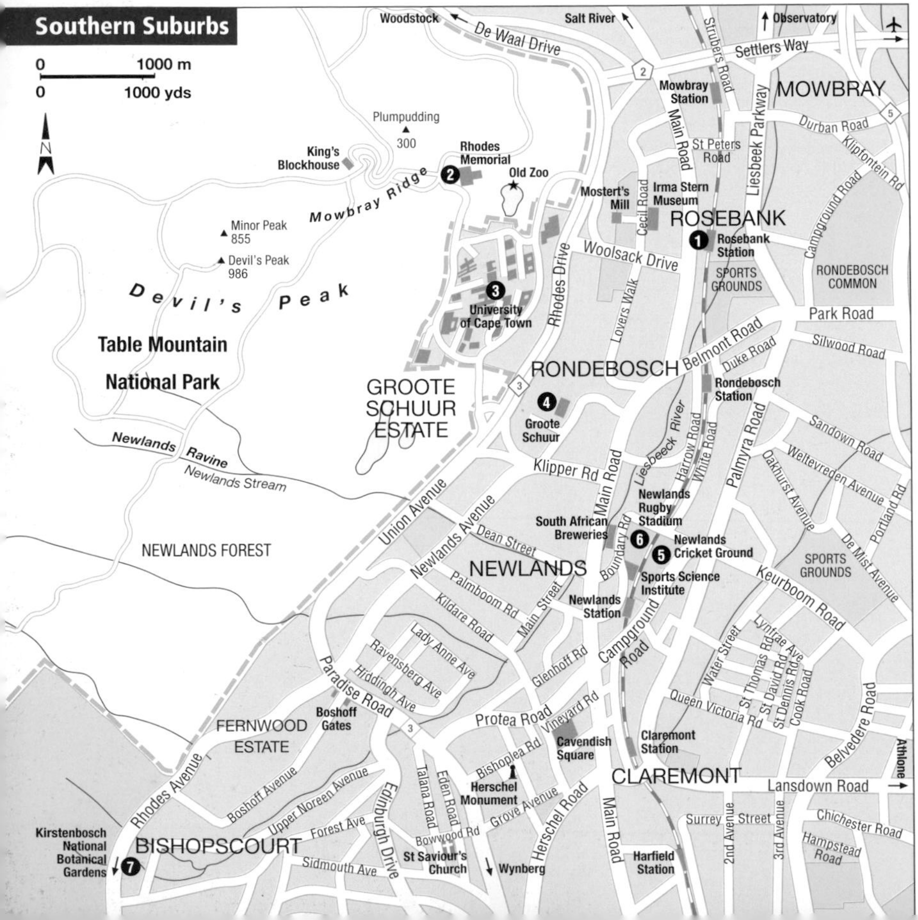

it also has plenty of character and is worth a closer inspection. In Victoria, Main and Albert roads there are down-at-heel bric-a-brac shops and factory outlets selling seconds from the many clothing manufacturers that populate the district.

Next to Salt River is **Observatory**, which derives its name from the Royal Observatory established there in 1821, and then **Mowbray**, named after the English town of Melton Mowbray. Mowbray developed around a crossroads where in 1724 a notorious murder took place in the Driekoppen tavern, owned by a certain Johannes Zacharias Beck. The murderers were caught and cruelly executed, their severed heads displayed on stakes.

Observatory is the most popular of these older neighbourhoods, and has a reputation as a bohemian quarter. Commonly known as Obz, it is filled with bars, cafés and cheap restaurants that are busy until the early hours. Its Victorian terraced houses are characterised by their ornate *broekie* (panty) *lace* decoration, elaborate cast-iron balconies and old gardens. Once a prosperous, middle-class area, it is now a popular area for students and those taking a first step onto the property ladder.

Beyond Observatory lie the Southern Suburbs proper – Rosebank, Rondebosch, Newlands, Claremont, Bishopscourt, Kenilworth, Wynberg, Plumstead and Constantia. You hit them once you've turned the corner and passed beyond Devil's Peak. Each one has its own character and style.

ROSEBANK

Rosebank ❶ is known as the "learned quarter" due to its proximity to the University of Cape Town and the large proportion of academics who live here. Substantial Victorian and Edwardian villas and palm trees characterise its old streets.

The easiest way to get to Rosebank from the city centre is to take the Eastern Boulevard or the parallel M3 De Waal Drive higher up the side of Devil's Peak. They join just above Groote Schuur Hospital, and together sweep around to the south. To the right is **Mostert's Mill**, a working windmill of a type that used to be common in the Cape. Dating from 1796 it has been restored, complete with a thatch cap that rotates to catch the wind. Visits are normally by appointment (tel: 021-762 5127; charge), though it is often open on Saturdays when volunteer millers operate it.

Irma Stern Museum

Address: Cecil Road, www.irmastern.co.za
Tel: 021-685 5686
Opening Hrs: Tue–Sat 10am–5pm
Entrance Fee: charge

Just below Mostert's Mill, this fascinating museum is set in the former studio and home of the great South African painter Irma Stern (1894–1966), who lived here for 40 years. Set in a tranquil garden, the 19th-century building is now a museum

Every day at noon an electronic signal is sent from the Royal Observatory to fire the Noon Gun on Signal Hill above Bo-Kaap (see page 119).

TIP

If you are interested in acquiring a work by Stern, watch the sales catalogues of South Africa's premier auction house, Stefan Welz (www.swelco.co.za), in association with Sotheby's.

OPPOSITE: Mostert's Mill, dating from the 18th century. **BELOW:** Irma Stern Museum.

ABOVE: an Edwardian terrace in Rosebank. **RIGHT:** a bust of Rhodes surveys the parkland setting of his memorial.

to her life. Stern, of German-Jewish descent, painted in the German Expressionist style mainly scenes from her travels around Africa, Asia, the Mediterranean, Europe and South America. Her subjects included exotic figures, portraits, lush landscapes and still lifes, conveyed in a variety of media that ranged from oils and watercolours to gouache and charcoal.

The rooms are filled with artefacts that she picked up on her travels. Most notable amongst these is a Buli Stool from the eastern region of the Democratic Republic of Congo, a pair of carved Zanzibar doors, and several fine examples of 17th-century Spanish furniture. The studio, with the artist's easel, palettes, paint and brushes left intact, is the focal point of the house.

Stern's home-decorating style is manifested in the paintwork of doors and cupboards throughout the house, not unlike the painted surfaces and panels of Charleston in Sussex, England, the country retreat of the Bloomsbury group. Stern's works are highly collectable today, and their prices are on the rise.

Rhodes Memorial ❷

Address: Residence Road, www.rhodes-memorial.co.za
Tel: 021-689 9151
Opening Hrs: open all hours
Entrance Fee: free

Way above Rosebank, on the other side of the M3 highway, just next to the campus of the University of Cape Town *(see page 132)*, stands Herbert Baker's classical monument to Cecil John Rhodes, who bequeathed all the land along the lower slopes of the mountain to the city of Cape Town. One of the most magnificently sited monuments in the world, it was built in 1912, and is an impressive U-shaped building fronted by Doric columns and a massive flight of 49 steps (one for each year of Rhodes's life) flanked by sleeping lions. Its design is based on that of the Greek temple at Segesta in Sicily, and the inscriptions were penned by Sir Rudyard Kipling.

It is said that the monument occupies one of Rhodes's favourite spots, where he would sit for hours and admire a view he believed was "unsurpassed anywhere in the world". At the base is a bronze horse and rider called *Energy*, by the Victorian artist and sculptor George Frederick Watts. Another version of it stands in London's Hyde Park.

The monument is enclosed by tall Stone pines and surrounded by vast open grasslands where an enclosure protects herds of the endemic black

Cecil John Rhodes

Cape and southern African history was shaped by the third son of an English parson, an Oxford graduate in poor health who would die before the age of 50. He was a consummate politician with a sharp eye for colonial real estate. In 1890, nine years after entering the House of Assembly in Cape Town, he was elected Prime Minister of the Cape Colony. He controlled De Beers Consolidated, a vast conglomerate of diamond mines, the Consolidated Goldfields of South Africa Company and the British South Africa Chartered Company, which would bring Bechuanaland (Botswana), Matabeleland and Mashonaland (most of Zimbabwe) under British protection.

Rhodes came to exemplify all that was wildly romantic and ruthless about colonial expansion. By the time of his death in 1902 he had added 2 million sq. km (772,200 sq. miles) to British possessions in Africa, established educational trusts (Rhodes scholarships, which continue to this day) and farming grants, left a Groote Schuur redesigned by Herbert Baker *(see page 67)* as the home of future South African heads of state, and created a new nation, the ill-fated Rhodesia (now Zimbabwe).

wildebeest and Cape mountain zebra – an area favoured for fashion shoots by magazines and advertising agencies because it looks like the grasslands of the Highveld in the north. The Rhodes Memorial Restaurant next to the monument occupies a small cottage also built by Herbert Baker.

This is a lovely place to walk. Park beside the monument and take a picnic up into the woods. From every vantage point there's a view out over northern Cape Town and the Cape Flats and to the jagged Hottentots Holland to the east.

Once Khoikhoi pastoralists used these slopes (they were recorded there in the 1600s), but in 1667 the Dutch East India Company (VOC) colonised them as a farming area and built a huge barn called Groote Schuur – today commemorated by the nearby hospital of the same name. The VOC planted the Stone pines in the 1700s.

When Rhodes arrived late in the 19th century, he cleared most of the indigenous landscape, leaving the pines, to create a parkland setting for his house (also called Groote Schuur) and grazing for animals. Between 1891 and 1899 Rhodes purchased most of the properties on the eastern slopes of Table Mountain, creating the Groote Schuur Estate, which was incorporated into the Cape Peninsula National Park in 1999.

Just below Rhodes Memorial is the old zoo, built in 1897 to house lions. Rhodes had a particular fondness for the lion as "king of beasts", because to him it symbolised the aspirations of the British Empire. The lions' descendants remained here until 1975 when the zoo closed. Until then donkeys were kept in a field behind the zoo – as lion fodder.

Today the estate serves as a gateway to Table Mountain National Park *(see pages 147–55)*. As well as access to the mountain, there are walks to Kirstenbosch, to the Cecilia Plantation and to the Newlands Forest. Paths and jeep tracks ascend the lower slopes of the mountain, and you can walk to the King's Blockhouse. If Rhodes's aim was to secure this landscape against encroachment, then he was successful. Today it is one of Cape Town's most important assets.

Cecil John Rhodes died in Rhodes cottage in Muizenberg on the False Bay coast in 1902. The last words of the archetypal colonialist were "So much to do, so little done". His grave lies at World's View in the Matopos Mountains of Zimbabwe.

BELOW: the Rhodes Memorial, nestling on the slopes of Table Mountain National Park.

The Groote Schuur Hospital is where Dr Christiaan Barnard made medical history by performing the world's very first heart transplant in 1967. The operating theatre he used is now part of the Heart of Cape Town Museum (tel: 021-404 1967; www.heartofcapetown.co.za; open 8am–7pm daily), which can only be explored on (costly) organised tours.

RONDEBOSCH

In the late 19th century Rondebosch was one of the city's smartest areas, popular with the English, who were keen to demonstrate their status in what had become a kind of rural suburbia. Houses with turrets and porte-cocheres and names chosen to remind their occupants of home – Ringmore, Silwood, Mayfield, for example – are the order of the day.

The name Rondebosch refers to a round thornbush found on the banks of the Liesbeeck River, and it grew up around a garden established by the early Dutch colonists because it was discovered to be virtually wind-free. It's thought that at the time the thornbushes were cleared from the land and made into a protective hedge around the garden, preventing wild animals and Khoikhoi from entering. Today Rondebosch is famous for its schools.

University of Cape Town ❸

Address: Residence Road, www.uct.co.za
Tel: 021-650 9111
Opening Hrs: daily tours by appointment only
Entrance Fee: free

Built on former Groote Schuur Estate land, the University of Cape Town (UCT) occupies a magnificent site, straddling the eastern foothills of Devil's Peak and facing out to the distant Hottentots Holland Mountain, Blouberg to the left and False Bay to the right. The first university in the country, it was founded in 1829, but didn't occupy its present site until 1911, after Rhodes had bequeathed the land to Cape Town. UCT is a distinguished institution; its architecture and medical faculties are world-renowned, and it was prominent in the struggle against apartheid. Today it attracts national and international students.

Groote Schuur ❹

Address: Groot Schuur Estate, Klipper Road
Tel: 021-701 8692
Opening Hrs: visits by appointment only
Entrance Fee: charge

Below the M3 highway, and accessible

BELOW: students at the University of Cape Town.

from Klipper Road in the higher reaches of Rondebosch, is **Groote Schuur**, the house remodelled for Rhodes in 1893 by Herbert Baker in a Cape Dutch Revival style. It's well worth a visit if you have the time. A tour takes in the public rooms and Rhodes's own bedroom, a small, Spartan chamber more in keeping with a boys' boarding school than the sanctuary of the man who named a country after himself and who dreamed of linking Cape Town with Cairo. The public rooms house the remains of Rhodes's magnificent collections of Cape Dutch and Batavian furniture, porcelain, silver and glassware, as well as carpets, tapestries and paintings. Rhodes's library is still here, as is one of the famous stone Great Zimbabwe birds, thought to have been removed from the ruins of ancient Great Zimbabwe.

Groote Schuur is a cross between a Victorian country house and a gentleman's club. For a long time it was the Cape Town residence of the prime minister and then of the state president. It's located in a secure complex of other important houses, including Genadendal (formerly Westbrooke), now the state president's Cape Town residence.

NEWLANDS

After Rondebosch comes Newlands, Claremont and Bishopscourt; high above Bishopscourt, where the Liesbeeck River begins, is Kirstenbosch.

The upper reaches of Rondebosch and Newlands are possibly the leafiest part of the city. In the early 1700s Willem Adriaan van der Stel created a new garden for the colony here. He also established oak plantations in the vicinity, the last vestiges of which you see throughout Newlands, particularly along Newlands Avenue, which was once the old wagon road to the south. The district is sprinkled with old farms, some with original houses and barns surviving in what is now dense suburbia. On the left as you drive down Paradise Road (now the M3), are the 19th-century Boshoff Gates, leading into leafy Boshoff Avenue for a short cut to Kirstenbosch. The air is cooler; in the summer you can feel the change in temperature as you round the mountain beneath Devil's Peak.

These days Newlands is associated with cricket and rugby. In Campground Road is the famous **Newlands Cricket Ground** ❺ (www.newlandstours.co.za; tel: 021-686 2150; tours by appointment Mon–Fri; charge), where several matches in the 2003 Cricket World Cup were held. Cricket was popularised by the British military in the 1850s, and in the 1860s there were organised matches pitching "the Army and Navy against South Africa", and between "Mother Country and Colonial Born". In 1871, during an international tour to the Cape, the England team suffered an innings defeat by the locals.

In Boundary Road is the equally renowned **Newlands Rugby**

ABOVE: Newlands property.

SHOP

In contrast to the slick surroundings and international brands at Cavendish Square is the Montebello Design Centre in Newlands (31 Newlands Avenue; www.montobello.co.za), where a cluster of farm outbuildings has been converted into studios and workshops for high-quality pottery, jewellery and other crafts.

TIP

To book tours online for Newlands Cricket Ground or Newlands Rugby Stadium (or the Super Tour, combining both), contact www.newlandstours. co.za

Stadium ❻ (tel: 021-686 2150; www.newlandstours.co.za; tours Mon–Fri; charge). The rugby field was first used in 1890, and is one of the oldest venues for the sport in the world. Its smart new stadium seats 51,000 spectators, and national and international matches are frequently held here. The **Rugby Museum** (tel: 021-659 6768; Mon–Fri 10am–4pm; free) here is dedicated to the history of Newlands and the South African game, with rugby memorabilia, news clippings, and so on. Also in Boundary Road is the **Sports Science Institute** (www.ssisa.com; tel: 021-659 5600; tours Mon–Fri; charge), where professional sportsmen and women go to train, receive dietary and nutritional advice, and see their coaches.

Nearby is **South African Breweries**, the second-largest brewery in the world. Newlands was chosen as the site of Cape Town's breweries because of the freshness of its mountain water. While the early breweries were higher up the slopes, closer to Newlands Avenue, the South African Breweries (SAB) are in Boundary Road. An old malt house and the old Ohlsson brewery on the site have been restored and can be visited by appointment (tel: 021-658 7511; free).

CLAREMONT

Beyond Newlands is **Claremont**, one of the commercial hubs of the Southern Suburbs. **Cavendish Square** (Dreyer Street; www.cavendish.co.za; tel: 021-657 5620; Mon–Sat 9am–7pm, Sun 10am–7pm) is a huge, exclusive shopping centre with a superb range of top-end fashion boutiques, smart interior-design businesses, bookshops, restaurants, coffee shops and two cinema complexes.

There's not much else to do in Claremont, although if you're passing along Bishoplea Road or Feldhausen Road behind Cavendish Square, have a look at the **Herschel Monument**, an obelisk in the grounds of Grove Primary School. It marks the site of the house where the astronomer Sir John Herschel (1792–1871) roamed the skies with his telescope. The telescope was a version of the one constructed by his father, William Herschel, of Bath, England, who discovered the planet Uranus. It was

BELOW: Newlands Cricket Ground.

considered the finest telescope of its time, and enabled William to re-survey the whole of the northern sky. Son John's version was used to survey the sky in the southern hemisphere. At the time John Herschel, who had no peer in his knowledge of the southern skies, was widely revered, and when he died he was buried near Sir Isaac Newton in Westminster Abbey, London. His house, Feldhausen, stood on this site.

Not far away, in Bowwood Road, is **St Saviour's Church**, designed by Sophie Gray and consecrated by her husband Bishop Gray in 1853. The little stone-built church was enlarged on two occasions as Claremont grew, the first time by William Butterfield (1880), the High-Church Gothic Revivalist responsible for Keble College in Oxford, England, and then again in 1903 by Herbert Baker.

BISHOPSCOURT

Claremont runs into Bishopscourt, an old suburb with enormous 20th-century mansions and massive gardens filled with shrubs and trees. The district is named after the seat of the Archbishop of Cape Town, which itself occupies a farm first granted to Jan van Riebeeck in 1658. Van Riebeeck never moved in and it was burned down soon after, but there's been a substantial house on the property ever since. Bishopscourt was renovated by Herbert Baker and made famous by Archbishop Desmond Tutu, who took up residence here in 1986. Even more famous is the graffiti once scrawled, in disaffection at the Archbishop's anti-apartheid activism, on a wall of a house in Edinburgh Drive near to Tutu's home. It said: "I was an Anglican until I put Tu and Tu together".

KIRSTENBOSCH NATIONAL BOTANICAL GARDEN ❼

Address: Rhodes Drive, www.sanbi.org
Tel: 021-799 8783
Opening Hrs: daily Sept–Mar 8am–7pm, Apr–Aug 8am–6pm
Entrance Fee: charge

Extending over 528 hectares (1,320 acres) along the southeast slopes of

ABOVE: office workers in Claremont.
BELOW: *Kniphofia uvaria*, commonly known as red-hot pokers, at Kirstenbosch Botanical Garden.

ABOVE: Kirstenbosch National Botanical Garden.

TIP

It is easy to spend the whole day in Kirstenbosch. If you don't have your own transport, you can get a bus to the gardens from the Golden Acre bus station near Cape Town railway station (timetables are posted at www.sanbi.org) or use the open City Sightseeing hop-on hop-off buses that visit the garden six times daily *(see page 240)*.

Table Mountain, with 36 hectares (89 acres) under cultivation, this famous botanical garden is only 13km (8 miles) from Cape Town city centre. To get there direct from the city, take De Waal Drive (M3) in the direction of Muizenberg, at the first traffic-light junction turn right (southwards) into Rhodes Drive (M63) and follow the signs to Kirstenbosch.

Established in 1913 to preserve and propagate rare indigenous plant species, Kirstenbosch is not only a national treasure, but also one of the most important botanical collections in the world.

Kirstenbosch means Kirsten's Forest, but although a Kirsten family once lived in the area, the precise link between the two is unclear. The site had been occupied for centuries before European settlers arrived in the 17th century. Large stone implements and round perforated stones used to weight pointed digging sticks are the only record of the existence of any earlier inhabitants. In 1660 a hedge of wild almond *(Brabejum stellatifolium)* and brambles was planted to form the boundary of the colony to keep livestock in and Khoikho locals out. It's known as van Rie beeck's Hedge, and you can still see the remaining sections of it.

In 1811, under the British Occupation, the landscape up here began to change when two large land grants were made, and a Colonel Bird buil a house at the foot of Window Gorge planted chestnuts and probably buil the lovely old "bath" in the Dell which still exists today. In 1823, the Ecksteen family acquired both properties, and they then passed to the Cloetes, who farmed here, planting oaks, fruit trees and vines. The old Ecksteen home stood on the site o the present Lecture Hall.

In 1895, Cecil Rhodes purchased the entire property from the Cloete family, and gradually it was allowed to grow wild again, though this time not without a large pig population that fed on the acorns and wallowed in big muddy pools. At this time th Camphor Avenue was planted (1898 – it still survives behind the restaurant buildings. In 1902 Rhodes died, equeathing Kirstenbosch to the eople as part of his Groote Schuur state. Professor Pearson, who came ɔ South Africa in 1903 to fill the ewly established Chair of Botany t the South African College, visited irstenbosch in 1911 and came to the onclusion that this wild, overgrown state would be a suitable site for a otanical garden.

On 1 July 1913, Kirstenbosch was et aside as a botanical garden, with earson as its first director, and a govrnment grant of £1,000 per annum ɔ keep it going. The Dell was the first ɔcation to be established, and cycads vere planted there. In 1916 Pearson ied of pneumonia – probably because he cottage in which he lived on the state was so damp. He is buried in the arden and his tombstone reads: "If ye eek his monument, look around."

ndigenous plants

Come here to learn about South frica's extraordinary floral heritage, in particular that of the Western Cape, which is the epicentre of the smallest of the world's six floral kingdoms. Known as the Cape Floristic Region, it supports more than 7,300 plant species, which is a greater variety per square metre than anywhere else on earth, and represents about 45 percent of southern Africa's flora squeezed into about 4 percent of its surface area.

The main vegetation type here is fynbos – a term first used by Dutch settlers to refer to its characteristic fine-leafed plants – and it is predominant not only in the mountains and coastal lowlands of the Western Cape, but also in parts of the Eastern Cape. In addition to fynbos, the garden also supports cycads, a herb garden, a fascinating medicinal garden with plants traditionally used by South Africa's indigenous people, and a fragrance garden.

The **Botanical Society Conservatory** Ⓐ displays indigenous plants

ABOVE: the Western Cape supports over 7,300 plant species. **BELOW:** helmeted guinea fowl.

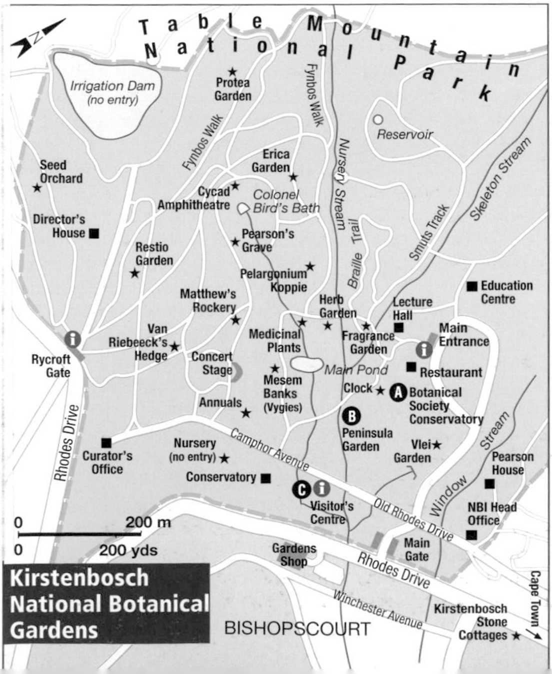

TIP

On Sundays from November to March, sunset musical concerts are held on the lawns of Kirstenbosch. Bring a picnic, a bottle of chilled wine and a rug, laze on the lawn and enjoy the music.

that cannot be grown in the outdoor gardens. Here are plants from typical South African habitats – from high mountain peaks, shady forests and hot, dry deserts. The main house, dominated by a large baobab tree, features succulents from the arid regions of southern Africa. Special collections of bulbs, ferns and alpines are displayed in corner houses.

There is also a Restio garden, focusing on the incredible variety of texture and form found in the reed family (*Restionaceae*), a "waterwise garden", designed to survive drought (a severe problem in South Africa in recent years), and the **Peninsula Garden** Ⓑ, displaying some of the 2,500 plant species found on the Cape Peninsula. The Protea Garden is most magnificent in winter and spring, when the proteas, conebushes and serrurias are in flower. Pincushions provide a colourful display in early summer.

Kirstenbosch's **Visitor's Centre** Ⓒ includes an information point as well as various retail outlets and a coffee shop. The Centre for Home Gardening sells plants, seeds, gifts and books. There's also an excellent café-restaurant called Fynbos Deli for breakfast and lunch, and the Silver Tree Restaurant for lunch and dinner.

RIGHT: wild dagga plant in Kirstenbosch botanical garden.

Tours of Kirstenbosch

There are many wonderful walking trails in Kirstenbosch, some of them reaching far up into the surrounding kloofs and peaks of the Table Mountain National Park. Others are simple meanders through beds of indigenous plants and along avenues – such as the great Camphor Avenue. There are also numerous guided "theme" walks and tours, nature walks for children, educational walks for those keen to learn more about the local fynbos, and there's a Braille Trail in which a guide rope leads visually impaired visitors along a route through a wooded area alive with scented, textured plants. Many of these are self-guided (you can pick up an audio guide at the entrance), but interesting free guided walks led by volunteers take place every day at 10am except Sundays. For more information, visit the website (www.sanbi.org) or call 021-799 8783. Group tours and special-interest tours can also be arranged for a fee.

For those unable to walk very far, shuttle cars for a maximum of seven people are available from 9am–3pm (booking is advisable and a fee is payable – call the number above).

Wynberg and the Constantia Valley

Continuing southwest along the M3, you come to **Wynberg**, which is worth a stop, despite having no particular monuments or museums of note. Wynberg grew up as a garrison village around a late 18th-century military camp, and its charming little streets are today lined with Regency-style cottages, many of which house interior-design shops and art galleries.

The next stop after Kenilworth and Plumstead is Constantia, dominated by the back of Table Mountain and the Constantiaberg. It contains some of the city's best hotels, guesthouses and restaurants, along with the Constantia Village shopping complex.

The **Constantia Valley** is, like Kirstenbosch, a national treasure, though its main claim to fame is its contribution to the country's viniculture rather than indigenous flora. The cultural landscape here derives from the earliest days of the colony, when the original land grants were handed out and farms were established to supply vegetables and fruit to the Dutch East India Company. An important relict of this era, **Alphen House,** is a two-storey homestead built in the mid-18th century and notable for the massive pediments at the front and back. It is now a hotel (tel: 021-794 5011) filled with period furniture and antiques, and even though its magnificent grounds are being encroached upon by spreading suburbia, the vineyards are still there, up the road behind the house.

Iziko Groot Constantia 8

Address: Groot Constantia Road, www.iziko.org.za
Tel: 021-794 5140
Opening Hrs: daily 10am–5pm
Entrance Fee: charge

The Constantia Valley is the cradle of South Africa's wine industry. Vines were first planted here by Simon van der Stel, who founded Groot Constantia in 1699 and lived in a magnificent Cape Dutch home there until his death in 1712. The property was subsequently bought by Hendrik Cloete, who built a wine cellar below the house. The Cloete family lived here for more than 200 years, during which time the house attracted plenty of famous travellers, including the English naturalist William Burchell, Charles Baudelaire, Anthony Trollope and the Prince of Wales, before he became King Edward VIII. It was sold to the government in 1925 and gutted by a terrible fire soon after that, but it reopened as a museum in 1927 following extensive restoration work.

Today, Groot Constantia gives visitors a feel for how a colonial gentleman-farmer would have lived in the 18th or 19th century. The main building is approached along an avenue aligned with a magnificent peak in the distance. Its main gable is thought to have been made by Louis Thibault, with a niche high above its window containing a figure of Abundance carved by Anton Anreith. Towering over the main entrance, it faces

TIP

Book in advance for wine-production and cellar tours at Groot Constantia (daily 10am–4pm, on the hour; charge). For further information about Groot Constantia Estate, visit www.grootconstantia.co.za.

BELOW: Groot Constantia Valley.

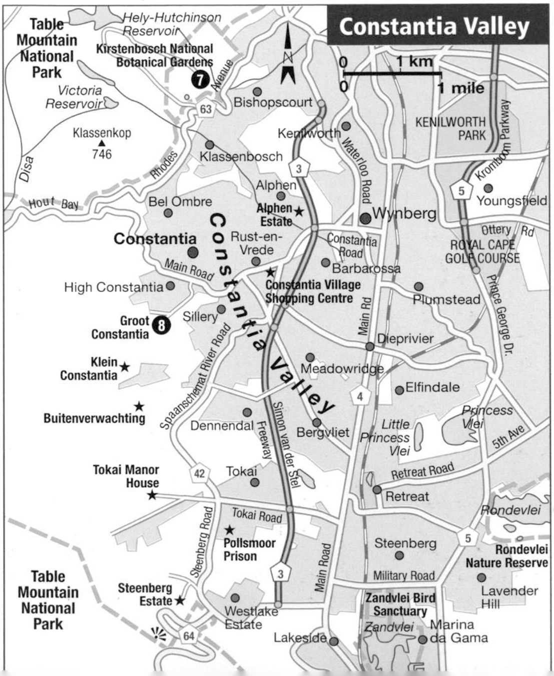

down a long elegant avenue lined on one side with outbuildings and the *jonkershuis* (where the son and heir would have lived), and on the other by vineyards sloping gently down into the Constantia Valley. There are magnificent views from here out over False Bay in the far distance.

The house contains a superb collection of Dutch furniture (in stinkwood, ebony and yellowwood), paintings, textiles, silver and ceramics, many of them donated by ship-owner Alfred de Pass. There are copper pots and pans in the kitchen, and underneath the house are vaulted cellars and workshops. The wine cellar that Cloete built behind the homestead has an interesting display of drinking and storage vessels and wine-making equipment. On the pediment is a magnificent 1791 sculpture of Ganymede by Anton Anreith.

In the grounds is an oval swimming pool with a gabled end and a niche a ship's figurehead of Triton The old coach house has a display of carriages, and it's worth popping into the orientation centre to learn about the development of the estate since 1685.

There are two restaurants – the Jonkershuis, with waiters dressed up in period clothing, and the superb Simon's at Groot Constantia *(see page 143)* – and a shop for wine sales and tastings, books and curios. The Gouveneurs Reserve, Gouveneurs Chardonnay and Gouveneurs Shiraz are very highly rated wines.

Steenberg Wine Estate

Address: Steenberg Road, www.steenberg-vineyards.co.za
Tel: 021-713 2211
Opening Hrs: Mon–Fri 9am–6pm, Sat and Sun 10am–6pm
Entrance Fee: free

ABOVE: Groot Constantia. **BELOW:** Groot Constantia contains a fine collection of Dutch furniture.

ABOVE: the scenic surroundings of Buitenverwachting.

Named after the surrounding rocky mountains – *steen* meaning stone – this estate was founded in 1662 by Catharina Ras, a formidable settler who, by the time she died, had had five husbands. When Catharina arrived here, there were still wild animals in the valley, including lions, leopards and elephants, and one of her husbands was murdered by the Khoikhoi, who objected to the colonisation of their lands. Steenberg is now at the centre of a large golf estate directly opposite Pollsmoor Prison, where Nelson Mandela was held for several years after being moved off Robben Island in 1982. The homestead at Steenberg is not the original one, but a later building dating from about 1740, by which time the farm had been taken over by the Russouw family. There's a good range of wines here, particularly the Sauvignon Blanc.

Other Constantia Wineries

Several other excellent wineries are dotted around the Constantia Valley, keeping similar tasting hours to Groot Contantia and Steenberg. Klein Constantia (Klein Constantia Rd, www.kleinconstantia.com; tel: 021-794 5188; Mon–Fri 9am–5pm; Sat 9am–1pm), a subdivision of the original van der Stel estate with a gabled homestead dating to 1824, produces some especially fine wines, including the Vin de Constance, a re-creation of the same estate's full-bodied dessert wine enjoyed by such 19th-century eminences as Charles Dickens, Jane Austen and Napoleon Bonaparte.

Also part of the original van der Stel estate, Buitenverwachting (Klein Constantia Rd, www.buitenverwachting.co.za; tel: 021-794 3522) has a beautiful 18th-century Cape Dutch homestead and a small museum. Its name literally means "Beyond Expectations," which was Ryk Cloete's assessment of the maiden grape harvest in 1825, and it still produces a fine selection of unblended reds and whites along with an award-winning Bordeaux blend called Christine, all of which can be tasted on the property. ❑

TIP

For information on Constantia's wine industry contact Constantia Valley Publicity and Tourism Association, tel: 082 332 7844, www.constantiavalley.com

RESTAURANTS, BARS AND CAFÉS

Restaurants

Old and established, the leafy Southern Suburbs have numerous fine-dining options, including several good hotel restaurants. Constantia is particularly well endowed in this regard. But there are also many less exclusive options, especially in bustling and youthful Observatory.

Constantia

Buitenverwachting
Klein Constantia Rd. Tel: 021-794 3522. www.buitenverwachting.co.za Open: L & D Tue–Sat. **$$$**
The food at Buitenverwachting Wine Estate is at once classic and unconventional, combining Austrian and contemporary influences with some local twists. The rather formal atmosphere complements the location in a typical Cape Dutch homestead, with lovely views of the vineyards. In summer Café Petit, serving light, less pricey meals, operates in the courtyard.

The Cape Malay
The Cellars-Hohenort Hotel, 93 Brommersvlei Rd. Tel: 021-794 2137. www.cellars-hohenort.com Open: D Thur–Mon. **$$$**
Probably the region's leading specialist in Cape Malay cuisine, this is housed in a Cape Dutch mansion with attractive period decor in the green ground of the five-star Cellars-Hohenort Hotel on the eastern slope of Table Mountain.

Catharina's Restaurant
Steenberg Hotel, Tokai Rd. Tel: 021-713 2222. www.steenberghotel.com Open: B, L & D daily. **$$$**
Come here for a close-up view of Steenberg, the oldest farm in the Constantia Valley. The architecture is Cape colonial, the decor earthily African, and the cuisine is strong on venison dishes. Enjoy a drink under the old oaks out at the front before dinner. Alternatively, there's a lighter lunch menu, and sundowners and tapas are served by the sexy poolside bar.

La Colombe
Constantia Uitsig Estate, Spaanschemat River Rd. Tel: 021-794 2390. www.constantia-uitsig.com Open: L & D daily. **$$$**
Constantia's other great restaurant, set on the lovely Constantia Uitsig Estate, was listed among San Pellegrino World's 50 Best Restaurants Awards in 2009. The decor, like that at Constantia Uitsig, is unpretentious and simple, while the set menu meals (with gourmand option inclusive of matching wines) is rooted in French country cooking, but also very experimental and aimed at discerning foodies with a generous budget.

Constantia Uitsig Restaurant
Spaanschemat River Rd. Tel: 021-794 4480. www.constantia-uitsig.com. Open: L & D daily. **$$$**
One of the most expensive restaurants in Cape Town, and winner of many awards since it opened in 1992, this is arguably the best place to eat in Constantia. It is essential to book in advance. The fusion menu draws from Italy, Asia and elsewhere, and there's an extensive wine list. Set in the heart of the vineyards.

The Greenhouse
The Cellars-Hohenort Hotel 93 Brommersvlei Rd. Tel: 021-794 2137. www.cellars-hohenort.com
Open: B, L & D daily. **$$$**
Set in one of the grandest hotels in the Southern Suburbs, occupying an old private mansion set in magnificent grounds bordering Kirstenbosch Botanical Garden, this French-style restaurant has one of the Cape's best "tasting menus", comprising seven courses, and a gourmand option, where every course comes with a different wine.

Jonkerhuis
Groot Constantia Estate, Groot Constantia Rd. Tel: 021-794 6255. www.jonkershuisconstantia.co.za Open: B & L daily, D Mon–Sat. **$$**
The renovated interior to this Cape Dutch farmhouse on Groot Constantia is an ideal setting for family lunches. The simple country fare is complemented by a good menu of salads and Cape Malay dishes.

River Café
Constantia Uitsig Farm, Spaanschemat River Rd. Tel: 021-794 3010. www.constantia-uitsig.com Open: B, L & D daily. **$**
A relaxed, laid-back and informal sort of place, with rooms opening onto a courtyard and a garden. Try the Eggs Benedict for breakfast, or have a glass of Constantia Uitsig wine for lunch. Salads, pasta, sausages – good café

LEFT: Jonkerhuis.

food characterises this popular venue.

Simon's at Groot Constantia
Groot Constantia Estate, Groot Constantia Rd. Tel: 021-794 1143. www.simons.co.za Open: L & D daily. **$$**
This is a relaxed venue serving big salads, fresh fish, Karoo lamb and game such as venison. It also has a good wine list, and reasonably priced mains. Take a table under the trees on the terrace. Also offers breakfast and tea on Sun.

Wasabi
Shop 17, Old Constantia Village. Tel: 021-794 6546. www.wasabi.co.za Open: L & D daily. **$$**
This is the sister restaurant of the excellent Wakame at Mouille Point *(see page 111)*. It's a trendy venue with an open-plan kitchen displaying flamboyant action. Serves a wide range of Japanese staples with interesting twists.

Newlands

Barristers Grill and Café on Main
Cardiff Castle, Kildare Rd. Tel: 021-671 7907. www.barristersgrill.co.za Open: L & D Mon–Sat. D Sun. **$$**
Celebrating its 30th anniversary in 2010, Barristers has long been revered for its large and succulent steaks, but it's also strong on fish. Offers relaxed eating at its best.

Myoga
Vineyard Hotel, 60 Colinton Rd. Tel: 021-657 4545. www.myoga.co.za Open: L & D Mon–Sat (L on request). **$$$**
This chic new restaurant in the Vineyard Hotel has a strong contemporary design with subtle Asian influences reflecting the main geographical component in the imaginative fusion menu designed by the renowned chef Mike Basset. Housed in an early Cape farmhouse, it has a live TV feed allowing diners to watch the chefs at work in the kitchen. The wine list is one of the best in the city, and you can also enjoy a drink in the gardens facing the eastern flank of Table Mountain.

Wijnhuis
Kildare Centre, Main St. Tel: 021-671 9705. www.wijnhuis.co.za Open: B, L & D Mon–Sat. **$$**
As you would expect of somewhere called Wijnhuis (wine house), it offers an extensive list of wines to go with good, modern Italian food. Offers a relaxed atmosphere with comfy sofas for post-prandial lounging.

Woodstock

Don Pedro
113 Roodebloem Rd. Tel: 021-447 4493. Open: B, L & D daily. **$**
Big, bustling and inexpensive, this student's stalwart has pizza, pasta and some South African specialities on the menu.

Prices for a three-course dinner per person with a half-bottle of house wine:
$ = under R200
$$ = R200–350
$$$ = more than R350

Bars and Cafés

The Southern Suburbs are awash with late-night drinking spots and clubs. The **Oblivion Wine Bar** (22 Chichester Rd, Harfield Village; tel: 021-671 8522; www.oblivion.co.za) is a funky little place with an excellent range of local, award-winning wines and a small menu if you get peckish – it's very popular for after-work drinks with over-23s. Another recommendation is **Obz Café** (115 Lower Main Rd; Observatory; tel: 021-448 5555; www.obzcafe.co.za), a buzzing bistro-bar, with a chalked-up menu and wooden furniture, where you can also enjoy live jazz.

In Newlands, head for **Cubana Havana Lounge** (Aska House, Main Rd; tel: 021-683 4040) for blaring music, cocktails and other daily drinks specials, and a reliable party atmosphere. Still in Newlands, **Forrester's Arms** (52 Newlands Ave; tel: 021-689 5949) is about as like a pub in the English shires as you'll get in Cape Town. It has comfortable sofas, the scuffed appearance of an old and favourite haunt, the smell of old leather, smoky nights and draught ales on tap. It's also a great venue for watching sport on a Saturday afternoon alongside the Newlands locals and university students.

Touch of Madness (Nuttall Rd, Observatory; tel: 021-448 2266; www.cafeatom.co.za) is located in a self-styled and somewhat tongue-in-cheek "Victorian Quaffery" set in a period house complete with comfy sofas, antiques and knick-knacks. **Peddler's on the Bend** (13 Spaanschemat Rd, Constantia; tel: 021-794 7747) has it all – a roaring fireplace in winters, an alfresco area for hot summer nights, an energetic bar and restaurant serving fine country cuisine.

Situated in the township of Langa, a short drive east of the Southern Suburbs, the legendary **Mzoli's** is a lively outdoor bar and *braai* (barbecue) venue where tourists can mingle easily with South Africans of all backgrounds over a chilled Castle beer and plate of grilled *pap en wors* (sausage and maize porridge). It's a good place to catch the latest local sounds too.

One of the best cafés in the area is **Melissa's** deli-café in Newlands (Cardiff Castle, Kildare Rd; tel: 021-683 6949; www.melissas.co.za), a popular meeting place for discerning locals. It sells the very best open sandwiches, salads and chicken pie. It also serves healthy breakfasts, croissants and coffee to start the day, as well as lunch and teas. Eat as much as you like and pay by weight. A popular meeting place for discerning locals.

VISA
VISA

TABLE MOUNTAIN NATIONAL PARK

The undoubted highlight of Cape Town's characterful topography is the flat-topped, often cloud-covered Table Mountain. Wherever you are in Cape Town it is a watchful presence, and at some point during your stay you will want to get to the summit

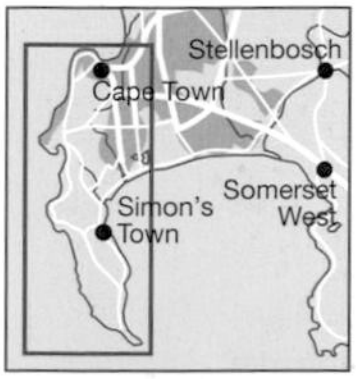

Main Attractions

TABLE MOUNTAIN CABLEWAY
PIPE TRACK
SKELETON GORGE
HOERIKWAGGO HIKING TRAIL
ADVENTURE SPORTS

Maps and Listings

MAP OF TABLE MOUNTAIN NATIONAL PARK, PAGE 148

Table Mountain and its companions, Devil's Peak, Lion's Head and Signal Hill, were known as the "mountains in the sea" – Hoerikwaggo – to the earliest inhabitants of the area, the indigenous Khoikhoi. The ensemble forms one of the most recognisable silhouettes in the world. To early mariners it was an important signpost on the shipping route to the east. A beacon of hope, it meant fresh water was close at hand.

These famous landmarks form the northern part of **Table Mountain National Park**, a vast but discontinuous protected area that covers some 73 percent of the Cape Peninsula, the narrow but mountainous strip of land that extends for 60km (36 miles) south of Cape Town to Cape Point. Characterised by vast panoramas with beautiful valleys and kloofs, rugged cliffs, wetlands and wooded hills, the park has many magnificent vantage points offering views across False Bay and the Cape Flats to the Hottentots Holland Mountains in the east, and to Blouberg and the beginning of the West Coast in the north.

Look at a map of Table Mountain National Park, and you'll recognise it has a somewhat patchwork nature, comprising several discreet or semi-contiguous blocs interspersed with the suburbs, coastal villages, port towns and wine estates of the Cape Peninsula. As a consequence, some of the park's most popular sections are featured in other chapters of this book. Kirstenbosch National Botanical Garden, for example, is covered as part of the Southern Suburbs *(see pages 135)*, from where it is most easily accessed, while the Cape of Good Hope and Boulders Beach slot best

PRECEDING PAGES: view of the Lion's Head and Cape Town. **LEFT:** the easy way to ascend Table Mountain. **RIGHT:** clouds surrounding Table Mountain.

Table Mountain National Park

into the circular tour of the coastline outlined in the chapter on the Cape Peninsula *(see page 159)*.

Dramatic topography

The Cape Peninsula comprises three types of rock – Malmesbury shale deposited here up to 540 million years ago (you can see it along the Sea Point shoreline and on Signal Hill), Cape granite (which forms a solid foundation for most of the Table Mountain chain) and Table Mountain sandstone, an incredibly hard sandstone that was laid down in successive layers over many millions of years.

When the supercontinent Gondwana broke up about 130 million years ago, the Peninsula was "block-faulted" into several giant blocks – hence Table Mountain's flat shape. Over the millennia, as the Table Mountain sandstone eroded, it produced sandy, shallow and nutrient-poor soils – not the best for vegetal growth. These are harsh conditions, and the plant species which have evolved in this spot, such as the indigenous fynbos, adapted to it. As a result, there are a great many endemic plant species in the park, and fynbos is so well adapted that, rather perversely, it reaches its greatest species diversity in places where the soil is at its poorest.

Table Mountain

Although it isn't known precisely when the first humans arrived at this dramatic spot under Table Mountain, it is thought that the first Khoikhoi pastoralists were here with their domestic animals about 2,000 years ago. Constant fresh water must have attracted them, just as it drew mariners on their way to the east.

Jan van Riebeeck was attracted by the sweet, fresh water flowing in an almost continuous stream from the steep Platteklip Gorge halfway along the face of Table Mountain. This

TIP

If you don't have your own transport, it is worth noting that the lower cableway station is a stop on the Cape Town Explorer open-top bus. A taxi to the cableway from the city centre will cost about R80. Your taxi driver may offer to wait for your return (no charge made for waiting time).

became the first water supply for the settlement, and early stone-built reservoirs can be seen from Tafelberg Road, the scenic drive running past the cableway station. During winter this cold mountain stream becomes a torrent.

Cape Town was supplied with water from this and other springs and streams on the north face of the mountain until about 1880. However, in 1887 work began on a plan to tap the Disa Stream in the Disa Gorge on Table Mountain's back table and take it through a tunnel (the Woodhead Tunnel) in the Twelve Apostles, bringing it to the Camps Bay side of the mountain from which it would be fed by gravity to Kloof Nek and then down to the city. The tunnel and the water's route have been altered and upgraded over the years, but it's still in use today, and can be seen if you go walking on the Pipe Track. During the late 18th and early 19th century, five storage dams were built on the mountain to augment the water supply to the suburbs developing along the eastern and western slopes of the mountain.

The tablecloth phenomenon

One of the most famous images of Table Mountain is of its famous white "tablecloth". For hours on end at certain times of the year, this sits on top of the mountain, falling over the edge and down the face, always threatening to cover it but never quite doing so. It is formed when warm, moisture-laden air is pushed in from the sea and driven over the mountain, where it cools and condenses into cloud.

Exploring the mountain

The quickest way to climb the mountain is to take the **cableway** *(see page*

ABOVE: Table Mountain cableway.

The Cableway

The cableway is completely dependent on the weather, and if you are in Cape Town out of season you are advised to make your trip to Table Mountain on the first clear day of your stay, in case you don't get another chance. Even on a clear day the cableway doesn't operate if it is very windy. It is best to call before you set out. Operating times vary according to the time of year (return fares: adults R160, senior citizens R80, children (under 18) R80; tel: 021-424 8181; tickets can be bought online, with an addition R10 processing fee, at www.tablemountain.net).

The cableway opened in 1929, and by the end of the 20th century had carried some 13.5 million people up to the summit. It was upgraded in 1997 and the cable cars in use today are capable of carrying 64 passengers each, as opposed to 28 previously. The cars rotate through 360° so that passengers get the most remarkable views of the rock face and out over the city and coastline way below. It takes between three and nine minutes to get to the top, depending on the wind resistance. **Note:** the cableway usually closes for annual maintenance for two weeks in July or August.

Conserving Table Mountain National Park

Subjected to piecemeal conservation policies for much of the 20th century following years of exploitation by European settlers, Table Mountain was set aside as a national park as recently as 1998

What you see today when you drive around Table Mountain National Park is a sophisticated, coordinated attempt to conserve this unique natural heritage in a busy modern environment. But it hasn't always been like this. In 1929, when the South African Wildlife Society first proposed according formal protection to much of the Cape Peninsula, things were complicated by the fact that 14 different public bodies and 200-plus private individuals owned parts of what is now the national park. In addition, much of the land had been devastated by alien vegetation and inappropriate farming methods.

The first part of the peninsula to be accorded formal protection was the southern tip, set aside as the Cape of Good Hope Nature Reserve in 1939. All of Table Mountain above the 152-metre/500ft contour line became a National Monument in 1958, and this was followed by the creation of several reserves by local authorities in the 1960s. Unfortunately, however, attempts to consolidate land management under one conservation body during the apartheid era met with repeated failure. It was only in May 1998 that the Cape Peninsula National Park was proclaimed and placed under the authority of South African National Parks. In 2004, it was renamed Table Mountain National Park.

The spin-off has been increased tourism. Cape Town's exceptional scenery and climate had to be put to good use to attract visitors and make a meaningful contribution to the socio-economic development of citizens living on and around the park's borders.

The outcome has been very successful indeed – more than 4 million people visit the Table Mountain National Park every year. But increased tourism brings its own problems, and the park is still threatened by a number of human-related factors, many of them the result of its proximity to a dense urban area. They include the spread of invasive alien plants, wildfires, encroaching urban development and informal settlements, increasing recreational use and the illegal exploitation of the area.

Still something of a work in progress, Table Mountain National Park is busy establishing partnerships with neighbouring communities, creating employment, and educating people about caring for the environment, all the while looking at the paucity of water resources, conservation strategies where development cannot be avoided, and management of the landscape in the face of income-generating tourist use of the Park's precious resources. It all goes to show that one of South Africa's most attractive treasures has, in effect, been under-utilised and underregarded for many years. ❑

LEFT: Boulders' Beach, home to colonies of African penguins, is one of the areas protected within the park.

ABOVE: far-reaching views from the top of Table Mountain.

149). Most people take this straight to the top, where they visit the restaurant or bar, have a quick walk around, then take the cable car down. But it is worth making a half-day or day of it. There are plenty of picnic spots, viewing platforms and a variety of walks, some of which continue down the Peninsula. Whatever you decide, take some warm clothing; it may be sunny and hot down below but is likely to be quite cold on top.

Climbers and hikers have opened over 350 separate routes to the summit of Table Mountain, ranging from easy to very difficult. One of the most popular walks is the **Pipe Track**, which starts at Kloof Nek, where there's parking, and continues on to Corridor Ravine. It's about 6km (4 miles) one way and the return trip takes about five hours. It's mostly (but not always) flat, running along the contours of the mountain, and the views down over the coast of the Atlantic Seaboard to Camps Bay and its surroundings are magical.

Another walk, popular with locals early in the morning before they go to work, is to the top of **Lion's Head**. At 669 metres (2,194ft), the summit takes an hour or so to reach if you're fit, and offers a breathtaking bird's-eye view of the city on all sides. It's a favourite at sunset as well, and during a full moon (bring a bottle of champagne). Quite steep at the beginning, it then pans out, before ladders and chains embedded in the rock aid the final stretch to the top. There is an alternative route using the contour path. It's a safe walk and well worth the effort.

The climb up **Platteklip Gorge** is another very popular (perhaps too popular) route. The track zigzags to the top of the mountain from Tafelberg Road. It is about 3km (1½ miles), and takes fit walkers about an hour to complete. If you want to take the cable car down, turn right at the

To the Xhosa, the earth goddess Djobela placed giants in the four corners of the earth and turned them into mountains to guard the world. The greatest of these was Umlindi Welingizunu, Table Mountain, Watcher of the South.

TIP

If you go hiking, it is important to be security conscious. Always stick to the paths and trails, and if the mist comes down stay where you are rather than try to make your way back down, which can be perilous. It is essential to let someone know where you are going before you set off and also to take a mobile phone.

top (Fountain Peak) and follow the path to Upper Cableway Station.

Skeleton Gorge is another popular Table Mountain climb. You can pick it up at the back of Kirstenbosch *(see page 135)* or along the Contour Path from Rhodes Memorial *(see page 130)* or from the Newlands Forest. The gorge, which is very steep, was a favourite walk of the former president Jan Smuts, who walked it regularly until he was well into his seventies. It leads through dense, lush forest (deliciously cool in summer), then climbs over steep rocky sections to Maclear's Beacon, at 1,086 metres (3,560ft). Erected in 1843 by the astronomer Sir Thomas Maclear, the beacon was part of an experiment to measure the circumference of the earth more accurately.

Up here you'll see the Hely-Hutchinson Dam (look for the red disas in late summer) and the aqueduct leading to it.

Serious hikes

The walks listed above can easily be done in a day. There are others which can take up to a week. The first overnight trail to be established was the **Cape of Good Hope Hiking Trail**, which takes two days and covers about 33km (20 miles) in all (call the Buffelsfontein Visitor Centre, tel: 021-780 9204, for more information and to book). The first day, which covers about 10.5km (6 miles) of rugged terrain, leads past lonely, windswept beaches on the Atlantic coastline, passes the wreck of the *Phyllisia*, and then follows the eastern boundary of the reserve to overnight huts near Cape Point. Herds of bontebok, eland and other antelope are usually seen grazing along this stretch. The second day, covering 19km (12 miles), concentrates on the Cape of Good Hope and Cape Point.

The overnight huts (ex-World War II observation points of the Coastal Defence Corps) are equipped with toilets, hot showers, bunks and mattresses, gas stoves and *braais*.

A new hiking trail, **Hoerikwaggo**, after the Khoikhoi name for Table Mountain, runs the full length of the peninsula (www.hoerikwaggotrail.org; tel: 021-683 7826). The full five-day trail starts at Deer Park,

BELOW: view of the Atlantic Coast.

above Vredehoek, and ends at the Goldfields Centre near Cape Point, with overnight stops, in huts or tents, on the Back Table, then at Silvermine, Red Hill, above Smitswinkel Bay. Several two- and three-day variations are also offered. Access to the **Orange Kloof Protected Area** – encircled by Constantia Corner Ridge and Bel Ombre, the Back Table and the Twelve Apostles – is strictly by permit only. Highlights of this lovely unspoilt area include the indigenous forest, with yellowwoods, milkwoods, red alder and Cape beech, and kloofs adorned with ferns.

Other guided hikes take visitors to remote and beautiful spots such as **Hell's Gate** with its tumbling waterfalls and pools, and **Disa Gorge**, up which one can ascend to the Back Table. Contact the Table Mountain National Park for information and permits.

Fabulous flora

The vegetation types in the Table Mountain National Park constitute a flora so rich in species that it is not only the most diverse section of the Cape Floral Kingdom *(see pages 156–7)*, but also, from a botanical point of view, the richest area, for its size, anywhere on the planet, surpassing even the tropical rainforests in its diversity.

The most common vegetation type is fynbos, including heaths *(Ericaceae)*, noted for its lovely colours ranging from butter yellow to red and purple. Fynbos also includes reeds *(Restionaceae)* and proteas *(Proteaceae)*. Some of the most conspicuous fynbos species on the mountain are from the protea family, and include the King protea *Protea cynaroides*, South Africa's national emblem. Of the 112 protea plants in the world, 69 occur in fynbos. Apart from the King Protea, there's the sugarbush, yellow pincushions, tree pincushions, golden cone bushes and silver trees which grow on the flank of Lion's Head.

ABOVE: the Mountain Café is a handy rest stop. **BELOW:** flowers abound on the mountainside in spring.

Among the shrubs below these larger species is evidence of the extraordinary species diversity for which fynbos is famous. This is particularly so with the geophytes, such as members of the disa, gladiolus, moraea, watsonia, babiana and iris genera. Many geophytes are well known for their spectacular displays when flowering en masse, particularly in the wake of fire. Strangely, fynbos needs fire to survive and flourish. It stimulates it to germinate and flower. Even smoke has the same effect.

While fynbos dominates, there are at least three other significant vegetation types in the park. The first of these is renosterbos ("rhinoceros bush"), which is rich in geophytes. Found principally on Signal Hill and on the lower slopes of Devil's Peak, it takes its name from the drab, grey shrub *Elytropappus rhinocerotis* that is common here. Also characteristic of renosterbos is the presence of grasses, which in this veld type take the place of restios, and the virtual absence of proteas.

Another vegetation type is Afromontane forest and thicket. This covers only around three percent of the Cape Peninsula, and is mainly established along the cooler, well-watered ravines on the eastern slopes of Table Mountain – above Constantia and Newlands, and in Orange Kloof.

From hyraxes to bontebok

Once upon a time you would have climbed Table Mountain at your peril. Lion, leopard and hyena lived here. Early callers at the Cape commented on the abundance of large animals they encountered here.

The large predators were shot or driven away in the early years of European settlement (the last lion, for example, was killed in 1802), but many of the smaller animals found here historically still survive, which is remarkable when you consider that Cape Town has experienced over 350 years of urban, agricultural and industrial development. The park still supports viable populations of bontebok, grysbok, caracal, mongoose, hyraxes, otter and Chacma baboons.

Baboons, part of the fynbos ecosystem on the Cape Peninsula for about a million years, are now locally endangered. The arrival of settlers, and subsequent development of the Cape Flats, has isolated the Cape Peninsula from the rest of the Western Cape, which effectively means that its baboon population has been stranded and is increasingly competing with humans for space. Although Chacma baboons are not threatened

ABOVE: Chacma baboons. **RIGHT:** Cape Point. **BELOW:** bontebok grazing near Cape Point.

as a species elsewhere, no more than 400 individuals survive in the park, living in about 10 troops mostly in the southern Peninsula. You will almost certainly see them as you drive around Scarborough to Cape Point, and if you do, slow down. They like to sit on the tarmac because it is warm, and they won't necessarily get out of your way. They live off fynbos plants, including sour fig, and forage on the shore for mussels and limpets. If you are caught feeding them you will be fined.

You will also almost certainly also chance upon the ubiquitous rock hyrax, locally known as the dassie, whose closest living relative is, strangely, the African elephant. Hyraxes thrive in areas of nutrient-poor unpalatable plant species. Look down from the cable car as it's travelling to and from the cable station and you'll see them sunning themselves on the rocks. They're diurnal – that is, they come out when the sun's up and retire when it goes down again.

Although snakes tend to be secretive and bites are very rare, the venomous Cape cobra and puff adder are a definite possibility on the footpaths of Table Mountain, though only in summer. You should wear stout shoes or hiking boots when out walking or hiking.

Best birds

A large variety of birds inhabit the park, but the relatively specialised nature of fynbos means that the species count is lower than in some other parts of South Africa. A few species have evolved specifically for the fynbos habitat, however, so the area is rich in endemics, most conspicuously the beautiful Cape sugarbird and orange-breasted sunbird, both of which are associated with blooming proteas, pincushions and other flowers. There are also plenty of raptors to be seen, including Verreaux's eagle, black sparrowhawk, and jackal buzzard. Some raptors, such as peregrine falcon, though rare in the rest of Africa, are quite common in the park, especially in the more rugged areas. The African fish eagle can be seen near water in both the central and the southern sections of the Cape Peninsula.

The best places for birdwatching are Kirstenbosch *(see page 135)*, particularly if you want to see the Cape sugarbird; Silvermine for other fynbos birds; and Cape Point for seabirds *(see page 168)*. On the summit of Table Mountain, where the vegetation is quite sparse, expect to see the orange-breasted sunbird, ground woodpecker, Cape rock-thrush, Cape grassbird, African black swift and Alpine swift.

Sports and activities

Lastly, Table Mountain National Park is a playground for adventure sports, from abseiling and rock climbing to mountain biking and hang-gliding. *For information on how to access such activities see page 240 of Travel Tips.* ❑

ABOVE: abseiling down Table Mountain.

EAT

The only place to eat on the mountain, a few minutes' walk from the upper cable station, is the Table Mountain Café, a self-service restaurant offering hot and cold meals, snacks, and the usual selection of drinks. The terrace, if you can find a free table, is nicer than the inside. Locals recommend coming here for breakfast before setting out on a day's hike. On a warm day, another option is to bring a picnic and enjoy the views. Alternatively, you could stop at one of the restaurants in Clifton or Camps Bay.

THE CAPE IN BLOOM

In spring the Cape bursts into flamboyant colour, but other seasons offer rich floral highlights, such as the winter-blooming Crane flower

The characteristic vegetation of the Cape Floral Kingdom is a low heath-like evergreen ground cover known as fynbos (fine bush). It can appear rather drab at first glance, especially during the dry summer months. On closer inspection, however, the apparent monotony of the summer fynbos landscape is transformed into a rich sprinkling of subtle pastel hues – and the entire region explodes into colour during the spring wildflower season. Most conspicuous in spring, especially along the Garden Route, are the brightly coloured blooms of various ursinia, senecio and cotula species of the daisy family.

Perhaps the best-known floral feature of the region, however, is its profusion of proteas, notably the spectacular King Protea, with its conical 30cm (12-inch) red flowers, and other members of the genera protea and mimetes. These proteas are at their most spectacular in winter.

ABOVE: the most iconic fynbos plant, the King Protea (*Protea cynaroides*), with its salmon pink bloom, is the national flower of South Africa.

LEFT: the brightly coloured flowers of the red-hot poker (genus *Kniphofia*) usually bloom profusely in winter.

LEFT: cycads are among the most ancient plants on earth, with fossil records dating back 300 million years.

BELOW: endemic to South Africa, the Agapanthus, with its long waxy leaves and beautiful blue flower, is now cultivated as a garden plant all around the world.

THE CAPE FLORAL KINGDOM

With its parched summers and damp winters, the so-called Mediterranean climate that characterises the southwestern coastal belt is an inversion of the summer rainfall pattern in the rest of southern Africa. And the borders of this isolated winter rainfall region also define those of what is by far the smallest of the world's six recognised floral kingdoms, an ecological island that extends over some 90,000 sq km (3,475 sq miles) yet supports a tally of almost 9,000 flowering plant species, most of which occur nowhere else in the world.

To place this in some perspective, although just one-tenth of these species occur within the 75-sq-km (29-sq-mile) Cape of Good Hope Nature Reserve on the southern tip of the Cape Peninsula, this still amounts to more than half the species indigenous to the entire European subcontinent.

Just north of the Cape Floral Kingdom, starting about 100km (60 miles) inland of Cape Town, the Karoo is a flat, dry semi-desert. Superficially it seems bereft of life. Yet it is one of the world's top biodiversity hotspots, dominated by succulents – a full 1,700 species, accounting for 10 percent of the global total. And in August and September, when the Karoo receives its meagre annual allocation of precipitation, its 400 species of spring annuals erupt into a riot of colour.

ABOVE: aloes and other succulents flourish in South Africa, and you will see them growing wild along the Garden Route.

BELOW: the slopes of Table Mountain are liberally covered in small fynbos flowers during spring.

BELOW: the Pincushion Protea, common on the slopes of Table Mountain, has smaller but more numerous flowers than the related King Protea.

THE CAPE PENINSULA

The Cape Peninsula is one of South Africa's great natural landscapes, a stunning sequence of glorious mountains and gorgeous sandy beaches culminating at Cape Point

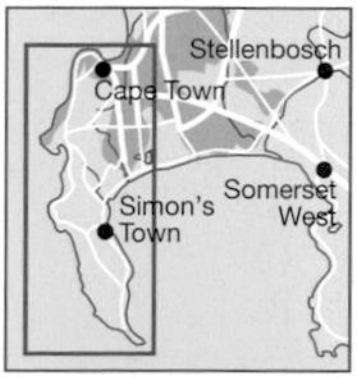

Main Attractions

CLIFTON BEACH
CAMPS BAY
DUIKER ISLAND
CAPE OF GOOD HOPE (TABLE MOUNTAIN NATIONAL PARK)
BOULDERS BEACH
SIMON'S TOWN
MUIZENBERG BEACH

Maps and Listings

MAP OF THE CAPE PENINSULA, PAGE 160
MAP OF SIMON'S TOWN, PAGE 172
SHOPPING, PAGE 177
RESTAURANTS, BARS AND CAFÉS, PAGES 178–9
ACCOMMODATION, PAGES 229–31

A circular trip around the coast of the Cape Peninsula will take you a day by car – that's if you want to stop along the way and swim, picnic or eat at a restaurant, admire a view, take in the flora and see animals, birds and historic buildings. There's all this, and more. You could do parts of the circuit on one day, and other parts on another. You could just travel to Cape Point for a swim, or to Scarborough for lunch on Sunday. But wherever you go, the one constant is the epic 60km (36-mile) mountain chain that runs from Table Mountain to Cape Point, forming the backbone not only to the Cape Peninsula but also to Table Mountain National Park *(see page 147)*. On the way to Cape Point, the main roads along the eastern and western sides of the Peninsula pass several famous peaks and formations, including the Twelve Apostles, Constantiaberg, Noordhoek Peak, Swartkop, Kalk Bay Peak and Steenberg.

The landscape

For the most part, the route around this famous spit of land jutting out at the bottom of Africa hugs the shoreline. Occasionally it rises to great heights, as at Chapman's Peak, and gingerly skirts a sheer cliff face which plunges some 200–300 metres (650–1,000ft) into the sea. The topography of the Cape Peninsula is stunning, and even if you set out simply to admire the various views, you'll return to base more than satisfied that you've seen one of the great sights of Africa. On the way you'll see a great variety of fynbos plant species, many of them endemic, while the Cape of Good Hope (the most southerly section of Table Mountain

LEFT: the colourful beach huts at the popular St James. **RIGHT:** heading out into the surf at Camps Bay.

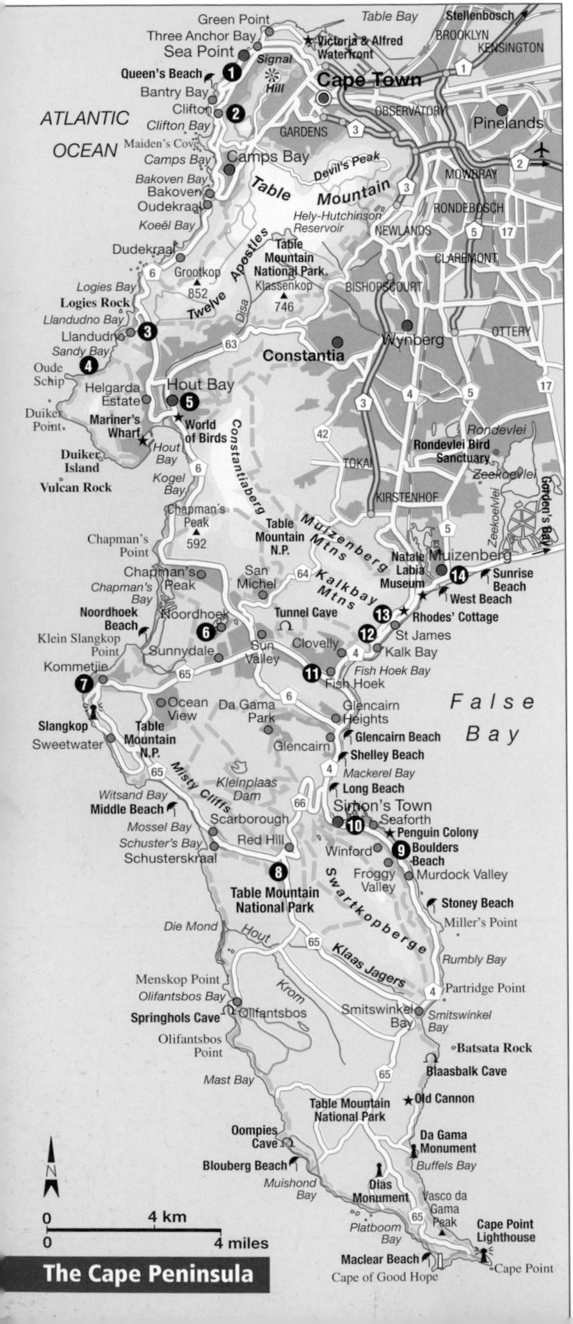

The Cape Peninsula

National Park) offers an opportunity to see some of the wildlife that once roamed this part of the world.

Around the coastline are coves, inlets and sandy beaches popular with the locals, not for swimming, because the water's mostly too cold, but for surfing, sunbathing and walking the dog. Some places, like the Atlantic Seaboard from Sea Point to Camps Bay, are built up. Indeed, Clifton, where Capetonians go to sunbathe on the beach, has some of the most expensive real estate in Africa – even for a very small property.

Other parts of the Peninsula are quiet and empty, and you can be quite alone on your walk – visit the coastline from Kommetjie via Scarborough to Cape Point. Other places, such as Simon's Town, are filled with historic buildings and museums, while Kalk Bay has a concentration of antique and bric-a-brac shops.

The False Bay coast is warmer than either the Atlantic Seaboard or Hout Bay, Noordhoek or Kommetjie. At Fishhoek, St James and, best of all, Muizenberg, you can swim for hours. And all along the coast, there are places to eat or relax over a drink, and there are many great hotels and guesthouses if you want to spend the night.

This route starts at Table Bay, rounds the tip of the Peninsula and ends in False Bay at Muizenberg. In all, it's about 100km (60 miles).

ATLANTIC SEABOARD

Between the seaward side of the rump of Lion's Head and the coastline of Table Bay, just before it merges with the Atlantic Ocean, is **Sea Point** ❶, a busy, brash, noisy and slightly seedy section of town noted for its apartment blocks, takeaways, dodgy nightclubs and porn shops. In the 19th century, wealthy Capetonians built holiday villas here, surrounded by gardens of exotic palms and pungent, scented

shrubs. Most of these have now gone, and the two main arteries, Main and Beach roads, now host a somewhat more downmarket cast of prostitutes, drug dealers and drunks, particularly after hours.

Nevertheless, after years of neglect, the neighbourhood is changing for the better. The widespread installation of street cameras has made Sea Point a much safer area in which to live, and its old apartment blocks, Victorian terraces and modern villas have shot up in value in the wake of the recent Cape Town property boom. The upgrading of Sea Point is well under way.

Along the seafront, under the various apartment blocks lining the landward side of Beach Road, some of them Art Deco, you'll also see joggers and cyclists making use of the wide promenade, nannies with prams, old ladies and their nurses, couples with dogs, and children from the townships playing football. **Graaff's Pool**, a wide, natural rock pool protected from view by a whitewashed wall, is a nudists' haven in the heart of the city.

Sea Point has an urban character entirely alien to the rest of the city. Along Main Road, at night a strip of flashing billboards, you can find something to eat virtually 24 hours a day, as well as the city's best video-rental stores. There are banks, supermarkets, delis, pubs, restaurants, chemists, hotels, guesthouses and backpackers' lodges, clothing and liquor stores, locksmiths, DIY centres and garages.

Sea Point even has the occasional stretch of beach where you can swim. There are some old tidal pools here, which at the weekend are very busy indeed. The restored **Sea Point Public Pool** has changing rooms and showers.

Between Bantry Bay and Clifton is a promontory (signposted) where igneous and sedimentary rock meets, thus forming the continental shelf. Charles Darwin stopped off to inspect the site on his round-the-world voyage on the Beagle *in 1836.*

Bantry Bay and Clifton

From Beach Road, the seaside drive enters Queen's Road and then Victoria Road, passes through Bantry Bay, overlooked from on high by one of the city's best hotels, Ellerman House, and continues on to Clifton, all the time hugging the steep mountainside beneath Lion's Head – which looks at its most monumental from here. This is known as the "lower road". The so-called "upper road", Kloof Road, can be entered by continuing to the top

LEFT: which way now?
BELOW: Lion's Head marks the start of the Atlantic Seaboard.

Kloof is originally an Afrikaans word for ravine or cliff, though it has now passed into English. You will come across it frequently in place names. The term "kloofing" refers to the adventure sport of following a river through a gorge, jumping into pools from great heights.

of Queen's Road and turning right, continuing until you descend to Victoria Road above Glen Beach on the approach to Camps Bay. The views from the upper road are some of best in Cape Town.

Bantry Bay is a lovely, small seaside neighbourhood characterised by sedate Victorian villas and old gardens filled with palms and bougainvillea. Its neighbour, **Clifton** ❷, is somewhat brasher. It has four little wind-free coves, each one an amphitheatre lined with characteristic bungalows. Don't be deceived, however. Bungalows they may be, simple they're not. Many have been redeveloped, and are luxurious. Clifton is a millionaire's playground, and if you can afford a pad here you've made it.

In summer, the stretch of Victoria Road running through Clifton is virtually impassable, and parking is impossible to find. Everybody wants to come to the beach here for a piece of the action, even though it is far too cold to swim anywhere along this coastline – except in the heated pools of the locals.

RIGHT AND BELOW: the sandy shores of Clifton.

Choose your beach

The four coves have become popular with different types of people. **Fourth Beach**, the furthest away, on the Camps Bay side, is longer and wider than the others, and generally packed with families with their children and dogs. The water is shallow for the first few metres, then slopes away gradually. It's safe to bathe here, if you can stand the icy-cold water, and there are lifeguards on duty during summer. A little further offshore, private yachts are at anchor and water-skiing and canoeing are on offer. You can also hire umbrellas and beach chairs, and there are little booths for cool drinks and ice cream.

Next door, at **Third Beach**, you'll find the city's most beautiful bodies on display. Tanned and taut, they parade up and down, with every curve and bulge on show. Third Beach is popular with gay men, all of whom seem to know each other. If you're an out-of-towner, this is where you'll make your friends. During the holidays there's a continuous round of beach, clubs and parties to go to, none of it worth much unless you are a regular at the gym. As on Fourth Beach there are umbrellas and chairs for hire, and ice cream and water sellers beat their weary path down here too.

At **Second Beach** you'll find a more laidback gay crowd, straight men playing ball, dogs gambolling in the waves and couples napping under their umbrellas. **First Beach** is much the same, but less busy, not least because it is accessed via 100 steps, which make for a long and arduous climb after a lazy day on the beach. If it's peace and quiet you're after, First Beach is where you should go.

Camps Bay

From the beaches at Clifton you can see Table Mountain in profile. To the right you get your first view of the **Twelve Apostles**, which, by the time you've rounded the wide bend of Victoria Road above Glen Beach on the approach to Camps Bay, are in full view. From the wide – and very windy – beach at Camps Bay, the sweep of mountains and sea is magnificent. Again, the water is so cold that it is hard even to dip your toes into the water, but brave souls do when the summer heat becomes too hot to handle.

Camps Bay is a popular beach all year round. It's wide, backed by lawns dotted with palms, and is easily accessible from the road. There are cold showers and toilets at either end. Everybody comes here, from families to singles, from beauties to those who couldn't give a damn, and there are umbrellas and chairs to rent. There is also a big tidal pool, which is great for a gentle wave-free swim.

There's plenty of parking up in the streets of Camps Bay, and all along the front are lots of popular, busy cafés, bars and restaurants, some simple, some swanky, for breakfast, lunch and dinner – or just a drink with a view. One hotel, the Bay Hotel *(see page 229)*, is attached to the Rotunda, built in 1903 as a roller-skating rink and dubbed the "best dance floor in South Africa". Today it's the hotel's function room. There are plenty of guest houses and B&Bs with their own swimming pools, all within easy distance of the beach.

Camps Bay itself is again a very expensive suburb, which isn't surprising given the panoramic views of the coastline from virtually every vantage point. Up on the Lion's Head side is the early 19th-century Round House, built on the circular foundations of one of the small batteries

TIP

If you have your own transport, Camps Bay is one of the best places to come for a sundowner. There are several good cocktail bars with ringside views of the sunset and the youthful passing scene.

BELOW: learning to fish in Camps Bay.

ABOVE: Llandudno is great for sunbathing.

which guarded one of the approaches to Cape Town. This was once Lord Charles Somerset's shooting box, and the interior is still kitted out with four gun cupboards. At the time wild animals, including lion and leopard, still roamed the mountainsides here – which is hard to believe when you take your dog for a walk up the "glen" surrounding it. In 2008, after years of semi-neglect, the Roundhouse *(see page 178)* opened as a restaurant with indoor and outdoor seating, and magnificent views over the Camps Bay coastline to Llandudno.

Llandudno and Sandy Bay

Between Camps Bay and Llandudno, Victoria Road continues on its way, skirting the last stretch of beach in the vicinity where the mountain launches an uninterrupted sweep down to the sea. At **Oudekraal**, just before Victoria Road rounds a corner and passes the Twelve Apostles Hotel, you can skin dive at an old wreck, and there are places to picnic or *braai*. There is also a tidal pool (charge). It's very popular in summer, so go early.

From here the road continues to **Llandudno ❸**. As it climbs towards the "nek" which opens the way to Hout Bay, take the right-hand fork and corkscrew your way down to a junction which, to the right, leads to Llandudno beach, and to the left, Sandy Bay. Llandudno is another expensive suburb of stylish modern beach houses built to maximise the view. Parking is minimal; be prepared to walk down the steep roads to the beach. This is a quiet beach, great for sitting and dreaming, or sunbathing. People come here to surf, although again the water is icy. There are no shops in Llandudno, and rarely do the ice-cream sellers make it this far, so make sure you bring snacks and drinks.

Sandy Bay ❹ is frequented by sun-worshippers who prefer to do it in the nude. The only way to reach Sandy Bay is to park in the small area at the end of the road, then walk, for up to 3km (2 miles), along the long

TIP

The Cape Peninsula offers some of the best surfing in South Africa. For the latest surf reports, visit www.wavescape.co.za or www.surfreport.co.za, or call 082-234 6370.

white beach. On the way, a section filled with huge boulders, little private inlets and overhangs is popular with gay nudists. But if you go early on a weekday morning you could have the whole area to yourself. It's a magical place. Strip off, oil yourself up, and settle down with a book or have a nap. When it gets too hot, take a dip in a rock pool. The beach itself is popular with couples, same-sex and straight, who make a day of it, taking an umbrella, a coolbox for food and drink, and the dogs. It's never too busy here, as the walk puts people off.

Hout Bay ❺

Victoria Road sweeps down into **Hout Bay**, a seaside district that takes its name from the fact that it was an important source of timber for the Dutch East India Company since the very earliest date of the colony (*hout* is an Afrikaans word meaning wood). A farm was established here in the 17th century, and a Cape Dutch house called Kronendal, dated *c*.1800, still stands there today, the only surviving example in the Cape Peninsula of an H-shaped house.

Hout Bay has been a fishing village for many years and has a busy little harbour and informal places to buy and eat fresh fish. **Mariner's Wharf** (www.marinerswharf.com; tel: 021-790 1100; daily 9am–5.30pm) is the best place to come. There are also little shops selling T-shirts, shells, postcards and buckets and spades, as well as self-service and takeaway restaurants.

The harbour here is also lined with kiosks offering 45–60-minute boat trips out to nearby **Duiker Island** to the impressive colony of Cape Fur Seals. Typically a boat

ABOVE: Hout Bay Harbour. **BELOW:** Cape Malay minstrels, Hout Bay.

leaves every 30 minutes or so in the morning, but departures are infrequent after lunch.

There's not much left of the village's old character, and few traditional buildings have survived. However, there's a pretty stone-built Anglican church of St Peter the Fisherman dating from 1895, and, as you leave town and enter Chapman's Peak, passing the popular Chapman's Peak Hotel on the left, you can visit what remains of the **East Fort**, erected to protect the bay when hostilities broke out between the Dutch and the British in 1781. Two batteries were built to protect the bay and a third was later added by the British. The site was abandoned in 1827 and partially dismantled, but enough remains for you to get an idea of what the complex looked like. It has tremendous views out over Hout Bay to Kapteinspiek and The Sentinel, its beach (popular with mothers and their children, and dog-walkers) and the harbour.

World of Birds

Address: Valley Road, Hout Bay, www.worldofbirds.org.za
Tel: 021-790 2730
Opening Hrs: daily 9am–5pm
Entrance Fee: charge

Reputedly the largest bird park on the continent, World of Birds' centrepiece is its walk-through aviaries, which shelter some 3,000 indigenous and exotic birds of about 400 different species. It also hosts an important breeding project for two endangered birds, the endemic southern bald ibis and stunning grey crowned crane, a monkey jungle with various South American primates, and a friendly family of meerkats.

ABOVE: colony of Cape Fur seals on Duiker Island. **BELOW:** Chapman's Peak Drive.

Chapman's Peak and Noordhoek

Leaving Hout Bay, Chapman's Peak Drive hugs the foothills of the **Constantiaberg** and **Noordhoek Peak** above **Kogel Bay**. The drive is one of the most impressive stretches of road in the country. It's a cliff road (also known as the M6), the construction of which defied all the odds in 1915. Joining Hout Bay and Noordhoek, it was built by convicts over the course of seven years. Rockfalls have marred it since the day it was built, and after expensive remedial work in 2000, it reopened in 2004 as a toll road (www.chapmanspeakdrive.co.za; R28 one-way for a light motor vehicle). At its summit there are wonderful panoramic views out over the coastline above Chapman's Point.

As you round the final curve of Chapman's Peak Drive, look straight ahead and you will see the vast expanse (4 miles/6km) of **Noordhoek Beach**, a location used in the filming of *Ryan's Daughter*, and perfect for horse riding. At its landward side, wetlands attract wild birds. This section, including Noordhoek Beach, is now owned by South Africa National Parks, ensuring its future protection.

If you want some idea of what the Peninsula must have been like before anyone settled here, visit **Noordhoek ❻**. There is little or no building on its edge, and the only humans you're likely to see are dog-walkers. There are a few shipwrecks to be seen on the sand. However, the isolation of this beautiful spot has attracted muggers, so leave your valuables at home and tell someone where you are going.

At the furthermost (southern) end past Klein-Slangkop Point, is **Kommetjie ❼**, another seaside village, reached at the junction of the M6 and M65. Once a village of holiday homes, it is becoming increasingly popular with commuters. It's sufficiently distant from the city to be a quiet haven, yet within reasonable commuting distance. Its beach, Long Beach, is lovely, white and wide, but as at Noordhoek, swimming is dangerous. There is a strong undercurrent that can carry you out to sea immediately.

A scenic walk takes in both beaches. On the way, look out for African black oystercatcher, sacred ibis, lapwings, plovers, egrets and other waders. Go when the tide is out so that you can walk on the harder sand at the shoreline.

The M65 continues on around the coast, passing the **Slangkop Lighthouse**, built in 1919, Witsand Bay, Misty Cliffs and on to the village of **Scarborough** which has two restaurants – Cobbs at the Cape and Camel Rock. If you want a simple lunch on your drive, this is the place to make a stop. Cobbs has a terrace with beautiful views over the surrounding area, including the beach, which is popular with surfers and Sunday dog-walkers. But, again beware: the currents are strong and swimming is very dangerous.

ABOVE: look out for African black oystercatchers and other waders at Noordhoek. **BELOW:** Chapman's Bay.

Hout Bay
Construction of Chapman's Peak Drive started in
1915 as a narrow, winding gravel road, and after
seven year's work the scenic drive "hewn out of
the face of sheer mountains" was officially
opened in 1922 by the Governor General
of the then Union of South Africa,
Prince Arthur of Connaught.

ABOVE: Cape Point. **BELOW:** wardens keep a watchful eye on the penguins of Boulders Beach.

TABLE MOUNTAIN NATIONAL PARK (CAPE OF GOOD HOPE SECTION) 8

Address: M65, about 40km (24 miles) south of Cape Town, www.sanparks.org
Tel: 021-701 8692
Opening Hrs: Oct–Mar daily 6am–6pm, Apr–Sept daily 7am–5pm
Entrance Fee: charge

From Scarborough, the M65 continues across the Peninsula to arrive at the entrance gate to the former Cape of Good Hope Nature Reserve, which was incorporated into Table Mountain National Park in 1998. Extending over 7,750 hectares (19,150 acres) to Cape Point at the southern tip of the Peninsula, this is an extraordinarily scenic area even by the Cape's high standards, and it is well worth dedicating a full day to exploring it. Its most famous viewpoint, reached either via a steep footpath or by funicular railway, is the Cape Point Lighthouse, which was built from 1913–19 and affords breathtaking views over sheer cliffs whose innate drama really does evoke the feeling you're at the edge of the continent (though in fact Cape Agulhas, *see page 195*, forms the most southerly point in Africa).

A visit to the Cape of Good Hope is also very rewarding for its fauna and flora. Fashioned from two old farms, Buffelsfontein and Blaauberg Vlei, in 1939, the vegetation is near-pristine and consists mainly of fynbos – the major vegetation type of the Cape Floral Kingdom, which is the smallest and, for its size, the richest of the world's six floral kingdoms. Scattered with attractive winter-blooming protea bushes, the reserve supports a wide selection of fynbos birds, while larger wildlife includes Chacma baboon, Cape mountain zebra, eland, bontebok, grey rhebok and grysbok. Marine wildlife is also well represented, from the seals, cormorants and oystercatchers that haunt the shore to the whales and dolphins that are frequently seen out at sea.

The beaches are magnificent (where else could you see wild game wandering along the beach as you lie in the sun and picnic?), and the Two Oceans Restaurant, with a magnificent terrace looking out over False Bay, is to hand for breakfasts and lunch.

The visitor centre at Buffelsfontein stocks maps of the reserve, and it can provide detailed information about walks, things to do and the various wild animals and birds that can be seen. Also worth a diversion is the little-used Rooikrans viewpoint, an excellent spot for whale-watching in False Bay, and the footpath from Cape Point Car Park to the attractive beach below Cape Point Lighthouse. Outside the park, the Cape Point Ostrich Farm (www.capepointostrichfarm.com; tel: 021-780 9294; daily 9.30am–5.30pm; free) opposite the entrance gate on the M65 offers

TIP

If you don't have your own transport, you can travel all the way to Simon's Town by rail from Cape Town's railway station *(see page 222)*. It is a lovely ride along the False Bay coast, with sea views and stops at Kalk Bay, St James and Fish Hoek. However, for safety reasons, be sure to take a train with a restaurant car and sit there.

affordable half-hour guided tours as well as light lunches.

FALSE BAY

From the entrance gate to Cape of Good Hope, the M65 continues eastward towards False Bay, and as it bears north, it becomes the M4 on its way to Boulders and Simon's Town.

Boulders Beach 9

Address: Kleintuin Road, Simon's Town, www.sanparks.org
Tel: 021-786 2329
Opening Hrs: daily 8am–6.30pm
Entrance Fee: charge

Boulders Beach is well known for its colony of endangered African (or jackass) penguins, which first started breeding here in 1982 and now number more than 3,000 individuals. Incorporated into Table Mountain National Park, the part of the beach where the penguins breed is now fenced off and reached by specially constructed boardwalks that offer

ABOVE: taking the funicular down to the view site at Cape Point. **LEFT:** the Cross of Vasca de Gama, Cape of Good Hope.

Cape of Storms or Cape of Good Hope?

All the romance of the sea route around the Cape of Storms to the east is vested in this tongue of land jutting out into a fierce, stormy ocean. Somewhere at Cape Point Bartolomeu Dias, who set sail from Lisbon in 1487 with three small ships, erected a *padrão* (a large stone cross) and became the first known European to reach the southern tip of Africa. Its location is uncertain, but only recently a small cross was found engraved on a rock, and it is thought this could be the location.

Dias called the Peninsula the Cape of Storms, while his contemporary, the Portuguese King João renamed it the Cape of Good Hope in anticipation of opening a sea route to the east. Vasco da Gama came later, reaching India in 1498. Sir Francis Drake also sailed by in 1580, and on a clear, still day you can see why he called it "the most stately thing and the fairest cape we saw in the whole circumference of the earth".

However, on a wild and windy day it is very much the Cape of Storms, as testified by the many shipwrecks littering the Cape, each one documented at the museum in Simon's Town *(see page 170)* and at the Maritime Museum in Cape Town *(see page 105)*.

TIP

The Battery in Simon's Town is a good place from which to spot the southern right whales that come to breed here between May and December. Other good places on False Bay are Kalk Bay and Fish Hoek.

great close-up views of these lovably daft creatures as they swim between the rocks, waddle around the sand, and bray dementedly at each other. If you visit outside opening hours, you can also see part of the colony from the wheelchair-friendly Willis Walk, which runs between the main beach used by the penguins and a second (equally stunning) beach where you can swim or sun yourself among the huge boulders that scatter the sandy shore, joined by the occasional wandering penguin.

Simon's Town ⑩

Boulders Beach lies on the outskirts of **Simon's Town**, the headquarters of the South African Navy. This is a seaside village rich in history and filled with character. It acquired its name back in 1687, when Simon van der Stel paid a visit to the harbour, which served as an alternative anchorage to Table Bay, especially in winter, when ships were often driven ashore and wrecked by the prevailing northwest wind. In 1795, during the aftermath of Napoleon's rampage across Europe, Britain took the Cape Colony from the Dutch, to prevent it falling into French hands, and the next year they erected a small fort known as a Martello Tower in Simon's Town's George Street to reinforce their defence.

The British handed the Cape back to the Batavian Government in 1803. Three years later they were back, this time for good, after the Battle of Blaauwberg in 1806. The Royal Navy established the South Atlantic base at Simon's Town in 1814, thus beginning its 143-year occupation of the port. The tiny settlement

RIGHT: Able Seaman Just Nuisance, the mascot of the Royal Navy during World War II. **BELOW:** penguins on Boulders Beach.

expanded rapidly from a far-flung winter anchorage to a strategic naval port that played an important role in the expansion of the British Empire. As a result, Simon's Town has one of the densest clusters of old buildings in the country, and many of them are still used, Admiralty House, the Residency, the Martello Tower and the British Hotel among them.

There's plenty to do and see here, with the main attractions easily accessible from the main road running through the town. At the centre of town is **Jubilee Square** Ⓐ with its tall palm trees and statue of Able Seaman Just Nuisance, a famous Great Dane who died in 1944. The mascot of the Royal Navy during World War II, Just Nuisance befriended and inspired the visiting sailors. His birthday is 1 April – known as Just Nuisance Day, which is celebrated with a parade of Great Danes and other dogs through the town to Jubilee Square. You can even visit the dog's grave (daily 9am–3.30pm), which lies above the town centre on Redhill Drive.

The are plenty of shops and cafés on Jubilee Square and in the town's main street, St George's Street, as well as several art galleries. The **Bronze Age Art Foundry, Gallery and Sculpture Garden** (www.bronzeageart.com; tel: 021-786 1816; Tue–Thur 10am–5pm, Fri 10am–4pm, Sat and Sun 10am–3pm; charge) is a wharfside complex where you can see artists at work in the foundry. The adjoining gallery, situated in the historic Alebertyn's Stables, displays work by top local artists.

Just south of Jubilee Square lies the **Heritage Museum** (tel: 021-786 2302; Tue–Fri 11am–4pm, Sun 11am–5pm; charge) in Amlay House, which was built in 1848. The house later became the home of the Amlays, in 1975 the last coloured family to be forcibly evicted from Simon's Town under the Group Areas Act, and in 1995 the first to return. The house became a museum in 1999, at the instigation of the Nooral Islam Historical Society, and it is a fascinating shrine to the local Muslim culture.

The waterfront below Jubilee Square overlooks the yacht basin and the town pier. Boat trips along the shore and into the naval harbour provide an interesting introduction to the town and its rich history as well as a glimpse of the South African Navy at work.

Worth a look for boat buffs, the **SA Naval Museum** Ⓑ (www.simonstown.com; daily 10am–4pm; tel: 021-787 4686; charge), in West Dockyard, has interesting displays on every aspect of the Cape's naval history, as well as displays relating to many shipwrecks that have taken place off the Peninsula. There is also a small church with murals in the museum.

Simon's Town Museum Ⓒ

Address: Court Road, www.simonstown.com

ABOVE AND BELOW: the bay and George Street, Simon's Town.

> **TIP**
>
> In March each year the Navy holds a festival in Simon's Town, when dockyard and naval vessels are opened to the public. The Penguin Festival in spring is another highlight in the town's calendar.

Tel: 021-786 3046
Opening Hrs: Mon–Fri 9am–4pm, Sat 10am–1pm, Sun 11am–3pm
Entrance Fee: charge

Housed in the historic Governor's Residency, this is one of the best museums of its kind in South Africa. It encapsulates the history of the town and its people, and their connection both to the Dutch East India Company and the Royal Navy, and it also arranges guided walks around the more historic parts of the town, including the mosque and the churches.

Constructed in 1777 as the winter residence for the Dutch East India Company's Governor at the Cape, this lovely old harbour-front building has subsequently served as a hospital, post office, school, customs house, police station, gaol and magistrate's court, and the exhibits reflect these composite functions. There are artefacts relating to the earliest inhabitants of the area, and tools and equipment of the Khoisan people are also exhibited. The early history of the Company and van der Stel is well documented. Displays point out the earliest buildings in the area – some the early farm buildings that still dot the mountain slopes around Simon's Bay. Many of these original buildings have been declared National Monuments.

Elsewhere, displays highlight the early development of schools (the first was Cradock's Dutch School, opened in the Residency in 1813) and the building of the town's churches and hospitals. The oldest church in Simon's Town is the Wesleyan Chapel (1828), which served the Anglicans as well as the Dutch Reformed Church congregation until their own church was built in 1856. The Roman Catholic Church of SS Simon and Jude was built in 1850, while the local Muslims completed the Noorul Islam Mosque in 1926. The latter had formerly been a house in which the faithful had met

BELOW: colour facade, Simon's Town.

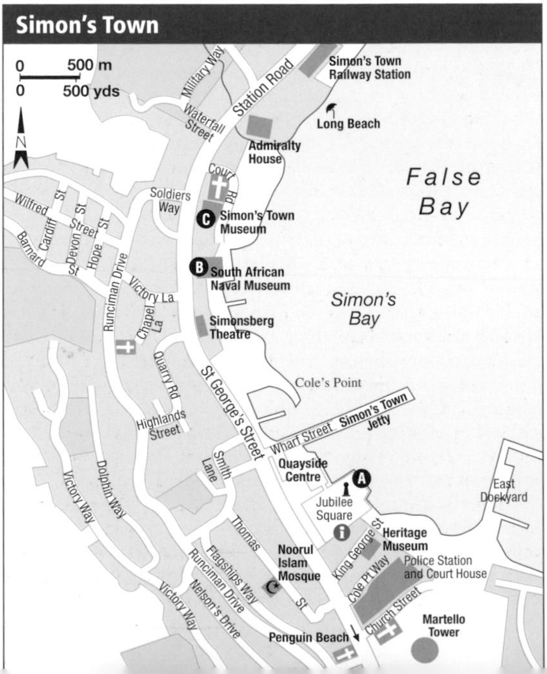

since 1888. The exhibition forms part of an attempt to record and preserve the history of some 7,000 people who were forcibly relocated to other parts of the Cape Peninsula and beyond under the Group Areas Act by the apartheid government in the 1960s.

Of the many hospitals in Simon's Town, the most impressive was the Dutch East India Company Hospital, with its three sea-facing gables. It was built on the mountainside above the Residency in 1764. More famous though, and of greater interest, is Old Hospital Terrace, built in 1814 for the Royal Navy. Here Lord Lister's new antiseptic methods were used for the first time in South Africa. The old Military Hospital was where Edgar Wallace, poet, author and playwright, served as a medical orderly in the late 1890s.

The new Royal Naval Hospital, built in 1901, had a very good reputation during World War II for treating patients with severe burns. Other local history displays refer to the Old Burying Ground, the oldest extant cemetery in South Africa (1813). A walk around here is a roll call of the many and varied communities who, down the centuries, made Simon's Town their home. There are also those who were just passing through and those who were lost at sea. Royal Navy matelots lie beside Russian sailors. There are slaves and aristocrats, Italian artisans and Boer prisoners-of-war. And there are generations of townspeople.

Most interesting of all are the town's links with the Anglo-Boer War and the two world wars. There are displays illuminating the horrors of the Anglo-Boer War prison ships, and the Boer prisoner-of-war camp at nearby Boulders (now known for its penguins; *see page 169*). Then there are the heroic stories of the World War I hunt for the German raider SMS *Konigsberg* in the Rufiji Delta (in present-day Tanzania) using a Curtis seaplane in 1914, and of the Royal Navy's search for the

ABOVE: a replica of the Africa Station Club in the Simon's Town Museum. **BELOW:** the Central Hotel building in Simon's Town.

ABOVE: African, or Jackass, penguins are an endangered species.
BELOW: musician performing in Kalk Bay.

German battleship, the *Admiral Graf Spee* on the River Plate off the coast of Argentina and Uruguay in 1939. At least 125 Allied ships were sunk by the Germans, Japanese and Italians in relatively close proximity to Simon's Town.

Also look out for memorabilia of royal visits to Simon's Town. The British royals were visitors, the Aborigine prince Metarai came in 1808, and Louis-Napoleon's corpse rested here on its way to Britain after this Prince Imperial's death in Natal in the Zulu wars. The Zulu king, Cetshwayo, also dropped in briefly en route to his imprisonment near Cape Town.

The shipwrecks around this stormy coast are of particular interest – their remains are often revealed at low tide, and legends abound right the way around the Cape Peninsula. Look in at the cells built to house the slaves of the colony's governor in the 18th century, the gaol, the stocks – generally used to hold women – and the punishment cell with whip marks on the ceiling.

Mineral World

Address: Dido Valley Road, www.scratchpatch.co.za
Tel: 021-786 2020
Opening Hrs: Mon–Fri 8.30am–4.45pm, Sat and Sun 9am–5.30pm
Entrance Fee: free, but you are required to spend a minimum of R14

On the northern edge of Simon's Town is **Mineral World**, a larger version of Scratch Patch at the V&A Waterfront in Cape Town *(see page 105)*. Visitors can choose and buy a variety of minerals and precious stones either in polished or unpolished form, or in jewellery and other artefacts. A good range of fossils is also on display. You can leave the children at the **Scratch Patch**, where they can play in the offcuts of smooth, polished gemstones, while you peruse the more precious objects upstairs.

Fish Hoek ⓫

Beyond Simon's Town, the M4 meanders around the coast through Glencairn to **Fish Hoek**. The idyllic beach

is cut off from the town by a railway line and poor development, but persevere and you can spend a delightful day on the sand here. Take care when entering the water. Shark attacks have happened here and the danger remains. It's a beautiful spot, though, and very quiet during the week.

There are two museums to visit in Fish Hoek. One, the **Fish Hoek Valley Museum** (59 Central Circle, www.fishhoek.com; tel: 021-782 1752; Tue–Sat 9.30am–12.30pm; charge), documents the history of whaling in the town, and displays Stone-Age implements relating to nearby Peers Cave. Excavated in 1926, the cave was found to contain nine ancient burial chambers. The skull of one of them, so-called Fish Hoek Man, was found to have the largest brain cavity of any other skull of similar age.

Apart from the museum and the beach, Fish Hoek is quite a bland place. More interesting is Kalk Bay.

Kalk Bay ⓬

After Fish Hoek, the road runs through **Clovelly** and then **Kalk Bay**, a pretty seaside village that acquired its name from the lime kilns located here in the early days of the colony. Capetonians come here for a lazy day ferreting through bric-a-brac shops and then lunching on freshly caught fish. It's well worth poking around through the furniture, books, ceramics, curios and a variety of other things old and not so old, because real treasures have been known to turn up from time to time. Beware of the silly prices, though; Kalk Bay is in danger of becoming over-commercialised.

TIP

If you are interested in seeing great white sharks (from a distance), several companies run excursions to Seal Island, a feeding ground for the sharks about 6km (4 miles) offshore. Enquire at the tourism office in Cape Town or Simon's Town.

ABOVE LEFT: antique shop, Kalk Bay.
BELOW: crashing waves at Kalk Bay.

ABOVE: surfing at Muizenberg. **BELOW:** a local resident.

There are also art galleries filled with the work of Sunday-afternoon painters, potters' shops and so on, and you can buy fresh fish at the quaint little harbour.

Kalk Bay is a busy weekend destination, particularly on Sundays when sleepy locals turn up at Olympia Café and Deli *(see page 179)* for the best brunch in Cape Town. Chaotic, busy and small, this café-restaurant – whose kitchens occupy an old theatre (ask to have a look) – is also noted for its bakery.

Kalk Bay evolved in the middle of the 19th century. Its little fishing harbour became a very successful whaling station. Here, the Brass Bell Restaurant *(see page 179)* is a good place to enjoy a meal while observing whales in season (May–December). The harbour is still the focus of the colourful local fishing fleet, and it has an interesting little fish market, as well as being home to several very relaxed Cape fur seals.

Victorian St James ⓭

Kalk Bay runs into **St James**, which has the same seaside character. Victorian villas line the seafront, and narrow cobbled alleys link the houses on the vertiginous slope beneath Ridge Peak and St James's Peak. There are warm tidal pools at Dalebrook and St James, the latter recognisable for its brightly painted beach huts lining the sands. The tidal pools here are great for small children.

Muizenberg ⓮

St James merges with **Muizenberg** a little further on. Here the coastline bears east, and a magnificent sweep of beach heads all the way to Gordon's Bay, 25km (15½ miles) away. The town itself has seen better days, but the beach is fantastic. The water is safe for swimming and its temperature is relatively warm. Surfers in particular love it here, but Capetonians of every description come here to ride the waves, paddle and picnic. You can buy surfing equipment, boogie boards and so on, have a meal, order a takeaway or simply relax over a drink.

Muizenberg has long been a favourite getaway for Capetonians. From 1882, when the suburban railway arrived, people came here in droves to sample the warm waters of the bay and the town quickly grew. Beach houses went up and it became a popular Sunday destination. Before that, Muizenberg was a military outpost which protected the back door to Cape Town from invasion through False Bay. However, in 1795, at the Battle of Muizenberg, the British succeeded in breaking through the defences, and thus began the First British Occupation of the Cape.

Architectural landmarks

The stretch of coast from Muizenberg to Kalk Bay is particularly interesting architecturally. In the late 19th century wealthy South Africans, including several mining magnates such as Oppenheimer, had their holiday homes here. Cecil John Rhodes loved this spot too, and owned the cottage at 246 Main Road. A very simple building under thatch, it was originally intended as a temporary home until Herbert Baker could build him his mansion at what is now Rust-en-Vrede at 244 Main Road. But Rhodes loved this cottage, and died here in 1902 aged 49. The cottage is now a museum (tel: 021-788 1816; daily 10am–4pm with reduced hours in winter; free) about Rhodes's life.

Rust-en-Vrede was in the end built next door in 1905, for another mining magnate Abe Bailey. It is considered one of Baker's best works, but it is a private residence and therefore not open to the public. A little further along, **Het Posthuys** (182 Main Road, tel: 021-788 7972; daily 10am–4pm) was built as a lookout post in 1670 and was later used as a naval warehouse, an alehouse and a private residence. Restored by the Anglo-American mining company in 1982–3, it is now a small maritime museum, complete with rusting old cannons in front.

At 190 Main Road is The Fort, built in 1929 by Frederick Mackintosh Glennie as a holiday home for Count Natale Labia, the Italian ambassador to South Africa. Now known as the **Natale Labia Museum** (Mon–Fri 10am–5pm; free), it gives an insight into a grand seaside lifestyle now vanished. It has original furniture and paintings on display, many of which were imported from Venice, the count's home. ❑

ABOVE: Cecil Rhodes's simple cottage at Muizenberg, now a museum.

SHOPPING

The Cape Peninsula lacks the focused shopping opportunities of Long Street *(see page 94)* or the V&A Waterfront *(see page 108)*, but there are interesting shops scattered around the peninsula, especially in Kalk Bay.

Art

Kalk Bay Modern
136 Main Rd, Kalk Bay. Tel: 021-788 6571. www.kalkbaymodern.com p352, A4
Situated above the ever popular Olympia Café, this vibrant gallery displays a varied selection of contemporary paintings, sculptures and ceramics made by up-and-coming local artists and community groups.

Books

Quagga Art and Books
Main Rd, Kalk Bay. Tel: 021-788 2752. www.quaggabooks.co.za p252, A4
An interesting collection of art, artefacts and books. The speciality is out-of-print Africana, but there are lots of more contemporary second-hand books too.

Crafts

Ethno Bongo
Mainstream Centre, 5 Main Rd, Hout Bay. Tel: 021-790 0802. www.ethno-bongo.co.za p253, D3
Good-quality contemporary handicrafts on sale here include the fabulous range of handmade jewellery crafted by Dolce & Banana from seashells, feathers, beads, ostrich eggshell, wood and other unusual materials.

Hout Bay Craft Market
Hout Bay Harbour
A good place for inexpensive gift shopping, the harbour from where boats depart to the seal colony on Duiker Island also hosts a few dozen stalls selling mass-produced batiks, beadwork and wooden carvings.

BEST RESTAURANTS, BARS AND CAFÉS

Restaurants

Sea Point

Harvey's at Winchester Mansions
221 Beach Rd. Tel: 021-434 2351. www.winchester.co.za Open: B, L & D daily. **$$$** 41 p252, A3
If there is such a thing as Euro-African food, you will find it here. New takes on South African dishes are the order of the day, plus simple staples such as fresh line-fish. The venue is pretty and quiet, in the courtyard of an old-fashioned seaside hotel. Jazz brunches and regular wine-and-dine evenings.

Camps Bay

Blues
The Promenade, Victoria Rd. Tel: 021-438 2040. www.blues.co.za Open: L & D daily. **$$$** 42 p258, A4
A popular seaside venue for locals and visitors since it opened in 1987, Blues attracts a smart-casual set who like to see and be seen. There's lots of seafood here, an extensive wine list and a great terrace overlooking Camps Bay.

Codfather Seafood Emporium
37 The Drive. Tel: 021-438 0782. www.codfather.co.za Open: L & D daily. **$$** 43 p258, A4
Come here for the seafood and sushi. Customers select what they fancy from the counter, where it is weighed and then cooked while they wait. Very popular, so make a reservation. There's a good, accessible wine list too.

Salt
Ambassador Hotel, Victoria Rd, Bantry Bay. Tel 021-439 7258. www.newmarkhotels.com Open: L & D daily. **$$$** 44 p254, A2
This is possibly the best seat on the Atlantic Seaboard for its spectacular views (you're basically suspended over the ocean) and good food. A small but well-chosen menu of modern international dishes and tapas. Good and relatively affordable local wines too.

The Roundhouse
The Glen. Tel: 021-438 4387. www.theroundhouserestaurant.com Open: L Wed–Fri, D Tue–Sat **$–$$$** 45 p258, B2
Situated in a historic building on the slopes above Camps Bay, this unique new restaurant has loads of character, great views, an inventive menu and a wine cellar of note. Dinner is a costly but sumptuous multi-course set menu eaten indoors, while lunch is a more casual and affordable al fresco affair.

Ristorante Posticino
3 Albany Mews, 323 Main Rd. Tel: 021-439 4014. www.posticino.co.za Open: L & D daily. **$$**
This local pizzeria offers a warm welcome, and has a vibrant pavement area. It serves some of the best pizza and pasta in town, with a well-priced wine list.

LEFT AND RIGHT: Camps Bay and Simon's Town have plenty of great restaurants and cafés.

Hout Bay

Chapman's Restaurant
Chapman's Peak Hotel, Chapman's Peak Drive. Tel: 021-790 1036. www.chapmanspeakhotel.co.za Open: L & D daily. **$**
Chapman's is a very popular hotel restaurant with a good seafood menu. It is most famous for its calamari, fries and seaside views. Also good for weekend lunches when it is okay to come in wearing shorts and flip-flops.

La Cuccina
Victoria Mall, Victoria Rd. Tel: 021-790 8008. Open: B & L daily. **$**
This is a great brunch venue. Choose from a huge buffet of Italian-style dishes. There are endless pots of coffee and great cakes. Vegetarians are unusually well catered for. Unlicensed.

Fish on the Rocks
Hout Bay Harbour. Tel: 021-790 0001. Open: B, L & D daily. **$**
Very basic, but serving superb fish and chips. The calamari and kingklip are especially good. Sit inside or out on the grass.

Wharfside Grill
Mariner's Wharf, Hout Bay Harbour. Tel: 021-790 1100. www.marinerswharf.com Open: B, L & D daily. **$$**
A busy, cheap venue right in the harbour. Eat your fish or calamari while you watch fish being unloaded on the quay. The waiters are dressed like sailors.

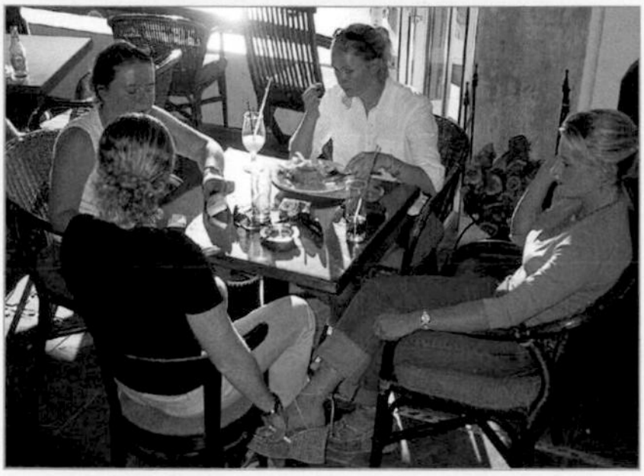

Simon's Town

Bertha's
1 Wharf Rd. Tel: 021-786 2138. www.berthas.co.za Open: B, L & D daily. **$**
This harbourside restaurant specialises in seafood but it is also good for burgers, pasta and salads. With its big open deck by the water, it gets very busy at the weekends.

Café Pescados
Main St. Tel: 021-786 2272. www.pescados.co.za Open: B, L & D daily. **$**
Situated opposite Jubilee Square in a historic building, the former Criterion Cinema, this relaxed and welcoming eatery is deservedly popular with locals for its good-value pizzas, seafood and breakfasts.

Tibetan Teahouse
2 Harrington St, Seaforth. Tel: 021-786 1544. www.sopheagallery.com. Open: L daily. **$**
Part of the Sophea Gallery, which lies along the main road connecting Simon's Town to Boulders, this is an excellent lunch venue, both for light, tasty and inexpensive Tibetan-style vegetarian fare, and for the superb view over False Bay.

Kalk Bay

Brass Bell
Kalk Bay Station. Tel: 021-788 5455. www.brassbell.co.za Open: L & D daily. **$$**
If you want to see the whales (May–Nov), come to the Brass Bell. To get here, pass under the railway line and climb up the steps to a warren of old station buildings. The views are amazing, even if the food is unexceptional. Ask them to grill the fish and serve it with oil and lemon.

Cape to Cuba
Main Rd. Tel: 021-788 1566. www.capetocuba.com Open: L & D daily. **$**
Serves a mixture of Cuban and seafood dishes. More important, though, is the location – practically straddling the railway line. It tries to evoke the shabby madness of Havana and is great for a theatrical-style night out.

Harbour House
Kalk Bay Harbour. Tel: 021-788 4133. www.harbourhouse.co.za Open: L & D daily. **$$**
Offers excellent and inexpensive dining in the heart of the harbour. Fresh fish imaginatively prepared, good salads and great wines.

Muizenberg

Fogey's Railway House
177 Main Rd. Tel: 021-788 3252. www.fogeys.co.za Open: L & D daily, closed Mon and Tue off season. **$**
Another restaurant in a defunct station, featuring a menu of contemporary South African cuisine, including really good linefish, all at very competitive prices.

Prices for a three-course dinner per person with a half-bottle of house wine:
$ = under R200
$$ = R200–350
$$$ = more than R350

Bars and Cafés

A host of buzzing cocktail bars lines the main road through Camps Bay. If you're looking for something to do on a Sunday night, the evergreen **Café Caprice** (tel: 021-438 8315; www.cafecaprice.co.za 13 p258, A3) is where it all happens, with the feel of Ibiza meets Cannes, but it's in a small space that spills out onto the pavement across from the beach, so arrive early to grab a table and enjoy the often spectacular sunset. Another institution for casual Sunday sundowners (as long as the wind isn't blowing) is **La Med** (tel: 021-438 5600; www.lamed.co.za 14 p258, A2), where you should come early to get a spot on the deck overlooking the ocean, before hitting the dance floor that opens later.

The Zanzibari-influenced **Baraza** (tel: 021-438 1758; www.baraza.co.za 15 p258, A4) is a good spot to chill, cocktail in hand watching the sun go down, or to party late into the evening with the resident DJ. The **Sand Bar** (31 Victoria Rd; tel: 021-438 8336; www.sandbar.co.za) is a pavement bar with great views but none of the pretentiousness that you'll find elsewhere on the strip.

For a pub-like atmosphere, Kalk Bay has two options: the **Brass Bell** (021-788 5455; www.brassbell.co.za) – waves practically wash over it on a stormy night – and the **Polana** (tel: 021-788 4133; www.harbourhouse.co.za), where you can eat or curl up in an old leather armchair.

For the perfect brunch the day after the night before, head to the **Olympia Café and Deli** (134 Main Rd; tel: 021-788 6396), which serves really great food in a bohemian atmosphere. Take the papers, order a jug of coffee and settle down with poached eggs and smoked salmon. Everything here from the shellfish to the cakes is first-class.

FURTHER AFIELD

There is plenty to see and do within a short distance of Cape Town. You can tour the wineries of the Boland, visit the picturesque towns of Stellenbosch and Franschhoek, or, in winter, enjoy land-based whale-watching from Hermanus

Main Attractions

STELLENBOSCH
VERGELEGEN WINE ESTATE
FRANSCHHOEK
BOSCHENDAL WINE ESTATE
HERMANUS
DE HOOP NATURE RESERVE
WEST COAST NATIONAL PARK

Maps and Listings

FURTHER AFIELD MAP, PAGE 184
MAP OF STELLENBOSCH, PAGE 186
SHOPPING, PAGE 199
RESTAURANTS, BARS AND CAFÉS, PAGES 200–1
ACCOMMODATION, PAGES 231–2

Cape Town's reputation as an outdoor-oriented city is enhanced by the beauty of the surrounding coastline and its mountainous hinterland. Scenically, the far southwest of the Western Cape Province is utterly magnificent – hazy blue peaks and heath-covered hills sloping down towards wide green valleys planted with leafy vineyards, quaint thatch-and-whitewash villages, and a seemingly endless stock of uncrowded and idyllically framed beaches.

Day trips from Cape Town

The part of the Western Cape that lies within realistic day-tripping distance of the provincial capital splits neatly into three tourist circuits, each with its own distinct character. Centred on the historic towns of Stellenbosch, Franschhoek and Paarl, the Cape Winelands of the Boland (literally "upland") is undoubtedly the most popular of these circuits, consisting of more than half a dozen different wine routes, each of which offers the opportunity to sample the produce of one of South Africa's oldest and most economically important agricultural industries. By contrast, the Overberg, a sheep-and-grain farming region situated to the southeast of Cape Town, is best known for the excellent whale-viewing out of Hermanus and as the site of Africa's most southerly point, Cape Agulhas. Finally, there is the West Coast, which attracts relatively few international tourists, yet offers those who do make the effort a winning combination of marine wildlife, low-key wine estates and fabulous mountain scenery.

In practice, with a rented vehicle, you could loop between all three of

PRECEDING PAGES: diving in Hout Bay.
LEFT: sheep farming in the Overberg.
RIGHT: the ornate Dutch Reformed Church in Swellendam.

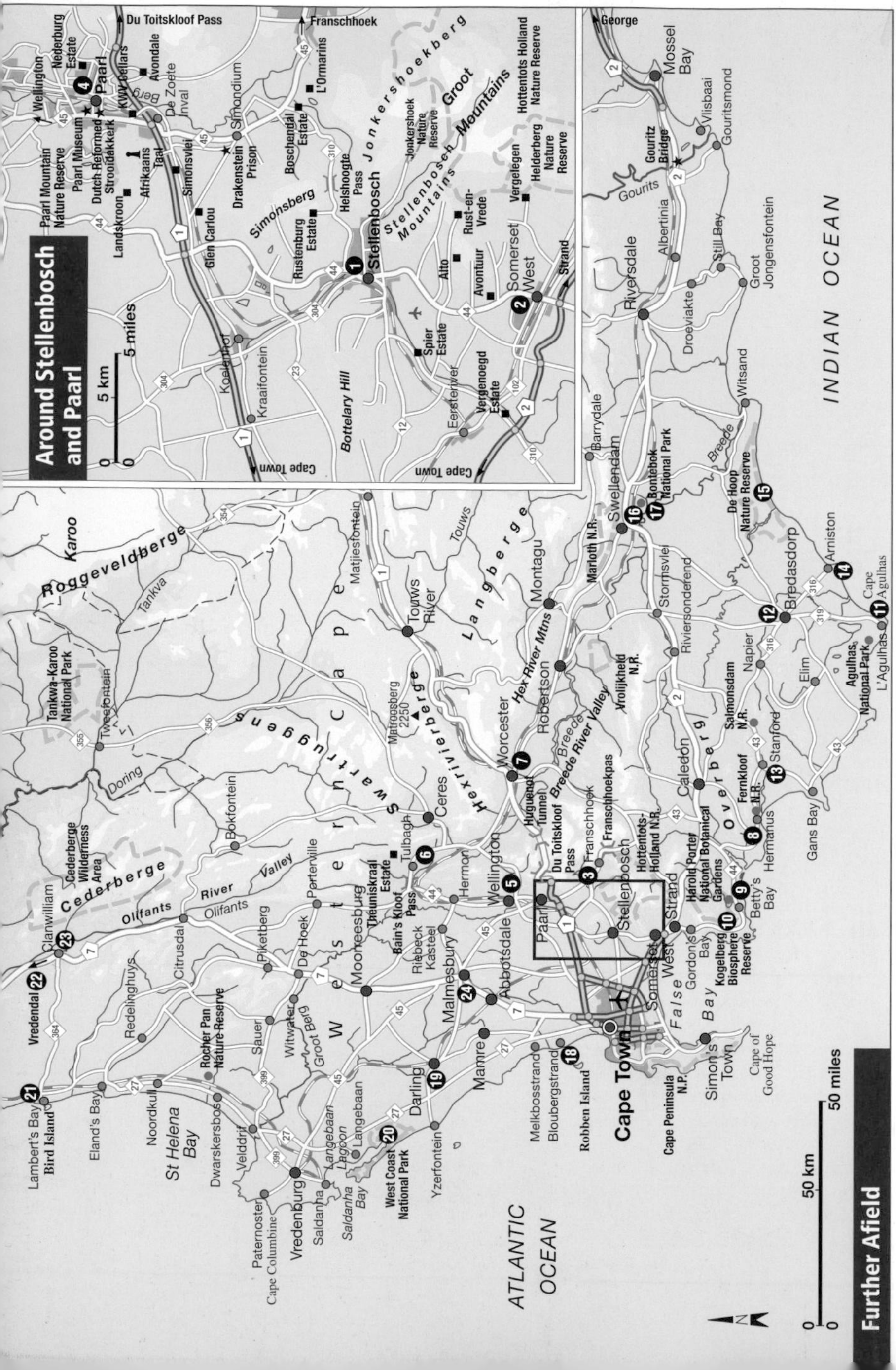
Further Afield
0 50 km
0 50 miles
Around Stellenbosch and Paarl
0 5 km
0 5 miles
ATLANTIC OCEAN
INDIAN OCEAN
Cape Town
Robben Island
Cape Peninsula N.P.
Simon's Town
Cape of Good Hope
False Bay
Somerset West
Strand
Gordon's Bay
Kogelberg Biosphere Reserve
Betty's Bay
Harold Porter National Botanical Gardens
Hermanus
Fernkloof N.R.
Stanford
Salmonsdam N.R.
Gans Bay
Elim
Agulhas National Park
L'Agulhas
Cape Agulhas
Arniston
Bredasdorp
Napier
De Hoop Nature Reserve
Witsand
Swellendam
Bontebok National Park
Marloth N.R.
Barrydale
Montagu
Robertson
Worcester
Breede River Valley
Vrolijkheid N.R.
Caledon
Riviersonderend
Stormsvlei
Overberg
Franschhoek
Franschhoekpas
Hottentots-Holland N.R.
Du Toitskloof Pass
Huguenot Tunnel
Paarl
Stellenbosch
Wellington
Hermon
Tulbagh
Theuniskraal Estate
Bain's Kloof Pass
Riebeck Kasteel
Malmesbury
Abbotsdale
Moorreesburg
Ceres
Hex River Mtns
Hexrivierberge
Matroosberg 2250
Touws River
Touws
Matjiesfontein
Langberge
Swartruggens
Western Cape
Roggeveldberge
Karoo
Tankwa
Tankwa-Karoo National Park
Tweefontein
Doring
Bokfontein
Cederberge Wilderness Area
Cederberge
Clanwilliam
Olifants River Valley
Olifants
Citrusdal
Porterville
Piketberg
De Hoek
Redelinghuys
Vredendal
Lambert's Bay
Bird Island
Eland's Bay
Noordkul
Rocher Pan Nature Reserve
St Helena Bay
Dwarskersbos
Velddrif
Sauer
Witwater
Groot Berg
Paternoster
Cape Columbine
Vredenburg
Saldanha
Saldanha Bay
Langebaan Lagoon
Langebaan
West Coast National Park
Yzerfontein
Darling
Mamre
Melkbosstrand
Bloubergstrand
Riversdale
Albertinia
Gourits
Gouritz Bridge
Mossel Bay
Vlisbaai
Gouritsmond
Still Bay
Droeviakte
Groot Jongensfontein
George
Du Toitskloof Pass
Franschhoek
Paarl Mountain Nature Reserve
Paarl Museum
Dutch Reformed Strooidakkerk
Landskroon
Afrikaans Taal
Wellington
Nederburg Estate
KWV Cellars
Avondale
Berg
De Zoete Inval
Simonsvlei
Simondium
Drakenstein Prison
Glen Carlou
Boschendal Estate
L'Ormarins
Simonsberg
Rustenburg Estate
Helshoogte Pass
Jonkershoekberg
Jonkershoek Nature Reserve
Groot
Stellenbosch Mountains
Hottentots Holland Nature Reserve
Helderberg Nature Reserve
Vergelegen
Rust-en-Vrede
Alto
Avontuur
Spier Estate
Bottelary Hill
Kraaifontein
Koelenhof
Eersterivier
Vergenoegd Estate
Cape Town
Strand

these circuits over the course of five or six days – the optimum route would entail following the R27 along the West Coast to Saldanha, then cutting east along the R45 through Malmesbury to Paarl, Stellenbosch and Franschhoek, before taking the R45/43 through Caledon to Hermanus and the Overberg. Equally, most individual destinations along these circuits would make for a straightforward day trip out of Cape Town, the one exception being the somewhat far-flung Cape Agulhas.

Using public transport, your options are more limited, although Stellenbosch and Paarl – the former arguably being the highlight of the whole region – are both connected to Cape Town by regular passenger trains. Another possibility is to join one of the organised wine-tasting day tours offered by numerous operators based in and around Cape Town, or to undertake other activities (ranging from hiking and kayaking to caged shark dives and bungee jumping) with specialist operators. Any hotel or backpacker hostel in Cape Town can provide details and make bookings at short notice.

THE CAPE WINELANDS

The second-oldest town in South Africa, **Stellenbosch** ❶ is 27 years younger than Cape Town, yet its compact, low-rise town centre projects a far more overt sense of architectural cohesion and antiquity than the Mother City, 45km (27 miles) to the east.

Founded on the banks of the Eersterivier (First River) by Governor Simon van der Stel in 1679 and accorded its own magistracy six years later, Stellenbosch started life as something of a frontier town, an isolated outpost of European urbanity. It lay days away from the Cape by ox-wagon, and was bounded to the north by kilometre after uncharted kilometre of lawless African wilderness.

Today, by contrast, it is the site of the country's premier Afrikaans university, as well as the epicentre of the burgeoning Cape wine industry. And it's less than an hour away from Cape Town by road or train.

Shaded by stately trees (some planted back in Van der Stel's day) from which its nickname "Eikestad" (Oak Town) derives, Stellenbosch is well worth a few hours' exploration, ideally on foot. There's no better place to start than Dorp (Village)

ABOVE LEFT: Hugenot monument, Franschoek. **ABOVE RIGHT:** baboon crossing. **BELOW:** Cape Dutch architecture abounds in Stellenbosch.

The University of Stellenbosch has provided higher education to two students who later became prime ministers of South Africa, Jan Smuts (1870–1950) and Daniel François Malan (1874–1959), who defeated Smuts in 1948 and was one of the main architects of apartheid.

Street, which runs roughly parallel to the Eersterivier at the southern end of the town centre, and contains what is probably the longest row of pre-20th-century buildings anywhere in South Africa. These include the quaint **Oom Samie's se Winkel** (Uncle Samie's Shop; tel: 021-887 0797; Mon–Fri 8.30am–5.30pm, Sat and Sun 9am–5pm) and a Lutheran Church built in 1851.

Nearby, on Alexander Street, the H-shaped **Burgherhuis** Ⓐ, built in 1797 and now listed as a National Monument, is one of the town's finest examples of traditional Cape Dutch architecture. It overlooks **Die Braak** – literally, "The Fallow", a commonage equivalent to the English village green – which is also where you will find the 19th-century Anglican and Rhenish churches, and the **Kruithuis** Ⓑ (Powder House; Mon–Fri 9am–2pm, closed June–Aug), a whitewashed munitions magazine that was built in 1777 and now serves as a low-key military museum.

Also situated in the town centre, off Ryneveld Street, is the **University of Stellenbosch** Ⓒ. It was formally established by Act of Parliament in 1918, but it started life 60 years earlier as the Theological Seminary of the Dutch Reformed Church. As of 1866, it became the secular Stellenbosch College (renamed Victoria College in 1887 in honour of the English queen's silver jubilee). Campus highlights include the Victorian Ou Hoofgebou (Old Main Building), which now houses the Faculty of Law, the **Sasol Art Museum**, and the small but beautiful **Botanical Garden** Ⓓ (daily 9am–4pm; free), which is the oldest such entity in South Africa and encloses a tranquil tea garden.

Stellenbosch Village Museum Ⓔ

Address: 37 Ryneveld Street

Stellenbosch

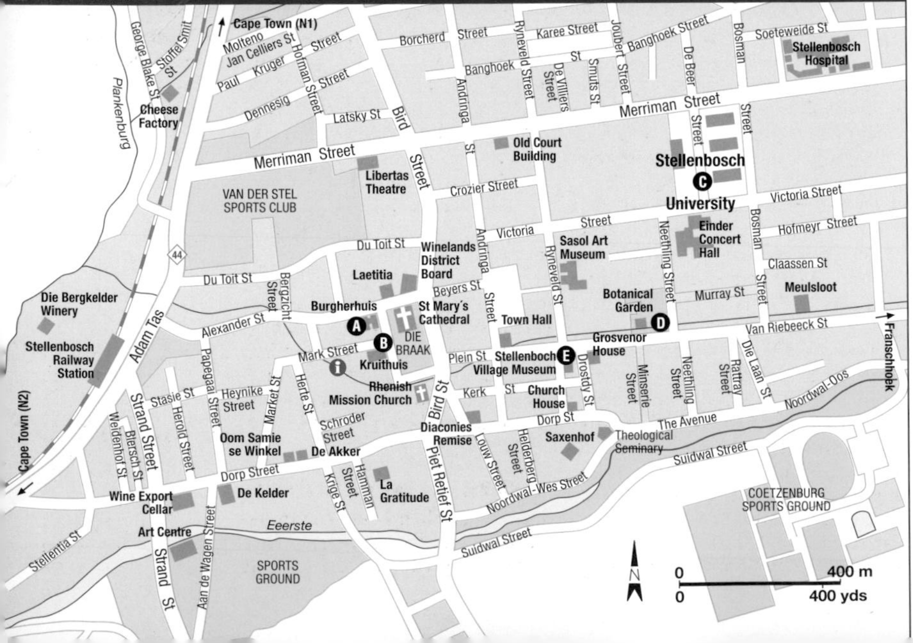

Tel: 021-887 2948
Opening Hrs: Mon–Sat 9.30am–5pm, Sun 10am–1pm and 1.30–4pm
Entrance Fee: charge

Situated immediately north of Dorp Street, Stellenbosch's premier museum comprises an entire block of impressive antique buildings, most notably the unpretentious Schreuderhuis, which is the oldest surviving town house in the country, built in 1709. Others in the row include the elegant **Cape Dutch Blettermanhuis** (1789), the Georgian-style **Grosvenor House** (1803) and the fine mid-Victorian **Murray House** (1850).

Lively nightlife

The significant student population of the town ensures that the sleepy olde-worlde ambience that engulfs Stellenbosch by day is complemented by an unexpectedly lively nightlife when the sun goes down, at least during term time. The longest serving pub is De Akker *(see page 200)*, set in a historic building on Bird Street, while the rowdier Tollies Pub and Grill *(see page 200)* stays open until late and occasionally hosts live music. Several other, mostly more ephemeral, drinking holes line Bird Street as it runs north from Dorp Street.

If "popular with students" isn't a recommendation in your book, the town centre is also liberally studded with classier restaurants serving fine Continental and Cape Malay fare accompanied by a varied selection of Cape wines. Revellers who are in the Cape area at the right time of year might want to ensure that their visit coincides with one of the local festivals, such as the Student Rag Carnival (February), the Stellenbosch Wine Festival (July or August), and the Stellenbosch Music Festival (September).

Trekking in the mountains

Situated less than 20km (12 miles) inland of False Bay as the crow flies, Stellenbosch lies at the relatively

ABOVE: Uncle Samie's Shop typifies the olde-worlde atmosphere of Stellenbosch. **BELOW:** the Kruithuis (powder house) in Stellenbosch.

SHOP

For serious wine buyers visiting Stellenbosch, a more efficient option than hopping between individual estates is to sample the more varied selection on offer at a specialist wine exporter, such as the Wine Export Cellar (Dorp Street, tel: 021-883 3814) or Die Bergkelder (Adam Tas Road; tel: 021-809 8283).

ABOVE: the Vergelegen winery **BELOW:** Mitchell's Pass.

modest elevation of 110 metres (360ft) above sea level, but it is encircled by several impressive mountain ranges. Notable among these is the 1,608-metre (5,275ft) **Groot Drakenstein** (Large Dragon's Rock), the 1,490-metre (4,889ft) **Stellenbosch Mountains** and 1,390-metre (4,560ft) **Simonsberg** (both named after Simon van der Stel), and the 1,224-metre (4,016ft) **Helderberg** (Clear Mountain).

In addition to providing a memorable backdrop to the town and the surrounding Winelands, the upper slopes of these mountains all support significant strands of indigenous fynbos, characterised by a wealth of proteas and colourful wild-flower displays in the spring.

Opportunities for a leg stretch range from the relatively undemanding circular 6km (4-mile) Swartboskloof–Sosyskloof Trail through the **Jonkershoek Nature Reserve**, which lies 8km (5 miles) east of the town centre along the Jonkershoek Road, to the more challenging 24km (15-mile) **Vineyard Trail** connecting the Papegaaiberg (Parrot Mountain) to the Kuils River, starting on the western outskirts of town behind the railway station. Several more arduous overnight hikes can be undertaken in the majestic **Hottentots Holland Nature Reserve**, the entrance to which lies off the R321 between Grabouw and Villiersdorp.

Exploring the wineries

The most popular attraction around Stellenbosch, however, is the Cape Winelands, the epicentre of the country's wine industry, with hundreds of estates nestling in the surrounding valleys and foothills. Divided informally into several different "wine routes", the first of which was established in 1971, most of these estates have a public wine-tasting room open from around 9am–4pm daily, though some operate shorter hours and may close altogether on Saturday or Sunday. Admission to some estates is free, but the more popular ones now charge a nominal tasting fee. Full details of the opening times and charges for individual estates are

provided in a free booklet issued at the tourist offices in Stellenbosch and Cape Town. It is perfectly possible to explore the Winelands under your own steam in a rented vehicle, but inadvisable to so without a spittoon-trained or teetotal designated driver in your party. Otherwise, if your whole party wants to enjoy a varied selection of wines with a clear conscience, it's best to hook up with one of the many inexpensive wine-tasting tours that run out of Cape Town or Stellenbosch every day.

Those who are touring independently are faced with some tough decisions regarding which of the plethora of different estates to visit. That selection will depend on your objectives and circumstances. If it's a genuine Cape Dutch atmosphere and mountain scenery you're after, there is no better place to start than the picturesque **Rustenberg Estate** (www.rustenburg.co.za; tel: 021-809 1200) on the northeastern outskirts of Stellenbosch. However, if you're travelling with children in tow, head southwest out of town for about 10km (6 miles) along the R310 to the fun-for-the-family **Spier Estate** (www.spier.co.za; tel: 021-809 1143), where fine wines and a quality Cape Malay restaurant are complemented by horse riding, a small zoo and playground, a picnic site, and regular steam-train connections to and from Cape Town.

Consistently voted South Africa's "top winery" by readers of *Wine* magazine, **Vergelegen** (www.vergelegen.co.za; tel: 021-847 1334; daily 9.30am–4.30pm) is a highlight of the **Helderberg Wine Route**, which centres on **Somerset West** ❷, some 20km (12 miles) south of Stellenbosch and 40km (24 miles) southeast of Cape Town. The farm of Vergelegen, which translates as "Far Away", was founded in 1700 by William van der Stel (son of Simon), and the first vines were planted there shortly afterwards. The Cape Dutch manor house, now a private museum decorated in period style, is set in tranquil gardens with a great little coffee shop, and the estate's multi-award-winning wines are equally inviting.

Other outstanding wineries along the Helderberg Wine Route include the venerable and very pretty **Vergenoegd Estate** (www.vergenoegd.co.za; tel: 021-843 3248), founded in 1696, as well as **Avontuur** (www.avontuur-estate.co.za; tel: 021-855 3450), **Alto** (www.alto.co.za; tel: 021-881 3884) and **Rust-en-Vrede** (www.rustenvrede.co.za; tel: 021-881 3881).

TIP

The winelands is as notable for its mountainous landscapes as its vineyards, and there's no finer scenic drive out of Stellenbosch than the R310, which skirts the northern slope of the Groot Drakenstein Mountains via the evocatively named Helshoogte (Hell's Heights) Pass, before descending via the R45 into the attractively sprawling village of Franschhoek.

ABOVE: Vergelegen manor house. **BELOW:** a tasting room at the Boschendal Estate.

TIP

Lovers of sparkling wines shouldn't miss out on the renowned Cabrière Estate, which lies on the outskirts of Franschhoek. Its Pierre Jourdan and Haut Cabrière are among the finest bubblies made in the Cape.

RIGHT: the picturesque grounds of the Boschendal Estate. **BELOW:** watch out for tortoises in Helderberg Nature Reserve.

For those who prefer walking to imbibing, there are seven trails, ranging from 15 minutes to three hours in duration, running through the **Helderberg Nature Reserve** (daily sunrise to sunset). The entrance is 4km (2½ miles) north of Somerset West and is signposted. Its floral wealth is capped by the endemic red disa, an exquisite orchid that blooms between January and March.

Franschhoek ❸

Only 28km (17 miles) from Stellenbosch by road, Franschhoek is blessed with the most spectacular setting of any Boland town, encircled by a series of tall, craggy peaks. Franschhoek was initially named Olifantshoek after the prodigious elephant herds that foraged in the valley, and while these mighty beasts are long gone from the Winelands, the town is distinguished by the tangible French influence alluded to in its present name, not least in its culinary tradition – there's surely no greater concentration of award-winning restaurants anywhere in South Africa *(see pages 200-1 for some of them)*.

The French influence extends to the name of several local wine estates, for instance Chamonix, Dieu Donné, La Bri and La Couronne, and you can sample more than 100 wines produced by these and other local wineries at the **Franschhoek Vineyards Co-op Cellar** (tel: 021-870 4200; Mon–Fri 9.30am–5pm, Sat, Sun and public holidays 10am–4pm) in the town centre.

Huguenot Memorial Museum

Address: Lambrecht Road, www.museum.co.za
Tel: 021-876 2532
Opening Hrs: Mon–Sat 9am–5pm, Sun 2–5pm
Entrance Fee: charge

Franschhoek acquired its present name (which means French Corner) due to the large number of French Huguenots who settled here in the 17th and 18th centuries. This museum and memorial, completed in 1943, recounts the history of these Protestant refugees, who fled France to avoid persecution by the Catholic King Louis XIV following the revocation of the Edict of Nantes in 1685. The Huguenots made an immense contribution to the Cape's wine industry, and while few if any of their descendants speak French, many common Afrikaans surnames – de Villiers and de Klerk, for instance – are of French origin.

Boschendal Estate

Address: R310, halfway between Franschhoek and Stellenbosch, www.boschendalwines.com
Tel: 021-870 4210
Opening Hrs: daily 8.30am–4.30pm
Entrance Fee: charge

Justifiably the most popular wine estate near Franschhoek, Boschendal was founded below the tall peaks of the Groot Drakenstein in 1685. The attractive Cape Dutch manor house, reached along a sweeping drive lined by ancient trees, has a good restaurant and also offers the option of a "pique-nique" between November and April. Rosé lovers should try the Blanc de Noir, an off-dry salmon-pink "white" wine blended from Pinot Noir and Merlot grapes. Also recommended are the bone-dry sparkling brut, highly rated reserve Shiraz, or an affordable Bordeaux blend called Lanoy.

Paarl ❹

The town of **Paarl** was founded on the banks of the Berg River in 1720, but much of the surrounding farmland (including the extant Laborie Estate) had been given to Huguenot settlers as early as 1687. Paarl is a 45-minute drive from Cape Town along the N1 Highway, and a similar driving distance north from Stellenbosch or Franschhoek.

The town centre is unmemorable, even dreary, by Boland standards, and the 11km (7-mile) main road – for what it's worth, vaunted by the local marketing machine as the longest in the country – takes ages to drive along. No original 1720s buildings survive, but the Oude Pastorie (Old Parsonage) on Main Street, now the **Paarl Museum** (tel: 021-872 2651; Mon–Fri 9am–5pm, Sat 9am–1pm; charge), was constructed in 1787, and the nearby **Dutch Reformed Strooidakkerk** (Thatched Roof Church) was consecrated in 1805.

Of greater interest than the town itself is the adjacent **Paarl Mountain Nature Reserve**, with a trio of lunar domes that can be reached via a relatively easy walking trail through slopes draped in protea-studded fynbos. A relatively modern landmark on the southern slopes of Paarl Mountain, the obelisk-like **Afrikaans Taal (Language) Monument** was erected in 1975 to commemorate the centenary of the local movement that led to the recognition of Afrikaans as the world's youngest official language.

Also situated just outside Paarl is **Drakenstein Prison**, formerly Victor Verster Prison, where Nelson Mandela was held captive for the last two years of his imprisonment.

The Paarl Wine Route

The Paarl Wine Route offers access to some of the country's most venerable wine estates, as well as a range of quality restaurants. A good place to start is the central **KWV Cellars** (www.kwv.co.za; tel: 021-807 3007) or the more outlying **Nederburg**

ABOVE: Hermanus boatman.

Paarl's name dates from 1657, when Abraham Gabbema followed the Berg River inland as far as the glistening granite-domed mountain he christened Peerlbergh – Dutch for "Pearl Mountain".

Nelson Mandela spent the last two years of his imprisonment (1988–90) in Victor Verster Prison, near Paarl. Unlike Robben Island, where conditions were harsh, Victor Verster was a comfortable and spacious villa, in his words "a gilded cage". Indeed, when he later had a new house built for himself, he based its design on that of Victor Verster.

Estate (www.nederburg.co.za; tel: 021-862 3104). The latter, probably the best known of all South Africa's wine producers, has received many awards for its reserve range, while its everyday drinking wines are ubiquitous restaurant fare.

Other prominent local cellars include **Avondale** (www.avondale.co.za; tel: 021-863 1976), **Landskroon** (www.landskroonwines.com; tel: 021-863 1039) and **Glen Carlou** (www.glencarlous.co.za; tel: 021-875 5528), while **Simonsvlei** (www.simonsvlei.com; tel: 021-863 3040 and the **Rhebokskloof Winery** (www.rhebokskloof.co.za; tel: 021-869 8386) both offer an extensive range of well-priced wines for everyday sipping, boosted in the latter case by a magnificent location below **Du Toitskloof Pass**, 16km (10 miles) east of Paarl.

The small town of **Wellington** ❺, on the R44 about 12km (7 miles) north of Paarl, is notable for its Dutch Reformed Moederkerk, built in 1838, and its imposing Town Hall.

Tulbagh and Worcester

Another 50km (30 miles) north of Wellington, crossing the Slanghoek (Snake Corner) Mountains via the magnificent **Bain's Kloof Pass**, the small town of **Tulbagh** ❻, founded on the banks of the Little Berg River in 1795, is a rare architectural gem. Its historic Church Street has been completely restored in Cape Dutch style following a series of earthquakes that virtually demolished the town and claimed the lives of nine residents in 1969–70. Designed by the French architect Louis Michel Thibault in 1804, the gracious **Oude Drostdy**, 4km (2½ miles) outside the village, now serves as a storeroom and sales floor for several nearby vineyards.

Further out of town is the **Theuniskraal Estate** (www.theuniskraal.co.za; tel: 023-230 0687), in the possession of the Jordaan family since 1927, which produces some excellent white wines, including an iconic dry Riesling.

Founded in 1820 and named after the Marquis of Worcester, the elder brother of then Governor of the Cape, Lord Charles Somerset, the attractive Boland town of **Worcester**

Afrikaans

A derivative of the Dutch spoken by the earliest Europeans to settle the Cape, Afrikaans, though readily intelligible to any Hollander today, is classified as a language in its own right thanks to its simplified grammar, pronunciation quirks and magpie vocabulary. It is rooted in the pidgin Dutch that formed the lingua franca of the early colonists and their Malay and indigenous subjugates. It was only in 1875, however, that the fledgling language's grammar was formalised.

In 1925 Afrikaans replaced Dutch as the country's second official language (alongside English), and it is now one of 11 official languages in South Africa. Perceptions of Afrikaans in the New South Africa are sometimes tainted by apartheid-era associations – it was, for instance, the Nationalist Party's insistence on using Afrikaans as a teaching medium that sparked the Soweto riots of 1976 *(see page 46)* – but Afrikaans is not an exclusively "white" language. Ironically, perhaps, roughly half of the six million South Africans who call Afrikaans their mother tongue are so-called coloureds of mixed racial descent.

BELOW: forest fires warning sign.

ABOVE: Cape Winelands scenery.
BELOW: the native aloe plant has renowned medicinal properties.

❼ lies in the Breede River Valley at the base of the Hex River Mountains. Rising to 2,250 metres (7,382ft), they form the highest peaks in the Western Cape. Some 50km (30 miles) southeast of Tulbagh, the town is notable for its elegant **Drostdy**, regarded by experts as the country's finest example of Cape Regency architecture. There's also a neo-Gothic Dutch Reformed **Moederkerk**, built in 1824.

The oldest wine producer along the Worcester Wine Route, the De Wet Wine Cellar (www.dewetcellar.co.za; tel: 023-341 2710), was founded as recently as 1946, so while the wines are good, the architecture doesn't compare to the more historic estates around Stellenbosch or Paarl. From Worcester, a straight 100km (60-mile) drive southwest along the N1 leads back to Cape Town.

Karoo Desert National Botanical Garden

Address: Roux Road, www.sanbi.org
Tel: 023-347 0785
Opening Hrs: daily 7am–7pm
Entrance Fee: free, except Aug–Oct

Situated along the northern edge of Worcester, this uncultivated garden lies in the semi-arid Karoo and protects some 400 plant species including the oddball kokerboom (quiver tree). It is known for its flowering succulents, which bloom most vividly after the spring rains, usually from August to October.

THE OVERBERG

Roughly 120km (72 miles) southeast of Cape Town via the N2 and R44, **Hermanus** ❽ is the main focus for tourism in the otherwise rather low-key and rustic region called the Overberg (literally, "beyond the mountain"). The town was founded in 1857 by German settlers who named it Hermanuspietersfontein (Hermanus Pieter's Spring) in remembrance of an itinerant shepherd who once used the site as his regular summer encampment. The fledgling resort town gained municipal status in 1904, two years after the official abbreviation of its name, and for much of the 20th century it served as a fashionable fishing, boating and beach retreat for a wealthy elite of holiday-home owners.

In recent years, this formerly rather exclusive resort town has assumed an altogether more egalitarian character – indeed, Hermanus can get quite crowded, especially at Christmas –

WHERE

The Western Cape isn't strongly associated with "Big Five" game viewing, since most of the region's large wildlife was hunted out in the 19th century. However, lion, leopard, cheetah, elephant, rhino and buffalo can all be seen in Aquila Private Game Reserve (tel: 021-431 8400; www. aquilasafari.com), with its four-star lodge set in the Little Karoo two hours' drive north of Cape Town.

ABOVE: Hermanus's official "whale crier".

but its clifftop setting near the mouth of the Klein (Small) River remains inspirational, and the town itself, all cobblestone alleys and open-air restaurants, retains the quaint feel of an olde worlde fishing village.

Whale-watching aside *(see below)*, Hermanus boasts an attractive sandy beach, and a good range of marine activities can be organised locally, from scuba dives and caged shark dives to sailing and kayaking. The 1,400-hectare (3,459-acre) **Fernkloof Nature Reserve** (www.fernkloof.com; tel: 028-313 0819; daily 9am–5pm; free), on the northern outskirts of town, protects the pretty fynbos-strewn slopes of the Kleinriviersberg, and is criss-crossed with a rewarding network of day trails.

Two other places are also worth a diversion – **Betty's Bay ❾**, a pretty resort town on the R44 back towards Cape Town, also known for the prodigious colony of African penguins at Stony Point, and the waterfall-strewn fynbos of the **Harold Porter National Botanical Gardens** (www. sanbi.org; tel: 028-272 9311; daily 8am–6pm; charge), below the Kogelberg Mountains.

Whale-watching off Hermanus

Hermanus's main claim to fame is as the world's top site for land-based whale-viewing. Every year, between June and November, up to 100 southern right whales congregate in Walker Bay for the mating and calving season, together with a smaller and less reliable number of humpback whales, and they often breach and lobtail in the water just 30 metres (100ft) below vantage points such as Castle Rock, which lies in the town centre overlooking the Old Harbour.

Whale activity generally peaks over September and October, when a wander along the 11km (7-mile) cliff walk leading west from Castle Rock is almost certain to yield whale sightings in the crystal-clear water. At this time of year, the tourist office (tel: 028-312 2629; www.hermanus.co.za) hires a special "whale crier" to keep visitors up to date on where the whales are best seen, and an underwater microphone transmits their strange "songs" live back to a room in the Old Harbour Museum. Boat-based whale-viewing in Walker Bay is permitted but strictly regulated – the only two licensed operators are Southern Right Charters (www. southernrightcharters.co.za; tel: 082-353 0550) and Hermanus Whale Cruises (www.hermanus-whale-cruises.co.za; tel: 028-313 2722).

Kogelberg Biosphere Reserve ❿

Address: 6km (4 miles) from Kleinmond on the R44 between Hermanus and Betty's Bay, www. kogelbergbiospherereserve.co.za
Tel: 028-271 4792
Opening Hrs: Sept–May 7.30am–7pm, June–Aug 8am–6pm
Entrance Fee: charge

Revered by dedicated hikers and botanists, this vast Unesco-registered reserve claims to protect the world's most bio-diverse habitat, with more than 1,880 plant species identified, 77 of which occur nowhere else on earth. It also harbours a wide variety of birds, a healthy Chacma baboon population, and a herd of wild horses, probably descended from beasts abandoned by soldiers of unknown affinities in the Anglo-Boer War of 1899–1902. Four hiking trails run through the reserve, from 6km (4 miles) to 23km (14 miles) in length, and there's canoeing on the Palmiet River.

The end of the continent

Situated in the **Eastern Overberg** almost 200km (120 miles) from the Cape of Good Hope as the crow flies, **Cape Agulhas ⓫** is not only the official meeting point of the Indian and Atlantic Oceans, but also, somewhat less arbitrarily, the most southerly point on the African continent. The cape is now protected within the 210-sq-km (82-sq-mile) Agulhas National Park (www.sanparks.org; tel: 028-435 6222; free), an entity that has little significance beyond the statute books at the time of writing, though formal nature trails, a museum, and interpretative and environmental centres are expected to open by 2013. Geographical significance aside, Agulhas can be rather underwhelming by comparison to, say, Cape Point, consisting of a flat, rocky, windswept peninsula punctuated by the Agulhas Lighthouse (daily 9am–5pm; charge), which is the second-oldest working lighthouse in South Africa, reached via 71 steps.

The name Agulhas, which translates as "Needles", was coined by one of the more prescient Portuguese navigators to enter the Indian Ocean in the 16th century: the treacherously jagged rocks that lie offshore have subsequently accounted for at least 250 shipwrecks. By contrast, the altogether more benign beach at nearby Struisbaai is magnificent, with its turquoise-blue sea and colourful fishing boats.

Diversions and backwaters

Agulhas lies about 100km (60 miles) southeast of Hermanus by any of several back roads, of which the most straightforward option is probably the R326/R316/R319 via **Napier** and **Bredasdorp ⓬** – the latter notable for its Shipwreck Museum (6 Independent Street; tel: 028-424 1240; Mon–Sat 9am–5pm, Sun 10am–4pm; charge), with treasures from ships wrecked off the Agulhas coast.

Various diversions are possible en route between Hermanus and Agulhas. For a gentle ramble, several undemanding walking trails run through the **Salmonsdam Nature Reserve** (www.capenature.co.za; tel: 028-314 0062; charge), which lies near **Stanford ⓭**, some 45km (28 miles) west of Hermanus. It protects a hilly area coloured by red fields of proteas and inhabited by bontebok, klipspringer and numerous birds. Altogether different is the small village of **Elim**, founded as a Moravian Mission in 1824 and now consisting of several

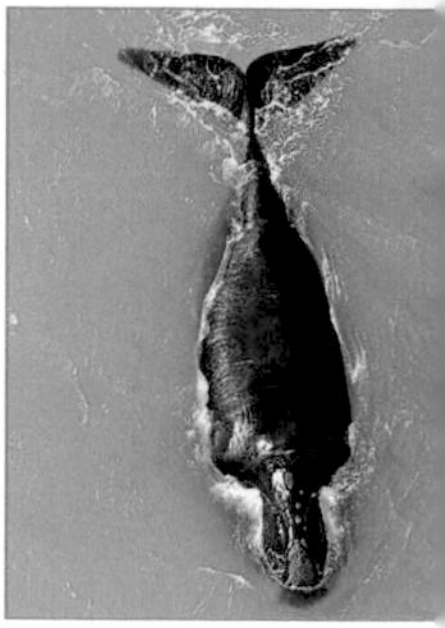

ABOVE: a southern right whale comes up for air.
BELOW: kayaking in the Kogelberg Biosphere Reserve.

ABOVE: sand dunes in De Hoop Nature Reserve. **BELOW:** mountain zebra.

picturesque, albeit increasingly run-down, whitewashed thatched dwellings, as well as a wooden waterwheel dating to 1828.

Just as rewarding is a detour from Bredasdorp to **Arniston** ⓮, named in memory of a ship that ran aground there in 1852, claiming 352 lives. The fishing village, with its thatched, whitewashed 19th-century fishermen's houses, has been declared a National Monument. The village is also sometimes referred to by its pre-1852 name Waenhuiskrans (Wagonhouse Cliff), in reference to a nearby cavern large enough to house several ox-wagons but accessible only at low tide.

De Hoop Nature Reserve ⓯

Address: northeast of Agulhas, www.capenature.co.za
Tel: 028-542 1253
Opening Hrs: daily 7am–6pm
Entrance Fee: charge

Running for some 50km (30 miles) along the coast east of Arniston, this attractive coastal reserve protects the world's largest remaining contiguous area of coastal fynbos. Walking trails range from the two-hour Klipspringer Trail to the 55km (34-mile), five-day Whale Trail. Terrestrial wildlife includes the endemic bontebok and Cape mountain zebra, while the offshore marine reserve forms a breeding ground for an estimated 120 southern right whales between June and November.

Swellendam

Some 60km (37 miles) north of Bredasdorp, you can rejoin the N2 near **Stormsvlei**, from where it's another 12km (8 miles) to **Swellendam** ⓰, the third-oldest town in South Africa (founded 1743). The town's Cape Dutch buildings include the **Town Hall** and a fine period-furnished **Drostdy** (www.drostdymuseum.com; tel: 028-514 1138), the latter built in 1746. An old prison and two other Victorian buildings form part of the same complex. Also of interest, on Voortrek Street, is the magnificent **Dutch Reformed Church,** built in 1911. Just 6km (4 miles) south of Swellendam, the **Bontebok National Park** ⓱ (www.sanparks.org; tel: 028-514 2735; Oct–Apr 7am–7pm, May–Sept 7am–6pm) is home to graceful bontebok, a fynbos-endemic antelope that was hunted to near-extinction in the early part of the 20th century, as well as springbok and the rare Cape mountain zebra.

THE WEST COAST

The Atlantic coastline north of Cape Town is characterised by relatively chilly and rough waters, making it a poor bet for a sedentary beach holiday. However, its combination of unspoilt beaches, sleepy fishing harbours, magnificent spring wild flowers and superb marine birdlife should recommend itself to active travellers seeking relief from the more popular tourist hotspots. The main road servicing this region is the N7, which runs about 50km (31 miles) inland for most of its length, but the more scenic option would be the coastal R27 via **Bloubergstrand** ⓲. The long sandy beach here offers a superb (and much photographed) view of Cape Town with Table Mountain in the background.

Evita se Perron

Address: Darling Station, www.evita.co.za
Tel: 022-492 3930
Opening Hrs: Tue–Sun 10am–4pm, with shows on Fri, Sat and Sun
Entrance Fee: charge

The small town of Darling ⓳, some 50km (31 miles) north of Bloubergstrand, pirouetted from obscurity in 1996 when gay icon Pieter Dirk Uys converted a former railway building into this cabaret theatre and museum. Evita Bezuidenhout is the name of Uys's Dame-Edna-esque alter ego, while "Perron" is an Afrikaans word for a railway platform. Uys's satirical one-man show has not only put Darling (named after Lt-Gen Sir George, not an itinerant "luvvie") on the tourist map, but also forms a worthwhile if rather irreverent introduction to contemporary South African politics.

West Coast National Park ⓴

Address: www.sanparks.org
Tel: 022-772 2144
Opening Hrs: daily 9am–5pm (Postberg section open during flower season only)
Entrance Fee: charge

Situated 20km (12 miles) further north, West Coast National Park protects a 30km (18-mile) stretch of coastline dominated by the

ABOVE: Tannie Evita, Pieter Dirk Uys's most well-known character.
BELOW: Bloubergstrand, with Table Mountain just across the bay.

ABOVE: colourful blooms in Namaqualand, north of Lambert's Bay.
BELOW: the Evita se Perron restaurant in Darling.

Langebaan Lagoon, one of the world's most important conservation areas for migrant marine birds, and home to significant breeding colonies of 10 species of marine bird. Even more impressive as natural phenomena go is the glorious eruption of spring wild flowers in August – the best displays are usually in the Postberg section of Langebaan, which also harbours large mammals such as springbok, bontebok and gemsbok. Langebaan Lagoon flows into **Saldanha Bay**, South Africa's deepest natural harbour, which is of limited interest to tourists since the eponymous town is also an important naval base, industrial centre and railway link.

Towards Lambert's Bay

In contrast to functional Saldanha, characterful **Paternoster**, which lies some 30km (18 miles) further north, is a largely unspoilt fishing village of traditional whitewashed cottages. Famed for its crayfish, which can be sampled at the local restaurants, the town also borders the Columbine Nature Reserve, an attractive peninsula noted for its spring wild flower displays.

Continuing north for 100km (60 miles) will bring you to the lonely fishing port of **Lambert's Bay** ㉑. It has a picturesque harbour, but is best known for **Bird Island** (tel: 027-432 1000; Sept–May daily 7am–7pm, June–Aug 7am–5pm; charge), with a nesting colony of around 14,000 Cape gannets and a few hundred African penguins. They can be viewed from an observation tower linked to the town by a short causeway.

Olifants River Valley and Cederberg

Lying inland from Lambert's Bay, **Vredendal** ㉒ is a small town set in the heart of the Olifants River Valley, an important emergent centre of viticulture. For wine-tasting, the best starting point is the vast **Namaqua Wines** (www.namaquawines.com; tel: 027-213 1080), whose output of almost 10 million cases annually makes it the largest single wine producer in the southern hemisphere – the popular

Gôiya export range is instantly recognisable by the stylised bushman painting that adorns its label.

Further south along the N7, **Clanwilliam** ㉓ is an orchard town that was founded at the beginning of the 18th century. It is the springboard for excursions into the craggy **Cederberg Wilderness Area** (www.cederberg.co.za; tel: 021-659 3500; daily; free), with a 2,000-metre (6,500ft) peak covered with snow during the winter. Several short walks on the lower slopes are particularly suitable for day visitors; one of the most worthwhile leads to a rock face bearing a well-preserved example of rock art *(see page 31)* depicting an elephant herd.

Back down in the Olifants River Valley, the drive along the N7 south of Citrusdal passes through a region known as the Swartland (Black Land) since the earliest days of European settlement, most probably in reference to the renosterbos (rhinoceros bush) that once grew here prolifically and turns black seasonally. Today, it might more accurately be known as the *geel* (yellow) land, since it produces about 15 percent of the national wheat crop.

The Swartland Cellar (www.swwines.co.za; tel: 022-482 1134) on the outskirts of **Malmesbury** ㉔ is the country's third-largest wine co-op, using grapes grown on almost 100 different farms to produce about 30 everyday wines.

If you're heading onward to the Cape Winelands, the R45 south of Malmesbury leads to Paarl after about 50km (24 miles). ❑

TIP

Working in conjunction with the SA Museum, the Travellers Rest, a small farm offering cottage accommodation and food 34km (21 miles) from Clanwilliam on the Wupperthal Road (tel: 027-482 1824; www.travellersrest.co.za), operates tours of 10 San art sites in the Cederberg.

SHOPPING

Huguenot Road, the commercial mainline through Franschhoek, is the top shopping destination in the winelands, dominated by independent specialist stores aimed at a discerning clientele. It's also a good place to buy wine, whether direct from the vineyard or from a specialist store in town.

Clothes

Green Sleeves
2 Crozier St, Stellenbosch.
Tel: 021-883 8374.
Budget-conscious fashionistas adore this hip second-hand clothes shop, which stocks an eclectic range of vintage clothing, specialising in 1960s and 70s retro gear.

Crafts

Oom Samie se Winkel
82–4 Dorp St, Stellenbosch.
Tel: 021-887 0797.
Having turned 100 in 2004, Stellenbosch's oldest and best-known *winkel* (shop) is arguably of greater interest for its time-warped decor than the oddball selection of local craftwork on sale inside.

Galerie Ezakwantu
Village Centre, Huguenot Rd, Franschhoek. Tel: 021-876 2162. www.ezakwantu.com
One of the top galleries of its type in the region, this will delight ethnic arts and crafts enthusiasts with its superb collection of quality artworks from all over Africa – but don't come here expecting a bargain.

Food

Huguenot Fine Chocolate
62 Huguenot Rd, Franschhoek. 021-876 4096.
www.huguenotchocolates.com
Indulge that sweet tooth in good conscience, as this purveyor of delicious handcrafted chocolates is the product of a Black Economic Empowerment scheme in which two local entrepreneurs were trained by Belgian chocolatiers.

Gifts

Touches and Tastes
Huguenot Rd, Franschhoek.
Tel: 021-876 2151. www.lequartier.co.za
Named "Best Shop in any Hotel Anywhere" by Tatler UK in 2005, the selection of brightly coloured handicrafts, jewellery and candles on sale at Le Quartier Francais makes this a fun place to browse.

Wine

Franschhoek Cellar
Main Rd, Franschhoek.
Tel: 021-876 2086.
On the right-hand side of the road as you enter town coming from Stellenbosch, this well-run cellar stocks pretty much every wine produced in the area, and most can be tasted before you buy.

La Cotte Inn
Corner of Main Rd and Louis Botha St, Franschhoek. Tel: 021-876 3775. www.lacotte.co.za
This is the finest cheese shop in the winelands, but even its cheese selection pales next to the extraordinary selection of (mostly South African) wines here. Ask about wine tastings.

BEST RESTAURANTS, BARS AND CAFÉS

The Winelands

Stellenbosch and Surroundings

Terroir
Kleine Zalze Wine Farm, off the R44. Tel: 021-880 8167. www.kleinezalze.co.za Open: L & D Tue–Sat, L Sun. **$$$**
An earthy, reed-roofed farmhouse restaurant, with terracotta floor tiles and crisp white linen tablecloths. Chef Michael Broughton's ever-changing menu celebrates seasonal, locally sourced ingredients, elegantly presented and delicious to eat. A string of awards testifies to its excellent quality.

De Oewer
Aan-de-Wagen Rd. Tel: 021-886 5431. www.volkskombuis.co.za Open: L & D daily. **$$**
Idyllically situated on the willow-lined banks of the Eersterivier. The light, alfresco Mediterranean meals here are accompanied by good local wines.

D'Ouwe Werf
30 Church St. Tel: 021-887 4608, www.ouwewerf.co.za Open: B, L & D daily. **$$**
This atmospheric small restaurant is located in South Africa's oldest inn (founded in 1802). It serves quality Cape and Continental food, with an excellent wine list.

Tokara
Hellshoogte Pass. Tel: 021-808 5959. www.tokara.co.za Open: L & D Tue–Sat. **$$$**
Set in a beautiful space overlooking vineyards and mountains. Quality ingredients, wonderful flavours, and attractive presentation, with the emphasis on fish and game dishes.

Blaauwklippen
Blaauwklippen Wine Estate, R44. Tel: 021-880 0133. www.blaauwklippen.co.za Open: L daily. **$$–$$$**
Upmarket yet informal dining in the winelands. Simple yet modern bistro dining with a German flavour and some South African specials.

Spier Deli
R310 south of Stellenbosch. Tel: 021-809 1100. www.spier.co.za Open: B & L daily. **$**
The family-oriented Spier Wine Estate has a popular deli serving tasty fresh snacks as well as generous picnic hampers to be enjoyed on the lawn overlooking a small lake.

Lady Phillips Restaurant
Vergelegen Estate, off the R44 near Somerset West. Tel: 021-847 1346. www.vergelegen.co.za Open: L daily. **$$–$$$**
Arguably the most beautiful wine estate in the Cape, Vergelegen has a superb restaurant with an adventurous Continental menu, as well as a cosy coffee shop, both annexes of the stately manor house.

Volkskombuis
Aan-de-Wagen Rd. Tel: 021-886 2121. www.volkskombuis.co.za Open: L & D daily. **$$**
An upmarket stable mate of De Oewer, the Volkskombuis – People's Kitchen – serves tasty traditional Cape and Malay dishes in a riverside Victorian Cape Dutch building with a beautiful view towards the mountains.

Wijnhuis Stellenbosch
Corner of Church and Andringa streets. Tel: 021-887 5844. Open: L & D daily. **$$$**
Top-notch Continental cuisine complemented by legendary wine list – connoisseurs can sample up to six different wines over the course of a meal for a sensible set fee. Many of the wines are from the Stellenbosch area.

Franschhoek and Surroundings

Boschendal Restaurant
R310 towards Stellenbosch. Tel: 021-870 4272. Open: L daily. **$$**
Situated on the lovely wine estate of the same name, this fine-dining restaurant offers first-class South African cuisine amid elegant surroundings. A cheaper and equally popular option is to enjoy one of their famous picnic hampers on the shady lawn.

Bread & Wine
Moreson Winery, Happy Valley Rd, La Motte. Tel: 021-876 3692. www.moreson.co.za Open: L daily. **$$**

Bars and Cafés

Stellenbosch has the liveliest nightlife in the winelands, thanks partly to the large student contingent. **De Akker** (corner of Herte and Dorp streets; tel: 021-883 3512) is a legendary old bar with appropriately fading decor, an older clientele, and a sociable atmosphere. **Tollies Pub and Grill** (15 Bird St; tel: 021-886 5497) is younger, livelier, and stays open into the wee hours; it has the best range of draught beer in town, inexpensive cocktails, and live music some weekends.

A favourite with locals in Franschhoek is **Taki's Restaurant and Cigar Bar** (Huguenot Rd; tel: 021-876 4161), which serves excellent and affordable Greek meze in addition to having a relaxed and friendly bar with a decidedly pre-21st-century attitude to smoking.

The aroma of fresh coffee permeates the oak-shaded courtyard at Paarl's **Kostinrichting Coffee Shop** (19 Pastorie Ave; tel: 021-871 1353). Located in a restored Victorian school hostel next to the Paarl Museum, it also offers a range of light meals. For an affordable snack or meal on the beachfront at Hermanus, try **Savannah Café** (25 High St; tel: 028-312 4259), opposite the old railway station.

Idyllically set among the estate's vineyards and orchards, Bread & Wine is a great place to stop for lunch. It has a courtyard and covered terrace, and a Mediterranean-inspired menu features a good range of meat and seafood, home-made sausages and pastas. Freshly prepared dishes are made with top-quality ingredients.

French Connection Bistro
Huguenot Rd. Tel: 021-876 4056. www.frenchconnection.co.za Open: L & D daily. **$$**
Set in the heart of the old town centre, this serves Continental snacks, pastry and coffee at lunch, and a more extravagant dinner menu dominated by French dishes. Steaks are something of a speciality.

La Petite Ferme
North of Franschhoek on the Franschhoek Pass Rd. Tel: 021-876 3016. www.lapetiteferme.co.za Open: L & D Mon–Sat. **$$**
This award-winning restaurant boasts an attractive terrace overlooking the Franschhoek Valley, a great and remarkably reasonably priced wine list, and a menu rooted in the Mediterranean but not afraid to do a spot of globe-trotting.

The Tasting Room
Le Quartier Français, 16 Huguenot St. Tel: 021-876 2151. www.lequartier.co.za Open: L & D daily. **$$$**
A regular on Restaurant Magazine's list of the World's Top 50, the Tasting Room does a set five- or eight-course menu with a degustation option that involves tasting a different wine with every course. The cuisine reflects the influence of the region's original French settlers, but also incorporates many South African elements. It's open for dinner only, but the lunch menu at the same hotel's iCi Bistro is similar in quality.

Prices for a three-course dinner per person with a half-bottle of house wine:
$ = under R200
$$ = R200–350
$$$ = more than R350

Paarl

The Goatshed
Fairview Wine Farm, Suid Agter Paarl. Tel: 021-863 3609. www.fairview.co.za. Open: B & L daily.
A charming, barn-style restaurant with a huge image of a goatherd on the wall. Choose from cheese and meat platters and daily specials, accompanied by carafes of the estate wine. It is one of the best lunching spots in the county, and very family friendly.

Noop Restaurant and Bar
127 Main Rd. Tel: 021-863 3925. www.noop.co.za Open: L Mon–Fri, D Mon–Sat. **$**
This popular eatery has a central location, a relaxed modern ambience, and a varied menu specialising in sushi and other seafood, as well as steaks and pizzas. Something for everyone – and a good inexpensive wine list too.

Tulbagh

Paddagang Restaurant
23 Church St. Tel: 023-230 0242. Open: B & L daily, D Fri–Sat. **$**
Known for its excellent wine list, the Paddagang – literally, and oddly, "Frogmarch" – serves wholesome South African fare in a restored Cape Dutch building.

The Overberg

Hermanus

Seafood at the Marine
The Marine Hotel, Main Drive. www.marine-hermanus.co.za Tel: 028-313 1000. Open: L & D daily. **$$–$$$**
A luxury hotel dining room with a fresh, modern appeal. Its small menu focuses solely on fish and other seafood, and it's superb. Prices are high for Hermanus.

Mogg's Country Cookhouse
Hemel en Aarde Rd. Tel: 028-312 4321. www.moggscookhouse.com Open: L Wed–Sun, D Sat. **$–$$**
At the end of a gravel road you'll receive a warm welcome. Simple farmhouse decor with a rustic menu on a small chalkboard: casseroles, lamb shanks, venison pie and a few desserts.

Agulhas

Agulhas Country Lodge
Main Rd. Tel: 028-435 7650. www.agulhascountrylodge.com Open: B, L & D daily. **$**
The nicest place to eat in Agulhas, this lodge has a restaurant and tearoom serving tasty unpretentious fare indoors or on a terrace with ocean views.

Swellendam

Stormsvlei Restaurant
Swellengrebel St. Tel: 028-261 1167. www.stormsvleifarmstall-restaurant.co.za Open: L Wed–Mon, D Fri–Sat. **$–$$**
Formerly Zanddrif, this farm stall and restaurant is set in a restored 18th-century building next to the Drostdy Museum. It still serves an all-day breakfast and other typical café fare, but it now opens for burgers and steaks two nights a week, and has added a hearty Sunday roast lunch to its repertoire.

The West Coast

Darling

Evita se Perron
Tel: 022-492 3930. Open: L daily, D usually Fri–Sun only. **$–$$**
Light snacks with a traditional Cape touch, dinners are accompanied by the one-man show performed most weekends by the legendary drag artist and sociopolitical satirist Pieter Dirk Uys.

Langebaan

Die Strandloper
Saldanha Rd. Tel: 022-772 2490. www.strandloper.com. L 5–6 days per week (check website for details). **$**
This legendary and very informal West Coast restaurant serves delicious and very filling seafood buffets in the open, on the beach.

Cape Wine

Shunned by international markets during the apartheid era, Cape wine has made great steps forward in subsequent years

Wine production dates back to the very earliest days of European settlement. The first recorded vintage was produced back in 1659 by none other than Jan van Riebeeck, the founder of the Cape Colony. The baton was taken up enthusiastically by his successor Governor Simon van der Stel, who founded the Constantia Estate on the Cape Peninsula in 1685. Constantia soon became known internationally for its sweet "Vin de Constance", a favourite tipple of Jane Austen, Frederick the Great and Napoleon.

Wine production spread to the interior of the Western Cape with the arrival of the first French Huguenots in the late 17th century. Country towns founded during this period, such as Stellenbosch, Franschhoek and Paarl, remain at the heart of South Africa's wine industry to this day, and the region's historic vineyards – the likes of Boschendal, Vergelegen, Nederberg and Meerlust – are still widely regarded to produce the country's finest wines. However, the last two decades has also seen production spread further afield to areas such as the more remote Breede, Olifants and Orange River Valleys, with more than passable results.

South Africa is the world's seventh-largest wine producer (approximately 1,000 million litres annually), while export volumes increased from 120 million litres in 1998 to 410 million in 2008, with the UK being the single largest importer. Hearteningly, increased volumes have done nothing to compromise quality – on the contrary, most wine experts believe that the overall standard of South African wine is higher than ever.

Above: Buitenverwachting (literally *beyond expectations*) is one of the most beautiful estates in the Cape, noted for its fine Cape Dutch architecture and setting below Constantia Mountain.

Left: a Bacchic mural adorns the exterior of a wine shop in Franschhoek.

Below: most estates in the vicinity of Cape Town offer wine tasting – though, unless you intend to make extensive use of the spittoon, an organised tour is a safer bet than self-drive.

ABOVE: for serious buyers, Le Cotte in Franschhoek is one of several specialist wine shops that offer regular tasting sessions involving wines produced by several different estates.

RIGHT: many of the best Cape wines are matured in oak barrels.

STYLES AND GRAPES

Until the 1970s, South Africa's wine-making tradition was strongly influenced by Germanic styles, despite Huguenot roots in the industry. As a result, South Africa was known predominantly as a producer of white wine. This has changed, however, and South African wine makers have been at pains to learn new skills and satisfy the demand for reds created by the recent growth in international markets. By 1998, some 25 percent of wine-yielding vineyards in the Cape were reds, a figure that had increased to 45 percent by 2008.

Cabernet Sauvignon is the most widely planted red in the Cape, and it tends to produce heavy wines that form an ideal complement to steak and other red meats. Shiraz and Merlot are also gaining popularity, while Pinotage is a unique South African cultivar, developed from a cross between Pinot Noir and Cinsaut, producing a fruity, purple wine that tends to be underrated by South Africans, and thus often represents good value.

As for whites, Chenin Blanc and Columbard dominate in terms of area planted, though the latter in particular is mostly used in blends. Chardonnay is traditionally the most popular white amongst dedicated enthusiasts, and also the priciest, though its place is rapidly being supplanted by Sauvignon Blanc, a zesty complement to Cape Town's excellent seafood.

BELOW: this road sign soon becomes a familiar sight on any excursion into the Cape Winelands.

THE GARDEN ROUTE

Wild forests and unspoilt beaches lead past hidden valleys and majestic mountains to the forested shores of Tsitsikamma National Park

Main Attractions

SEAL ISLAND (MOSSEL BAY)
SAFARI OSTRICH FARM
CANGO CAVES
GARDEN ROUTE NATIONAL PARK
KNYSNA
ROBBERG NATURE RESERVE
TSITSIKAMMA NATIONAL PARK

Maps and Listings

MAP OF THE GARDEN ROUTE, PAGES 208–9
RESTAURANTS AND CAFÉS, PAGE 217
ACCOMMODATION, PAGE 233

Lush and bountiful, the relatively short stretch of coastline between Mossel Bay and Tsitsikamma is popularly referred to as the Garden Route, and its timeless appeal both to foreign travellers and to South African holiday-makers is reflected in a booming guesthouse and hotel industry, not to mention the region's ever-escalating property prices. This, however, is a distinctly African garden – no European-style manicured lawns with neat and formal layouts, but an exhilaratingly rugged coastline flanked by indigenous rainforests, blue lagoons, parallel rows of serrated mountain peaks and fields bright with fynbos.

MOSSEL BAY ❶

Coming from Cape Town, the eastbound N2 runs inland through **Swellendam** *(see page 196)* and **Riversdale** to reconnect with the coast after some 400km (240 miles) at **Mossel Bay**. Generally regarded as the beginning of the Garden Route, Mossel Bay also has the distinction of being the place where Portuguese navigator Bartolomeu Dias dropped anchor in 1488, becoming the first European to set foot on South African soil. From that time onwards, passing ships often stopped at Mossel Bay for water and to trade with the local Hottentots, but it would be another 300 years before a permanent settlement was founded there.

Today, Mossel Bay is a popular holiday resort, thanks to its many beaches and calm swimming pools between rocks. It has also become a sprawling industrial centre since the discovery of oil and natural gas off the coast. As a result, it has sacrificed something of its charm to industrial

PRECEDING PAGES: the spectacular Outeniqua Choo Tjoe railway.
LEFT: Knysna Heads.

development, though it still offers some of the most alluring marine activities in the region, full details of which can be obtained from the tourist office next to the old post office.

Most popular, and relatively inexpensive, is a boat excursion to nearby **Seal Island** (www.mosselbay.co.za; tel: 044-690 3101; hourly departures 9pm–5am), where hundreds of Cape fur seals can be seen basking on the rocks and foraging in the surrounding waters. Rather more daunting (and not just financially) are the caged shark dives arranged by Shark Africa (www.whitesharkafrica.com; tel: 044-691 3796) to view predatory great whites in their natural habitat. More conventional dives can be arranged too, as can kayaking expeditions.

Bartolomeu Dias Museum Complex

Address: 1 Market Street, www.diasmuseum.co.za
Tel: 044-691 1067
Opening Hrs: Mon–Fri 9am–4.45pm, Sat and Sun 9am–3.45pm
Entrance Fee: charge

Housed inside a converted granary, this waterfront museum complex is dedicated to the memory of Bartolomeu Dias, the first European known to sail round the tip of South Africa, and its most memorable exhibit is a full-scale replica of his surprisingly small caravel. Other displays are dedicated to sea shells and local maritime history, and it also the site of the renowned Post Office Tree, a giant milkwood on which the Portuguese sailor Pedro d'Ataidea hung an old boot containing a letter in 1500. A year later, another sailor found the letter and was kind enough to forward it. The tradition continued as the tree became a message board for passing sailors. If you post your mail in the boot-shaped letterbox provided (with a suitable stamp), the "oldest post office in South Africa" will process them promptly.

GEORGE ❷

Leaving Mossel Bay, the scenery grows increasingly wild as the N2 continues east towards the former lumber village of **George**, founded in 1811 at the base of the Outeniqua Mountains and described a few decades later by Anthony Trollope as "the prettiest village on the face of the earth". A few kilometres inland, George today is anything but a village – indeed, its population of 210,000 is twice that of any other town on the Garden Route – and few would regard it as especially pretty. On the plus side, George does offer a good range of

TIP

For thrill seekers, the Bloukrans Bridge, 215 metres (710ft) above the Storms River, is the site of the world's highest bungee jump. At the other end of the Garden Route, 35km (22 miles) from Mossel Bay, the Gourits Bridge bungee jump is also popular with adrenaline junkies. Both jumps are run by Face Adrenalin. For more information call 044-697 7001 (Gourits) or 042-281 1458 (Bloukrans) or visit www.faceadrenalin.com.

LEFT: Bartolomeu Dias Museum Complex.
BELOW: catamarans, Mossel Bay.

ABOVE: the George Museum, housed in the Old Drosdty.

tourist facilities at lower prices than you'll find elsewhere in this popular area, and it's well placed as a base for numerous day trips along the Garden Route or into the Little Karoo.

Within George's historic town centre stand several fine buildings. These include the **Dutch Reformed Moederkerk** with its magnificent carved stinkwood pulpit, and the elegant **Public Library** (1840) – although the latter's books have sadly all been moved to Cape Town. Outside the library is the mighty **Slave Tree**, one of the broadest oak trees in the southern hemisphere, beneath which a slave market was once held.

A popular excursion from George is the **Outeniqua Choo Tjoe** (www.outeniquachootjoe.co.za; tel: 044-801 8288), a steam locomotive from 1928 that used to follow a narrow-gauge railway all the way to Knysna but now only runs as far as Mossel Bay, as a result of irreparable storm damage to the track further east. The Outeniqua Mountains to the north of George offer some excellent hiking possibilities, while motorists can explore the fynbos- and forest-covered slopes along a road loop via the sensational Outeniqua and Montagu passes to Oudtshoorn.

George Museum

Address: Courtenay Street
Tel: 044-873 5343
Opening Hrs: Mon–Fri 9am–4pm
Entrance Fee: charge

Touching on a dark chapter of South African history, this modest museum has an exhibition devoted to the presidency of P. W. Botha, the last of the hard-line apartheid leaders, who retired to this part of the country in 1989 and lived there until his death in 2006. It is housed in the Old Drosdty, which was built in 1811, rebuilt after fire damage in 1826, and served as a hotel from 1890 until 1972, when it was bought by the municipality and converted into a museum.

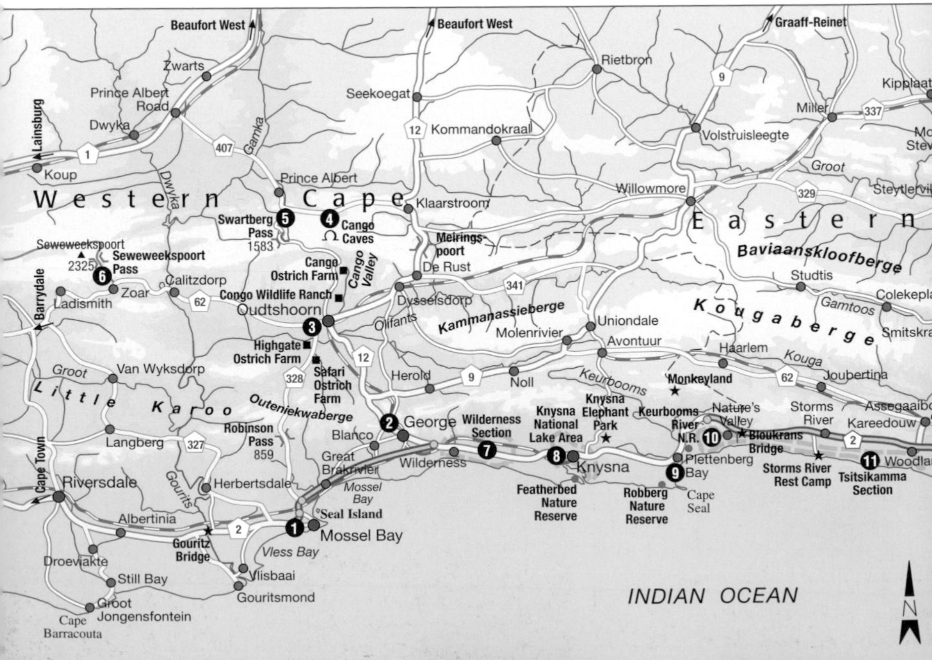

Oudtshoorn and around

Situated roughly 60km (36 miles) north of George, **Oudtshoorn** ❸ is an increasingly popular day or overnight trip out of the Garden Route proper. It is the principal town of the Little Karoo, a rather arid region whose name derives from a Khoi word for dry. It can get blisteringly hot in summer, but it also has an austere beauty that comes in many guises – the serenity of far horizons, a black eagle soaring above a silent plain, a cool breeze after a stifling day, or just a donkey-cart crunching slowly along an old farm road.

Oudtshoorn was once a celebrated ostrich-feather centre. Between 1880 and 1910 Jewish traders from eastern Europe came here, set up ostrich farms and made a small fortune exporting the feathers to fashion-conscious Europe. The trade brought vast riches – 1kg (2lb) of feathers could fetch up to R200. All this revenue pouring into what had hitherto been nothing more than a remote hamlet helped build a number of "feather palaces", several of which have survived the decline in the market.

Today, the ostrich industry still thrives, but the feathers are used more for dusters than millinery, and it's the skins that are sought after in the world of high fashion. Ostrich skins for expensive shoes, handbags and purses now command prices comparable to the highly prized skins of baby crocodiles. Farms where the ostriches are bred form the lynchpin of an increasingly lucrative tourist industry. Why Oudtshoorn? Ostriches are happiest in a hot, dry climate, like a type of alfalfa that grows here, and find here some of their favourite dietary supplements – sand, stones and insects.

ABOVE: Oudtshoorn residence. **BELOW:** ostrich in Oudtshoorn.

EAT

If you visit an ostrich farm at lunchtime, try dining on an ostrich steak – the red meat, with a fat content of 3g per 100g, is more than three times leaner than beef, and about half as lean as turkey or chicken.

Most visitors approach Oudtshoorn via the N12 from George, either returning the way they came, or using the R328 to Mossel Bay via the 859-metre (2,818ft) **Robinson Pass**, or the rougher **Montagu Pass** to the east. Coming to or from Cape Town, however, a rewarding alternative is to travel between Swellendam and Oudtshoorn on the R324 through Tradouw Pass to **Barrydale**, then follow the R62 through fertile valleys and pretty orchard villages such as Ladysmith and Calitzdorp.

C. P. Nel Museum

Address: Baron van Rheede Street, www.cpnelmuseum.co.za
Tel: 044-272 7306
Opening Hrs: Mon–Fri 8am–5pm, Sat 9am–1pm
Entrance Fee: charge

Set in a Victorian building in the heart of the town centre, this diverting museum has many displays covering the history of the ostrich boom. The admission fee includes entrance to the **Le Roux Townhouse**, on the corner of Loop and High streets, a former "feather palace", complete with period fittings and furnishings.

Safari Ostrich Farm

Address: On the Mossel Bay Road, on the outskirts of town, www.safariostrich.co.za
Tel: 044-272 7311
Opening Hrs: daily 8am–5pm
Entrance Fee: charge

The most rewarding of several ostrich farms open to the public, this is notable for its fine old homestead, built with teak from Burma, Belgian roof tiles and marble floors. Here you can

RIGHT: C. P. Nel Museum. **BELOW:** breathtaking scenery along the Garden Route.

try riding on the back of the world's largest bird, or watch jockeys take part in a mock Ostrich Derby. Similar entertainment is offered at other ostrich farms, such as **Highgate** (www.highgate.co.za; tel: 044-272 7115) and **Cango** (www.cangoostrich.co.za; tel: 044-272 4623).

Cango Wildlife Ranch

Address: about 2km (1¼ miles) from the town centre along the R328, www.cango.co.za
Tel: 044-272 5593
Opening Hrs: daily 9am–5pm
Entrance Fee: charge

Established in the 1980s to breed endangered wildlife, this ranch might come across as a zoo – albeit a very good one – offering the opportunity to hold hand-reared cheetahs and to see a variety of indigenous and exotic animals, including white Bengal tigers, white lions, pumas, jaguars and meerkats. But it is also one of the world's most productive breeding centres for cheetah, and other creatures that have bred successfully here include serval, aardwolf, African wild dog and pygmy hippo (the latter a West African rainforest species). There's a snake park, curio shop and restaurant attached.

Cango Caves 4

Address: 32km (20 miles) from Oudtshoorn on the R328, www.cango-caves.co.za
Tel: 044-272 7410
Opening Hrs: daily 9am–4pm, guided tours hourly
Entrance Fee: charge

Part of a massive cave system that extends into the Swartberg Mountains north of Oudtshoorn, Cango once sheltered San bushmen, whose paintings *(see page 90)* were found on the walls. It is a fascinating place to visit, and a guided tour into three of the biggest caves passes some amazing subterranean rock formations. At the end of the main tour, you can either turn back or else continue on a more adventurous route that involves squeezing through narrow, hot, damp and stifling shafts where the seat of your trousers will get as much wear as your shoes.

ABOVE: stalactites in the Cango Caves.
BELOW: Southern Black Koorhaan, endemic to the Western Cape.

LITTLE KAROO

Past the Cango Caves, the R328 continues towards the whitewashed village of **Prince Albert** over one of the most beautiful of all the mountain passes in South Africa – the 1,436-metre (4,700ft) **Swartberg Pass** 5. Built between 1881 and 1888 and now a National Monument, the gravel road climbs 1,000 metres (3,281ft) in 12km (7 miles) over the mighty Swartberg Range, with very sharp, blind hairpin bends. The views are magnificent, but not for those who suffer from vertigo.

If that's not challenging enough, you could take an alternative route via the **Seweweekspoort Pass** 6, across the mountains, or by the

ABOVE: relaxing on the beach.

main road (the R29) through Meiringspoort. First opened in 1857, this pass crosses the Groot River some 30 times along its 17km (11-mile) length, snaking through bare walls of vertical rock which at times stretch hundreds of metres high. Twisted bands of red sandstone and milky quartz loom above the road, their yellow-lichened crags glowing in the sun. Check the status of the road before you set out to drive through the gorge, though – it's often closed after heavy rains.

National Parks and Nature Reserves

Heading east from George, the railway and the N2 both pass through **Wilderness**, a bustling little resort town fringed on one side by a magnificent 8km (5-mile) sandy beach and on the other by the Wilderness Section of the Garden Route National Park. Shortly before the N2 enters Wilderness, it offers a superb view over a photogenic riverine gorge spanned by a disused railway bridge (part of the line once used by the Outeniqua Choo Tjoe). Immediately after this, you can pull up at a viewpoint from where dolphins are regularly observed playing in the surf below.

TIP

Wheelchair access in the Wilderness Section of the Garden Route National Park is limited. The Wilderness Rest Camp *(see page 233)* has one accessible chalet and one accessible forest hut. Most of the boardwalk along the Touws River is wheelchair-friendly, although the access ramps are intimidating. The bird hide at Rondevlei is harder to reach (the pathway is a mixture of sandy soil and thick grass).

Garden Route National Park (Wilderness Section) 7

Address: 2km (1 mile) from the N2 through Wilderness, www.sanparks.org
Tel: 044-877 0046
Opening Hrs: daily 8am–5pm
Entrance Fee: charge

Formerly Wilderness National Park, this beautiful area was amalgamated with nearby Tsitsikamma in 2009 to form the Garden Route National Park. Bordering the small town of Wilderness, it protects a series of freshwater pans – the largest are Swartvlei, Langvlei, Groenvlei and Rondevlei – connected by various tributaries of the Touws River, which empties into the ocean in the town. The combination of open waterways, reed beds and marshes provides a rich source of food and varied habitats for a wide array of birdlife, as

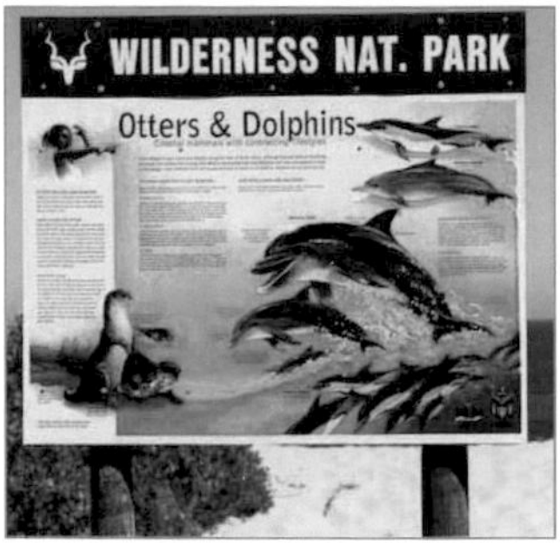

does the surrounding bush and forest. Most attractive of all are the large wading birds that scour the shallows for food. Pink flamingos drift across the shimmering water, straining the surface for tiny algae and crustaceans, and African spoonbills rake the mud with their broad, flat beaks. Of the 95 water bird species recorded in South Africa, 75 have been seen bobbing about on the lakes here.

Understandably popular with birdwatchers, the Wilderness Section also offers some great rambling opportunities in the form of a network of non-strenuous day trails, each of which is named for one of the park's six kingfisher species. The Half-Collared Kingfisher Trail is a good one to begin with, an 8km (5-mile) circuit that leads through riparian woodland fringing the Touws River to an attractive waterfall that tumbles over a group of gigantic round boulders. Forest birds such as the beautiful Knysna loerie and yellow-throated warbler are likely to be seen here, and bushbuck and duiker are present too. A similar route can be followed on the water by renting a canoe from the main rest camp and paddling gently upstream to the base of the falls.

Knysna 8

A short distance east of Wilderness lies the busiest resort on the Garden Route: **Knysna**, founded at the beginning of the 19th century by George Rex, who was rumoured to be an illegitimate son of King George III. Wooded hills, dotted with holiday homes, surround pretty **Knysna Lagoon**, connected to the ocean by a single narrow waterway. The mouth of this canal is flanked by two huge sandstone cliffs known as **The Heads**, which ensured that Knysna never became a harbour town. Access by sea was simply too dangerous. The eastern cliff is the only one open to cars (along George Rex Drive), and the view from the top is fantastic.

A good place for crafts, such as pottery and woven fabrics, is **Thesen House**, a historic town house named after one of Knysna's oldest and most influential families. The area is chiefly known for natural wood products, especially hardwood furniture. The best-quality products are made by hand by master craftsmen, using yellowwood, dark stinkwood and ironwood judiciously culled from the surrounding forests. Another popular photo opportunity – albeit a rather surreal one for Africa – is the **Holy Trinity Church** in the leafy settlement of Belvedere, looking much

EAT

Don't leave Knysna without sampling the product of the legendary Mitchell's Brewery (Arend Street; www.mitchellsknysnabrewery.com; tel: 044-382 4685), one of the few private breweries in South Africa, for the sumptuous oysters that are farmed in the lagoon and served fresh at various dockside restaurants. Tours Mon–Fri 10.30am and 3pm; tastings Mon–Fri 8.30am–4.30pm, Sat 9.30am–12.30pm,

LEFT: information board in the Wilderness Section. **BELOW:** coastline near Knysna.

like an 11th-century Norman implant. By contrast, May sees Knysna hosting a five-day gay, lesbian, transsexual and transgender carnival, the **Pink Loerie Mardi Gras** (www.pinkloerie.com), the only one of its kind on the African continent.

Like Mossel Bay, Knysna is a popular base for marine and other activities, including scuba diving, sailing, hiking, mountain biking, canoeing, whale and dolphin safaris, and abseiling down the Knysna Heads. The excellent **tourist office** (Main Road; tel: 044-382 5510; www.visitknysna.co.za) can provide details of costs and booking contacts. There are also some great overnight hikes through the surrounding hills, details of which can be obtained from the Department of Forestry office on Main Road. **Thesen Town Island**, a short drive from Knysna waterfront, is a new upmarket holiday and retirement complex, built in Cape-Cod style on the lagoon. The island features good restaurants, delis, boutiques and lots of boating activity.

ABOVE: Featherbed Nature Reserve.
BELOW: windsurfing in Plettenberg Bay.

Featherbed Nature Reserve

Address: Featherbed Ferry Terminus Building, Knysna
Tel: 044-382 1693/7, www.featherbed.co.za
Opening Hrs: one 4-hour excursion departs daily
Entrance Fee: charge

Sitting on the western cliff of the formation known as The Heads, this private reserve can only be reached by joining a ferry excursion across the lagoon mouth from the eastern cliff. Protecting a mosaic of terrestrial and marine habitats, it is home to the shy blue duiker, various birds and the endangered Knysna sea horse.

Plettenberg Bay 9

South Africa's most upmarket seaside resort, **Plettenberg Bay** lacks the charm of Knysna, 32km (20 miles) to its west, but its perfectly rounded Baia Formosa (Beautiful Bay), with its golden beaches, has long been a favourite. Sadly, the hideous multi-storey Beacon Isle Hotel now dominates Plettenberg Bay's beachfront from its rocky promontory. A better option for those who like their beaches relatively unspoilt is the lengthy **Keurboomstrand**, 10 minutes' drive east near the Keurbooms River mouth. It also forms a good base for visits to several nature reserves and more contrived wildlife sanctuaries, as described below. During the Christmas holiday, "Plett" is extremely popular, but out of season it can be surprisingly quiet.

Robberg Nature Reserve

Address: 9km (5 miles) south of Plettenberg Bay, www.capenature.org.za
Tel: 044-533 2125
Opening Hrs: Feb–Nov daily 7am–5pm; Dec and Jan 7am–8pm
Entrance Fee: charge

A bracing day hike leads through this spectacular reserve on the Robberg ("seal mountain") Peninsula, whose dramatic cliffs rise almost vertically from the choppy blue sea, interspersed with several small sandy coves. The full circuit covers an undulating 11km (7 miles), but shorter variations are available. The peninsula is home to an impressive colony of Cape fur seals – along with marine birds such as the African black oystercatcher. Look out, too, for the whales and dolphins that pass by seasonally.

Keurbooms River Nature Reserve

Address: along the N2 about 7km (4 miles) east of Plettenberg Bay, www.capenature.org.za
Tel: 044-802 5300
Opening Hrs: daily 8am–6pm
Entrance Fee: charge

A contrasting scenic gem is this small reserve protecting the wide tranquil Keurbooms River and its lushly forested banks. Ferry cruises run along the river several times daily, and it's also possible to follow a hiking trail into the spectacular wooded gorge. But for those who have the time and the energy, there is no better way to explore this reserve than to take one of the canoe trips that overnight at a rustic riverside hut deep in the forested gorge. The tourist office in Plettenberg Bay has all the details.

Knysna Elephant Park

Address: about 10km (6 miles) west of Plettenberg Bay on the Knysna Road, www.knysnaelephantpark.co.za
Tel: 044-532 7732
Opening Hrs: daily 8.30am–4.30pm
Entrance Fee: charge

This rather zoo-like setup does not – as might be expected – protect the few survivors of the wild herds that once roamed these coastal forests, but instead offers the opportunity to touch and feed a few semi-domesticated tuskers relocated from elsewhere in the country.

Monkeyland

Address: 16km (10 miles) east of Plettenberg Bay, before the turn-off to Nature's Valley, www.monkeyland.co.za
Tel: 044-534 8906
Opening Hrs: daily 8am–5pm; guided tours hourly
Entrance Fee: charge

As contrived as Knysna Elephant Park, but great fun all the same, is this private primate sanctuary, which hosts about 200 monkeys of a dozen species, ranging from the South American spider monkey to various Madagascan lemurs, all of them rescued from domestic captivity. A visit can be combined with one to the neighbouring **Birds of Eden**, where a 1km (½-mile) walkway and suspension bridge leads through a huge free-flight aviary.

ABOVE AND BELOW: get up close to the elephants at Knysna Elephant Park.

ABOVE: Plettenberg Bay.

Garden Route National Park (Tsitsikamma Section)

Address: immediately south of the N2, between Nature's Valley and Storms River, www.sanparks.org
Tel: 044-302 5600
Opening Hrs: daily 7am–7pm
Entrance Fee: charge

From Plettenberg Bay you can take either the fairly straight N2 toll road through forests and across the high coastal plain, or the byway (the R102) winding down past the Grootrivier and Bloukrans gorges and through **Nature's Valley** ❿ on the western boundary of what was formerly Tsitsikamma National Park, but became part of the Garden Route National Park in 2009. Nature's Valley is a tiny forested village overlooking an isolated beach that remains practically undeveloped for tourism – there are few more attractive places to pitch a tent than at the magical National Park campsite on the edge of town.

Taking the back road is a rewarding experience, sinking deep into the forest's cool microclimate. Beneath giant yellowwoods, the shaded floor is thick with proteas, arum lilies and watsonia; vividly coloured loerie birds dart through the dense forest canopy, while shy duiker and bushbuck hide in the undergrowth. Back on the N2, the concrete bridges over the Storms, Groot and Bloukrans rivers were once the biggest such structures in the world.

Either option – the N2 or the R102 – will bring you to the turn-off to **Storms River Mouth**, with its forests and unspoilt, rocky shore, its log cabins and suspension bridge at the eastern border of the Tsitsikamma Section. Stretching 35km (20 miles) between Nature's Valley and Storms River, this scenic park protects coastal lagoons, dunes, cliffs, beaches and coral reefs, with an interior of steep ravines, thickly clothed with ancient yellowwoods up to 50 metres (164ft) high.

The well-run **Storms River Rest Camp**, 1.5km (1 mile) west of the river mouth, has chalet lodgings and campsites, and forms a good base for swimming, snorkelling and hiking. The short walk from the rest camp to the bridge across the river mouth is a must (look out for seals below the bridge), and you can ascend from here to a viewpoint on the surrounding cliffs. ❑

Hiking Tsitsikamma

The Tsitsikamma Section ⓫ of the Garden Route National Park is legendary in South African hiking circles as the location of the Otter Trail, which follows the coast all the way from Storms River Camp to Nature's Valley, a distance of 26km (14 miles) as the crow flies and 41km (25 miles) on foot. It is one of the country's oldest and most challenging hikes, and one of the most scenic in the world, encompassing some wild coastal scenery and crossing 11 rivers – sometimes you will need to swim rather than just wade.

Though not especially notable for wildlife, the Cape clawless otter is often seen along the way, as are marine, forest and fynbos birds, notably the endemic Knysna loerie and African black oystercatcher. The hike takes five days (sleeping in huts along the way). Only 12 people are allowed to start daily, and because it is so popular it should be booked as far in advance as possible (www.sanparks.org). For those who don't have the time to spare, a justifiably popular day hike effectively follows what would be the first day of the Otter Trail, running for about 4km (2½ miles) east along the rocky coast from Storms River Camp to a small waterfall.

BEST RESTAURANTS AND CAFÉS

Restaurants

Mossel Bay

Café Gannet
Church St. Tel: 044-691 1885. Open: L & D daily. **$$**
Part of the Bartolomeu Dias Museum Complex, this popular café is known for its excellent and good-value seafood, all delivered fresh from the harbour daily.

Bahia dos Vaqueiros
Diaz Strand Hotel, Beach Boulevard. Tel: 044-692 8400. www.diazbeach.co.za Open: B & D daily. **$$**
Great for its views and sounds of the ocean. An interesting menu, with unusual combinations like ostrich *bobotie* spring rolls with fruit chutney and mint sauce. Popular gourmet food and wine evenings.

Rose and Vine
5 Amy Searle St, Great Brak River. Tel: 044-442 3590. Open: L & D daily. **$–$$**
In a 19th-century cottage, just five minutes from the N2 between Mossel Bay and George, this friendly family-run restaurant specialises in country cooking, light lunches and cakes.

George

La Laconda
124a York St. Tel: 044-874 7803. www.lalocanda.co.za Open L Mon–Fri & D Mon–Sat. **$**
Possibly the finest Italian along the Garden Route, this central restaurant has acquired a great reputation for thin pizzas and home made pasta, and the meat and seafood dishes are pretty good too, as is the wine list.

Prices for a three-course dinner per person with a half-bottle of house wine:
$ = under R200
$$ = R200–350
$$$ = more than R350

Oudtshoorn

Jemima's
94 Baron von Rheede St. Tel: 044-272 0808. www.jemimas.com Open: L Mon–Fri & D daily. **$$**
Robust, generous portions of Karoo fare, including a selection of ostrich dishes. A focus on seasonal ingredients with a fun, modern twist. A broad wine list matches the flavourful food you'll enjoy.

Knysna

34° South
Knysna Quays, Waterfront Drive. Tel: 044-382 7331. www.34-south.com Open: B, L & D daily. **$**
Pleasantly laid-back and very popular with visitors. Sit out on the deck and order platters of oysters, sardines, freshly grilled line fish, seafood paella or Mediterranean-style meze. Good wine selection too.

JJ's Restaurant
Knysna Waterfront. Tel: 044-382 3359. www.jjsrestaurant.co.za Open: D daily. **$$**
This relaxed and likeable restaurant is arguably the leading light on Knysna's waterfront, has hands-on management, a great quayside location, and an equally good seafood and venison menu, with a varied wine list to go with it.

Plettenberg Bay

Sand at the Plettenberg
The Plettenberg Hotel, 40 Church St. Tel: 044-533 2030. www.plettenberg.com B, L & D daily. **$$$**
Set in one of the most prestigious hotels on the Garden Route, Sand offers a great à la carte selection of contemporary South African and seafood dishes, though the (costly) speciality is the gourmand set menu, with a different wine accompanying every course.

Lookout Deck
Lookout Beach. Tel: 044-533 1379. www.lookout.co.za Open: L & D daily. **$–$$**
This superb beachfront restaurant offers great sea views, and there is a good chance of spotting dolphins frolicking in the waves while you dine. Specialities include seafood and prime steak matured on the premises, accompanied by a wide selection of wines.

Cafés

For the best freshly baked breads and pastries on the Garden Route, head to **Ile de Pain Bread and Café** in Knysna (10 The Boatshed, Thesen Harbour Town; tel: 044-302 5707; www.theboatshed.co.za). Locals sip coffee and munch on croissants, quiches and sandwiches layered with local cheeses, meats and home made relishes. A memorable location on the waterfront makes the **East Head Café** (Knysna Heads; tel: 044-384 0933; www.eastheadcafe.co.za) a great spot for a relaxed and inexpensive breakfast or a lunchtime sandwich accompanied by crisp white wine. On Market Square, **Mugg and Bean** (tel: 044-533 1486) has a great sandwich and snack menu and plenty of tempting cakes and pastries. A good breakfast spot, it also stays open until late.

RIGHT: dining al fresco.

INSIGHT GUIDES TRAVEL TIPS
CAPE TOWN

Transport

Getting There 220
By Air 220
By Rail 220
By Bus 220
By Car 221
By Sea 221
Getting Around 221
From the Airport 221
Orientation 221
By Bus 222
By Car 222
By Train 222
By Taxi 222
Cycling 222
Motorbike Hire 222

Accommodation

Choosing a Hotel 223
House and Apartment Rentals 223
Townships 224
City Centre and the City Bowl 224
Victoria & Alfred Waterfront 226
Southern Suburbs 228
Atlantic Seaboard 229
False Bay 230
Further Afield 231
Garden Route 233

Activities

Festivals 234
The Arts 235
Ballet/Dance 235
Cinemas 235
Opera and Concerts 235
Theatres 236
Nightlife 237
Casinos 237
Live Music Venues 237
Nightclubs 238
Sightseeing Tours 239
Bicycle Tours 239
Boat Tours 239
Bus Tours 240
Helicopter Tours 240
Walking Tours 240
Sports 240
Participant Sports 240
Spectator Sports 240
Children's Activities 241

A – Z

Admission Charges 242
Budgeting for Your Trip 242
Children 243
Climate 243
Crime and Safety 243
Customs Regulations 244
Disabled Travellers 244
Electricity 244
Embassies/Consulates 244
Emergencies 245
Gay and Lesbian 244
Health and Medical Care 245
Internet 246
Lost Property 246
Media 246
Money 246
Opening Hours 247
Postal Services 247
Public Holidays 247
Religious Services 247
Student Travellers 247
Tax 248
Telephones 248
Time Zone 248
Toilets 248
Tour Operators 248
Tourist Information 249
Visas and Passports 249
What to Bring 249
Women Travellers 249

Language

History and Biography 250
Culture 250
Fiction 250
Natural History 250
Food and Wine 250
Special Interest 250
Other Insight Guides 250

TRANSPORT

GETTING THERE AND GETTING AROUND

GETTING THERE

By Air

Cape Town International Airport is operated by the **Airports Company of South Africa** (ACSA, tel: 086-727 7888; www.acsa.co.za). It is located 22km (15½ miles) east of Cape Town along the N2 highway, and it takes between 15 and 20 minutes to reach the city centre from the airport outside rush hours. These are 7–9am and 4–6pm, and during these hours your journey time will increase to around 30–45 minutes (bear this in mind when returning to catch a flight).

From UK, US and Europe

International airlines that fly to Cape Town include:
South African Airways, tel: 021-936 1111, www.flysaa.com
British Airways, tel: 021-936 9000, www.britishairways.com
Singapore Airlines, tel: 021-674 0601, www.singaporeair.com
KLM Royal Airlines, tel: 086-024 7747, www.klm.com
Lufthansa, tel: 086-184 2538, www.lufthansa.com
Virgin Atlantic, tel: 011-340 3400, www.virgin-atlantic.com
Emirates, tel: 021-403 1111, www.emirates.com

Internal

There are daily flights to Cape Town from Durban, Johannesburg, Bloemfontein and Port Elizabeth. Tickets can cost anything from R600 to R2,500 for a return ticket to Johannesburg. One from Kulula, 1 Time or Mango will usually be the cheapest option and it is worth shopping around on their user-friendly websites, which also allow you to combine the flight with good accommodation and car rental deals. Domestic airlines flying into Cape Town include:
South African Airways, tel: 021-936 1111, www.flysaa.com
BA/Comair, tel: 021-921 0111, www.comair.co.za
Kulula, tel: 086-158 5852, www.kulula.com
1time, tel: 086-134 5345, www.1time.aero
Mango, tel: 086-116 2646, www.flymango.com

By Rail

The state-owned long-distance rail passenger operator, **Spoornet's Shosholoza Meyl**, offers a daily Trans-Karoo service linking Cape Town to Johannesburg and Pretoria, and the weekly Trans-Oranje from Cape Town to Bloemfontein, Pietermaritzburg and Durban. For bookings and timetables, tel: 083-123 2010 or visit www.shosholozameyl.co.za, which also has online booking facilities.

For extreme luxury there is the privately owned **Rovos Rail** (tel: 021-421 4020; www.rovos.com). Its beautifully restored trains consist of four royal suites and 32 de luxe suites, accommodating a maximum of 72 passengers, and its variety of routes includes a two-day trip between Cape Town and Pretoria, and a 24-hour journey between Cape Town and George.

Another alternative is the famous **Blue Train** (tel: 021-449 2672/2991; www.bluetrain.co.za), with its swish sleeper compartments. It offers two scheduled routes: Cape Town to Pretoria or vice versa (one day, one night) and Cape Town to Port Elizabeth (the Garden Route), taking one day and two nights.

By Bus

Luxury coaches linking major cities across South Africa every day are run by **Greyhound** (tel: 083-915 9000; www.greyhound. co.za), **Translux** (tel: 0861-589 282; www.translux.co.za) or **Intercape Mainliner** (tel: 0861-287 287; www.intercape.co.za). The trip from Cape Town to Johannesburg is about 1,400km (870 miles), and takes about 18 hours by bus. Expect to pay between R300–500 depending on the carrier you use.

The **Baz Bus** (tel: 021-439

2323; www.bazbus.co.za) runs less frequently from Cape Town to Johannesburg via KwaZulu–Natal and the uKhukhlamba-Drakensburg. It's popular among backpackers and younger travellers who want the hop-on/hop-off option of getting around the country. Tickets cost about R3,400 (one way from Cape Town to Johannesburg) – and you can get on and off as much as you like along the route.

By Car

Roads in and around the Western Cape are good and well signposted. Vehicles of all types can be rented from major car companies such as **Avis** (tel: 086-1021 111; www.avis.co.za), **Budget** (tel: 086-102 6622; www.budget.co.za), **Hertz** (tel: 021-935 4800; www.hertz.co.za) and **Europcar** (tel: 086-113 1000; www.europcar.co.za). To hire a car you will require an international driving licence or, for UK citizens, an EU-style photo-card licence (not the old-style green paper licence). Car-rental desks can be found inside the International and Domestic Arrival terminals at the airport.

Driving conditions

The roads in the Cape area are excellent. In South Africa you drive on the left-hand side of the road. Speed limits are generally 60–80km/h (35–50 mph) in towns and up to 120km/h (75 mph) on national highways. Each province operates independently in terms of law enforcement, and some are stricter than others when it comes to speed limits, parking limitations and so on. Always beware of speed traps (and pedestrians) as you approach country towns and big housing developments alongside the highways.

The journey between Johannesburg and Cape Town takes about 15 hours via Bloemfontein through the Karoo. For those who want to take it at a more leisurely pace, it is best to make a one-night stopover at a bed-and-breakfast in Colesburg or Beaufort West.

ABOVE: Cape Town's railway station.

If you are following the Garden Route from Port Elizabeth to Cape Town your journey should take about eight hours, with a quick meal break, but no sightseeing.

By Sea

RMS *St Helena* (tel: 021-425 1165 or (UK) 020-7575 6480; www.rms-st-helena.com) carries up to 128 passengers on Portland (UK) to Cape Town route, via Tenerife, Ascension Island and St Helena, though it usually only sails from the UK once or twice annually. A number of cruise companies offer Cape Town as a port of call, including Crystal Cruises, Princess Cruises and Silversea Cruises.

GETTING AROUND

From the Airport

There is no rail or bus service from Cape Town International Airport, so you will either need to take a taxi or one of the shuttle buses. Licensed taxis are easy to locate at the airport, and display regulated charges on a meter.

The other way of getting into town is to use one of the shared shuttle services. These include **Magic Bus** (tel: 021-505 6300; www.magicbus.co.za), **Citi Hopper** (tel: 021-386 0077; www.citihopper.co.za) and **Way 2 Go** (tel: 021-638 0300; www.way2gotransfers.co.za). They will drop you outside your hotel. Tickets can be bought in the arrivals hall.

Orientation

Cape Town has a layout defined by the dramatic topography of the Cape Peninsula. The city centre runs uphill from Table Bay towards Table Mountain. At its heart is a neat grid of roads that forms the oldest and most business-oriented part of the city, centred upon the Company's Garden originally founded by Jan van Riebeeck. The V&A Waterfront lies at the northern end of the city centre, while the upper slopes to the south are more residential.

West of this, a striking pair of formations called Lion's Head and Signal Hill separates the city centre from the built-up seafront suburbs running southwest from Green Point to Camps Bay, via Sea Point and Clifton. Meanwhile, to the southeast of the city centre, a series of increasingly upscale residential suburbs, such as Kirstenbosch and Newlands, follows the eastern slopes of Table Mountain. More remote from the city centre, the central spine of the Cape Peninsula divides Atlantic Seaboard settlements such as Hout Bay and Kommetjie from their Indian Ocean counterparts like Muizenberg and Simon's Town.

Walking is the easiest way to get around the city centre by daylight, though taxis are also easy to find and might be safer at night. A new Integrated Rapid Transit (IRT) system is under development and due to open in 2011.

By Bus

The city bus service is fairly basic, but if you don't have your own transport and don't want the continual expense of taking taxis, buses can be useful. **Golden Arrow** (tel: 0800-656463; www.gabs.co.za) runs services within the city as well as around the Peninsula. You can pick up a timetable at their terminus in Strand Street.

By Car

Although the city centre is best explored on foot, to get the most out of the Cape Peninsula you will need to rent a car. The driver must be at least 25 years old and have a valid driver's licence (an international licence is not necessary). If you are planning to rent in Cape Town, shop around, as some rental companies offer deals and special rates for foreign tourists.

Parking is always a problem, so ensure that your hotel has guarded parking places and check the cost. When parking on the street look out for official, uniformed parking attendants whom you pay per hour (you'll also find unofficial parking guards looking for money). The City of Cape Town is very strict about cars parked illegally, and tows them away to the local pound; retrieving them costs a small fortune in towing fees and fines. for a parking ticket. *See also Driving conditions, page 221.*

By Train

Metrorail (tel: 080-065 6463; www.capemetrorail.co.za) is another transport option, especially for getting down to Kalk Bay and Simon's town on the False Bay Coast, but it has been associated with unreliable schedules and crime issues in the past. That said, most commuters use the train every day to and from Cape Town, and trains are jam-packed at peak hours during the week. If you do take the train, always travel in the first-class coach (Metroplus) – a third-class ticket costs less but you're more at risk of being mugged or pick-pocketed, especially at off-peak times when security is less tight. The railway station is at the junction of Adderley and Strand streets.

By Taxi

Sedan taxis

These can be hired by telephone or at designated taxi ranks, but cannot be hailed on the street. They are more expensive than the minibus taxis *(see below)*, and it is best to ask the driver for a quote before getting in. Your hotel concierge or guesthouse owner will be able to recommend a reliable taxi service. If you're stuck, **Rikki's Intercity** (tel: 086-174 5547; www.rikkis.co.za) operates in the city centre and V&A Waterfront area.

Minibus taxis

The legendary minibus taxi is South Africa's trademark method of transport. However, the vehicles are often overcrowded and their drivers have a reputation for driving recklessly. That said, they transport thousands of people to and from the surrounding townships and from Cape Town to the Southern Suburbs, and cost very little. Simply flag one down in the street, or go to a designated taxi rank in Adderley Street, or the upper deck of the Cape Town railway station. Take care if you are travelling alone, especially if you are a woman, and make sure you know exactly where you are going. Don't carry any valuables.

Cycling

For those fit enough to cycle around the Cape Peninsula, **Daytrippers** (tel: 021-511 4766; www.daytrippers.co.za) offers half-day tours on mountain bikes or extended tours around the Cape. **Downhill Adventures** (tel: 021-422 0388; www.downhilladventures.com) also offers mountain bike rentals and tours through the Cape Point Nature Reserve, Constantia Winelands, Tokai Forest and Table Mountain.

Motorbike Hire

For a ride on a BMW motorbike or Honda 100cc scooter, **Moto Berlin** (tel: 021-421 0396; www.motoberlin.co.za) is a reliable company that rents out bikes on a daily, weekly and monthly basis.

Below: the world famous Table Mountain cablecar.

ACCOMMODATION

SOME THINGS TO CONSIDER BEFORE YOU BOOK THE ROOM

Choosing a Hotel

Cape Town has a wide range of accommodation, which includes luxury hotels, smaller boutique hotels that have all the frills of the larger establishments, comfortable B&Bs and guesthouses, self-catering apartment and villa rentals, as well as youth hostels for the young at heart. Whether you are looking for a hip hang-out or a snug home-from-home with sea views, you won't be disappointed. Cape Town has also become known for its excellent standards of service in all areas of accommodation.

In Cape Town, hotels range from new and funky to old and traditional, with style, charm and pizzazz. Most of the big luxury hotels are centrally located in the City Bowl, on the V&A Waterfront and along the Atlantic Seaboard, and are relatively pricey. However, a number of smaller boutique hotels, often with no more than 20 rooms, have sprung up over the last few years in the City Bowl and Southern Suburbs such as Bishopscourt and Constantia. They offer everything you would expect from a larger-chain hotel, but are often better priced and a little bit more intimate. Of course, the location is important, too. If you want the the best cosmopolitan experience, close to a wide range of restaurants and all the popular beaches, find a place in the City Bowl or along the Atlantic Seaboard. For a more tranquil environment, where you can take it easy in leafy, more homely surroundings, head for the Southern Suburbs, on the other side of Table Mountain but still only a 20-minute drive to the city (depending on traffic).

Some of the guesthouses can be quite luxurious, too, and there are plenty of less expensive B&Bs for total informality, plus basic backpacker retreats. For greater freedom and your own front door, there are some excellent villa and apartment rentals, which are also ideal if you plan to stay in the city for an extended period of more than three weeks.

Always negotiate prices, especially in low season when there's greater availability. At any time of year, though, published rates are never cast in stone, so it's worth shopping around.

Low season is, of course, over the winter months, from early May to mid-September. High season can occupy the whole of the remaining months, when the weather is generally good, but the peak season is from mid-December to the end of January. If you plan to visit at this time, make reservations well in advance, as hotels fill up quickly with both local and international guests. You'll be most likely to get the best peak-season rates by booking early – though, conversely, many chain hotels offer bargain rates to walk-in clients and last-minute internet bookings when occupancies are low.

Rates given in the listings provide an indication of the price of a double room. However, some smaller establishments (like B&Bs and youth hostels) have a per-person rate (based on two people sharing a room); single travellers will usually be charged a supplement.

House and Apartment Rentals

If you're looking for a place of your own for a long or short

INFORMATION

The following websites are worth checking for a range of accommodation, from luxury hotels to self-catering apartments and villas, in and around Cape Town:
www.sa-venues.com
www.portfoliocollection.com
www.bookabed.co.za
www.cape-venues.co.za
www.wheretostay.co.za
www.capestay.co.za

rental, there is no shortage of agencies and private companies in Cape Town that will organise anything from luxury, seafront villas that are serviced daily to small, economical bachelor lofts in the city centre.

Village and Life (tel: 021-438 4444; www.villageandlife.co.za) rents out holiday accommodation across the city, including Waterfront, Camps Bay, Mouille Point and De Waterkant. They have more than 80 properties that range from luxurious beachside villas on Camps Bay to small garden studios in De Waterkant.

Icon Villas and Vistas (tel: 021-424 0905; www.icape.co.za) offers private and luxurious self-catering luxury accommodation, from city penthouses to small cottages, available on a daily, weekly or monthly basis.

Townships

For a truly African experience, try to spend at least one night at a township B&B in Langa or Khayelitsha, where you'll enjoy warm and modest lodging with welcoming hosts. Enter the township either with an arranged transfer, or a recognised tour operator or guide.

At **Malebo's B&B** (tel: 021-361 2391; www.malebos-bed-and-breakfast.com) in Khayelitsha, host Lydia Masoleng offers comfortable beds and a traditional African breakfast with the family in the morning. Double rooms from R500.

Established in 1998, **Vicky's B&B** (tel: 082-225 2986; www.vickysbedandbreakfast.com) is the oldest B&B in Khayelitsha, run by the affable Vicky, a hard working mother of three, and winner of two local awards for hospitality in 2009. From R250 per person per night.

For a traditional African buffet with local dishes and beer, eat at **Eziko Cooking School**, where trainee chefs destined for some of the leading hotels and guesthouses in Cape Town have the opportunity to show off their skills. For further information and bookings, tel: 021-694 0434 or visit www.ezikorestaurant.com.

ACCOMMODATION LISTINGS

CITY CENTRE AND THE CITY BOWL

Luxury

Mount Nelson Hotel
76 Orange St, Gardens
Tel: 021-483 1000
www.mountnelson.co.za
1 p255, E3
Traditionally one of the "Big Five" luxury hotels in Cape Town, and still the grande dame of Cape Town's historic hotels. Illustrious past visitors include Sir Winston Churchill and Lady Colefax. Luxury, opulence, world-class service and out-of-this-world food make this a favourite among celebrities, world leaders and royalty. Recently renovated suites are a modern take on 1950s glamour. Enjoy a pre-dinner drink at the Planet Champagne Bar and Lounge, where hip and well-heeled Capetonians spend their Friday and Saturday evenings.

Expensive

Alta Bay
12 Invermark Crescent, Higgovale
Tel: 021-487 8800
www.altabay.com
2 p259, E2
This six-bedroom guesthouse (sleeps 12) is a real find. On the slopes of Table Mountain in the leafy suburb of Higgovale, its designer-chic ambience blends contemporary style with comfort, and the classic modern furniture is in neutral, warm colours. This is a place that's both smart and relaxing, with a lovely pool area and a first-floor terrace. Available on an exclusive basis for longer stays.

Cape Milner
2A Milner Rd, Tamboerskloof
Tel: 021-426 1101
www.capemilner.com
3 p255, E3
Situated in Tamboerskloof, between Table Mountain and the City Bowl, this hotel offers a peaceful, Zen-inspired setting with contemporary furnishings, impressive views and tranquil surroundings. There's a swimming pool, restaurant and outside bar.

Four Rosmead
4 Rosmead Ave, Oranjezicht
Tel: 021-480 3810
www.fourrosmead.com
4 p259, E1
This boutique guesthouse, built in 1903, has been stylishly renovated to its former glory. It's a Cape contemporary classic with a rich history. Accommodation includes

a suite, as well as four deluxe and three luxury en-suite bedrooms that exude a sophisticated African feel. Upstairs bedrooms have views across the city, Table Mountain and Lion's Head, whilst the rooms downstairs lead onto a quiet landscaped garden. Spend the day lounging around the pool, or enjoy one of many spa treatments on offer.

Westin Grand Cape Town Arabella Quays
1 Lower Long St, Convention Sq

Tel: 021-412 9999
www.starwoodhotels.com
5 p256, B1
Opposite the Cape Town International Convention Centre with views of the V&A Waterfront and Table Mountain, the former Arabella Sheraton is an ultra-cool glass-and-granite structure and conforms to the luxury and style of the worldwide brand. At the end of the day, cool down at the spa or swim in the heated pool.

ABOVE: the stylish interior of the Cape Milner boutique hotel.

Moderate

Abbey Manor
3 Montrose Ave, Oranjezicht
Tel: 021-462 2935
www.abbey.co.za
6 p259, E2
Set against the slopes of Table Mountain in the City Bowl suburb of Oranjezicht, this five-star luxury guesthouse was once the home of an early-20th-century shipping magnate. It has lovely views across the city, and each spacious en-suite room has been individually decorated in rich, textured fabrics and with a mix of contemporary and traditional furnishings. Rooms are air-conditioned, and have a minibar and free access to wireless internet (laptops are available for hire). There's a large heated swimming pool in a landscaped garden, as well as a spa bath on the upper terrace.

The Cape Cadogan
5 Upper Unions St, Gardens
Tel: 021-480 8080
www.morehotels.co.za
7 p255, E3
Close to vibey Kloof Street, with its selection of restaurants, decor boutiques, cinemas and café society, this 12-room hotel has an equally bohemian yet contemporary feel. It occupies a stately two-storey Georgian and Victorian building that has left its farmhouse origins far behind, and provides many comforts and luxuries that you would expect of a bigger hotel.

Cape Heritage Hotel
90 Bree St, City Centre
Tel: 021-424 4646
www.capeheritage.co.za
8 p256, A2
This hotel is centrally located in Cape Town's Heritage Square, an 18th-century courtyard that's alive with bars, restaurants and boutiques. It's small, but the 15 spacious rooms all feature high ceilings, hardwood floors and stylishly individual decor. The range of services includes free internet access and valet parking, and the hotel is convenient for all the major sights and entertainments.

Cape Riviera Guest House
31 Belvedere Ave, Oranjezicht
Tel: 021-461 8535
www.caperiviera.co.za
9 p259, E1
Ideally located in the City Bowl, this period home set at the foot of Table Mountain is perfect for a one-night stay, or it can be rented out as a whole guest house. It comes with everything from internet connection to reliable baby-sitting services. Decor is modern, with dark wood veneers and clean, simple lines, and luxurious accessories include goose-down duvets and faux-fur throws. Generous breakfasts are served. There's a comfortable lounge, well-stocked reading room and a 9-metre (30ft) swimming pool.

Cape Town Hollow Boutique Hotel
88 Queen Victoria St, Gardens
Tel: 021-423 1260
www.capetownhollow.co.za
10 p256, A3
Despite its quiet location opposite the Company's Garden, this small and well-run hotel is ideally located for museum enthusiasts or those who want to be close to the lively nightlife scene associated with Long Street. The rooms are very comfortable at the price, and several have views of the gardens to the mountains.

Derwent House Boutique Hotel
14 Derwent Rd, Tamboerskloof
Tel: 021-422 2763
www.derwenthouse.co.za
11 p255, E4
Combining classical elegance with contemporary African decor, this owner-managed ten-room hotel wins the affections of all who stay there, thanks to the excellent service, relaxed ambience, top-notch facilities, overall attention to detail, and convenient location within walking distance

PRICE CATEGORIES

Price categories are based on the summer (high season) rate for the cheapest double room. This usually includes breakfast and typically drops by 25–50 percent in winter.
Luxury = over R3,000
Expensive = R2,000–3,000
Moderate = R1,000–2,000
Budget = under R1,000

of dozens of restaurants. The rates are very competitive for this level of quality.

The Grand Daddy
38 Long St, City Centre
Tel: 021-424 7247
www.granddaddy.co.za
12 p256, B2
Formerly the Metropole, this upmarket relative of nearby Daddy Longlegs is the latest, hippest and most flamboyant addition to Long Street. Set inside an Old Victorian building, the upbeat interiors of the standard rooms are where Manhattan-glam meets sassy Afro-chic, while the six units in the Airstream Penthouse Trailer Park are the last word in tongue-in-cheek kitsch. Daddy Cool is where you'll find a funky crowd chilling amidst the self-styled "blingest" decor in the country. The ground-floor café serves breakfasts and ready-to-go, lighter deli-style meals and buffet lunches.

The Village Lodge
49 Napier St, De Waterkant
Tel: 021-421 1106
www.thevillagelodge.co.za
13 p253, D4
Comprises a 15-bedroom boutique hotel, private villa and several self-catering townhouses in trendy De Waterkant Village, close to shops, bistros, restaurants and more. All the rooms are simply decorated and come with internet access, telephone, air conditioning and safes. The rooftop swimming pool at the main lodge is a great feature, with panoramic views across the harbour and city, and the SOHO restaurant serves Thai-style meals at lunch and dinner, plus a hearty English-style breakfast to start your day.

Budget

Ashanti Gardens Lodge
11 Hof St, Gardens
Tel: 021-423 8721
www.ashanti.co.za
14 p255, E4
You won't be roughing it at Ashanti – they offer a laundry service, internet facilities, travel consultants and a vibrant bar and restaurant. Rates are a little higher than other backpackers' in the area, but you're getting small home comforts you wouldn't normally find at this end of the market.

Daddy Long Legs Art Hotel
134 Long St, City Centre
Tel: 021-422 3074
www.daddylonglegs.co.za
15 p256, A2
An arty, boutique hotel for backpackers, with a difference. Each of the 13 rooms has been individually decorated by a Cape Town artist. Well priced and central to all the hotspots, restaurants and tourist attractions in the mother city. Also has self-catering apartments at 263 Long Street (tel: 021-424 1403).

Long Street Backpackers'
209 Long St, City Centre
Tel: 021-423 0615
www.longstreetbackpackers.co.za
16 p256, A2
This small, modern hotel offers cheap and cheerful lodging for the young adventurous spirit on a tight budget. It's central and close to all the happening hotspots on Long Street. Private rooms or small bunk-bed dormitories; also has kitchen, lounges, video and cable TV, pool room, and courtyard with BBQ. Tours organised.

VICTORIA & ALFRED WATERFRONT

Luxury

Cape Grace Hotel
West Quay Rd
Tel: 021-410 7100
www.capegrace.com
17 p253, E3
As a member of the Leading Small Hotels of the World, the Cape Grace combines world-class service and standards with an understated elegance and charm enhanced by extensive refurbishment in 2009. The hotel's 122 rooms and suites are all luxuriously furnished and well supplied with the usual treats to pamper their guests. Surrounded by water, with views of the harbour and Table Mountain, it includes a spa that incorporates various facets of African traditional healing. Have a drink downstairs at the Bascule whisky bar and wine cellar, followed by a gourmet meal at the Signal restaurant.

Radisson Waterfront
Beach Rd, Granger Bay
Tel: 021-441 3000
www.radissonblu.com
18 p253, D2
Sipping a gin and tonic at the water's edge at the Radisson's own marina in Granger Bay, right next door to the V&A Waterfont, is rather like being on a cruise liner. It's comfortable, stylishly decorated and has plenty of modern amenities, including a rim-flow swimming pool and wireless internet access.

The Table Bay
Quay 6
Tel: 021-406 5000
www.suninternational.com
19 p253, E2
This luxurious chain hotel is perfect for those who want big service, big views and big rooms. The services on offer range from a personal butler to a fully equipped state-of-the-art gym. Little wonder that it attracts so many international celebrities.

Take time out in the Camelot Spa after a day's sightseeing followed by a sumptuous meal at the Atlantic Grill.

Expensive

Victoria & Alfred Hotel
Corner of Dock and Alfred roads
Tel: 021-419 6677
www.vahotel.co.za
20 p253, E3

Located at the heart of the Waterfront Complex, the V&A Hotel is a welcoming and comfortable place in a lovely setting. Views extend across the marina and its yachts to Table Mountain. The hotel has 94 spacious, air-conditioned en-suite bedrooms, and a wide selection of restaurants including the hotel's own brasserie-style eatery, the Waterfront Café downstairs.

ABOVE: the Cape Grace Hotel on the V&A Waterfront.

Moderate

City Lodge Waterfront
Corner of Dock and Alfred roads
Tel: 021-419 9450
www.citylodge.co.za
21 p253, E4
Revamped and refurbished, this 204-room hotel now has a fitness room, an internet café and a jacuzzi-pool for guests. It's in a central location, and though there's nothing special about the decor, it's a clean and comfortable place, and is well priced, with outstanding rates often offered at the last minute.

La Splendida
121 Beach Rd, Mouille Point
Tel: 021-439 5119
www.lasplendida.co.za
22 p252, B2
Situated on the Mouille Point beachfront promenade opposite the Mouille Point Lighthouse, this small hotel is ideally placed between Sea Point and the V&A Waterfront (with the best views of sunrise and sunset in town) and it offers a winning combination of boutique-style character and affordable rates. Interiors feature a pleasing blend of Art Deco and African style, with lovely warm tones. Rooms and suites are comfortable and spacious, each with a fridge, bar and safe, and there's a luxurious two-storey penthouse with two balconies. The attached Café Splendida, which serves Italian food, is buzzing in the evening.

Budget

Braeside Bed and Breakfast
15 Braeside Rd, Green Point
Tel: 021-439 7909
www.braesidebnb.co.za
23 p252, C3
Conveniently situated on a quiet road in Green Point, this is set in neighbouring houses that were built for the harbourmasters of Cape Town in 1870 and 1903 and retain period features such as high pressed ceilings and Oregon pine floors. The large and comfortable bedrooms have private bathrooms, TV and tea tray, and some even have a fireplace – great for off-season visits. When it's fine you can breakfast on the patio. Easy access to the V&A Waterfront, city and Sea Point.

Breakwater Lodge
Portswood Rd
Tel: 021-406 1911
www.breakwaterlodge.co.za
24 p253, D3
Those who wouldn't relish spending time in a prison should think again. This distinctive hotel, the cheapest option bordering the V&A Waterfront, is a restored and converted 19th-century prison building that now offers good, friendly service and great value for money, especially if you take advantage of the last-minute rates sometimes offered on their website. The decor and furnishings are fairly standard modern-hotel-style, and the light, airy rooms couldn't be less cell-like, with en-suite bathrooms, TV and some good views. There are some suites, too, plus a pleasant restaurant and a bar with a terrace.

Romney Lodge
10 Romney Rd, Green Point
Tel: 021-434 4851
www.romneylodge.co.za
25 p252, C3
There's a relaxed and comfortable atmosphere at this pleasant place in the heart of Green Point, conveniently within walking distance of the V&A Waterfront, restaurants and Cape Town's vibrant nightlife. Formerly Launic House, it has ethnic decor with a colonial twist, and all rooms have a television and a safe. Breakfast is served on the terrace.

PRICE CATEGORIES

Price categories are based on the summer (high season) rate for the cheapest double room. This usually includes breakfast and typically drops by 25–50 percent in winter.
Luxury = over R3,000
Expensive = R2,000–3,000
Moderate = R1,000–2,000
Budget = under R1,000

Southern Suburbs

Luxury

The Bishops' Court
18 Hillwood Ave, Bishopscourt
Tel: 021-797 6561
www.thebishopscourt.com
An exclusive residence with jaw-dropping views of Table Mountain and rates to match. If the beach is not your thing, this is a perfect location to stay. Each of the five luxury suites features king-size beds, huge marble bathrooms and private sitting areas that are separate from the bedroom. For recreation there's a rim-flow swimming pool and tennis court. A full English breakfast is served every morning.

The Cellars-Hohenort
93 Brommersvlei Rd, Constantia
Tel: 021-794 2137
www.cellars-hohenort.com
A Cape colonial building, quietly tucked away in Constantia, the Cellars-Hohenort is a charming and stylish hotel set in lush gardens bordering Kirstenbosch Botanical Garden, with fantastic mountain views. Enjoy the excellent menu at the Green House or Cape Malay restaurant, looking out to the gardens through enormous plate-glass windows.

The Constantia
Spaanschemat River Rd, Constantia
Tel: 021-794 6561
www.theconstantia.com
Spacious, well-appointed rooms are a feature of sister hotel to the Bishop's Court set in the heart of Constantia's winelands. Here you can enjoy country-style accommodation with all the frills, from air conditioning to heated towel rails and a full English breakfast (and rates include both breakfast and drinks). It's just a short drive to local shopping centres and beaches.

Expensive

Andros Boutique Hotel
Corner Phyllis and Newlands rds, Claremont
Tel: 021-797 9777
www.andros.co.za
Situated in an elegant 100-year-old Cape Dutch homestead designed by Sir Herbert Baker, this sedate hotel comprises 12 rooms (four in the old manor house) and one suite set in leafy gardens around a swimming pool. The rather isolated location makes this unsuitable for travellers without a vehicle, but otherwise it's a perfect retreat for those seeking suburban peace and quiet.

The Vineyard Hotel and Spa
Colinton Rd, Off Protea Rd, Newlands
Tel: 021-657 4500
www.vineyard.co.za
A wide variety of rooms and suites is available at this 207-unit hotel, many with river or mountain views. Some suites feature a modern, Zen style of decor that contrasts with the more traditional rooms within the main building. Other rooms are arranged around a Japanese-style courtyard, and Mountain rooms are named for their impressive views. Interiors are understated, with natural stone tiles, muted fabrics and mahogany wood furnishings. Wall-length sliding doors front each ground-floor unit, with a sunny outdoor terrace. An added bonus is that you're only steps away from the superb Myoga Restaurant or a mind-blowing, authentic Thai massage available at the Angsana Spa next door.

Moderate

Constantia Valley Lodge
18 Wycombe Ave, Upper Constantia
Tel: 021-794 6061
www.constantiavalleylodge.co.za
A lovely, colonial-style B&B lodge set in leafy grounds in a secure part of the Constantia Valley close to wine estates and golf courses. Light, airy, spacious rooms offer every comfort for the business and leisure traveller. It also has an honesty bar, self-catering options and conference facilities.

Medindi Manor
4 Thicket Rd, Rosebank
Tel: 021-686 3563
www.medindi.co.za
This renovated Victorian home is well suited to both business travellers and holiday makers who want easy access to the Cape's main attractions. It offers a relaxed and informal setting filled with a collection of Cape antiques and three inviting fireplaces. The seven rooms have bar fridges, and there's a pool if you fancy a dip on a warm summer's day. Bathrooms are kitted out with Victorian tubs.

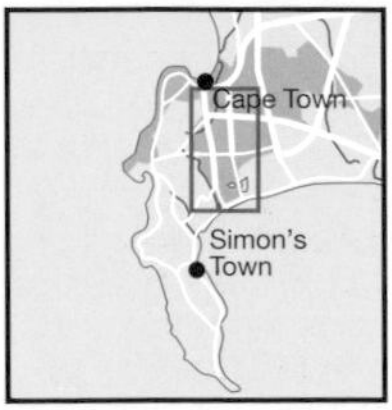

Budget

The Green Elephant
57 Milton Rd, Observatory
Tel: 021-448 6359
www.capestay.co.za/greenelephant
Set in Cape Town's lively Observatory area that's popular with students, and near the city centre, this backpackers' lodge has lots of luxuries, including a heated swimming pool and hot tub, internet and email access and four-poster beds, yet it's really well priced, with some cheaper beds available in dorms. Run by a backpacker, it's a very sociable place, complete with pet dog.

Paradiso Guesthouse
6 Purcell Way, Kreupelbosch, Constantia
Tel: 021-715 8701
In a tranquil garden setting with views of the Constantiaberg Mountains, this B&B has spacious rooms, two of which offer a self-catering option. All have satellite TV, fridges and tea trays.

Atlantic Seaboard (Bantry Bay, Camps Bay, Clifton, Hout Bay, Kommetjie)

Luxury

The Bay Hotel
69 Victoria Rd, Camps Bay
Tel: 021-430 4444
www.thebayhotel.co.za
26 p258, A4
This Miami-style hotel is on Cape Town's prime strip of beachfront in Camps Bay. Decor is cool, crisp and minimalist, but there's nothing minimal about the amenities, which include a hair salon, boutique shops, and restaurants. The Sandy B Cocktail Bar is great for sundowners overlooking the beach on a hot summer's evening.

O on Kloof
92 Kloof Rd, Bantry Bay
Tel: 021-439 2081
www.oonkloof.co.za
27 p254, B3
Situated in a quiet spot in the sheltered Bantry Bay, with views across to Lion's Head, this trendy boutique hotel is nevertheless convenient for the beach and local shops. The winner of several awards, it has large rooms with comfortable beds, huge bathrooms, high-tech modern finishes and wireless internet access. 24-hour security and parking are available and there is an indoor swimming pool.

Twelve Apostles Hotel and Spa
Victoria Rd, Oudekraal, Camps Bay
Tel: 021-437 9000
www.12apostleshotel.com
Gold-listed as one of *Condé Nast Traveler's "Best Places to Stay in the World" for 2010*, this elegantly laid-back hotel is set between mountain and sea on the Atlantic coast and has a variety of chic sea-view rooms. The spa offers indulgent body-and-health treatments inside a cave-like space, with flotation tanks and steam rooms. South African food is served at the Azure restaurant, overlooking the ocean, and the service is friendly.

Expensive

Atlantic House
20 St Filians Rd, Camps Bay
Tel: 021-437 8120
www.atlantichouse.co.za
28 p258, B4
A luxury hideout in Camps Bay offering wonderful sea views and exceptional service for its modest size. Within the modern-contemporary interior, comfortable en-suite bedrooms are well equipped. The heated pool has underwater music.

Atlantic View
31 Francolin Rd, Camps Bay
Tel: 021-438 2254
(London reservations: 020-7620 2600)
www.atlanticviewcapetown.com
A contemporary villa set high above Camps Bay, with spectacular views of the Atlantic Ocean. Luxurious suites have queen- or king-sized beds, fine cotton linen, bar fridges, high-speed internet and TV. For the active there's a gym, or you can arrange for a relaxing massage. There are beaches and restaurants very close by. Rates include breakfast, aperitifs and hors d'oeuvre. No smoking.

Bali Bay Apartments
113 Victoria Rd, Bantry Bay
Tel: 021-438 1893
www.balibay.com
Set against the Twelve Apostles Mountains along the Atlantic coast, Bali Bay is a luxury retreat offering a studio with kitchenette (perfect for the business traveller), a spacious apartment that sleeps six people, and a penthouse with its own private pool deck. All accommodation offers fully equipped kitchens, underfloor heating, air conditioning in the main bedrooms, satellite TV, music systems and telephones. Sliding doors open out onto small balconies right above the sea. Shops and restaurants are within walking distance. Accommodation is serviced daily.

The Long Beach
1 Kirsten Ave, Kommetjie
Tel: 021-783 6561
www.thelongbeach.com
In the quaint fishing village of Kommetjie on an 8-km (5-mile) stretch of white beach with turquoise waters, you'll feel a million miles from city life, which makes this the perfect getaway. Accommodation is available on an individual daily room basis or as an entire beach villa to share with family and friends. There are five stylishly appointed suites, all with sea

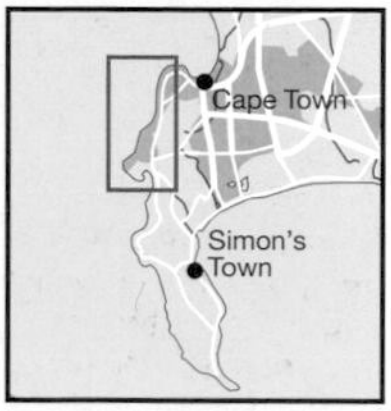

views, and each room includes a safe, satellite TV, air conditioning, heated towel rails, and underfloor heating during the cooler months.

Winchester Mansions Hotel
Beach Rd, Sea Point
Tel: 021-434 2351
www.winchester.co.za
29 p252, A3
This is a stylish and elegant hotel right on the Sea Point promenade, with a colonnaded courtyard and 76 rooms and suites that combine traditional decor with ultra-modern facilities. The personal attention to detail is exemplary, and a good range of treatments is offered at the adjoining Gingko

Price Categories

Price categories are based on the summer (high season) rate for the cheapest double room. This usually includes breakfast and typically drops by 25–50 percent in winter.
Luxury = over R3,000
Expensive = R2,000–3,000
Moderate = R1,000–2,000
Budget = under R1,000

Above: the Twelve Apostles overlooking Camps Bay.

Spa. A huge bonus is that this hotel is only minutes away from the V&A Waterfront.

Moderate

Hout Bay Manor
Main Rd, Hout Bay
Tel: 021-790 0116
www.houtbaymanor.co.za
Built in 1871, this hotel is one of many national monuments in Hout Bay. Recently extensively refurbished and updated with a more modern feel, where all the rooms are individually decorated and now offer affordable luxury with all the mod-cons, as well as gourmet food and deluxe amenities, including massage treatments. The hotel is only 20 minutes from the city and waterfront, with beaches and restaurants a short stroll away.

Peninsula All Suites Hotel
313 Beach Rd, Sea Point
Tel: 021-430 7777
www.peninsula.co.za
Situated on the city's Platinum Mile, this large, modern hotel comprises 110 large, luxurious, sea-facing rooms and suites (mini, studio and luxury), some with two bedrooms and all with self-catering facilities, making it especially well suited to family parties seeking central accommodation. Its newly refurbished Sunset restaurant offers a wide range of international and Cape Malay cuisine.

Budget

Hout Bay Hideaway
Skaife St, Hout Bay
Tel: 021-790 8040
www.houtbay-hideaway.com
Blissfully secluded and exclusive, in gorgeous gardens, only a few minutes from the beach and the village. Its suites and apartments are all tastefully furnished; spacious bedrooms with extra large beds and an eclectic mix of furniture, antique and modern. Has ADSL internet connection, sundecks, barbecue area and a solar-heated saltwater swimming pool.

The Lavender Lodge
Corner of Ave Fresnaye and Ave De Longueville, Fresnaye
Tel: 021-439 8328
www.lavenderlodge.co.za
This is a very friendly and hospitable place, offering comfortable Provençal-style rooms that all have private patios. Each room has a fridge, satellite TV, tea tray and fan, and the bathrooms have heated towel rails for added comfort during the chilly months. Lavish buffet breakfast spreads are served every morning.

The Villa Rosa
277 High Level Rd, Sea Point
Tel: 021-434 2768
www.villa-rosa.com
At the foot of Lion's Head, this is a restored Victorian mansion, with friendly service and delicious breakfasts. Comfortable rooms, with phone, TV, ceiling fans and safe, and it's close to shops, restaurants and beaches.

False Bay (Muizenberg, Kalk Bay, Simon's Town)

Expensive

Colona Castle
1 Verwood St, Off Boyes Drive, Lakeside
Tel: 021-788 8235
www.colonacastle.co.za
Located between Sandvlei Lake and Muizenberg, on sheltered False Bay, this Tuscan-style villa built in the 1920s is lavishly furnished with antiques and paintings. The eight suites are kitted out with satellite TV, heated towel rails, minibar and safe. Delicious gourmet breakfasts and dinners are served on the patio when the weather permits.

Moderate

The Inn at Castle Hill
37 Gatesville Rd, Kalk Bay
Tel: 021-788 2554
www.castlehill.co.za
This inn occupies a restored Edwardian villa overlooking the pretty little fishing village of Kalk Bay. Rooms are clean and comfortable, and the inn is close to some fabulous antiques shops and restaurants on the Kalk Bay strip.

Simon's Town Quayside Hotel
Off Jubilee Sq, St George's St, Simon's Town
Tel: 021-786 3838
www.relaishotels.com
If you don't mind the slightly dated nautical decor, you can wake up to the sound of the sea in one of this good-value hotel's comfortable rooms overlooking the harbour. There are

some great restaurants within walking distance. Check the website for last-minute specials pushing it into the budget range.

Whale View Manor
402 Main Rd, Murdock Valley,

Simon's Town
Tel: 021-786 3291
www.whaleviewmanor.co.za
On the Main Road in Simon's Town, overlooking a secluded beach, Whale View Manor is authentically decorated with a colourful mix of Asian and African fabrics, sculptures and accessories. Six rooms have sea views, while the other four look towards the mountains. Leisurely breakfasts are served in the dining room, from where you can watch whales and penguins splash about in the bay.

Budget

Cape Point Cottages
59 Cape Point Rd, Castle Rock, Simon's Town
Tel: 021-786 3891
www.capepointcottages.co.za
Only five minutes from the Cape of Good Hope sector of Table Mountain National Park, the two isolated cottages here can be taken as a self-catering or bed-and-breakfast basis. It's a perfect spot for nature-lovers.

Clovelly Lodge
40 Montrose Ave, Clovelly, Fish Hoek
Tel: 021-782 3000
www.clovellylodge.com
Bordering the Cape Peninsula National Park, you'll find yourself in a tranquil setting surrounded by lush greenery and birdsong, with mountain and sea views. The lodge has comfortable double bedrooms, a separate TV room and a lounge with a fireplace.

Lord Nelson Inn
58 St George's St, Simon's Town
Tel: 021-786 1386
www.lordnelsoninn.co.za
Set along Simon's Town's characterful historic mile, this is the longest serving hostelry on the Cape Peninsula, with a determinedly unpretentious feel, good-value accommodation, lively old pub, and a great location for dining out and exploring the southern peninsula.

FURTHER AFIELD

Stellenbosch

Luxury

Lanzerac
Jonkershoek Rd
Tel: 021-886 5641
www.lanzeracwines.co.za
Established in 1692 on what now forms the eastern outskirts of Stellenbosch, this renowned wine estate, complete with restored manor house, is also one of the most sumptuous small hotels in the Winelands, with a restaurant to match.

Expensive

Devon Valley Hotel
Devon Valley Rd
Tel: 021-865 2012
www.protea-hotels.co.za
Set on Sylvanvale, a boutique estate known for its pinotage reserve and vine-dried Chenin blanc, this medium-sized hotel has a scenic Winelands ambience, a fine restaurant, good facilities for disabled guests, and many other facilities, including a swimming pool. Check the website for bargain last-minute full-board packages.

D'Ouwe Werf
30 Church St
Tel: 021-887 4608
www.ouwewerf.com
Established in the heart of old Stellenbosch in 1802, this plush inn is a real gem – notable for its authentic Cape Dutch architecture, period decor, personal service, sumptuous traditional Cape cuisine and quality wine list.

Moderate

Stellenbosch Protea Hotel
Techno Park, off the R44 about 5km (3 miles) south of Stellenbosch
Tel: 021-880 9500
www.protea-hotels.co.za
This efficient modern hotel, consisting of 180 spacious rooms, lies in the vicinity of the award-winning Blaauwklippen and Kleine Zalze Estates, in the shadow of the craggy Helderberg (Clear Mountain).

Budget

Rolands Uitspan
1 Cluver Rd
Tel: 021-883 2897
www.rolands.co.za
Neat, central guesthouse with pleasant pool and sundeck offering en-suite accommodation at very reasonable rates.

Stumble Inn
12 Market St
Tel: 021-887 4049
www.stumbleinnstellenbosch.hostel.com
Lively, central backpacker hostel sprawling over two houses. Facilities include a swimming pool, satellite TV and discounted wine-tasting tours.

Franschhoek

Luxury

Le Quartier Francais
16 Huguenot Rd
Tel: 021-876 2151
www.lequartier.co.za
A small but exceptional guesthouse in the heart of the Winelands' most scenic village. Its focus is an award-winning restaurant.

Moderate

Auberge La Dauphine
Excelsior Rd
Tel: 021-876 2606
www.ladauphine.co.za
Cosy and attractively

PRICE CATEGORIES

Price categories are based on the summer (high season) rate for the cheapest double room. This usually includes breakfast and typically drops by 25–50 percent in winter.
Luxury = over R3,000
Expensive = R2,000–3,000
Moderate = R1,000–2,000
Budget = under R1,000

located guesthouse comprising two rooms, three suites and one cottage on La Dauphine Estate in the Franschhoek Valley on the southeastern outskirts of town.

Paarl

Luxury

Grand Roche Hotel
Plantasie St
Tel: 021-863 5100
www.granderoche.com
A superb vineyard setting, luxury accommodation, good service, fine food and prize-winning cellar (plus swimming pool, tennis and gym) place this restored 18th-century Cape Dutch homestead among the best hotels in South Africa.

Moderate

Roggeland Country House
Roggeland Rd, Northern Paarl
Tel: 021-868 2501
www.roggeland.co.za
This superb eight-room Cape Dutch-style guesthouse, in the shadow of the Drakenstein Mountains, has been rated as one of the 50 best country-house hotels in the world and features excellent South African regional cuisine.

Hermanus and The Overberg

Luxury

Marine Hermanus
Marine Drive, Hermanus
Tel: 028-313 1000
www.marine-hermanus.co.za
Expanded and renovated on several occasions since it spearheaded Hermanus's first tourist boom back in 1902, this superb cliffside hotel now has 42 individually decorated bedrooms and suites with views across Walker Bay or the Kleinriviersmond Mountains.

Below: the delightful gardens at Marine Hermanus.

Moderate

Die Herberg
Arniston
Tel: 028-445 9420
www.dieherberg.co.za
This resort-like hotel in sleepy Arniston offers comfortable en-suite accommodation and good facilities.

Budget

Bontebok National Park Rest Camp
6km (4 miles) south of Swellendam
Tel: 012-428 9111
www.sanparks.org
This tranquil camp outside Swellendam consists of a campsite and some inexpensive six-berth "chalavans" with wooden ante-room and basic kitchen, using communal washrooms.

De Hoop Nature Reserve
Northeast of Agulhas
Tel: 086-133 4667
www.dehoopcollection.co.za
Low-key and inexpensive, the accommodation dotted around this reserve includes several self-catering cottages and a campsite.

Salmonsdam Nature Reserve
Northeast of Stanford
Tel: 028-341 0018
www.capenature.org.za
Basic hutted accommodation here has a wonderful location and is very inexpensive.

Zoete Inval Lodge
23 Main St, Hermanus
Tel: 028-312 1242
www.zoeteinval.co.za
Excellent backpacker hostel on the west side of town. Good facilities and local day tours.

West Coast

Luxury

Kagga Kamma
Near Citrusdal
Tel: 021-872 4343
www.kaggakamma.co.za
A private reserve, with craggy scenery, ancient rock art and a San village, offering lodging in luxury chalets or tents, and there's a restaurant and swimming pool.

Moderate

Lambert's Bay Protea
Voortrekker, St Lambert's Bay
Tel: 027-432 1126
www.lambertsbayhotel.co.za
This bland but comfortable 47-room hotel facing the old harbour is the best option in Lambert's Bay, a quaint village known for its bird colonies and fine seafood.

Citrusdal Country Lodge
66 Voortrekker Rd, Citrusdal
Tel: 022-921 2221
www.citrusdallodge.co.za
A comfortable place to stay in the Olifants River Valley, with air conditioning, telephone in rooms, restaurant and pool.

Saldanha Bay Protea
51B Main Rd, Saldanha
Tel: 022-714 1264
www.proteahotels.com
This unpretentiously comfortable harbour-front hotel forms a good base from which to explore the nearby West Coast National Park.

Budget

Columbine Beach Camp
Columbine Nature Reserve
Tel: 082-926 2267
www.beachcamp.co.za
This private camp offers tented and A-frame accommodation, plus organised sea-kayaking, diving and boat trips to seal and seabird colonies, as well as hiking excursions.

Garden Route

Mossel Bay

Moderate

The Point Hotel
Point Rd
Tel: 044-691 3512
www.pointhotel.co.za
This four-star hotel dominates the rocky seafront, and while its presence is somewhat intrusive from a scenic point of view, the views from the rooms are lovely and the location is great for exploring the town's many walking trails and museums.

Protea Hotel Mossel Bay
Corner of Church and Market streets
Tel: 044-691 3738
www.proteahotels.com
Built as a warehouse in 1846, this historic hotel, in an attractive waterfront location, has all modern amenities.

George

Moderate

Protea Hotel Outeniqua
123 York St
Tel: 044-874 4488
www.proteahotels.com
This is a comfortable 50-room hotel with a convenient location in the historic heart of town.

Oudtshoorn

Moderate

Eight Bells Mountain Inn
On the R328 between Mossel Bay and Oudtshoorn
Tel: 044-631 0000
www.eightbells.co.za
This family-run country inn, set amid stunning scenery south of Oudtshoorn, has been in operation for more than 80 years, and combines character with comfort, plus sports facilities.

Protea Hotel Riempie Estate
Corner of Baron Van Rheede and North streets
Tel: 044-272 6161
www.riempieestate.co.za
Cosy country atmosphere and tranquil setting in the heart of ostrich country.

Wilderness

Moderate

Fairy Knowe Hotel
Tel: 044-877 1100
www.fairyknowe.co.za
Built in 1874, this homely resort on the Touws River has comfortable rooms in a location suited to walking and birdwatchers.

Moontide
Touws River Rd
Tel: 041-877 0361
www.moontide.co.za
With a shady deck set below an ancient milkwood tree overlooking the Touws River, this owner-managed guesthouse has a setting to match its individualistic character and attractive rates.

Budget

Wilderness Rest Camp
Wilderness Section, Garden Route National Park
Tel: 044-302 5600
www.sanparks.org
Camp sites and affordable self-catering cabins and chalets are available at this idyllic rest camp (also known as Ebb and Flow) on the Touws River.

Knysna

Moderate

Eden's Touch
Fisanthoek Rd, off the N2
Tel: 083-253 6366
www.edenstouch.co.za
This idyllic retreat just off the road towards Plettenberg Bay has large wooden chalets with kitchen, satellite TV and lots of activities. It's fringed by privately protected indigenous forest.

Knysna River Club
Sun Valley Drive
Tel: 044-382 6483
www.knysnariverclub.co.za
This award-winning resort has 35 fully equipped, self-catering chalets on the grassy verge of Brenton Lagoon. Facilities include a restaurant, swimming pool and canoeing.

Budget

Knysna Backpackers
42 Queen St
Tel: 044-382 2554
www.knysnabackpackers.co.za
This Victorian manor houses one of the more sedate of the half-dozen hostels around central Knysna. It offers private rooms as well as dorms.

Plettenberg Bay

Luxury

The Plettenberg
40 Church St
Tel: 044-533 2030
www.plettenberg.com
This iconic hotel combines English country-house decor with superb food, memorable sea views, and five-star amenities and facilities.

Moderate

Bitou River Lodge
Tel: 044-535 9577
www.bitou.co.za
Winner of six AA awards since 2003, this luxurious owner-managed guesthouse with five rooms is on the forested banks of the Bitou River.

Tsitsikamma

Moderate

Tsitsikamma Lodge
N2 National Rd
Tel: 042-280 3802
www.tsitsikammalodge.com
A former hunting lodge with good-value log cabins in a forest setting. Honeymoon suites have spa baths and fireplaces.

Budget

Storms River Mouth Rest Camp
Tsitsikamma Section, Garden Route National Park
Tel: 044-302 5600
www.sanparks.org
Magnificently sited on the Storms River, with beachfront campsites and comfortable but affordable self-catering chalets.

Price Categories

Price categories are based on the summer (high season) rate for the cheapest double room. This usually includes breakfast and typically drops by 25–50 percent in winter.
Luxury = over R3,000
Expensive = R2,000–3,000
Moderate = R1,000–2,000
Budget = under R1,000

Activities

Festivals, The Arts, Nightlife, Sightseeing Tours, Sports and Children

Festivals

January

Cape Town Minstrel Carnival
City Bowl and Bo-Kaap
Tel: 021-761 5239
Cape Town's biggest and most raucous carnival sees the city celebrating the advent of the New Year with festivals, competitions and extravagant parades.

Jazzathon
V&A Waterfront
Tel: 021-696 6961
www.jazzathon.co.za
Highly recommended festival held over several days in mid-summer. Free entry.

February

Cape Town Pride Festival
Tel: 021-425 6461
www.capetownpride.co.za
The most flamboyant date on Cape Town's gay calendar. Pride Parade Day is the centrepiece of a fortnight-long festival that includes pageants, balls, wine-tasting sessions, tea parties and a season of gay films.

March

Cape Town Festival
Tel: 021-465 9042
www.capetownfestival.co.za
A wave of sizzling talent comes to 20 different venues throughout the region during March.

Dragon Boat Festival
Tel: 021-447 2820
www.dragonboat.org.za
An exciting weekend of dragon boating on the V&A Waterfront, plus lion dancers.

Cape Town International Jazz Festival
Tel: 021-422 5651
www.capetownjazzfest.com
Renowned international jazz festival with an impressive programme of African and international artists.

July

Encounters South African Independent Documentary Festival
Cinema Nouveau, V&A Waterfront
Tel: 021-465 4686
www.encounters.co.za
An interesting programme of documentaries from top film-makers.

August

Cape Town Fashion Week
Cape Town International Convention Centre
Tel: 011-269 6960
www.africanfashioninternational.com
Fashionistas gather to see the top African (and some international) designers showcase their ready-to-wear collections. Early/mid-August for one week.

V&A Waterfront Winter Food Fair
Market Square, V&A Waterfront
Tel: 021-556 8200
www.waterfront.co.za
A feast of hot and tasty local cuisine and wine in mid-August.

September

Cape Town Comedy Festival
Tel: 021-425 5792
www.comedyfestival.co.za
During the first three weeks of the month, the world's leading stand-ups share the stages of various venues with top local talents to give you their hilarious take on life.

October

Cape Town International Kite Festival
Zandvlei, Muizenberg
Tel: 021-447 9040
www.capementalhealth.co.za
Kites of all shapes and sizes fly high in the Cape's southeaster in this festival sponsored by the Cape Mental Health Society.

Outsurance Gun Run
Beach Road, Mouille Point
www.outsurance.co.za/gunrun
This popular half-marathon is run along the Atlantic seaboard.

December

Mother City Queer Parade

www.mcqp.co.za
Another highlight of Cape Town's pink calendar.

The Arts

Ballet/ Dance

Cape Town City Ballet
Artscape Theatre Complex, DF Malan Street, Foreshore
Tel: 021-650 2400
www.capetowncityballet.org.za
Bookings through Computicket or Dial-a-Seat *(see box below)*.
This ballet company is the oldest of its kind in Cape Town. The company's dancers also perform at several other events in Cape Town, like the Spier Summer Festival (Jan–Feb) in Stellenbosch. Apart from staging some classical ballets, the Cape Town City Ballet is also exploring more contemporary-style productions, like *Queen at the Ballet*, which is a powerful mix of dance, opera and rock singers, and the Cape Town Philharmonic Orchestra.

Jazzart Dance Theatre
Artscape Theatre Centre, DF Malan Street, Foreshore
Tel: 021-410 9848
www.jazzart.co.za
Bookings through Computicket or Dial-a-Seat *(see box below)*.
While this dance company offers training in African dance (gumboot and contemporary), it's worth making a note of the fundraiser production that they put together every year, called Danscape. It features mostly community dance groups who are still in training, and gives them the chance to get some on-stage performing experience.

Cape Dance Company (CDC)
The Space, Bell Crescent, Westlake Business Park, Westlake Tokai
Tel: 021-701 0599
www.capedancecompany.co.za
This particular dance company runs in association with the Academy of Dance. It puts on performances annually at the Grahamstown Festival, and has also danced at the Artscape Theatre, as well as at the Edinburgh Festival in Scotland.

Cinemas

Cape Town's cinemas are of an excellent standard, and show international releases (both art-house films and blockbusters) with a minimum delay time. The choice of films on mainstream cinema screens remains international.

Cavendish Nouveau
Cavendish Square, Claremont
Tel: 0861-300 444 or 082-16789
www.sterkinekor.com
Box office: 11am–11pm. Tickets about R35. Not strictly an art-house theatre, but they do screen the majority of non-mainstream films released in South Africa.

Cinema Nouveau Waterfront
Victoria Mall, V&A Waterfront
Tel: 0861-300 444 or 082-16789
www.sterkinekor.com
Box office: 11am–11pm. Tickets about R35. International releases and arthouse films.

Canal Walk Nu Metro
Canal Walk, Century City.
Tel: 0861 CINEMA
www.numetro.co.za
Box office: 8.30am–11pm daily. Tickets about R40 (half price on Wednesdays). If you feel like catching an arty film, followed by some late-night shopping, this is a good choice. And you're almost guaranteed a seat everytime, as most people there are going to see more mainstream films.

Independent Cinemas

The Labia and Labia on Kloof
Next door to Mount Nelson Hotel
Tel: 021-424 5927
www.labia.co.za
Box office: daily noon–midnight. Tickets R30.
The Labia is a nice old cinema that shows both mainstream and arthouse film. Its sister cinema around the corner is more modern. Set inside a shopping centre, with a good selection of restaurants and coffee shops (and ample parking), the Labia on Kloof makes going to the cinema a real pleasure. And you can take your coffee, wine and beer inside with you. The popcorn comes in old-fashioned bags.

Opera and Concerts

You'll be spoilt for choice in Cape Town with the range of opera productions, symphony concerts and chamber-orchestra events on offer. The Cape Town Philharmonic Orchestra is a full-time professional symphony orchestra that often hosts internationally known conductors and soloists. It's really been put on the map in terms of the growing global music culture, and has 45 permanent musicians performing over 100 concerts each year.

Artscape Theatre Centre
DF Malan Street, Foreshore
Tel: 021-410 9800
www.artscape.co.za
Box office: Mon–Fri 9am–5pm. Bookings can also be made through Computicket and Dial-a-Seat *(see box below)*.
Throughout the year you can enjoy the Cape Town Opera at the Opera House (which seats 1,200)

Buying Tickets

Tickets can be booked at the relevant theatre box office, which is generally open during the week and on show days – either by telephone or in person. Alternatively, you can book through the following companies:
Computicket: open Mon–Fri 9am–5pm, Sat 9am–6am. Tel: 083-915 8000, www.computicket.co.za
Dial-a-seat: for bookings at Artscape productions only. Tel: 021-421 7695
Prices vary according to the production, and can range from R60 to R500. Look out for specials on quieter nights (usually early in the week) or matinée performances.

Above: the acclaimed Jazzart Dance Theatre.

and has excellent acoustics. The company is best known for its light classical productions and opera in foreign languages (with subtitles displayed on an overhead digital screen).

Baxter Theatre Centre
Main Road, Rondebosch
Tel: 021-685 7880
www.baxter.co.za
Box office: 9am – start of performance.
As part of the University of Cape Town, the Baxter Theatre Centre provides an exciting platform for live music that reflects a mix of cultural talents. It's an excellent venue for international and national productions that appeal to all devotees of fine music.

What's On Listings

The Friday editions of the *Cape Times* and *Cape Argus* newspapers have arts and entertainment sections that will keep you up to date with performances and events. The bimonthly *Cape Etc* and associated website www.capeetc.com are also excellent sources for listings information. You can also get information online at www.tonight.co.za.

City Hall
Darling Street, opposite the Grand Parade (Cape Philharmonic Orchestra)
Tel: 021-410 9809
www.cpo.org.za
The Cape Philharmonic Orchestra performs throughout the year, but Thursday nights are traditionally concert nights. The City Hall's acoustics are excellent and the Edwardian setting splendid. Bookings through Computicket or Dial-a-Seat *(see box, page 235)*.

Outdoor Concert Venues

Kirstenbosch Botanical Garden Centre
Kirstenbosch Botanical Gardens, Rhodes Drive, Newlands
Tel: 021-799 8783
www.sanbi.org
Bookings through Computicket *(see box, page 235)*.
During the summer, Kirstenbosch Botanical Gardens hosts concerts every Sunday evening, featuring everything from jazz to classics. For the best experience, pack a picnic and enjoy the music under the stars, with Table Mountain as the backdrop. The New Year's Eve concert with the Cape Philharmonic Orchestra is a delightful alternative to the celebrations in the city.

Theatre

There is a whirlwind of mixed talent and energy that sweeps through Cape Town's theatre scene, from the City Bowl through to the townships. In addition to the established venues where big productions usually take centre-stage, there are also a number of privately owned theatres, nurturing the city's passion for the arts, that have proved to be a huge success over the years. Venues vary from old church halls to restaurants and small Victorian theatres. Going to the theatre in Cape Town is also an affordable night out on the town, in comparison to London's West End or New York's Broadway strip. There's something to suit everyone, from light-hearted comedy to serious drama.

Major Theatre Venues

Artscape Theatre Centre
DF Malan Street, Foreshore
Tel: 021-410 9800/01
www.artscape.co.za
Expect to see anything from an Andrew Lloyd-Webber musical extravaganza to contemporary African dance, classical ballet or opera. Artscape is also home to the Cape Philharmonic Orchestra (tel: 021-410 9809; www.cpo.org.za), Cape Town City Ballet (tel: 021-650 2400; www.capetowncityballet.org.za), Cape Town Opera (tel: 021-410 9807; www.capetownopera.co.za) and the modern dance company Jazzart Dance Theatre (tel: 021-410 9848; www.jazzart.co.za).

Barnyard Theatre
Willowbridge Lifestyle Centre, Carl Cronjé Drive
Tel: 021-914 8898
www.barnyardtheatres.co.za
This is the Cape Town branch of a popular countrywide chain of theatre/restaurant venues specialising in nostalgic musical revues.

Baxter Theatre Centre
Main Road, Rondebosch
Tel: 021-685 7880
www.baxter.co.za
Aside from its very ugly 1970s

exterior, this theatre is always buzzing inside. You can enjoy a meal at the theatre restaurant before the show, followed by a few drinks at the bar afterwards; you might even get to meet some of the cast. There are two main venues at the Baxter – the Main Theatre and Concert Hall. Productions include light musicals, heavy dramas and hilarious comedians. Special deals are available for pensioners, students and for block bookings over 10 people.

The Fugard Theatre
Cnr of Harrington Street and Caledon Street
Tel: 021-461 4554
www.thefugard.com
Cape town's newest theatre is named after the eminent playwright Athol Fugard and it hosted the premiere of his play *The Train Driver* in 2010. Situated in District Six, in the handsomely restored Sacks Futeran Building, it has a very pleasant roof terrace and is a good place to see arty local productions.

Theatre on the Bay
1 Link Street, Camps Bay
Tel: 021-438 3301
www.theatreonthebay.co.za
This vibey theatre definitely has the best setting in Cape Town. It's situated on the trendy strip on Camps Bay, where you can enjoy a light drink or supper before making your way to the show.

On Broadway
88 Shortmarket Street
Tel: 021-424 1194
www.onbroadway.co.za
A dinner theatre in the lively suburb of Green Point which features brilliant drag shows, cabaret and stand-up comedy shows. You're guaranteed to leave laughing. It's best to book well in advance as it's a popular venue and fills up quickly. Booking is essential and can be done online.

Kalk Bay Theatre
52 Main Road, Kalk Bay
Tel: 073-220 5430
www.kbt.co.za
The oldest theatre in Cape Town is situated in a Victorian church hall in the quaint village of Kalk Bay. It puts on some hilarious interactive productions. It's most fun if you go in a big group. Dinner available; booking essential.

Grand West Casino
1 Vanguard Drive, Goodwood
Tel: 021-505 7777
www.suninternational.com
Even though it's not close to the city, you will probably catch a few good shows here, so it's worth calling to find out what's on. It's also the venue for the annual Cape Town International Comedy Festival, featuring some talented local stand-up acts.

Nightlife

When the sun sets in the "Mother City", temperatures may start dropping, but the heat is on with bars and party venues that line up exciting events and shows all year round. Welcome to party town! It's known for varied and vibrant nightlife – a lot of clubs don't open until 11pm and are bound by law to close at 4am sharp. Many are open seven nights a week.

Start your evening early in Kloof Street or at a bar in Green Point/De Waterkant (which also has a string of gay and gay-friendly clubs and restaurants). After you've chilled out and absorbed the beautiful sunsets, you can hit the city and choose from an endless list of sizzling club venues to suit your taste in music. Long Street is the happening place for the young and hip, and you could spend all night wandering between the pubs and clubs. The dress code is almost always as casual as you wish, although shorts and trainers are not welcome at some venues.

Admission prices to clubs vary between R20–120, often free before 11pm. The legal drinking age is 18, although some clubs impose an age limit of 21 years.

Clubbing Websites

Check out these clubbing websites for more information on parties, promotions, etc:
www.topclubs.co.za
www.thunda.com
www.clubbersguide.co.za
www.e-vent.co.za

Casinos

Grand West Casino and Entertainment Centre
1 Vanguard Drive, Goodwood
Tel: 021-505 7777
www.suninternational.com
There are three casinos in the Cape region and this is the best. A massive complex incorporating various reconstructed historic buildings, it has two hotels, an Olympic-size ice rink, several restaurants and, of course, the casino. This features 1,750 slot machines and 66 tables, plus bars, restaurants, lounges, a nightclub and revue bar. Gambling areas are open to those over 18 years, dress is smart casual in the gaming halls (and a passport or ID is required).

Live Music Venues

Jazz

Cape Town is big on jazz, with two annual festivals, four jazz-only venues and several jazz events that take place during the year. Venues vary from stylish restaurant-type supper clubs to more relaxed pubs that get quite loud and noisy. To stay informed on the jazz scene, check out the jazz column in the Wednesday *Cape Argus* or visit www.tonight.co.za. Tickets for the bigger jazz events can be booked through Computicket *(see box, page 235)*.

Dizzy Jazz Café
The Drive, Camps Bay
Tel: 021-438 2686
www.dizzys.co.za
A pavement café bar in Camps Bay that carries on into the early hours of the morning. There are

usually live jazz performances that get foot-stomping and very festive every night of the week.

Green Dolphin
Victoria and Albert Arcade, V&A Waterfront
Tel: 021-421 7471
With live jazz sets seven days a week, usually starting at around 8pm, the Green Dolphin really does uphold its motto, "Dedicated to the preservation of jazz". High-quality line-ups feature unique collaborations of local jazz artists. Sunday blues nights are very popular, so book in advance.

Marimba Restaurant
Corner of Heerengracht and Coen Steytler Avenue, Entrance 5, Cape Town International Convention Centre
Tel: 021-418 3366
www.marimbasa.com
The place for world music, big band, blues, soul and contemporary African sounds. Book early, because on big nights the restaurant is booked weeks in advance. There's usually live music on Thursday, Friday and Saturday evenings, with groups coming from as far afield as the Congo and East Africa.

Rock

Cape Town Stadium
Fritz Sonnenberg Road, Green Point
Tel: 021-430 7300.
This new stadium was built for the 2010 World Cup on the site of the former Green Point Stadium, which was the city's grand old dame of rock concerts, having hosted Michael Jackson, U2, Robbie Williams and the Mandela 46664 concert. Indications are that the new stadium will resume that role post-World Cup. Bookings through Computicket *(see box, page 235)*.

Jo'burg Bar
218 Long Street
Tel: 021-422 0142
Mon–Thur 5pm–late; Fri and Sat 3pm–late, Sun 6pm–late.
A drinking den on the Long Street strip where you'll find a mixed bag of people, especially when they're hosting a live band on a Sunday night. Free admission.

Acoustic Café
Main and Camp Road, Muizenberg
Tel: 021-788 1900
http://acousticcafe.tripod.com
A new venue that's really starting to make some noise (in a good way). There's a colourful mix of surfers, hippies and laid-back locals who gather here on Thursday, Friday and Saturday evenings for the live band.

The Assembly
61 Harrington Street, District Six
Tel: 021-465 7286
www.theassembly.co.za
Open 9.30pm–4am Fri and Sat.
This excellent live venue is the place to catch up-and-coming contemporary indie, techno and Afro-fusion groups, though more established acts also play here regularly.

The Melting Pot
15 Church Street, Muizenberg
Tel: 021-788 9791
Open 7pm–late Wed, Fri–Sun.
This new and very laid back venue, close to Muizenberg Beach, hosts an interesting mix of live acts, ranging from folk and jazz to African and reggae.

Nightclubs

Hemisphere
31st floor, ABSA Building, 2 Riebeek Street, City Centre
Tel: 021-421 0581
www.hemisphere.org.za
Open Tue–Sat 10pm–late.
Being 31 floors up gives this glitzy venue the edge, with its 180° views of the city and harbour. Suburban party-goers flock here until the early hours, dancing to a musical mix of 70s retro, commercial house and more. Also has a cocktail lounge. Strict dress code: smart casual. Over-25s only.

Club 91
4th Floor, Stadium on Main Parkade, 91 Main Road, Claremont
Tel: 021-674 9191
www.club91.co.za
Open 8pm–4am Tue, Thu–Sat.
Set out over 750 sq metres (2,475 sq ft), this trendsetting new venue has an awesome sound system, a large dance floor, lavish finishes, ample parking, and great views over suburban Claremont. It serves up a mixture of live music and DJ evenings with the emphasis on commercial R&B and house.

Zula Sound Bar
196 Long Street, City Centre
Tel: 021-424 2442
www.zulabar.co.za
Open noon–late daily.
Hip-hop and old school beats are the perfect mix in this ethnic and earthy venue. Often live music and a good lineup of DJs to keep you grooving through the night. Great balcony where the crowds gather.

Mercury Live and Lounge
43 De Villiers Street
Tel: 021-465 2106
www.mercuryl.co.za
Open Mon, Wed, Fri and Sat 8pm–4am.

Gay Clubs and Bars

Cape Town's gay clubs are mostly situated in De Waterkant and Green Point but come and go depending on the season – during peak season (Dec and Jan) they often reinvent themselves.

Adam and Eve Lounge Bar
1st floor, 24 Napier Street, Greenpoint
Tel: 079-502 7083
www.adam-and-eve.co.za
Open 4pm–late daily.
Relaxed vibes, contemporary decor and 80s/90s music are hallmarks of this funky new gay and lesbian bar opposite the Cape Quarter.

Bronx Action Bar
22 Somerset Road, Green Point
Tel: 021-419 9216
www.bronx.co.za
An old favourite gay and lesbian venue that's been on the strip the longest. Excellent music; karaoke on Monday. Free admission.

A retro-style venue that feels like you're dancing in a friend's living room, except that the music is better. There are two floors, with live music either upstairs or downstairs most nights, and a DJ playing classic pop, disco and house anthems on the other floor. Monday is the night for new unsigned talent.

Liquid
84 Sir Lowry Road
Tel: 021-461 9649
Open Fri and Sat 9pm–8am.
If you're looking for all-night dancing to hard house and trance, look no further. There's nothing glamorous about this nightclub situated on the outskirts of town, but you're sure to get your dance fix, considering the impressive line-up of well-known local and international DJs.

Club Deluxe
Unity House, Corner of Long and Longmarket streets
Tel: 021-422 4832
Open Fri and Sat 10pm–4am.
The city's best venue for deep house has retro-glam decor, with an outside patio and an intimate lounge area for taking time out. Here you'll find leggy models drinking at the bar or shaking it up on the dance floor.

Club Galaxy/West End
College Road, Rylands
Tel: 021-637 9132
www.superclubs.co.za
Open Thur–Sat 9pm–4am.
Founded in 1978, Cape Town's oldest and arguably best-known nightclub has weathered the decades with unexpected sprightliness, and it remains a very popular venue, with four different floors offering an eclectic mix of dance music old and new.

Chrome
6 Pepper Street, City Centre
Tel: 083-700 6078
www.chromect.com
Open 10pm–late Wed–Sun.
An exclusive clubbing experience with a VIP lounge kitted out in chandeliers and plasma screens. A swanky crowd comes to drink exotic cocktails long into the night. Well-known Cape Town DJs play funk and commercial house music; VIP lounge and private parties Privé; students' night on Wednesdays, with special promotions.

Above: boat trip to Seal Island.

Fiction
226 Long Street, City Centre
Tel: 021-424 5709
www.fictionbar.com
Open Tue, Thur–Sat 8pm–4am.
A lounge meets DJ bar that's a hotspot in summer. Ironic decor, underground beats (strictly not commercial and R&B policy) and a balcony overlooking buzzing Long Street make this one of the coolest hangouts in town. Free admission.

Karma Lounge
The Promenade, Camps Bay
Tel: 021-438 7773
www.karmalounge.co.za
Open Wed–Sat 9pm–2am, Sun 5.30pm–2am.
The hottest party venue in Camps Bay combines a chic beachfront lounge bar with a dance floor featuring different DJs and styles every night of the week. In keeping with its upscale mood (and prices) it enforces a rigid no under-23 policy.

The Bang Bang Club
70 Loop Street
Tel: 021-426 2011
www.thebangbangclub.co.za
Owned by DJ Shaun Duvet, this hot new venue combines retro decor with the very latest sounds, spread across three dance floors in a national heritage building in the heart of central Cape Town.

Sightseeing Tours

Bicycle Tours

Daytrippers (tel: 021-511 4766; www.daytrippers.co.za) organise bicycle tours, including the popular full-day "Cape Point Tour". This scenic tour follows the Atlantic Coast to the Cape of Good Hope Nature Reserve. The cost includes bicycle rental, a picnic lunch and any admission charges.

Boat Tours

Waterfront Boat Company (tel: 021-418 5806; www.waterfront-boats.co.za) offers harbour tours, educational excursions and champagne cruises, all of which depart from Quay Five on the V&A Waterfront. Tours range from a one-hour cruise to a full day's fishing trip.

The Waterfront Information Office (tel: 021-408 7600; www.waterfront.co.za) can provide information on a variety of other tours from the V&A Waterfront.

Boat trips to see the Cape fur seals on Duiker Island near Hout Bay can be arranged through **Drumbeat Charters** (tel: 021-791 4441; www.drumbeatcharters.co.za). They depart from Hout Bay Harbour, and there is also a one-way trip from Hout Bay to the Waterfront Harbour.

ABOVE: kite surfing, Muizenberg.

Bus Tours

The open-top **City Sightseeing** bus (tel: 021-511 6000; www.citysightseeing.co.za) links the main places of interest within the city centre. It leaves the V&A Waterfront (Ferryman Pub or, 10 minutes later, the Clock Tower) at 45-minute intervals from 9.30am–3pm (until 3.30pm from mid-Oct to mid-Apr). Stops include all the major museums, the Convention Centre on the Foreshore, Cape Town Tourism on Burg Street, the Cableway, Camps Bay and Sea Point. The fare is very competitive and you can hop on and off as you wish.

Helicopter Tours

Civair (tel: 021-934 4488; www.civair.co.za) offers breathtaking but very pricey 20-min, 30-min, and 1-hr scenic helicopter tours along the Atlantic coast.

Walking Tours

Cape Town is ideal for exploring on foot. **Cape Town Tourism** operate Wanderlust's "Cape Town on Foot" tours (tel: 021-426 4260; www.wanderlust.co.za), which take 2½ hours to cover the main sights and history of the city centre. These tours are very popular, so book in advance.
Grassroute Tours (tel: 021-462 4252; www.grassroutetours.co.za) and **Roots Africa Tours** (tel: 021-913 9553; www.rootsafrica.co.za) both offer tours of Cape Town's cultural sites and organise excursions to townships.

SPORTS

Participant Sports

Abseiling

Abseiling is a daring way of experiencing Table Mountain. Contact **Abseil Africa** (tel: 021-424 4760; www.abseilafrica.co.za).

Canoeing and Rafting

White-water enthusiasts can experience the turbulent rivers of the Western Cape such as the Breede, Berg, Dorings and Orange. Reliable operators include the **African Rafting Company** (tel: 021-853 2453; www.africanrafting.co.za) and **Aquatrails** (tel: 21-782 7982; www.aquatrails.co.za).

Golf

There are 18 golf clubs in the Cape Town area. Here are a few of the most central courses:

Mowbray
Raapenberg Road
Tel: 021-685 3018
www.mowbraygolfclub.co.za
Good central 18-hole course at the foot of Table Mountain.

Rondebosch
Klipfontein Road, Rondebosch, Southern Suburbs
Tel: 021-689 4176
www.rondeboschgolfclub.com
Another 18-hole course at the foot of Table Mountain.

Royal Cape Golf Course
174 Ottery Road, Wynberg, Southern Suburbs
Tel: 021-761 6551
www.royalcapegolf.co.za
Excellent 18-hole course used for professional tournaments.

Atlantic Beach Golf Club
1 Fairway Drive, Melkbosstrand
Tel: 021-553 2223
www.atlanticbeachgolfclub.co.za
Beautifully sited course on the Atlantic seafront 30 minutes' drive from the city centre.

Mountain Climbing

The Mountain Club of South Africa offers guides and group mountaineering experiences. To find out more contact www.mcsa.org.za.

Running

The Old Mutual Two Oceans Marathon, usually held in April, attracts international athletes as well as local enthusiasts. To join the competitors, apply six months in advance. Visit www.twooceansmarathon.org.za.

Surfing

The Cape Peninsula has several great beaches for surfing. Which one is best will depend on the wind direction. A local radio station, KFM 94.7, broadcasts a daily surf report. Popular spots include Long Beach, Noordhoek, Fish Hoek and Muizenberg. See also www.wavescape.co.za.

Spectator Sports

Cricket

Newlands Cricket Ground in the Southern Suburbs is one of the finest in the world, not least on account of its magnificent location. If you fancy seeing a match while you are in town, contact Newlands Ticket Hotline, tel: 021-657 2003.

Football

The most successful football team in Cape Town is Ajax Cape Town FC, which has never won the country's premiership division, but managed to take the runner-up position in the 2003/4 and 2007/8 seasons. It also won the knockout Rothmans Cup in 2000 and was the original home club of the Everton player Seven Pienaar. It uses the Cape Town Stadium, build especially to host the 2010 FIFA World Cup, as its home ground. For details of fixtures see www.ajaxct.com.

Rugby

If you would like to watch a game of rugby at the Newlands Stadium, contact the Western Province

Child-Friendly Shopping Centres

British Airways: Cavendish Square
1 Dreyer Street, Claremont
Tel: 021-657-5600.
Children's activities in the central courtyard, Zip Zap Circus, fashion shows and cinemas.

Canal Walk
Century Boulevard, Century City, Milnerton
Tel: 021-555 4444
Children's promotional events, cinema complex, fashion shows and other activities.

V&A Waterfront
Tel: 021-408 7600
www.waterfront.co.za
Concerts and events during the holidays and children's entertainment monthly, plus year-round free street performances, with jugglers, mime artists, clowns, busking musicians and the like.

Rugby Association (tel: 021-659 4600; www.wprugby.co.za) for fixtures and ticket information.

Children's Activities

Cape Ostrich Farm
Cape of Good Hope Nature Reserve
Tel: 021-780 9294
www.capepointostrichfarm.com
Open daily 9.30am–5.30pm.
Even though you won't be able to ride on the ostriches, you can take a tour of the breeding stations and see the baby ostrich chicks in incubators. Also a variety of ostrich paraphernalia for sale, such as feathers, eggs and leather accessories.

World of Birds
Valley Road, Hout Bay
Tel: 021-790 2730
www.worldofbirds.org.za
Open daily 9am–5pm.
Admission: R65 (children under 16 yrs R39, students and pensioners R50).
Walk-through aviaries that house more than 4,000 birds and some monkeys.

Grand West Casino and Entertainment Centre
1 Vanguard Drive, Goodwood
Tel: 021-505 7777
www.grandwest.co.za
Games, rides, go-karting and minigolf at the Magic Company. The ice station has two rinks (one for smaller children), and there's a cinema complex and The Grand Kids Corner crèche, where you can leave the children while you play the slots or tables.

Laserquest
Lower Level, Stadium on Main, Claremont
Tel: 021-683 7296
www.lazerquest.co.za
Open 10am–10pm Mon–Fri, 8.30am–11pm Sat, Sun
Run around in the dark shooting little points of light at your friends. A good place to come when the weather is wet. Exhausting, but lots of fun.

Action Paint Ball
Imhoffs Gift. Ou Kaapse Weg,
Tel: 021-790 7603
www.actionpursuit.co.za
Children of 11 or older can play this game. Strict safety rules and regulations and first-aid standards are followed by the trained managers and field marshals.

Planetarium
South African Museum, 25 Queen Victoria Street
Tel: 021-481 3900
www.iziko.org.za
Open daily (show times vary).
Admission: R20 (under 17s R6).
Sit inside a dark room and watch the night sky appear before your eyes. A variety of shows cater for all age groups – little children love the interactive "Twinkle" show, while teenagers might enjoy "The Sky Tonight" to check out what the sky will look like that evening. The reclining seats are a comfortable bonus.

Two Oceans Aquarium
Dock Road, V&A Waterfront
Tel: 021-418 3823
www.aquarium.co.za
Open 9.30am-6pm daily
Admission: R94 (children 4–17 yrs and pensioners R73).
Everything that lives underwater from kelp to sea horses. Seeing the sharks being fed in the predator tank is especially popular. Lots of hands-on activities too, as well as seals and penguins, and plenty of friendly staff on hand to explain what the children are seeing.

MTN ScienCentre
407 Canal Walk, Century City, Entrance 5
Tel: 021-529 8100
www.mtnsciencentre.org.za
Open daily 9am-6pm.
This is an interactive educational science centre that's fun for the whole family. Workshops, talks and films, many with an environmental slant, are held during school holidays.

Below: feeding one of the inhabitants of Hout Bay.

A – Z

An Alphabetical Summary of Practical Information

A Admission Charges 242
B Budgeting for Your Trip 242
C Children 243
Climate 243
Crime and Safety 243
Customs Regulations 244
D Disabled Travellers 244
E Electricity 244
Embassies/Consulates 244
Emergencies 245
G Gay and Lesbian 244
H Health and Medical Care 245
I Internet 246
L Lost Property 246
M Media 246
Money 246
O Opening Hours 247
P Postal Services 247
Public Holidays 247
R Religious Services 247
S Student Travellers 247
T Tax 248
Telephones 248
Time Zone 248
Toilets 248
Tour Operators 248
Tourist Information 249
V Visas and Passports 249
W What to Bring 249
Women Travellers 249

Admission Charges

Most museums and galleries charge admission fees but these are inexpensive by European and US standards, with most charging between R10 and R50. Some larger establishments are free of charge on certain days and offer special deals for large groups.

High-profile attractions are more expensive. The boat trip to and tour of Robben Island, for example, costs R200 for an adult (R100 for a child), and the cable-car ride up Table Mountain costs R160 return for an adult (R80 for a child).

Senior citizens and students are entitled to reduced-rate admissions at most museums and galleries, although they may need to produce a student card or passport as proof of age. Children are usually admitted for half-price.

Budgeting for Your Trip

If you're looking for accommodation with an acceptable level of comfort, cleanliness and facilities (TV, en-suite bathroom and breakfast) at reasonable cost, your best bet is a bed and breakfast, where the price of a double room starts at less than R1,000. For budget hotels you'll pay around R1,000, while more luxurious or designer hotels in the city centre or on the seafront will have a much higher room rate.

For between R1,500 and R3,000 there's a range of good hotels, from boutique establishments to business-traveller favourites with luxury facilities and amenities. Anything over R3,000 is certainly in the de luxe league.

Food costs are very reasonable, and range from about R15 for a ready-made sandwich to R150 per head for a three-course meal without wine at a bistro-style eatery, and from R300 upwards at a fine-dining restaurant (with good wine). A 1-litre bottle of mineral water will cost you between R8 and R15. Spirits are very cheap (as well as widely available: even modest cafés seem to have a licence), though the price of wine, will, of course, depend on the quality. Expect to pay about R80–100 for a bottle of house wine and R100–150 for an easy-drinking wine.

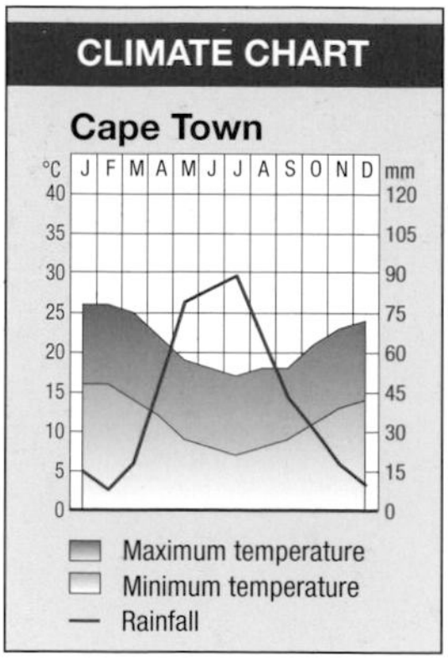

A hire car will cost from R170 per day (depending on special rental deals), and petrol costs about R7 a litre. Metropolitan train and bus tickets are very inexpensive.

Taxi fares are relatively expensive at around R10–12 per kilometre, and a one-way ticket for the airport shuttle is around R200 per person. A taxi to, say, Kirstenbosch, from the city centre, will cost about R120.

Children

Cape Town is a very child-friendly destination, with a good choice of activities to suit youngsters of all ages. Children are typically charged lower entrance fees than adults, and many places let young children in for free. Hotels also usually offer discounted rates (or don't charge at all) for children sharing with an adult, and many restaurants, especially the chains, have dedicated children's menus or offer cheaper dishes aimed at unadventurous palates. Most hotels can also provide child-sitting services, though it is advisable to check this before you make a booking.

Climate

The seasons in the southern hemisphere are, of course, the opposite to those in the northern hemisphere. Cape Town has a Mediterranean climate with four seasons. Winter runs from June to August, when temperatures range from 7–18°C (45–65°F), with pleasant, sunny days scattered between cold, wet ones. From September to November the weather is extremely unpredictable, with anything from hot summer days to a howling south-easterly wind that blows at around 120 km/h (75 mph). December to March is considered mid-summer. In the interior it becomes very hot in the summer months, and during winter snow falls on the mountain peaks. For the weather forecast bureau, tel: 082-231 1640; www.weathersa.co.za, or consult the daily newspapers.

When to Visit

The best time to visit climatically is the southern hemisphere summer, which runs from October to April. This is also the dry season, so the warm temperatures and long days are complemented by rainless skies. The weather is often at its best in March and April, when there is little wind or rain, and temperatures are not too stifling. For those combining a visit to Cape Town with game viewing elsewhere in Southern Africa, the spring months of September or October are the best time to go on safari. Winter is less predictable, alternating between periods of temperate weather and clear skies to spells of rainy, windy weather that might last for several days – a bit of a lottery, but with the advantage of significantly cheaper low season rates at most hotels.

What to Wear

South Africa used to be fairly old-fashioned in its attitude to what to wear, with people dressing up for even quite modest social occasions and women opting for full make-up. This is no longer the rule, however, and Cape Town is informal, particularly in summer. That said, many businessmen will wear a suit and tie except on hot days, when it is acceptable to go without the jacket. These days, for an informal lunch or shopping expedition you can get away with shorts and T-shirts. In the evening most restaurants expect smart-casual attire.

It rains quite often in Cape Town between May and August, so bring a raincoat. Summers are long and dry, which calls for light clothing and a swimsuit, but bring a warm jacket or sweater for trips up Table Mountain, boat trips or for travelling around the Peninsula.

Crime and Safety

Even though South Africa's crime statistics are notoriously high, most of Cape Town's crime is concentrated in the townships, or occurs late at night in the quieter, darker areas of the city. In the downtown areas closed-circuit TV cameras have been installed on most street corners, keeping an electronic eye on the city, and these have proved to be an effective deterrent.

Avoid walking alone after dark in unpopulated streets and do not draw attention to your money and jewellery. If you are dining out, ask the restaurant staff to call a taxi for you. Be extra careful with your belongings wherever you go, whether it's a restaurant, inner-city flea market or nightclub. Keep your handbag and wallet close by at all times. Petty theft such as pickpocketing is especially prevalent at flea markets. If you're parking in town at night, try to find a well-lit area near busy restaurants, with a car guard close by. When drawing money from an ATM do not accept help from any person or stranger that offers assistance, as it's likely they'll clean out your account. Some banks employ a guard to watch over their ATMs. Credit cards are welcome at most shops and restaurants, so it is not necessary to carry around a lot of cash. Lost or stolen credit cards should be reported to the following 24-hour services:

American Express, tel: 0800 110929
Diners Club, tel: 0860 DINERS
MasterCard, tel: 0800-990 418
Visa International, tel: 0800-990 475

Police

If you've been subjected to a serious crime such as mugging, robbery, rape or assault, contact the Flying Squad on 10111. For petty crime (such as pickpocketing), call the local police station (look under Regional Offices of National and Governmental in the blue section of the Yellow Pages directory). *See also Emergencies, (page 245).*

To claim for theft or loss on an insurance policy it is necessary to notify the local police, usually within a specified time limit.

Customs Regulations

Money

Visitors are permitted to import a maximum of R5,000 in South African banknotes, but can bring unlimited quantities of traveller's cheques denominated in South African rand. Large amounts of foreign currency should be declared on arrival.

On departure, visitors can export a maximum of R5,000 in South African notes. It is advisable to keep bank-exchange receipts.

Goods

Travellers (aged 18 and over only in the case of alcohol and tobacco) are allowed to import the following items duty-free:

- **Alcohol** – 2 litres of wine, 1 litre of spirits.
- **Tobacco** – 200 cigarettes, 20 cigars, 250g tobacco.
- **Perfume** – 50 ml perfume, 250 ml eau de toilette.
- **Gifts** up to the value of R3,000 per person.

Duty is levied at 20 percent on anything over these limits.
The following are prohibited: drugs and narcotics; pornographic materials; plants, seeds, bulbs, raw cotton; uncooked meat and poultry; uncut diamonds; unwrought gold; ammunition.

Disabled Travellers

Hotels and tourist attractions in Cape Town have a good reputation for meeting the needs of travellers with disabilities. SAA provides Passenger Aid Units (PAU) at all major airports, and larger car-rental companies can provide vehicles with hand controls. For further information, contact the Johannesburg-based Association for the Physically Disabled (www.apdjhb.co.za), tel: 011-646 8331. The visually impaired can contact the SA National Council for the Blind (www.sancb.org.za), tel: 012-452 3811.

Several tour operators provide services for travellers with disabilities, including suitable hotels and itineraries. These include Flamingo Tours (tel: 021-557 4496, www.flamingotours.co.za).

Embassies/Consulates

In South Africa

Most of the major consulates and embassies are situated in Pretoria, but several countries do have representatives or consulates in Cape Town.

Australian Consulate
Suite 2B, The Wellington,
96 Longmarket Street
Tel: 021-465 3346
www.australia.co.za
British Consulate
15th Floor, Southern Life Centre,
8 Riebeeck Street
Tel: 021-405 2400
www.ukinsouthafrica.fco.gov.uk
Canadian High Commission
SA Reserve Bank Building,
60 St George's Mall
Tel: 021-423 5240
www.canadainternational.gc.ca/southafrica-afriquedusud/index
New Zealand Consulate
2 Lente Road, Sybrand Park
Tel: 021-696 8561
http://new-zealand.visahq.com/embassy/south-africa
US Consulate General
Postnet Suite 50, Private Bag X 26, Tokai 7966
Tel: 021-702-7300
http://southafrica.usembassy.gov

Abroad

Visa requirements are subject to change, so it is important to check with the South African High Commission in your own country before travelling.

UK
South African High Commission
South Africa House
Trafalgar Square
London WC2N 5DP
www.southafricahouse.com
Consular section:
15 Whitehall
London SW1
Tel: 020-7925 8900
Australia
South African High Commission
Corner of Rhodes Place and State Circle, Yarralumla
Canberra, ACT 2600
Tel: 02-6272 7300
www.sahc.org.au
USA
Embassy of South Africa
3051 Massachusetts Avenue, NW, Washington, DC 20008
Tel: 202-232 4400
www.saembassy.org

Electricity

The supply is 220/230 volts AC at 50 cycles per second. Three-pronged round-pin plugs are universal, so to use UK or US appliances you'll need to take a plug adaptor, sold at airport terminals in your home country, but also available at electrical appliance stores in Cape Town. Most rooms have 110-volt outlets for electric shavers.

Gay and Lesbian

If South Africa is the rainbow nation, then the Mother City is definitely the reigning queen. The Cape gay scene is lively and friendly, whilst continually making a cultural, political and economic contribution to the city. It attracts both local and international gay visitors.

The gay scene is most pronounced in De Waterkant gay village in Green Point, which is a popular meeting spot thanks to a number of gay-friendly cafés, clubs, steam rooms, restaurants, hotels and designer shops. However, if you travel further along the Atlantic Seaboard you'll find a colourful array of smaller, intimate restaurants, boutique hotels and cafés also catering for the gay market.

Cape Town's gay scene is noted for certain annual festivals and parties, including the Cape Town Pride Festival and the Mother City Queer Project *(see page 234)*, destination parties throughout the year and relaxed (but very social) beach time recreation over the summer. The lesbian scene is less extensive, confined to organised parties and selected gay bars around the Green Point area.

For further information on the gay scene contact Cape Town Tourism, tel: 021-405 4500. Also visit www.gaydar.co.za for safe online dating. Lesbians should visit www.lushcapetown.co.za to find out more about the lesbian party circuit.

Health and Medical Care

Precautions

No special precautions are necessary unless you are also travelling to Mpumalanga Province (including the Kruger National Park), the Northern Province or northeastern KwaZulu-Natal, where you will need to take malaria tablets, especially during the wet summer months of November to May.

You can drink tap water anywhere in Cape Town unless a notice warns you otherwise. The sun in South Africa is much stronger than in Europe, and it is essential for visitors to use a good sun screen for protection, and wear a hat when out and about. Venomous snakes and spiders are present in many places, especially in lush, mountainous areas (like Table Mountain National Park), so be careful when tramping around. Watch where you are walking, and wear protective footwear rather than open sandals.

EMERGENCIES

Ambulance, tel: 10177
Fire, tel: 021-480 7700
General emergencies, tel: 107 (mobile-phone users dial 112)
Flying Squad, tel: 10111
Mountain Rescue Services, tel: 021-948 9900
Police Station, tel: 021-467 8000
Poison Crisis Centre, tel: 021-931 6129
Sea Rescue, tel: 021-449 3500

HIV/Aids

HIV infection and Aids have become huge problems in South Africa, which currently has the world's largest population of people living with HIV/Aids disease, estimated at more than 5 million. It is thus especially important to exercise caution and take necessary precautions in any sexual relations. Hospitals are extremely vigilant in ensuring that HIV does not spread during medical procedures.

Medical Facilities

Cape Town has excellent medical facilities. Indeed, the first heart transplant was conducted here by Christiaan Barnard in 1967*(see page 132)*. The city also has an international reputation for excellent, low-cost cosmetic surgery. Visitors are advised to take out medical insurance for the duration of their trip, as all medical care must be paid for.

Most hospitals have a 24-hour accident and emergency department with highly trained doctors and fully equipped operating theatres. Hospitals are classified as government hospitals or private hospitals/clinics. The latter are better equipped. Outpatient treatment may be obtained at hospitals for a nominal fee.

Groote Schuur Hospital
Tel: 021-414 9111
www.gsh.co.za

Netcare Christiaan Barnard Memorial Hospital
Tel: 021-480 6111
www.netcare.co.za

Red Cross Children's Hospital
Tel: 021-658 5111
www.childrenshospitaltrust.org.za

UCT Hospital
Tel: 021-442 1800
www.ucthospital.co.za

Doctors and Dentists

For a list of doctors or dentists consult Directory Enquiries on 1023 or speak to your hotel receptionist or concierge. You might have to call in advance to organise an appointment. Also, as a tourist you will have to pay cash for medicines and consultation fees, so be sure to keep receipts for insurance purposes.

Late-night Pharmacies

Glengariff Clicks Pharmacy
2 Main Road, Sea Point
Tel: 021-434 8622
Open Mon–Sat 8am–10pm, Sun 9am–9pm

Lite-Kem
24 Darling Street
Tel: 021-461 8040
Open Mon–Fri 8am–11pm, Sat and Sun 9am–11pm

M-Kem Medicine City
Corner of Durban and Raglan roads, Belville
Tel: 021-948 5707
Open daily 24 hours

SAA-Netcare Travel Clinic
11th Floor, Picbel Arcade, 58 Strand Street
Tel: 021-419 3172
www.travelclinic.co.za
Open Mon–Fri 8am–5pm, Sat 9am–1pm
Offers traveller's vaccinations, first-aid kits and travel medical advice, especially on malaria which occurs in northern areas. Credit cards accepted.

Internet

Most ISPs (Internet Service Providers) will provide a programme that allows you to connect to the internet and email services anywhere in the world. Most hotels now have broadband Wi-fi and/or a fixed internet point in the bedrooms, and others have a business centre or a few computers for the use of guests. If you intend to stay in South Africa for an extended period, you may want to contact a local ISP which will provide you with a user name, password and internet dial-up. This can be done through the national telephone provider Telkom (www.telkomsa.net) or any of several private providers.

Internet Cafés

There are innumerable internet cafés in Cape Town, especially around Long Street. You will also find internet access in most public libraries, backpacker hostels, hotels and guest lodges. Broadband speeds are not generally as fast as in Europe or the USA, but this is constantly improving

Lost Property

Report your loss at the local police station and leave your contact details and address. Missing items of luggage can be located at the Lost and Found division of the Cape Town International Airport, tel: 021-937 1200. It may also be worth checking the "lost and found" section in the classified section of the local daily newspapers.

Media

Newspapers

The *Cape Argus*, an afternoon newspaper, and *Die Burger*, an Afrikaans-language morning newspaper, are the most widely read daily papers in the area. They provide general interest news with a dash of politics and an emphasis on human-interest stories. The *Cape Times*, a morning newspaper, carries more international news and provides readers with greater depth of information on South African and international political developments.

The three major Sunday newspapers, the *Sunday Times*, *Weekend Argus* and *Rapport*, include a mix of detailed analyses of political developments, summary of the week's news and saucy sensation. The *Mail & Guardian*, published on a Friday, is an excellent read, and focuses on South African, African and international politics. It is read by business people and decision-makers throughout southern Africa. Its online version (www.mg.co.za) is excellent, as is the Independent On-Line (www.iol.co.za).

South Africa also offers a wide range of local and international magazines, ranging from fashion to fishing. You will find them at leading newsagents, supermarkets and bookstores throughout the Western Cape.

You can also pick up a copy of the *Big Issue* magazine at most traffic intersections. Proceeds from the sales go to the vendors, who are usually homeless people in need of an income.

Radio

The Western Cape has a range of local, regional and national radio stations. Most broadcast in English. KFM (94.5 FM), the most popular radio station in the Western Cape, plays a mix of '70s, '80s, '90s and current hits. Good Hope FM and P4 Radio are two of the most popular radio stations in Cape Town. Community radio stations have boomed in South Africa in recent years. Stations such as Christian station CCFM in Cape Town and the Muslim community station Voice of the Cape are among the community stations aimed at serving the Western Cape's diverse population.

Television

The South African Broadcasting Corporation (SABC) provides three television channels: SABC 1, 2 and 3. SABC 1 and 2 broadcast programmes in English, Afrikaans and Xhosa, while SABC 3 broadcasts only in English, and includes many award-winning American and British hit TV shows. Privately owned free-to-air e-TV broadcasts a mix of local and international programmes. DSTV is a multi-channel satellite subscription service whose flagship pay station M-Net shows good films, live sport and chat shows, and is supplemented by a varied range of other stations, ranging from BBC, CNN, MTV, Discovery and National Geographic to the local Super Sport 1-6 and Movie Magic 1-2. Most hotels and guesthouses and even backpackers' hostels provide up to 12 DSTV channels.

Money

Most banks are open Mon–Fri 9am–3.30pm, Sat 8–11am. The unit of currency in South Africa is the rand (R), divided into 100 cents (c). Notes are issued in R200, R100, R50, R20, R10; coins R5, R2, R1, 50c, 20c, 10c, 5c, 2c and 1c. Currency-exchange rates are available at banks and are published in the daily press, or contact your closest bureau de change. In the last year or so rates have been around R11.50 to £1 and R7 to $1. *See also Customs Regulations (page 244) and Tax (page 248).*

Credit Cards

Credit cards are widely accepted for goods and services. The most universally accepted brands are Visa, Maestro and MasterCard, with Diners Club and American Express also being accepted at most chain and other large outlets. International credit cards cannot be used to buy petrol, and while some filling stations do now accept debit cards, cash remains the most reliable option when it comes to fuelling up.

ATMs

ATMs are common in the downtown areas, and are also present in all shopping malls and many filling stations, supermarkets and convenience stores. Some have on-site security guards outside normal hours. The machines accept most major credit cards and some debit cards. Beware when using ATMs, especially of "helpful" strangers, who try to involve themselves in your transaction.

Tipping

Gratuities are the norm in South Africa because of the very low wages of service staff. You'll be expected to tip hotel porters up to R5 per item, registered taxi drivers 10 percent, petrol attendants get around R3 for washing your windscreen and car guards are usually happy with about R3–5. Waiters or service attendants in restaurants should be tipped a minimum of 10 percent of the total bill (also subject to quality of service), but check your bill to ensure a service charge hasn't already been included.

Opening Hours

Most shops in the city centre and suburbs are open 9am–5pm on weekdays and at least until 1pm on Saturdays, though some will stay open later. Activity in the city centre comes to an end around 1pm on Saturdays. However, shopping malls such as the V&A Waterfront, Cavendish Square in Claremont and Canal Walk at Century City keep much later hours, staying open from 9am–9pm throughout the week (from 10am Sunday). On public holidays the city centre is completely dead, but you will find plenty of life at the Waterfront.

Government agencies are open Mon–Fri 9am–5pm. Most liquor stores close at 6pm (Mon–Sat). Supermarkets generally close at 6pm (according to the seasons), until 5pm on Saturday and until 2pm on Sunday, though there are a few 24-hour supermarkets around.

In mid-summer sunrise is around 5.30am and sundown at around 8.30pm. In mid-winter it gets dark at about 5.45pm and light at about 7.30am, depending on cloud cover.

Postal Services

You'll find that sending mail from South Africa to anywhere in the world is relatively inexpensive. A postcard or standard letter to Europe or the United States costs around R5. Postage stamps are sold at the Post Office and selected newsagents and retail outlets. The Post Office (tel: 0860 111 502, www.sapo.co.za) handles local and international post and offers 24-hour door-to-door (Speed) services, including insurance, between major cities. Opening times are: weekdays 8.30am–4.30pm, Saturday 8am–noon. Cape Town's General Post Office is a huge Art Deco building in Darling Street.

Courier and freight

The Post Office and local courier companies can help you ship your purchases home and deal with the formalities. There are many freight companies in Cape Town that will assist you with the shipping of goods and you'll find them in the Yellow Pages under "Courier Services".

Religious Services

Most South Africans are Christians. The largest denominations are Anglican (Church of England), Roman Catholic and Dutch Reformed. There are also large Jewish and Muslim communities living in the Western Cape. To find the place of worship of your choice, consult your hotel staff or the weekend press.

Otherwise contact these places of worship for information on services:

Buddhist Information
Kenilworth
Tel: 021-761 2978

Central Methodist Mission
Corner of Longmarket and Burg streets, Greenmarket Square
Tel: 021-422 2744

Dutch Reformed Church
Groote Kerk, Adderley Street, Cape Town
Tel: 021-422 0569
www.grootekerk.org.za

Evangelical Lutheran Church
98 Strand Street
Tel: 021-421 5854

Jewish Cape Town Hebrew Congregation
88 Hatfield Street, Gardens
Tel: 021-465 1405

Palm Tree Mosque
185 Long Street
Tel: 021-444 4613

St George's Anglican Cathedral
Corner of Queen and Wale streets
Tel: 021-424 7360
www.stgeorgescathedral.com

St Mary's Roman Catholic Cathedral
Roeland Street
Tel: 021-461 1167

PUBLIC HOLIDAYS

New Year's Day 1 January
Constitution Day 27 February
Human Rights Day 21 March
Good Friday March/April
Family Day (Easter Monday) March/April
Workers' Day 1 May
Youth Day 16 June
National Women's Day 9 August
Heritage Day 24 September
Day of Reconciliation 16 December
Christmas Day 25 December
Day of Goodwill 26 December

Student Travellers

Young people under the age of 26 are entitled to many concessionary rates, including air fares, hostel accommodation and admission to museums and galleries, although a valid passport or international student card may be required (visit www.isic.co.za for information on internationally recognised student cards).

STA Travel is the world's largest travel company specialising in the needs of young people and students, ranging from travel insurance to discount cards, budget travel packages and more. For information visit www.sta travel.co.za.

A popular student magazine in South Africa is *SL Magazine* (www.slmagazine.co.za), which is available from most newsagents and bookstores. It's a hip and funky read that's filled with information on current films, exhibitions, music concerts and all cultural events.

Tax

The only tax that affects tourists is VAT (value-added tax), which is charged at 14 percent and included automatically in practically all prices quoted by shops and other service providers. Foreign visitors can reclaim the VAT on goods that cost more than R250. This must be done within 90 days of purchase. To make a claim, it is necessary to request a tax invoice for the goods from the sales assistant when you make your purchase. This must include a tax-invoice number, the seller's VAT registration number, the date of issue, the seller's name and address, the buyer's name and address, a description of the goods, the cost of the goods and the amount of VAT charged. On your departure from South Africa this should be presented, along with the goods, at the airport's VAT Goods Inspection Desk prior to check-in (allow plenty of time for this). An administration charge of 1.5 percent is made. For further information, contact: www.taxrefunds.co.za.

Telephones

The dialling code for South Africa is 27 followed by the local regional codes. These include Cape Town (0)21, Johannesburg (0)11, Pretoria (0)12 and Durban (0)31. Telephones have direct dialling to most parts of the world. If you have a problem getting through to an international number contact Directory Enquiries on 1023.

Public Phones

International calls from hotel rooms are often very expensive (be sure to check the rates before dialling). It is usually considerably cheaper to buy a phone card and use a call box. You will find telephone booths all over town, particularly near shopping malls and hotels.

Public phones are either coin- or card-operated. Phone cards of varying values (R10, R20, R50, R100 and R200) are available from newsagents, post offices and Telkom offices.

To phone abroad from South Africa, dial 00 followed by the relevant country code:
Australia 61
US and Canada 1
UK 44
Ireland 353

Mobile Phones

South Africa's booming mobile-phone industry is served by three service providers: MTN (www.mtn.co.za), Vodacom (www.vodacom.co.za) and Cell C (www.cellc.co.za). All three operate on GSM digital. It may be that your phone is compatible, so speak to your network provider about international roaming. Alternatively, you can hire a mobile phone at the airport or from tourist information centres. It's also very inexpensive to purchase a local SIM card (some international mobile phones will work here if you purchase a local SIM card). Most network providers deliver excellent service that allows you to call or exchange text messages at any time.

Toilets

The best bet is the toilets in shopping malls, which will include toilets for disabled and baby-changing facilities. Most garages also have clean toilets.

Time Zone

Standard time is two hours in advance of GMT and seven hours in advance of United States Eastern Standard Time throughout the year.

Tour Operators and Travel Agents

There are a huge number of tour operators in the Eastern Cape. The tourist information centres on the corner of Castle and Burg streets and near the Clocktower on the Waterfront are stuffed with leaflets advertising every kind of tour, from township tours to horse-riding tours through the Peninsula. As a rule, prices are quite high, and it may work out cheaper to hire a car and undertake excursions independently. Here is a selection of the many and varied options on offer:

African Pathfinder
11 Stoneybrook Estate,
Valley Road, Hout Bay
Tel: 021-790 6061
www.africanpathfinder.com
Tailor-made honeymoons, holidays, safaris, etc.

Southern Destinations
46 Main Road, Claremont
Tel: 021-671 3090
www.southerndestinations.com
Specialists in tours, safaris and honeymoons to some of the top lodges, hotels and camps.

Cape Rainbow Tours
PO Box 51372, Waterfront
Tel: 021-551 5465
www.caperainbow.com
This company has a fleet of luxury, air-conditioned micro-buses, offering day tours, Garden Route tours and country tours.

Cruise Travel and Tours
14 Jefferson Road, Noordhoek
Tel: 021-785 6994
www.cruisesa.co.za
As the name suggests, they can organise an underwater adventure amongst shipwrecks or a swim with dolphins and seals.

Embassy Travel
17 Wale Street
Tel: 021-424 1111
www.embassytravel.co.za
One of the leading travel agencies. Excellent arrangements for car hire, air travel, conference organising, day tours, etc.

Mike Bosch Tours
PO Box 27365, Rhine Road
Tel: 021-434 1956

www.mikeboschtours.co.za
For the discerning traveller wanting mountain, coastline, beach and vineyard tours.

Cape Town Private Tours
Tel: 021-790 5477
www.capetownprivatetours.co.za
Small hands-on company offering personalised private tours in greater Cape Town and the Winelands.

Take 2 Tours and Safaris
PO Box 364, Plumstead 7801
Tel: 082-650 0545
www.take2tours.co.za
Customised private tours to everywhere from the Cape Flats townships to Hermanus and the West Coast.

Tourist Information

Cape Town Tourism (www.capetown.travel) operates 18 visitor centres, which are one-stop sources of information for everything you need to know, from maps and brochures to accommodation, tours and events. The most important offices are in the city centre (Corner of Castle and Burg streets; tel: 021-426 4260), at Cape Town International Airport (tel: 021-935 6060) and at the V&A Waterfront (tel: 021-408 7600). Opening times of most visitor centres are Mon–Fri 8.30am–5.30am, Sat 8.30am–1pm and Sun 9am–1pm.

Confusingly, the separate **Western Cape Tourism** also has a visitors' centre at the V&A Waterfront (tel: 021-405 4500, www.tourismcapetown.co.za; open 9am–9pm daily) providing a similar service but with more information about parts of the province outside metropolitan Cape Town.

For information about travel further afield in South Africa, **South Africa Tourism** (www.southafrica.net) has an information office at 80 St George's Mall (tel: 021-426 5639).

Smaller independent sites worth checking out are www.capetourism.co.za and www.capetown.gopassport.com – the latter is a directory that covers Cape Town accommodation, restaurants, property, car hire, tour operators and nightlife, among other specials and travel deals.

Visas and Passports

All visitors need a valid passport to enter South Africa. Nationals from the EU, Australia, Canada, the USA, New Zealand and Japan do not require a visa for stays of less than 90 days, though they technically need to provide a return ticket (or the means to purchase one) at their point of entry, a requirement that is very seldom checked in practice.

If you are subject to visa requirements, you will need to apply for your visa at least four weeks before your intended departure. You can apply at your nearest South African Embassy, High Commission or Consulate. Visas are issued upon completion of the necessary forms, payment of a fee, proof of sufficient financial means and possession of a return ticket (or proof of the means to purchase one). You will also need to supply two passport-size photographs. Your passport must be valid for at least 30 days after the expiry date of your intended visit. To check the latest on visa requirements, visit www.home-affairs.gov.za.

Arriving with Children

If your child's passport shows a different surname to your own, you will need to provide evidence that the child is yours, such as a birth certificate.

What to Bring

If you take a prescription drug on a regular basis, be sure to bring supplies with you; as an added precaution, bring a copy of your prescription too. In winter bring a warmish waterproof coat and an umbrella. Also bring a pair of flat, comfortable shoes, and possibly walking boots if you are planning to hike (though trainers will suffice for most hikes in summer). If you are planning to extend your trip with a safari, or even if you just want to enjoy the amazing birdlife of the Cape, bring a pair of binoculars.

If you bring a laptop, make sure that it can operate on 240 volts or that you have the necessary transformer. You will also need to purchase an adaptor plug *(see Electricity, page 244)*, though these can also be bought in electrical stores in South Africa. Make sure that your laptop and any other electronic equipment you bring along is adequately insured against loss or theft and be vigilant about protecting your property at all times.

Women Travellers

In most respects, Cape Town – or at least those places regularly frequented by tourists – feels more like a Western city than part of the developing world. As such, women travellers who take the same sort of precautions they would at home, especially with regard to avoiding quiet unlit areas after dark or hanging out on isolated beaches and hiking trails by day, are unlikely to hit gender-specific problems. Crime is a greater problem than in most European or North American cities, but solo women are not specifically targeted.

When it comes to the place and role of women in society, South Africa is somewhat more conservative than Europe or North America, a perspective that is prevalent across all race groups. Fortunately, Cape Town is considerably more liberal than the rest of the country on matters of sex and sexuality, and women are unlikely to feel themselves discriminated against in places that regularly host tourists. It might be very different if you find yourself socialising over a few drinks with South Africans outside the cocoon of the tourist industry – not that a situation like that is likely to be threatening in any sense, but it might well be rather eye-opening!

FURTHER READING

History and Biography

Long Walk to Freedom by Nelson Mandela. A compelling, must-read autobiography for anyone coming to South Africa.
Desmond Tutu: A Biography by Steven D. Gish. Inspiring life story of the tireless anti-apartheid campaigner Archbishop Desmond Tutu.
My Traitor's Heart by Rian Malan. Outstanding autobiography of a white South African coming to terms with his heritage and his country's future.
Beyond the Miracle: Inside the New South Africa by Allister Sparks. Delves into various aspects of post-Mandela South Africa, identifying its challenges and successes.
Biko by Donald Woods. Portrait of the Black Consciousness Movement leader killed in police custody in 1977.
Every Secret Thing: My Family, My Country by Gillian Slovo. Fascinating memoir by the daughter of white activists Joe Slovo and Ruth First.
The History of South Africa by Leonard Monteath Thompson. Now in its third edition, this is the best overall introduction to South African history, and remarkably comprehensive given its relative compactness.
The Boer War by Thomas Packenham. Masterly and thorough account of the protracted Anglo-Boer hostilities.
Of Warriors, Lovers and Prophets and ***Of Tricksters, Tyrants and Turncoats*** by Max du Preez. Collections of stories offering a fresh, lively and rather quirky anecdotal look at South Africa's history.
Country of My Skull by Antjie Krog. Definitive account of the Truth and Reconciliation Commission in the immediate aftermath of apartheid.
Bring Me My Machine Gun: The Battle for the Soul of South Africa, from Mandela to Zuma by Alec Russell. A modern history of the ANC.
Kaffir Boy: The True Story of a Black Youth's Coming of Age in Apartheid South Africa by Mark Mathabane. The subtitle of this riveting autobiography says it all.
Ways of Staying by Kevin Bloom. A journalist's examination of the rising tide of violence in South Africa, from a personal and social perspective, and how it has affected the white community.

Culture

The Lost World of the Kalahari by Laurens van der Post. A poetic interpretation of the San culture.
Indaba My Children by Vusamazulu Credo Mutwa. An extraordinary compilation of history, legend, folk tales, customs and beliefs by an author who grew up in KwaZulu-Natal.

Fiction

The Conservationist by Nadine Gordimer. 1974 Booker Prize winner, by one of South Africa's highly acclaimed fiction writers.
Disgrace by J.M. Coetzee. A cynical look at South African society, which won the 1999 Booker Prize.
Cry, The Beloved Country by Alan Paton. A classic, profoundly compassionate tale of a Zulu pastor and his son, set in the 1940s.
Power of One by Bryce Courtenay. A moving story of a young English boy's search for love and friendship.
The Heart of Redness by Zakes Mda. Modern retelling of the story of 19th-century Xhosa prophetess Nongqawuse.
Welcome to Our Hillbrow by Phaswane Mpe. Hard-hitting tale of the arrival of a rural innocent in Johannesburg's most notoriously seedy suburb.

Natural History

Sasol Birds of Southern Africa by Ian Sinclair, Phil-Hockey and Warwick Tarboton. An excellent field guide with good colour plates.
Mammals of Southern Africa by Charles and Tilde Stuart. A useful guide for wildlife spotters.

Food and Wine

Traditional South African Cooking by Magdaleen van Wyk and Pat Barton. A definite collection of traditional South African recipes.
Tasting the Cape by Jean-Pierre Rossouw. The ideal companion to touring the Cape Winelands.

Special Interest

The Bigfoot Family Guide to Cape Town by Andre Plant. A small, inexpensive book with lots of fun ideas for families.
Holistic Holidays in South Africa by Janine Nepgen and Sharyn Spicer. Life-changing holidays to rejuvenate body, mind and soul.

Other Insight Guides

The *Insight Guide South Africa* makes an excellent companion to this guide. Other African destinations in the Insight series include *Morocco*, *Egypt*, *The Nile*, *Gambia and Senegal*, *Kenya* and *Namibia*.

CAPE TOWN STREET ATLAS

The key map shows the area of Cape Town covered by the atlas section. An index of street names and places of interest shown on the maps can be found on the following pages. For each entry there is a page number and grid reference

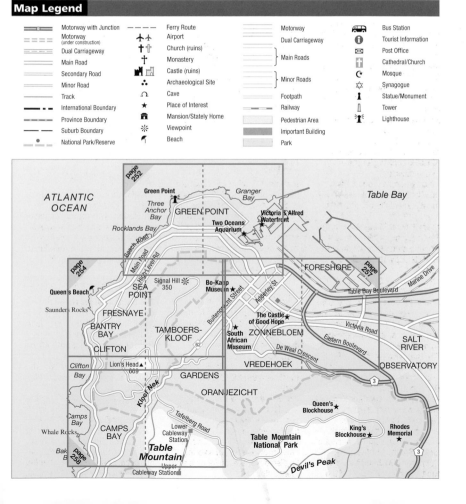

Map Legend

- Motorway with Junction
- Motorway (under construction)
- Dual Carriageway
- Main Road
- Secondary Road
- Minor Road
- Track
- International Boundary
- Province Boundary
- Suburb Boundary
- National Park/Reserve
- Ferry Route
- Airport
- Church (ruins)
- Monastery
- Castle (ruins)
- Archaeological Site
- Cave
- Place of Interest
- Mansion/Stately Home
- Viewpoint
- Beach
- Motorway
- Dual Carriageway
- Main Roads
- Minor Roads
- Footpath
- Railway
- Pedestrian Area
- Important Building
- Park
- Bus Station
- Tourist Information
- Post Office
- Cathedral/Church
- Mosque
- Synagogue
- Statue/Monument
- Tower
- Lighthouse

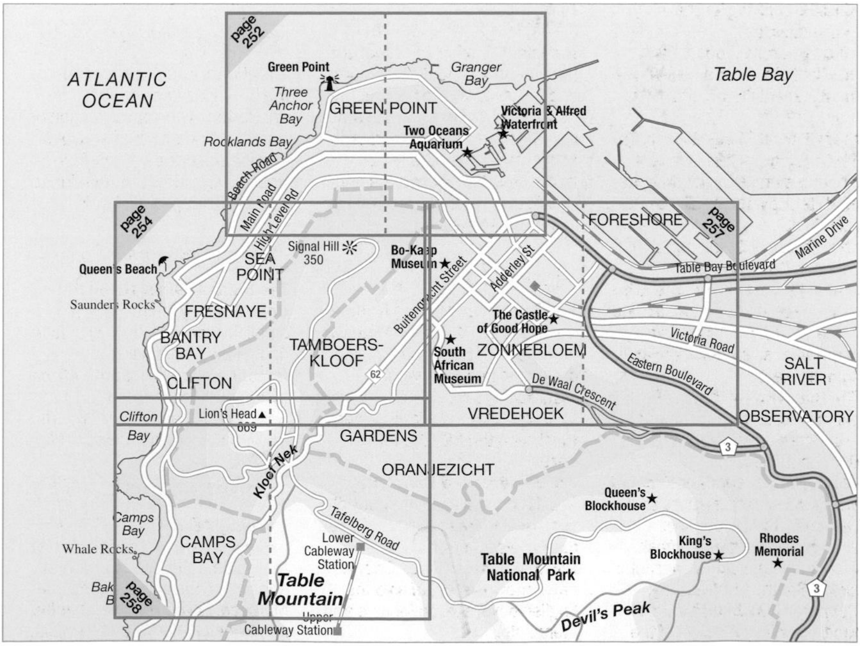

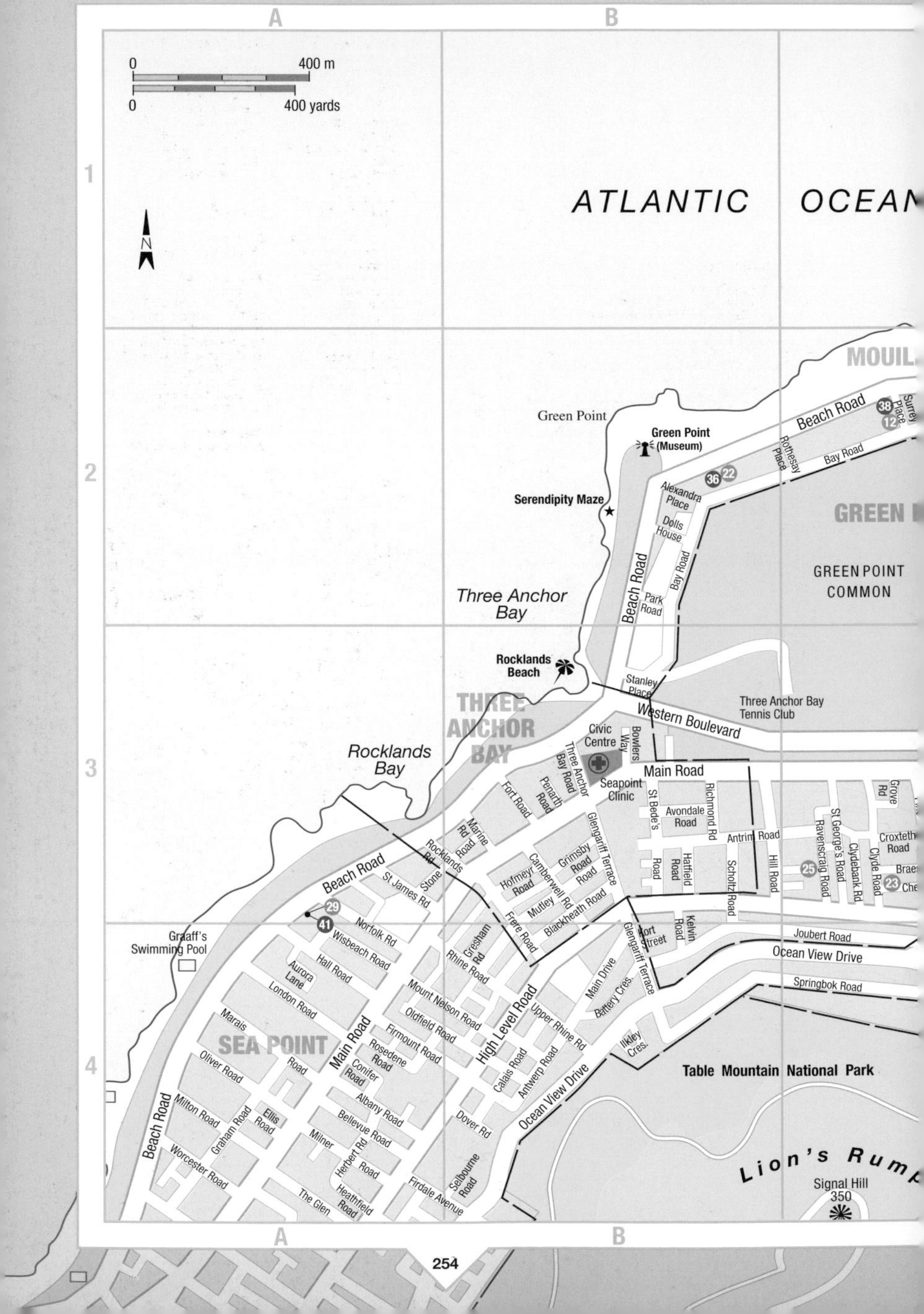
A
B
1
2
3
4
0
400 m
0
400 yards
N
ATLANTIC OCEAN
MOUILLE
Green Point
Green Point (Museum)
Serendipity Maze
Beach Road
Rothesay Place
Bay Road
Surrey Place
Alexandra Place
Dolls House
Park Road
GREEN POINT COMMON
Three Anchor Bay
Rocklands Beach
Stanley Place
THREE ANCHOR BAY
Western Boulevard
Three Anchor Bay Tennis Club
Rocklands Bay
Civic Centre
Bowlers Way
Three Anchor Bay Road
Seapoint Clinic
Main Road
Penarth Road
Fort Road
St Bede's Road
Avondale Road
Richmond Rd
Antrim Road
Hatfield Road
Scholtz Road
Hill Road
Ravenscraig Road
St George's Road
Clydebank Rd
Clyde Road
Croxteth Road
Grove Rd
Marine Road
Rocklands Rd
Stone Road
St James Rd
Hofmeyr Road
Camberwell Rd
Grimsby Road
Glengariff Terrace
Mutley
Blackheath Road
Frere Road
Gresham Rd
Fort Street
Kelvin Road
Joubert Road
Ocean View Drive
Springbok Road
Graaff's Swimming Pool
Norfolk Rd
Wisbeach Road
Hall Road
Aurora Lane
London Road
Rhine Road
Mount Nelson Road
Oldfield Road
Firmount Road
High Level Road
Upper Rhine Rd
Main Drive
Battery Cres.
Ilkley Cres.
Table Mountain National Park
Marais Road
SEA POINT
Main Road
Rosedene Road
Conifer Road
Calais Road
Antwerp Road
Oliver Road
Albany Road
Dover Rd
Milton Road
Graham Road
Ellis Road
Bellevue Road
Milner Road
Herbert Rd
Worcester Road
The Glen
Heathfield Road
Firdale Avenue
Selbourne Road
Lion's Rump
Signal Hill
350
254
29
41
36
22
38
12
25
23

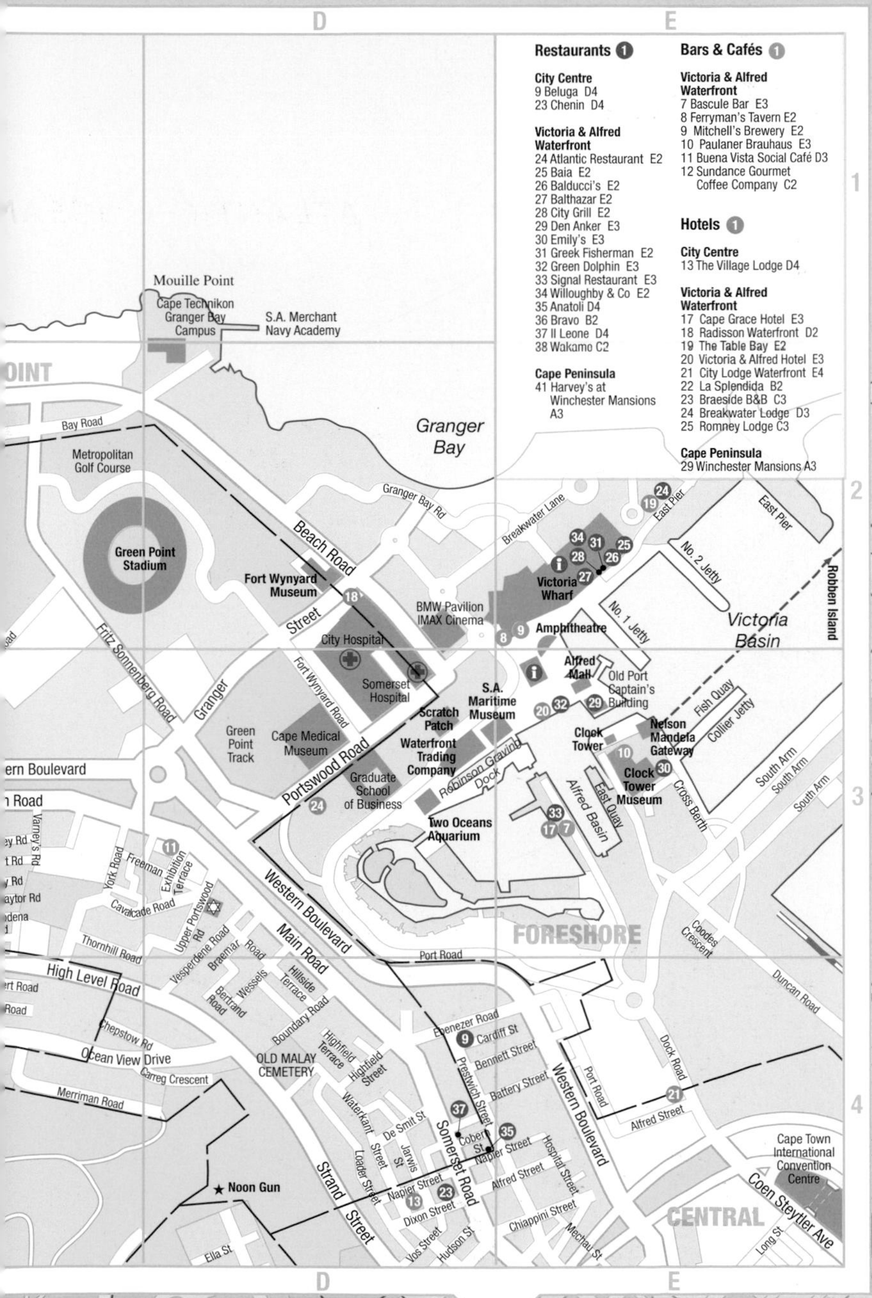
D
E
Restaurants 1
City Centre
9 Beluga D4
23 Chenin D4
Victoria & Alfred Waterfront
24 Atlantic Restaurant E2
25 Baia E2
26 Balducci's E2
27 Balthazar E2
28 City Grill E2
29 Den Anker E3
30 Emily's E3
31 Greek Fisherman E2
32 Green Dolphin E3
33 Signal Restaurant E3
34 Willoughby & Co E2
35 Anatoli D4
36 Bravo B2
37 Il Leone D4
38 Wakamo C2
Cape Peninsula
41 Harvey's at Winchester Mansions A3
Bars & Cafés 1
Victoria & Alfred Waterfront
7 Bascule Bar E3
8 Ferryman's Tavern E2
9 Mitchell's Brewery E2
10 Paulaner Brauhaus E3
11 Buena Vista Social Café D3
12 Sundance Gourmet Coffee Company C2
Hotels 1
City Centre
13 The Village Lodge D4
Victoria & Alfred Waterfront
17 Cape Grace Hotel E3
18 Radisson Waterfront D2
19 The Table Bay E2
20 Victoria & Alfred Hotel E3
21 City Lodge Waterfront E4
22 La Splendida B2
23 Braeside B&B C3
24 Breakwater Lodge D3
25 Romney Lodge C3
Cape Peninsula
29 Winchester Mansions A3
1
2
3
4
Mouille Point
Cape Technikon Granger Bay Campus
S.A. Merchant Navy Academy
Granger Bay
Bay Road
Metropolitan Golf Course
Green Point Stadium
Granger Bay Rd
Beach Road
Breakwater Lane
East Pier
No. 2 Jetty
Robben Island
Fort Wynyard Museum
Victoria Wharf
BMW Pavilion IMAX Cinema
Street
City Hospital
Amphitheatre
No. 1 Jetty
Victoria Basin
Fritz Sonnenberg Road
Granger
Fort Wynyard Road
Somerset Hospital
Alfred Mall
Old Port Captain's Building
Fish Quay
Collier Jetty
S.A. Maritime Museum
Scratch Patch
Green Point Track
Cape Medical Museum
Waterfront Trading Company
Clock Tower
Nelson Mandela Gateway
Portswood Road
Robinson Graving Dock
Clock Tower Museum
South Arm
Graduate School of Business
Alfred Basin
East Quay
Cross Berth
Two Oceans Aquarium
York Road
Freeman
Exhibition Terrace
Cavalcade Road
Upper Portswood Rd
Western Boulevard
FORESHORE
Coodes Crescent
Thornhill Road
Vesperdene Road
Braemar Road
Main Road
Hillside Terrace
Port Road
Duncan Road
High Level Road
Bertrand Road
Wessels
Boundary Road
Ebenezer Road
Cardiff St
Chepstow Rd
Highfield Terrace
Highfield Street
Bennett Street
Dock Road
Ocean View Drive
OLD MALAY CEMETERY
Prestwich Street
Battery Street
Western Boulevard
Port Road
Carreg Crescent
Merriman Road
Waterkant Street
De Smit St
Jarvis St
Coben St
Alfred Street
Somerset Road
Napier Street
Hospital Street
Cape Town International Convention Centre
Loader Street
Napier Street
Alfred Street
Coen Steytler Ave
Noon Gun
Strand Street
Dixon Street
Chiappini Street
CENTRAL
Ella St
Vos Street
Hudson St
Mechau St
Long St

256

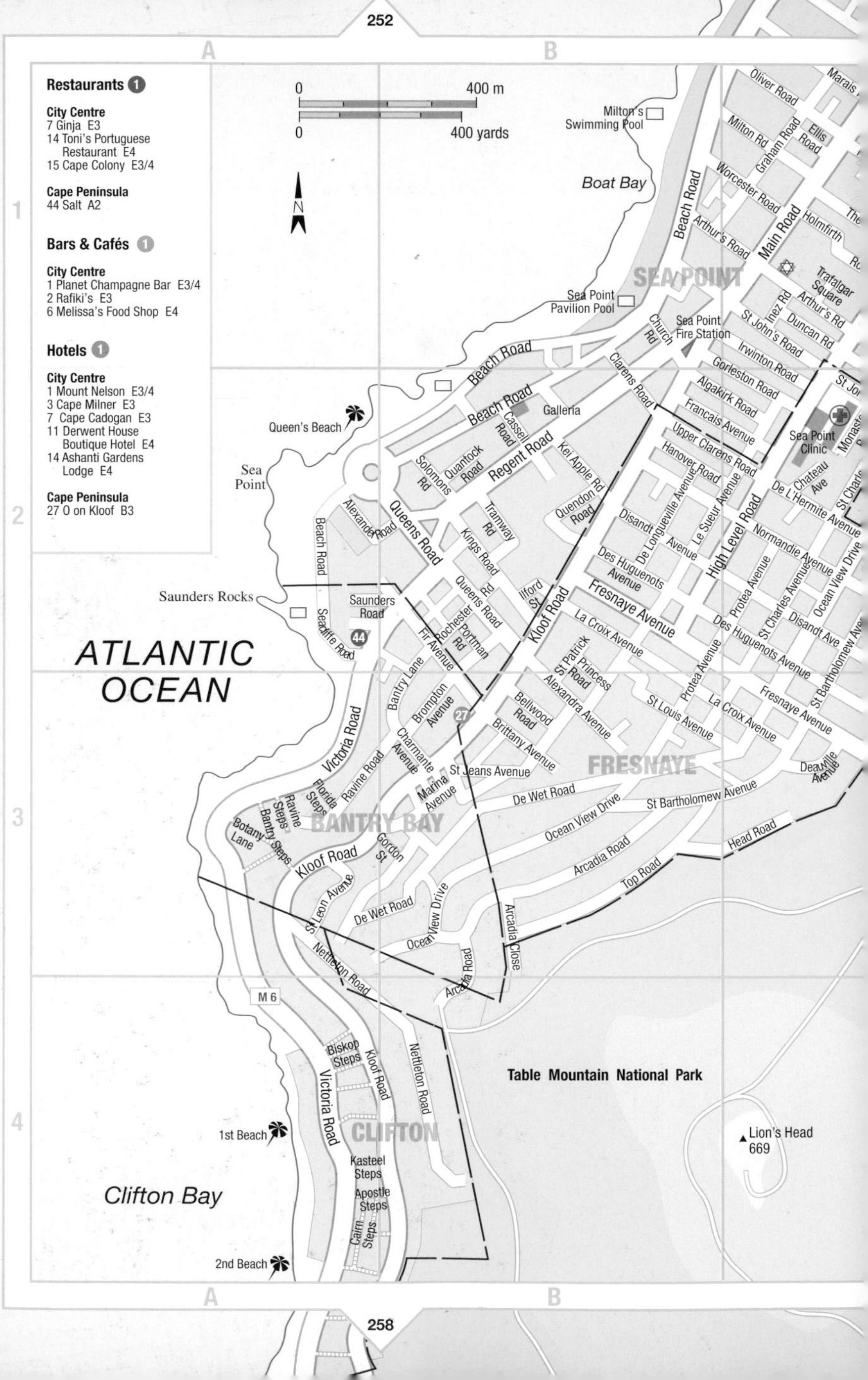
252
A
B
Restaurants 1
City Centre
7 Ginja E3
14 Toni's Portuguese Restaurant E4
15 Cape Colony E3/4
Cape Peninsula
44 Salt A2
Bars & Cafés 1
City Centre
1 Planet Champagne Bar E3/4
2 Rafiki's E3
6 Melissa's Food Shop E4
Hotels 1
City Centre
1 Mount Nelson E3/4
3 Cape Milner E3
7 Cape Cadogan E3
11 Derwent House Boutique Hotel E4
14 Ashanti Gardens Lodge E4
Cape Peninsula
27 O on Kloof B3
0
400 m
0
400 yards
N
1
2
3
4
ATLANTIC OCEAN
Boat Bay
Milton's Swimming Pool
SEA POINT
Sea Point Pavilion Pool
Sea Point Fire Station
Sea Point Clinic
Queen's Beach
Sea Point
Saunders Rocks
Galleria
FRESNAYE
BANTRY BAY
CLIFTON
Clifton Bay
1st Beach
2nd Beach
M 6
Table Mountain National Park
Lion's Head 669
Beach Road
Main Road
Regent Road
Queens Road
Kloof Road
Victoria Road
High Level Road
Fresnaye Avenue
Nettleton Road
Biskop Steps
Kasteel Steps
Apostle Steps
Cairn Steps
258

253
D
E
1
2
3
4
256
259
Table Mountain National Park
Signal Hill
350
Lion's Rump
Signal Hill Road
SCHOTSCHE
KLOOF
TAMBOERSKLOOF
GARDENS
St Mary
Maternity
Volks
Hospital
DE WAAL
PARK
Fresnaye
Sports Club
Conradie
Recreation
Ground
Leeuwenhof
& Bo-Tuin
Calais Rd
Antwerp Rd
Ocean View Drive
Dover Rd
High Level Road
Selbourne
Road
Firdale Avenue
Edward Road
Deane Road
Clifford Road
Friars Road
Sparta Road
Military Road
Voetboog Road
Yusuf Drive
Tanabaru
St
Astana
Street
Pentz Road
Upr Pepper St
Upper Bloem Street
Lion Street
Bryant Street
Jordaan Street
Military Road
Whitford
Street
Carisbrook
Road
Bennington
Road
Military Rd
Victoria
Street
Carisbrook
Street
Poyser Road
Kenmore Road
Milner Road
Devonport Road
Queens Road
Brownlow Road
Leeukloof
Leeuwenvoet Road
Milner Road
Hillside Road
Carstens Street
Brunswick Rd
Upper Buitengracht
New Church Street
Frederick
Close
Burnside Road
Woodside Road
Gilmour Hills
Leith Hill
Tamboerskloof Road
Belle Ombre Road
Hildene Road
Albert Road
Bond Street
Camden Street
Warren Street
Upper Albert Road
Bay View
Rael Street
St Michael's Rd
Hastings Street
De Hoop
Cambridge
Avenue
Avenue
Avenue
Varsity Street
Regent
Square
Leeukop Street
Kloof Nek Road
Quarry Hill
Quarry Hill
Park Lane
Park House
Road
Kloof Street
Kloo
Nek
Road
Faure Street
Eaton Road
Wilkinson Street
Upper Union St
King St
Nicol
Street
Barnabas St
Weltevreden St
Union
Krynauw St
Street
Vine
Street
Morkel St
Camp Street
De Lorentz Street
Kloof Avenue
Derwent Road
Kelvin St
Bath St
Newport
St
Malan
St
Leeuwendal
Stephen Road
Welgemeend Street
Lingen Street
Street
Tuin St
Cotswold
Ave
Firdale Road
Cresc.
Ivy St
Kloof Street
Hofmeyr Street
Hof
Molteno Road
Ivanhoe
Street
Kotze Street
Constantia Road
Kloof Nek Road
Hof Street
Rayden
Street
Bellevue Street

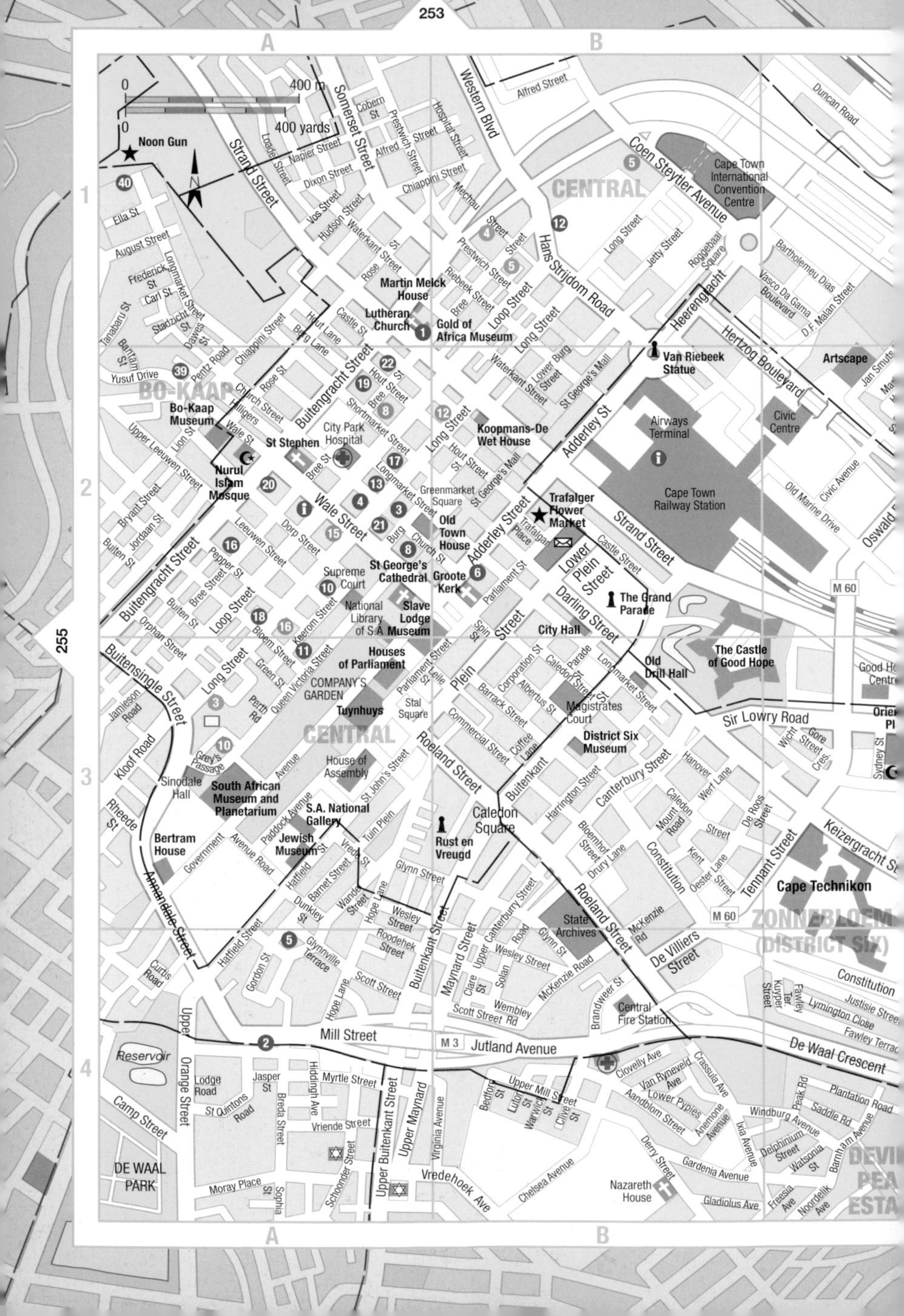
253
255
A
B
1
2
3
4
0
400 m
0
400 yards
Noon Gun
CENTRAL
BO-KAAP
ZONNEBLOEM (DISTRICT SIX)
Cape Town International Convention Centre
Artscape
Civic Centre
Airways Terminal
Cape Town Railway Station
Van Riebeek Statue
Martin Melck House
Lutheran Church
Gold of Africa Museum
Bo-Kaap Museum
Nurul Islam Mosque
St Stephen
City Park Hospital
Koopmans-De Wet House
Greenmarket Square
Trafalger Flower Market
Old Town House
St George's Cathedral
Groote Kerk
Supreme Court
National Library of S.A
Slave Lodge Museum
Houses of Parliament
COMPANY'S GARDEN
Tuynhuys
Stal Square
The Grand Parade
City Hall
Old Drill Hall
The Castle of Good Hope
Magistrates Court
District Six Museum
House of Assembly
South African Museum and Planetarium
Sinodale Hall
S.A. National Gallery
Jewish Museum
Bertram House
Rust en Vreugd
Caledon Square
State Archives
Cape Technikon
Central Fire Station
Nazareth House
Reservoir
DE WAAL PARK
Good Hope Centre
M 60
M 3
Alfred Street
Duncan Road
Western Blvd
Coen Steytler Avenue
Somerset Street
Strand Street
Hans Strijdom Road
Heerengracht
Hertzog Boulevard
Bartholomeu Dias
Vasco Da Gama Boulevard
D.F. Malan Street
Long Street
Jetty Street
Roggebaai Square
Riebeek Street
Prestwich Street
Loop Street
Waterkant Street
Lower Burg Street
St George's Mall
Adderley St
Buitengracht Street
Bree Street
Shortmarket Street
Longmarket Street
Hout Street
Wale Street
Church Street
Burg St
Dorp Street
Leeuwen Street
Pepper St
Keerom Street
Bloem Street
Queen Victoria Street
Parliament Street
Plein Street
Darling Street
Lower Plein Street
Castle Street
Corporation St
Caledon Street
Barrack Street
Commercial Street
Roeland Street
Buitenkant
Canterbury Street
Harrington Street
Hanover
Constitution Street
Tennant Street
Keizergracht Street
Sir Lowry Road
De Villiers Street
Mill Street
Jutland Avenue
De Waal Crescent
Buitensingle Street
Kloof Road
Annandale Street
Government Avenue
Orange Street
Camp Street
Upper Buitenkant Street
Upper Maynard
Vredehoek Ave
Chelsea Avenue
Gardenia Avenue
Gladiolus Ave
Plantation Road
Windburg Avenue
Yusuf Drive
Chiappini Street
Rose St
Upper Leeuwen Street
Loader Street
Napier Street
Dixon Street
Vos Street
Hudson Street
Cobern St
Alfred Street
Hospital Street
Chiappini Street
Mechau
Ella St
August Street
Frederick St
Carl St
Longmarket Street
Stadzicht St
Dawes St
Tanabaru St
Bantam St
Pentz Road
Hilligers
Lion St
Bryant Street
Jordaan St
Buiten St
Orphan Street
Green St
Perth Rd
Grey's Passage
Jamieson Road
Rheede St
Hatfield Street
Barnet Street
Dunkley St
Wandel Street
Hope Lane
Wesley Street
Roodehek Street
Scott Street
Glynn Street
Tuin Plein
St John's Street
Paddock Avenue
Vrede St
Gordon St
Glynnville Terrace
Curtis Road
Maynard Street
Upper Canterbury Street
Clare St
Solan Road
Wembley Road
Scott Street Rd
McKenzie Road
Brandweer St
Glynn St
Bloemhof Street
Drury Lane
Mount Road
Kent Street
Oester Lane
De Roos Street
Werf Lane
Wicht Cres.
Gore Street
Sydney St
Jan Smuts
Civic Avenue
Old Marine Drive
Oswald
Constitution
Justisie Street
Lymington Close
Fawley Terrace
Kuyper Street
Fawley Ter.
Clovelly Ave
Van Ryneveld Ave
Lower Pypies
Aandblom Street
Anemone Avenue
Crassula Ave
Ixia Avenue
Derry Street
Peak Rd
Saddle Rd
Barnham Avenue
Delphinium Street
Watsonia St
Freesia Ave
Noordelik Ave
Upper Mill Street
Bedford St
Luton St
Warwick St
Clive St
Virginia Avenue
Myrtle Street
Hiddingh Ave
Jasper St
Lodge Road
St Quintons Road
Breda Street
Vriende Street
Schoonder Street
Moray Place
Sophia St
Coffee Lane
Albertus St
Parade St
Spin St
Lelie St
Trafalgar Place
Castle St
Berg Lane
Hout Lane
Rose St
Bree St

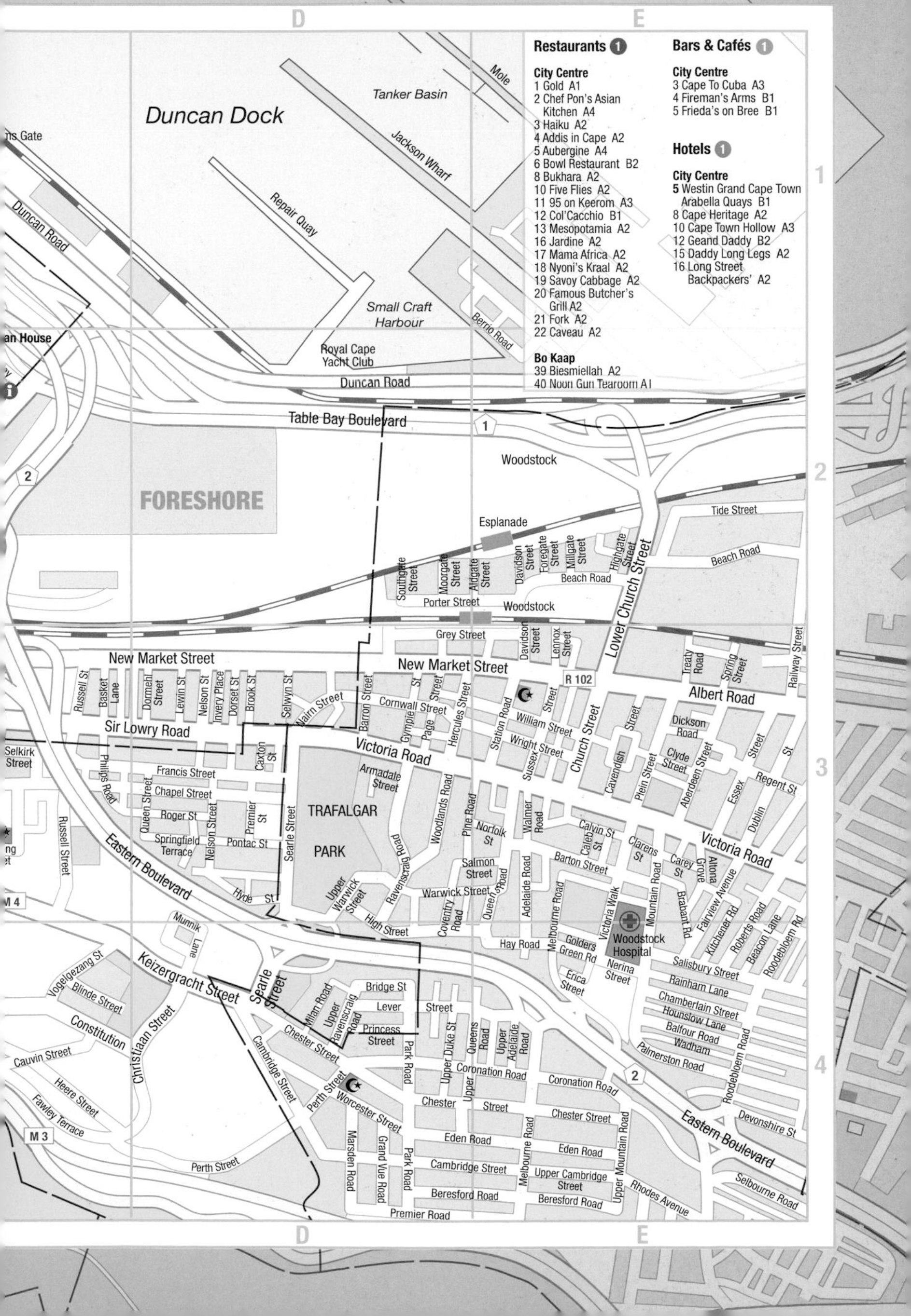
D
E
Restaurants 1
City Centre
1 Gold A1
2 Chef Pon's Asian Kitchen A4
3 Haiku A2
4 Addis in Cape A2
5 Aubergine A4
6 Bowl Restaurant B2
8 Bukhara A2
10 Five Flies A2
11 95 on Keerom A3
12 Col'Cacchio B1
13 Mesopotamia A2
16 Jardine A2
17 Mama Africa A2
18 Nyoni's Kraal A2
19 Savoy Cabbage A2
20 Famous Butcher's Grill A2
21 Fork A2
22 Caveau A2
Bo Kaap
39 Biesmiellah A2
40 Noon Gun Tearoom A1
Bars & Cafés 1
City Centre
3 Cape To Cuba A3
4 Fireman's Arms B1
5 Frieda's on Bree B1
Hotels 1
City Centre
5 Westin Grand Cape Town Arabella Quays B1
8 Cape Heritage A2
10 Cape Town Hollow A3
12 Geand Daddy B2
15 Daddy Long Legs A2
16 Long Street Backpackers' A2
Duncan Dock
Tanker Basin
Mole
Jackson Wharf
Repair Quay
Small Craft Harbour
Royal Cape Yacht Club
Berrio Road
Duncan Road
Table Bay Boulevard
Woodstock
FORESHORE
Esplanade
Tide Street
Beach Road
Lower Church Street
Porter Street
Grey Street
New Market Street
Sir Lowry Road
Victoria Road
Albert Road
TRAFALGAR PARK
Eastern Boulevard
Keizergracht Street
Searle Street
Christiaan Street
Constitution
Woodstock Hospital
Coronation Road
Chester Street
Eden Road
Cambridge Street
Beresford Road
Premier Road
Perth Street
Devonshire St
Selbourne Road
Rhodes Avenue
Salisbury Street
Rainham Lane
Chamberlain Street
Hounslow Lane
Balfour Road
Wadham
Palmerston Road
Roodebloem Road
R 102
M 3
M 4
1
2
3
4

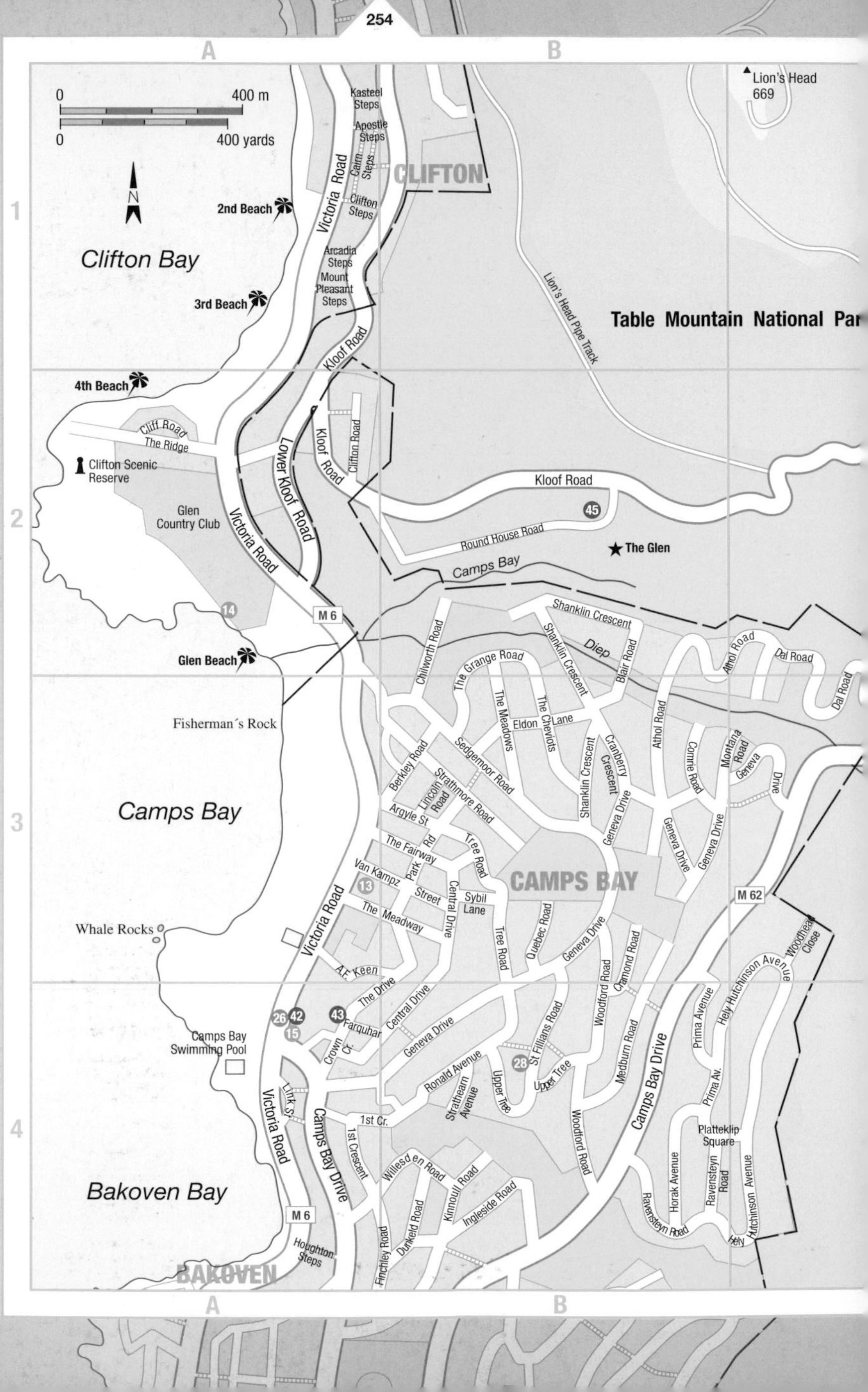
254
A
B
1
2
3
4
0
400 m
400 yards
N
Clifton Bay
2nd Beach
3rd Beach
4th Beach
Glen Beach
Kasteel Steps
Apostle Steps
Cairn Steps
Clifton Steps
Arcadia Steps
Mount Pleasant Steps
CLIFTON
Victoria Road
Kloof Road
Lower Kloof Road
Clifton Road
Cliff Road
The Ridge
Clifton Scenic Reserve
Glen Country Club
Lion's Head 669
Lion's Head Pipe Track
Table Mountain National Par
Round House Road
The Glen
Camps Bay
M 6
Shanklin Crescent
Diep
Chilworth Road
The Grange Road
Blair Road
Athol Road
Dal Road
The Meadows
The Cheviots
Eldon Lane
Cranberry Crescent
Montana Road
Geneva Drive
Comrie Road
Fisherman´s Rock
Berkley Road
Sedgemoor Road
Strathmore Road
Lincoln Road
Argyle St
The Fairway
Park Rd
Tree Road
Van Kampz Street
Central Drive
Sybil Lane
CAMPS BAY
Camps Bay
M 62
The Meadway
Quebec Road
Diamond Road
Woodhead Close
Whale Rocks
A.F. Keen
The Drive
Woodford Road
Hely Hutchinson Avenue
Prima Avenue
Farquhar Cr.
Crown Cr.
St Fillians Road
Medburn Road
Camps Bay Swimming Pool
Ronald Avenue
Upper Tree
Strathearn Avenue
Camps Bay Drive
Prima Av.
Link St
1st Cr.
1st Crescent
Platteklip Square
Willesden Road
Kinnoull Road
Horak Avenue
Ravensteyn Road
Hely Hutchinson Avenue
Bakoven Bay
Dunkeld Road
Ingleside Road
Finchley Road
Houghton Steps
BAKOVEN
Hely

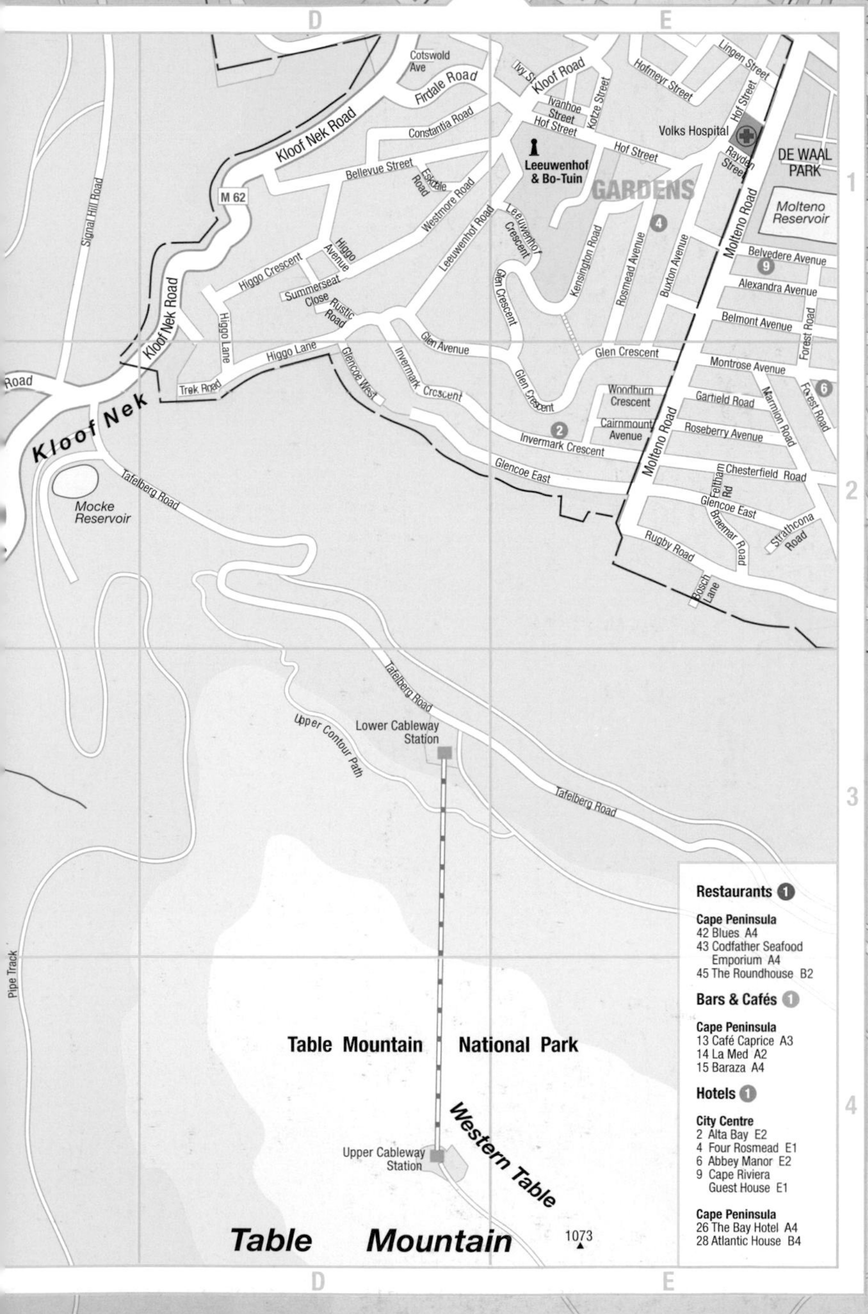

Restaurants 1

Cape Peninsula
42 Blues A4
43 Codfather Seafood Emporium A4
45 The Roundhouse B2

Bars & Cafés 1

Cape Peninsula
13 Café Caprice A3
14 La Med A2
15 Baraza A4

Hotels 1

City Centre
2 Alta Bay E2
4 Four Rosmead E1
6 Abbey Manor E2
9 Cape Riviera Guest House E1

Cape Peninsula
26 The Bay Hotel A4
28 Atlantic House B4

Street Index

1st Beach **254** A4
1st Crescent **258** A4
2nd Beach **254** A4
3rd Beach **258** A2
4th Beach **258** A2

A

A.F. Keen **258** A3
Aandblom Street **256** B4
Aberdeen Street **257** E3
Adderley Street **256** B2
Adelaide Road **257** E3
Airways Terminal **256** B2
Albany Road **252** A4
Albert Road **255** D3, **257** E3
Albertus Street **256** B3
Aldgate Street **257** D2
Alexander Road **254** A2–B2
Alexandra Avenue **254** B3, **259** E1
Alexandra Place **252** B2
Alfred Street **253** E4
Algakirk Road **254** B2
Alkmaar Road **257** E1
Altona Grove **257** E3
Amphitheatre **253** E2
Anemone Avenue **256** B4
Annandale Street **256** A3
Antrim Road **252** B3
Antwerp Road **252** B4
Apostle Steps **254** A4
Arcadia Close **254** B3
Arcadia Road **254** B4–B3
Arcadia Steps **258** A1
Argyle Street **258** B3
Armadale Street **257** D3
Arthur's Road **254** B1–C1
Artscape **256** C2
Aspeling Street **257** C3
Astana Street **255** E2
Athol Road **258** B3–B2–C2
August Street **256** A1
Aurora Lane **252** A4
Avenue Road **256** A3
Avondale Road **252** B3

B

Balfour Road **257** E4
Bantam Street **256** A2
Bantry Lane **254** B3–B2
Bantry Steps **254** A3
Barkly Road **255** C1
Barnabas Street **255** E4
Barnet Street **256** A3
Barnham Avenue **256** C4
Barrack Street **256** B3
Barron Street **257** D3
Bartholemeu Dias **256** C1
Barton Street **257** E3
Basket Lane **257** C3
Bath Street **255** E4
Battery Crescent **252** B4
Battery Street **253** D4
Bay Road **252** B2–C2, **253** C2
Bay, The **258** A4
Bay View Avenue **255** D3
Beach Road **252** A4–A3–B2–C2, **253** D2, **254** A2–B2–B1, **257** E2
Beacon Lane **257** E4
Bedford Street **256** B4
Belle Ombre Road **255** D3
Bellevue Road **252** A4
Bellevue Street **255** D4
Bellwood Road **254** B3
Belmont Avenue **259** E1
Belvedere Avenue **259** E1
Bennett Street **253** D4
Bennington Road **255** E3
Beresford Road **257** D4–E4
Berg Lane **256** A1
Berkley Road **258** B3
Berrio Road **257** E1
Bertram House **256** A3
Bertrand Road **253** D4
Bill Peters Drive **252** C3
Biskop Steps **254** A4
Blackheath Road **252** B4
Blair Road **258** B3
Blinde Street **257** C4
Bloem Street **256** A2
Bloemhof Street **256** B3
BMW Pavilion IMAX Cinema **253** D2
Bo-Kaap Museum **256** A2
Bond Street **255** D3
Bordeaux Road **255** C2
Bosch Lane **259** E2
Botany Lane **254** A3
Boundary Road **253** D4
Bowlers Way **252** B3
Brabant Road **257** E3
Braemar Road **253** D4–D3
Braeside Street **252** C3
Brandweer Street **256** B4
Breakwater Lane **253** E2
Breakwater Lodge **253** D3
Breda Street **256** A4
Bree Street **256** A2–B1
Bridge Street **257** D4
Brittany Avenue **254** B3
Brompton Avenue **254** B3
Brook Street **257** D3
Brownlow Road **255** E3
Brunswick Road **255** E3
Bryant Street **255** E2
Buiten Street **256** A2
Buitengracht Street **256** A2
Buitenkant Street **256** A4–B3
Buitensingle Street **256** A3
Burg Street **256** A2
Burnside Road **255** E3
Buxton Avenue **259** E1

C

Cableway Station **259** D4
Cairn Steps **254** A4
Cairnmount Avenue **259** E2
Calais Road **252** B4
Caleb Street **257** E3
Caledon Square **256** B3
Caledon Street **256** B3
Calvin Street **257** E3
Camberwell Road **252** B3
Cambridge Avenue **255** D4
Cambridge Street **257** D4
Camden Street **255** D3
Camp Street **255** E4
Camps Bay Drive **258** A4–B4, **259** C3–C2
Camps Bay Swimming Pool **258** A4
Canterbury Street **256** B3
Cape Gardens Lodge **256** A3
Cape Grace **253** E3
Cape Medical Museum **253** D3
Cape Swiss **255** E4
Cape Technikon **256** C3
Cape Technikon Granger Bay Campus **253** D1
Cape Town Inn **256** A2
Cape Town Railway Station **256** B2
Capetonian **256** B1
Cardiff Street **253** D4
Carey Street **257** E3
Carisbrook Road **255** E2
Carisbrook Street **255** E3
Carl Street **256** A1
Carreg Crescent **253** D4
Carstens Street **255** E3
Cassell Road **254** B2
Castle of Good Hope, The **256** B3
Castle Street **256** A1–B2
Cauvin Street **257** C4
Cavalcade Road **253** C3–D3
Cavendish Street **257** E3
Caxton Street **257** D3
Central Drive **258** B3–B4
Central Fire Station **256** B4
Chamberlain Street **257** E4
Chapel Street **256** C3, **257** C3–D3
Charmante Avenue **254** B3
Chateau Avenue **254** C2
Chelsea Avenue **256** B4
Chepstow Road **253** C4
Chester Street **257** D4–E4
Chesterfield Road **259** E2
Cheviot Place **252** C3
Cheviots, The **258** B3
Chiappini Street **253** E4
Chilworth Road **258** B3
Christiaan Street **257** D4
Church Road **254** B1
Church Street **256** A2, **257** E3
City Hospital **253** D2
City Lodge **253** E4
City Park Hospital **256** A2
Civic Avenue **256** C2
Civic Centre **252** B3, **256** C2
Clare Street **256** B4
Clarens Road **254** B1
Clarens Street **257** E3
Claridges International **253** D3
Cliff Road **258** A2
Clifford Road **255** C1
Clifton Road **258** A2
Clifton Scenic Reserve **258** A2
Clifton Steps **258** A1
Clive Street **256** B4
Clock Tower **253** E3
Clock Tower Museum **253** E3
Clovelly Avenue **256** B4
Clyde Road **252** C3
Clyde Street **257** E3
Clydebank Road **252** C3
Cobern Street **253** D4
Cobern Street **256** A1
Coen Steytler Avenue **253** E4
Coffee Lane **256** B3
Collier Jetty **253** E3
Commercial Street **256** B3
Comrie Road **258** B3
Conifer Road **252** A4
Conradie Recreation Ground **255** D3
Constantia Road **255** D4
Constitution **256** B3–C4, **257** C4
Coodes Crescent **253** E3
Cornwall Street **257** D3
Coronation Road **257** D4–E4
Corporation Street **256** B3
Cotswold Avenue **255** D4
Coventry Road **257** D4
Cramond Road **258** B4–B3
Cranberry Crescent **258** B3
Crassula Avenue **256** B4
Cross Berth **253** E3
Crown Crescent **258** A4
Croxteth Road **252** C3
Curtis Road **256** A4
Customs Gate **257** C1

D

D.F. Malan Street **256** C1
Dal Road **258** C3–C2
Darling Street **256** B2
Davidson Street **257** E2, E3
Dawes Street **256** A1
De Barrange Avenue **255** C2
De Hoop Avenue **255** D3
De L'Hermite Avenue **254** C2
De Longueville Avenue **254** B2
De Lorentz Street **255** E4
De Roos Street **256** B3
De Smit Street **253** D4
De Tuynhuys **256** A3
De Villiers Street **256** B4
De Waal Crescent **256** C4
De Wet Road **254** B3
Deane Road **255** C1
Deauville Avenue **254** C3
Delphinium Street **256** B4
Derry Street **256** B4
Derwent Road **255** E4
Des Huguenots Avenue **254** B2
Devonport Road **255** D3
Devonshire Street **257** E4
Dickson Road **257** E3
Disandt Avenue **254** B2–C2
District Six **256** B3
Dixon Street **253** D4
Dock Road **253** E4
Dolls House **252** B2
Dormehl Street **257** D3
Dorp Street **256** A2
Dorset Street **257** D3
Dover Road **252** B4
Drelingcourt Avenue **255** C2
Drive, The **258** A4
Drury Lane **256** B3
Dublin Street **257** E3
Duncan Road **253** E4, **254** C1, **256** C1, **257** C1–D2
Dunkeld Road **258** B4
Dunkley Street **256** A3
Dysart Road **253** C3

E

East Pier **253** E2
East Quay **253** E3
Eastern Boulevard **257** C3–D3–E4
Eaton Road **255** E3
Ebenezer Road **253** D4
Eden Road **257** D4–E4
Edward Road **255** C1
Eldon Lane **258** B3
Ella Street **253** D4
Ellis Road **252** A4
Erica Street **257** E4
Eskdale Road **259** D1
Esplanade **257** E2
Essex Street **257** E3
Exhibition Terrace **253** D3

F

Fairview Avenue **257** E4
Fairway, The **258** B3
Farquhar **258** A4
Faure Street **255** E3
Fawley Terrace **256** C4, **257** C4
Feltham Road **259** E2
Finchley Road **258** B4
Fir Avenue **254** B2
Firdale Avenue **252** A4
Firdale Road **255** D4–E4
Firmount Road **252** A4
Fish Quay **253** E3
Florida Steps **254** A3
Fontainebleau Avenue **255** C2
Foregate Street **257** E2
Forest Road **259** E2
Fort Road **252** B3

Fort Wynyard Museum **253** D2
Fort Wynyard Road **253** D2
Francis Street **257** D3
Frederick Close **255** D3
Frederick Street **256** A1
Freeman **253** C3
Freesia Avenue **256** C4
Frere Road **252** B3
Fresnaye Avenue **254** B2–C3
Fresnaye Sports Club **255** C2
Friars Road **255** C1
Fritz Sonnenberg Road **253** C2

G

Galleria **254** B2
Gardenia Avenue **256** B4
Garfield Road **259** E2
Geneva Drive **258** B3–B4–C3
Gilmour Hills **255** E3
Gladiolus Avenue **256** B4
Glen Avenue **259** D1–D2
Glen Beach **258** A2
Glen Country Club **258** A2
Glen Crescent **259** E1–E2
Glen, The **252** A4, **258** B2
Glencoe East **259** D2–E2
Glencoe West **259** D2
Glengariff Terrace **252** B3
Glynn Street **256** A3–B4
Glynnville Terrace **256** A4
Gold of Africa Museum **256** A1
Golden Acre **256** B2
Golders Green Road **257** E4
Good Hope Centre **256** C3
Gordon Street **254** B3
Gore Street **256** C3
Gorleston Road **254** B1
Government Avenue **256** A3
Graaff's Swimming Pool **252** A4
Graduate School of Business **253** D3
Graham Road **252** A4
Grand Parade, The **256** B2
Grand Vue Road **257** D4
Grange Road, The **258** B3–B2
Granger Bay Road **253** D2
Granger Street **253** D2
Greenmarket Square **256** B2
Green Point (Museum) **252** B2
Green Point Stadium **253** C3
Green Point Track **253** D3
Green Street **256** A3
Gresham Road **252** B4
Grey Street **257** D3
Grey's Passage **256** A3
Grimsby Road **252** B3
Grove Road **252** C3
Gympie Street **257** D3

H

Hall Road **252** A4
Hanover **256** B3
Hanover Road **254** B2
Hans Strijdom Road **256** B1
Harrington Street **256** B3
Hastings Street **255** D3
Hatfield Road **252** B3
Hatfield Street **256** A4–A3
Hay Road **257** E4
Haytor Road **253** C3
Head Road **254** C3
Heathfield Road **252** A4
Heere Street **257** C4
Heerengracht **256** B1
Hely Hutchinson Avenue **258** B4–C4
Herbert Road **252** A4
Hercules Street **257** D3
Hertzog Boulevard **256** B1
Hiddingh Avenue **256** A4
Higgo Avenue **259** D1
Higgo Crescent **259** D1
Higgo Lane **259** D1–D2
High Level Road **252** A4–B4–C3, **253** C4, **254** B2, **255** C1
High Street **257** D4
Highfield Street **253** D4
Highfield Terrace **253** D4
Highgate Street **257** E2
Hildene Road **255** D3
Hill Road **252** B3
Hilligers **256** A2
Hillside Road **255** E3
Hillside Terrace **253** D4
Hof Street **255** E4
Hofmeyr Road **252** B3
Hofmeyr Street **255** E4
Holiday Inn **256** A4, **257** E4
Holiday Inn Garden Court **256** A2
Holiday Inn St George's **256** B2
Holmfirth Road **254** C1
Hope Lane **256** A4–A3
Horak Avenue **258** B4
Hospital Street **253** E4
Houghton Steps **258** A4
Hounslow Lane **257** E4
House of Assembly **256** A3
Houses of Parliament **256** A3
Hout Lane **256** A1
Hout Street **256** A2–B2
Hudson Street **253** D4
Hyde Street **257** D3

I

Ilford Street **254** B2
Ilkley Crescent **252** B4
Inez Road **254** C1
Ingleside Road **258** B4
Invermark Crescent **259** D2–E2
Invery Place **257** D3
Irwinton Road **254** C1
Ivanhoe Street **255** E4
Ivy Street **255** E4
Ixia Avenue **256** B4

J

J. Craig Street **256** C2
Jackson Wharf **257** D1
Jamieson Road **256** A3
Jan Smuts Street **256** C2
Jarwis Street **253** D4
Jasper Street **256** A4
Jetty Street **256** B1
Jewish Museum **256** A3
Jordaan Street **255** E2
Joubert Road **252** C4, **253** C4
Justisie Street **256** C4
Jutland Avenue **256** B4

K

Kasteel Steps **254** A4
Keerom Street **256** A3
Kei Apple Road **254** B2
Keizergracht Street **256** C3 **257** D4
Kelvin Road **252** B3
Kelvin Street **255** D4
Kenmore Road **255** D2–E2
Kensington Road **259** E1
Kent Street **256** B3
Kiewiet Lane **252** B2
King Street **255** E3
Kings Road **254** B2
Kinnoull Road **258** B4
Kitchener Road **257** E4
Kloof Avenue **255** E4
Kloof Nek **259** C2
Kloof Nek Road **255** D4–E3, **259** C2–D1
Kloof Road **254** A4–A3–B2, **255** E4–E3, **256** A3, **258** A1–A2–B2, **259** C2, E1
Koopmans De Wet House **256** B2
Kort Street **252** B4
Kotze Street **255** E4
Krynauw Street **255** E4
Kuyper Street **256** C4

L

L. Gradner Street **257** C2
La Croix Avenue **254** B2–B3
Le Sueur Avenue **254** B2
Leeukloof **255** D3
Leeukop Street **255** D4
Leeuwen Street **256** A2
Leeuwendal Crescent **255** D4
Leeuwenhof & Bo-Tuin **259** E1
Leeuwenhof Crescent **259** E1
Leeuwenhof Road **259** D1
Leeuwenvoet Road **255** E3
Leile St **256** B3
Leith Hill **255** E3
Lennox Street **257** E3
Lever Street **257** D4
Lewin Street **257** D3
Lincoln Road **258** B3
Lingen Street **255** E4
Link Street **258** A4
Lion Street **255** E2
Lion's Head Pipe Track **258** B1
Loader Street **253** D4
Lodge Road **256** A4
London Road **252** A4
Long Street **253** E4, **256** A3–A2–B1
Longmarket Street **256** A1–A2–A3
Loop Street **256** A2–B1
Lower Burg Street **256** B2
Lower Cableway Station **259** D3
Lower Church Street **257** E3
Lower Kloof Road **258** A2
Lower Plein Street **256** B2
Lower Pypies **256** B4
Lutheran Church **256** A1
Luton Street **256** B4
Lymington Close **256** C4

M

Magistrates Court **256** B3
Main Drive **252** A4–B3, B4, **253** C3, **254** C1
Main Drive **253** D3
Malan House **257** C2
Malan St **255** E4
Marais Road **252** A4
Marina Avenue **254** B3
Marine Road **252** B3
Marmion Road **259** E2
Marsden Road **257** D4
Marseilles Avenue **255** C2
Martin Hammerschlag Way **256** C2
Martin Melck House **256** A1
Maynard Street **256** B4
McKenzie Road **256** B4–B3
Meadows, The **258** B3
Meadway, The **258** A3
Mechau Street **253** E4
Medburn Road **258** B4
Melbourne Road **257** E4–E3
Merriman Road **253** C4
Metropole **256** B2
Metropolitan Golf Course **253** D2
Mijlov Manor **255** E3
Milan Road **257** D4
Military Road **255** E3–E2
Mill Street **256** A4
Millgate Street **257** E2
Milner Road **252** A4, **254** C1, **255** E3–E2, C1
Milton Road **252** A4
Milton's Swimming Pool **254** B1
Modena Road **253** C3
Mole **257** E1
Molteno Road **255** E4, **259** E2–E1
Monastery Road **254** C2
Montana Road **258** C3
Montrose Avenue **259** E2
Moorgate Street **257** D2
Moray Place **256** A4
Morkel Street **255** E4
Mount Nelson **255** E3
Mount Nelson Road **252** A4
Mount Pleasant Steps **258** A1
Mount Road **256** B3
Mountain Road **257** E4
Muir Street **256** C3
Munnik Lane **257** D3–D4
Mutley Road **252** B3
Myrtle Street **256** A4

N

Nairn Street **257** D3
Napier Street **253** D4
Nazareth House **256** B4
Nelson Street **257** D3
Nelson Mandela Gateway **253** E3
Nerina Street **257** E4
Nettleton Road **254** A3–A4
New Church Street **255** E3
New Market Street **257** C3–D3–E3
Newport Street **255** D4
Nicol Street **255** E3
No. 1 Jetty **253** E2
No. 2 Jetty **253** E2
Noon Gun **253** D4
Noordelik Avenue **256** C4
Norfolk Road **252** A3
Norfolk Street **257** E3
Normandie Avenue **254** C2
Nurul Islam mosque **256** A2

O

Ocean **257** E1
Ocean View Drive **252** B4, **253** C4–D4, **254** B3–C2, **255** C2–C1–D1
Oester Lane **256** B3
Old Drill Hall **256** B3
Old Marine Drive **256** C2
Old Port Captain's Building **253** E3
Old Town House **256** A2
Oldfield Road **252** A4
Oliver Road **252** A4
Oriental Plaza **256** C3
Orphan Street **256** A2
Oswald Pirow Street **256** C2

P

Paddock Avenue **256** A3
Page Street **257** D3
Palmerston Road **257** E4
Parade Street **256** B3
Park House Road **255** E3
Park Lane **255** E3
Park Road **252** B2, **257** D4, **258** B3
Parliament Street **256** A3–B2
Peak Road **256** C4
Penarth Road **252** B3

Peninsula All Suite 254 B2
Pentz Road 255 E2, 256 A2
Pepper Street 256 A2
Perth Road 256 A3
Perth Street 257 D4
Philips Road 257 C3
Pierhead 253 E3
Pine Road 252 C3, 257 D3–E3
Pipe Track 259 C3
Planet Hollywood 253 D3
Plantation Road 256 C4
Platteklip Square 258 B4
Plein Street 256 B3, 257 E3
Pontac Street 257 D3
Port Road 253 D3–E4
Porter Street 257 D2
Portman Road 254 B2
Portswood Road 253 D3
Poyser Road 255 E2
Premier Road 257 D4
Premier Street 257 D3
Prestwich Street 253 D4, 256 A1–B1
Prima Avenue 258 B4
Princess Road 254 B2
Princess Street 257 D4
Private Road 255 C1
Protea Avenue 254 B3–C2

Q

Quantock Road 254 B2
Quarry Hill 255 D4
Quebec Road 258 B3
Queen Street 257 D3
Queen Victoria Street 256 A3
Queen's Beach 254 A2
Queens Road 254 B2, 255 E3, 257 E3
Quendon Road 254 B2

R

Rael Street 255 D3
Railway Street 257 E3
Rainham Lane 257 E4
Ravenscraig Road 252 C3, 257 D3
Ravensteyn Road 258 B4
Ravine Road 254 A3
Ravine Steps 254 A3
Rayden Street 255 E4
Reform Street 257 C3
Regent Road 254 B2
Regent Square 255 D4
Regent Street 257 E3
Repair Quay 257 D1
Rheede Street 256 A3
Rhine Road 252 B4
Rhodes Avenue 257 E4
Richmond Road 252 B3
Ridge, The 258 A2
Riebeek Street 256 B1
Ritz Protea 252 B3
Roberts Road 257 E4
Rochester Road 254 B2
Rocklands Beach 252 B3
Rocklands Road 252 A3
Roeland Street 256 A3–B3
Roger Street 257 D3
Roggebaai Square 256 B1
Ronald Avenue 258 B4
Roodebloem Road 257 E4
Roodehek Street 256 A3
Roos Road 253 C4
Rose Street 256 A2–A1
Roseberry Avenue 259 E2
Rosedene Road 252 A4
Rosmead Avenue 259 E1
Rothesay Place 252 C2
Round House 258 B2
Round House Road 258 B2
Royal Cape Yacht Club 257 D2
Rugby Road 259 E2
Russell Street 257 C3
Rust en Vreugd 256 B3
Rustic Road 259 D1

S

Saddle Road 256 C4
Salisbury Street 257 E4
Salmon Street 257 D3
Saunders Road 254 A2
Scholtz Road 252 B3
Schoonder Street 256 A4
Scott Street 256 A4–B4
Sea Point Clinic 254 C2
Sea Point Fire Station 254 B1
Sea Point Pavilion Pool 254 B1
Seacliffe Road 254 A2
Seapoint Clinic 252 B3
Searle Street 257 D4–D3
Sedgemoor Road 258 B3
Selbourne Road 252 B4
Selkirk Street 257 C3
Selwyn Street 257 D3
Serendipity Maze 252 B2
Shanklin Crescent 258 B2–B3
Shortmarket Street 256 A2
Signal Hill Road 255 C4–C3–D2–D1, 259 C1
Sinodale Hall 256 A3
Sir Lowry Road 256 B3–C3, 257 C3
Slave Lodge Museum 256 A2
Solan Road 256 B4
Solomons Road 254 B2
Somerset Hospital 253 D3
Somerset Street 253 D4
Sophia Street 256 A4
South African National Library 256 A2
South African Maritime Museum 253 D3
South African Museum 256 A3
South African National Gallery 256 A3
South African Navy Academy 253 D1
South Arm 253 E3
Southgate Street 257 D2
Sparta Road 255 C1
Spin Street 256 B2
Spring Street 257 E3
Springbok Road 252 C4
Springfield Terrace 257 D3
St Bartholomew Avenue 254 B3–C3
St Bede's Road 252 B3
St Charles Avenue 254 C2
St Denis Road 255 C2
St Fillians Road 258 B4
St George's Mall 256 B2
St George's Road 252 C3
St George's Cathedral 256 A2
St James Road 252 A3
St Jeans Avenue 254 B3
St John's Road 254 C1–C2
St John's Street 256 A3
St Leon Avenue 254 A3
St Louis Avenue 254 B3
St Mary Maternity 255 E2
St Michael's Road 255 D3
St Patrick 254 B2
St Quintons 256 A4
St Stephen 256 A2
Stadzicht Street 256 A1
Stal Square 256 A3
Stanley Place 252 B3
State Archives 256 B3
Station Road 257 E3
Stephan Way 252 C2
Stephen Road 255 E4
Stone Road 252 A3
Strand Street 256 B2
Strathcona Road 259 E2
Strathearn Avenue 258 B4
Strathmore Road 258 B3
Summerseat Close 259 D1
Supreme Court 256 A2
Surrey Place 252 C2
Sussex Street 257 E3
Sybil Lane 258 B3
Sydney Road 253 C3
Sydney Street 256 C3

T

Table Bay 253 E2
Table Bay Boulevard 257 D2
Tafelberg Road 259 C2–D3–E3
Tamboerskloof Road 255 E3
Tanabaru Street 255 E2–E1
Tennant Street 256 B3
Thornhill Road 253 C3
Three Anchor Bay Road 252 B3
Three Anchor Bay Tennis Club 252 B3
Tide Street 257 E2
Top Road 254 B3
Torbay Road 253 C3
Town House 256 B3
Trafalgar Place 256 B2
Trafalgar Square 254 C1
Tramway Road 254 B2
Treaty Road 257 E3
Tree Road 258 B3
Trek Road 259 D2
Tuin Plein 256 A3
Tuin Street 255 E4
Two Oceans Aquarium 253 D3

U

Union Street 255 E4
Upper Adelaide Road 257 E4
Upper Albert Road 255 D3
Upper Bloem Street 255 E2
Upper Buitengracht 255 E3
Upper Buitenkant Street 256 A4–A4
Upper Cambridge Street 257 E4
Upper Canterburry Street 256 B4–B3
Upper Contour Path 259 D3
Upper Clarens Road 254 B2
Upper Duke Street 257 D4
Upper Leeuwen Street 256 A2
Upper Maynard 256 A4
Upper Mill Street 256 B4
Upper Mountain Road 257 E4
Upper Orange Street 256 A4
Upper Pepper Street 255 E2
Upper Portswood Road 253 D3
Upper Queens Road 257 D4
Upper Ravenscraig Road 257 D4
Upper Rhine Road 252 B4
Upper Tree 258 B4
Upper Union Street 255 E3
Upper Warwick Street 257 D3

V

Van Kampz Street 258 A3
Van Riebeek Statue 256 B2
Van Ryneveld Avenue 256 B4
Vanguard 257 E1
Varney's Road 253 C3
Varsity Street 255 D4
Vasco Da Gama Boulevard 256 C1
Vesperdene Road 253 D4
Victoria & Alfred 253 E3
Victoria Road 254 A4–A3, 257 D3, 258 A1–A2–A3–A4,
Victoria Street 255 E3
Victoria Walk 257 E4
Victoria Wharf 253 E2
Viktoria Road 257 E3
Vine Street 255 E4
Virginia Avenue 256 A4
Vlei Road 253 C3
Voetboog Road 255 E1
Vogelgezang Street 257 C4
Volks Hospital 255 E4
Vos Street 253 D4
Vrede Street 256 A3
Vredehoek Ave 256 A4–B4
Vriende Street 256 A4

W

Wadham 257 E4
Wale Street 256 A2
Walmer Road 257 E3
Wandel Street 256 A3
Warren Street 255 D3
Warwick Street 256 B4 257 D3
Waterkant Street 253 D4, 256 A1–B1
Watsonia Street 256 C4
Welgemeend Street 255 E4
Weltevreden Street 255 E3
Wembley Road 256 B4
Werf Lane 256 B3
Wesley Street 256 A3–B4
Wessels 253 D4
Western Boulevard 252 B3, 253 C3–D3–E4
Westmore Road 259 D1
Whitford Street 255 E2
Wicht Crescent 256 C3
Wigtown Road 253 C3
Wilkinson Street 255 E3
Willesden Road 258 B4
William Street 257 E3
Winchester Mansions 252 A4
Windburg Avenue 256 C4
Wisbeach Road 252 A4
Woodburn Crescent 259 E2
Woodford Road 258 B4–B3
Woodhead Close 258 C3
Woodlands Road 257 D3
Woodside Road 255 E3
Woodstock Hospital 257 E4
Worcester Road 252 A4
Worcester Street 257 D4
Wright Street 257 E3

Y

York Road 253 C3
Yusuf Drive 255 E1

Art and Photo Credits

AKG London 32B, 38, 39, 42/T, 44, 47T
Alamy 8TL, 11B, 55, 57, 83T, 133, 135B, 183, 208, 201T
Bridgeman Art Library 33T
courtesy CapeTown Opera 64
Courtesy Cape Milner 225
Corbis 28/T, 29, 43, 45, 46, 48, 49/T, 60, 65B
Mary Evans 22R, 26B, 32, 33B, 34T, 36, 37APA Alex Havret 4B, 6BR, 9T, 10TL, 11M/TL/TR, 18, 19, 20, 22L, 23/T, 25, 26T, 56, 58, 67, 79, 80TR, 83BR, 86, 95TR, 96T, 99, 104, 108, 116TL, 118T, 129, 135T, 138, 144/145, 147, 149, 162, 163, 188T, 215R, 227, 240, 241, 242
William Fehr Collection 30, 35
Getty Images 34B, 134, 197T
Roger de la Harpe/Gallo 185T
Holler (Schirmer) Hermanus 194
Istockphoto 116B, 210, 214B
courtesy Jazz Art Theatre 65t, 236
Kobal 66
Courtesy Marine Hermanus 232
Bill Parkinson 8BL
Randy OHC 136
Photolibrary 57T, 58T, 182, 185, 204/205, 206
Pictures Colour Library 54
Redferns 61
David Sanger 168B
South African Tourism 153, 196B
South African Tourism/Thea Grenfell 215B
South African Tourism Lanz Von Hörsten 154/TL, 196T, 198T, 209T, 211T, 213
South African Tourism/Walter Knirr 207T
South African Tourism/Colin Mead 209
South African Tourism/Mike Skinner 174
South African Tourism/Jill Sneasby 211B
South African Tourism/Hein Waschefordt 207
Dorothy Stannard 80
Erhardt Thiel/Struik Image Library/Images of Africa 117, 140
Superstock 119L
Topfoto 27M/T, 41
APA Ariadne Van Zandbergen 1, 4T, 5, 6BL/L/MR, 7BL/BR/ML/MR/TL/TR, 8BL, 10B/M/TR, 9B/M, 12/13, 14/15, 16, 17/T, 21, 27B, 50/51, 59, 68/69, 70/71, 72, 73L/R, 76, 77, 81, 82/T, 84L/R/T, 85B/T, 87T, 88, 89/T, 90, 91L, 92/B, 93/T, 95, 96, 100, 101, 102/T, 103/T, 105/T, 107/T, 109/T, 110, 114, 115/T, 116TR, 118B, 119R, 121, 123,114/T, 125, 126, 128, 130L/R, 132, 137, 139, 140T, 141, 142, 146, 150, 151, 152T, 153R, 154TR, 155, 158, 159, 161/T, 162T, 164, 165/T, 166/T, 167, 168T, 169/T, 170/T, 171/T, 172, 173/T, 174B, 175T, 176/T, 177/T, 178, 179, 180/181, 182, 185TL/TR, 187/T, 188, 189/T, 190/TL, 193/T, 213T, 234, 237, 239
Ariadne Van Zandbergen 110, 131, 191
APA Bill Wassman 8BR, 24/T, 62, 80TL, 83BL, 87B, 88T, 91R, 95TL, 106, 175, 185, 190TR, 197, 198B
Geoff Wilson 137T

Photo Features

52–53
Corbis 52/53, 53BL/BR/T, Getty Images 52BL, APA Ariadne Van Zandbergen 52BR, APA Alex Havret 53M

112–113
AKG London 112/113, Getty Images 112B, Corbis 112B/L, APA Alex Havret 113TR

156–157
APA Alex Havret 156/157, 156BL/BR/M, 157BL, South African Tourism/Maureen Craig-Cooper 156TL, Alamy 157BR

202–203
APA Ariadne Van Zandbergen 202/203, 202BL/BR/M, 203BL/BR/M, APA Alex Havret 203TR

Map Production: original cartography Stephen Ramsay, updated by APA Cartography Department

Production: Tynan Dean, Linton Donaldson and Rebeka Ellam

General Index

A

Abalimi Bezekhaya Peace Park and Community Garden 125
Abdurahman, Dr 43
abseiling 52, 155, 240
Abubakr Effendi 118, 119
accommodation **223–33**
Action Paint Ball 241
activities 155, 185, 214, **234–41**
Adderley Street 83
admission charges 242
Africa Nations Cup 52
African Indigenous Churches (AIC) 23–4
African Music Store 94, 95
Afrikaans
language 192
literature 62, 63
Afrikaans Taal (Language) Monument (Paarl) 191
Afrikaner nationalism 39, 41, 42
Afrikaner population 19, 20, 21–2
afro-montane forest 154
Agulhas National Park 195
air travel 220
Alfred, Prince 102
Alfred Mall 104
Alphen House 139
Alto winery 189
Amphitheatre 183–4
ANC (African National Congress) 20, 21, 41, 45, 46, 47, 48, 49, 62, 86
Anglo-Boer War **39**, 102, 173
Anreith, Anton 80, 87, 89, 93, 96, 139, 140
Antoni, Stefan 67
apartheid 20, 22–3, 25, 41, 42, **43–7**, 92
and the arts 61–2
Bo-Kaap 118
dismantling of 47–8
Robben Island 112–13
sport under 52
townships 121–5
apartments 223–4
Aquila Private Game Reserve 9, **194**
architecture 11, **67**, 81
Arniston **196**, 232
Art Deco 67, **81**, 83
art galleries
see also **museums and galleries**
commercial 176, 177
arts **61–6**, **235–7**
Arts and Crafts movement 85
Artscape Theatre Centre 235–6
Ataidea, Pedro d' 207
Atlantic Seaboard **160–8**, 229–30
ATMs 246–7
Auge, Jan Andries 89
Auwal Mosque 118–19
Avondale 192
Avontuur 189

B

Baartman, Saartjie 35
Bailey, Abe 177
Bailey, Brett 63
Bain, Thomas 40
Bain's Kloof Pass 192
Baker, Sir Herbert 37, 67, 135, 177
Groote Schuur 67, **133**
Rhodes Memorial 67, **130–1**
St George's Cathedral 86
ballet 63, 64, 235
banks 246–7
Bantry Bay 161, **162**, 229
Barnard, Christiaan 132
Barnyard Theatre 236–7
Barry, Dr James 25
Barrydale 210
bars *see* **restaurants, bars and cafés**
Bartolomeu Dias Museum Complex (Mossel Bay) 207
Basson, Marthinus 63
Battery (Simon's Town) 170
Baxter Theatre Centre 236, 237
beaches 10, 162–70, 175, 176–7, 193–4, 195, 197, 206, 212, 214
beadwork 118
bed and breakfast 122
beer 213
Berg River 191
Betty's Bay 194
bicycle tours 239
Biehl, Amy 124
Biko, Steve 46
Bill of Rights 61
Bird, Colonel 136
Bird Island 198
birds *see* **wildlife**
Birds of Eden 215
Bishop Lavis Town 121
Bishopscourt 135
Blaauwberg, Battle of 170–1
Black Peoples Convention 46
black protest 40–1
Blank, Claas 25
Bloubergstrand 8, **197**
Bloukrans Bridge 207
BMW Pavilion 102
Bo-Kaap 36, 81, 86, **114–19**
restaurants 119
boat trips 104, 239–40
Duiker Island 166
Robben Island 101
Simon's Town 171
Boer Republics 36–7
Boer War *see* **Anglo-Boer War**
Boland 183
bontebok 154
Bontebok National Park **196**, 232
Bonteheuwel 121
bookshops 94, 108, 177
Boom, Hendrik 88
Boschendal Estate 11, **191**, 202
Botanical Garden (Stellenbosch) 186
Botanical Society Conservatory (Kirstenbosch) 137–8
Botha, Louis 40
Botha, P.W. 47, 48, 208
Botha, Wim 65
Boulders Beach 9, 147, **169–70**, 173
braai **(barbecues)** 58–9
Bredasdorp 195
Breede River Valley **192–3**, 202
Breytenbach, Breyten 63
Brink, André 22, 63
Britain
colonialism 130, 171
occupation of Cape 35–6, 118, 170, 177
British Empire 42
Bronze Age Art Foundry, Gallery and Sculpture Garden (Simon's Town) 171
budgeting 242–3
Buitenverwachting 141
bungee jumping 207
Burgherhuis (Stellenbosch) 186
bus travel 220–1, 222
sightseeing buses 11, 79, 240
Buthelezi, Mangosuthu 47
Butterfield, William 135

C

Cabrière 11
cafés *see* **restaurants, bars and cafés**
Camps Bay 7, 20, 149, **163–4**, 178–9, 229
Canal Walk 21
Cango Caves 211
Cango Wildlife Ranch 211
canoeing 240
Cape Agulhas 168, 183, **195**, 201
Cape Care Route 124
Cape Colony 36, 39
Cape Coloured community 24, 43–4
Cape Dance Company 235
Cape Dutch style 36, 37, 67, 114
Cape Flats 24, 44, 121, 127
Cape Floral Kingdom 137, 153, **156–7**, 168
Cape of Good Hope 6, 9, 147, 159–60, **168–9**
beaches 10

Cape of Good Hope Hiking Trail 152
Cape of Good Hope Nature Reserve *see* **Table Mountain National Park**
Cape Malays 24, 114–19
cuisine 119
Cape Peninsula 147–8, 154, **159–77**
restaurants, cafés and bars 178–9
shopping 177
Cape Peninsula National Park *see* **Table Mountain National Park**
Cape Philharmonic Orchestra 63–4, 81
Cape Point 147, 152, 153, 155, 159, **168–9**
Cape Point Lighthouse 168
Cape Point Ostrich Farm 169, 241
Cape of Storms 169
Cape Town City Ballet 64, 235
Cape Town Holocaust Centre 91–2
Cape Town Opera 64
Cape Town Pass 11
Cape Town Stadium 11, **109**, 238
Cape Winelands 183, **185–93**, 200
car rental 221
casinos 237
Castle of Good Hope 11, **79–80**
Cavendish Square 134, **135**
Cecilia Plantation 131
Cederberg Wilderness Area 199
censorship 22, 46
Chacma baboons 154–5
Chapman's Peak 166, **167**
Chapman's Peak Drive 8, **167**
Chaskalson, Arthur 25
Chavonnes Cannon Battery Museum 108–9
children 243, 249
activities for 9, **241**
Church Street (Tulbagh) 11
churches and cathedrals
Dutch Reformed Church (Swellendam) 196
Groote Kerk 87
Holy Trinity Church (Knysna) 213
Lutheran Church 96
Moederkerk (George) 208
Moederkerk (Worcester) 193
St George's Cathedral 67, **85–6**
St Peter the Fisherman (Hout Bay) 166
St Saviour's Church 135
Strooidakkerk (Paarl) 191
cinema *see* **film**
cinemas 235
City Centre 77–96
accommodation 224–6
restaurants, bars and cafés 97–9
shopping 94
City Hall 80–1, 236
Clanwilliam 199
Claremont 134–5
Clifton 10, 160, 161, **162**
climate 157, 243
Clock Tower 107
Clock Tower Centre 107
Cloete family 136, 139, 140, 141
clothing
shops 94, 108, 199
what to wear 243
Clovelly 175
clubs 238–9
Coetzee, Basil 66
Coetzee, J.M. 63
comedy 9, 64
Communist Party 41, 43
Company's Garden 32, 35, 59, **88–9**
Congress of the People (COPE) 44, 49
Congress of Vienna 36
conservation, Table Mountain National Park 150
Constantia 20, 138, 202
Constantia Valley 138–9
restaurants, cafés and bars 142–3
Constantiaberg 167
constitution 47–8
Convention for Democratic South Africa 47
Corridor Ravine 151
corruption 49
C.P. Nel Museum (Oudtshoorn) 210
crafts 65–6
shops 94, 102, 108, 133, 177, 199, 213
credit cards 246
cricket 52, 53, 134, 240
crime 122, **243–4**
Crossroads 121
cuisine 55–9
customs regulations 244
cycling 53, 222, 239

D

dance 64, 96, 235
Darling 197, 201
day trips 183–99
De Hoop Nature Reserve 196, 232
de Klerk, F.W. 47, 48, 104
de Pass, Alfred 140
de Waal, Jan 115
De Waterkant Village 25
de Wet, Reza 63
De Wet Wine Cellar 193
Defiance Campaign 44
Delville Wood, Battle of 40
democracy, transition to 47–8, 86
Democratic Alliance (DA) 20, 49
dentists 245
Depression era 41–2
Devil's Peak 127, 135, 147
diamonds 37, 39, 40
Dias, Bartolomeu 31–2, 169, 206, **207**
Disa Gorge 149, 153
disabled travellers 212, **244**
District Six 24, 43, **44**
District Six Museum 8, 44, 59, **81–3**
diving 164
Drake, Francis 169
Drakenstein Prision (Paarl) 191
driving 221, 222
Drostdy (Swellendam) 196
Drostdy (Worcester) 193
Du Toitskloof Pass 192
Duiker Island 166
Dutch East India Company 32, 33, 80, 85, 86, 88, 172, 173
Dutch Reformed Church 41, 85
Dutch Reformed Church (Swellendam) 196
Dutch settlement 32–7
duty-free 244

E

East Fort (Hout Bay) 166
Eastern Overberg 195
eating out *see* **restaurants, bars and cafés**
Ebrahim, Noor 81
Ecksteen family 136
economic sanctions 45, 47
electricity 244
Elim 195–6
Elizabeth II, Queen 42
embassies and consulates 244
English-speaking community 19, 20–1
Evita se Perron (Darling) 64, **197**, 201
excursions 183–217

F

Fagan, Gawie 67, 102
Fagan, Gwen 67
faith-healers 24
False Bay 147, 160, **169–77**, 230–1
Featherbed Nature Reserve 214
Fernkloof Nature Reserve 194
festivals and events 9, **234–5**
Cape Carnival 117, 234
Cape Gourmet Festival 55
Cape Town Fashion Week 234
Cape Town Festival 234
Cape Town International Kite Festival 9, 234
Cape Town Jazz Festival 9, 234
Cape Town Pride Festival 234
Dragon Boat Festival 234
Encounters South African Independent Documentary Festival 234
International Comedy Festival 9, **106**, 234
Jazzathon 234
Kirstenbosch summer concerts 138, 236

Mother City Queer Parade 234–5
Naval Festival (Simon's Town) 172
New Year 9, **117**
Out in Africa Gay and Lesbian Film Festival 66
Outsurance Gun Run 234
Penguin Festival (Simon's Town) 172
Pink Loerie Mardi Gras (Knysna) 213–14
Stellenbosch Music Festival 187
Stellenbosch Wine Festival 9, 187
V&A Waterfront 106
Winter Food Festival 234
Fifa World Cup 2010 53, 109
film 61, **66**
First Beach 163
Fish Hoek 160, **175**, 231
Fish Hoek Valley Museum 175
flora
see also **parks and gardens**
Cape Floral Kingdom **156–7**
Kirstenbosch National Botanical Garden 137–8
Table Mountain National Park 153–4
food and drink 55–9
shops 94, 199
football 52–3
Foreshore 102
Fourie, Jopie 42
Fourth Beach 162
Franschhoek 22, 183, **190**, 202
accommodation 231–2
restaurants, bars and cafés 200–1
shopping 199
Franschhoek Vineyards Co-op Cellar 190
Freedom Charter 44
Fugard, Athol 63
fynbos 137, 153, 156

G

Gabbema, Abraham 191
Galeta, Hotep Idris 66
Galgut, Damon 63
Gama, Vasco da 32, 169
Garden Route 206–16
accommodation 233
restaurants and cafés 217
Garden Route National Park
Tsitsikamma Section 215–16
Wilderness Section 212–13
gay community 25
clubs and bars 238
festivals and events 66, 234–5
gay and lesbian travellers 244–5
gemstones 107, 174–5
Genadendal 133
George 207–8, 217, 233
George Museum 208
George V, King 86
gift shops 108, 199
Glen Carlou 192
Glennie, Frederick Mackintosh 177
Gobbato, Angelo 64
Gola, Loyiso 64
gold 37, 39, 95–6
Gold of Africa Museum 8, 59, **95–6**
golf 240
Gondwana 148
Goodwood 21
Gool, Cissie 43
Gordimer, Nadine 63
Graaf, Jan 87
Graaf's Pool 161
Grand Parade 81
Grand West Casino and Entertainment Centre 237, 241
Gray, Bishop and Sophie 135
Great Synagogue 91
Great Trek 36–7, 42
Great Zimbabwe 133
Green Point 109
Green Point Flea Market 109
Greenmarket Square 81, **84**
Greenmarket Square Flea Market 94
Greyson, John 25
Griquas 24, 35
Groot Constantia *see* **Iziko Groot Constantia**
Groot Drakenstein Mountains 188, 189, 191
Groot River 211–12
Groote Kerk 87
Groote Schuur 37, 67, 130, 131, **132–3**
Groote Schuur Hospital 131, **132**
Group Areas Act (1950) 23, 82, 118, 127, 171, 173
Guga sThebe Arts and Cultural Centre 124
Gugulethu 121, **124–5**
Gugulethu Seven 124
guided tours
Bo-Kaap 115
Groot Constantia 139
Kirstenbosch 138
townships 122–3

H

hang-gliding 155
Hanover Park 121
Harold Porter National Botanical Gardens 194
health 245
Heart of Cape Town Museum 132
Helderberg 188
Helderberg Nature Reserve 190
Helderberg Wine Route 189
helicopter tours 104, 240
Hell's Gate 153
Helshoogte Pass 189
Hely-Hutchinspm Dam 152
Hermanus 183, **193–4**, 200, 201, 232
Herschel, William and John 134–5
Herschel Monument 134–5
Heritage Museum (Simon's Town) 171
Het Posthuys (Muizenberg) 177
hiking and trekking 10
Cape Winelands 189–90
Cederberg Wilderness Area 199
De Hoop Nature Reserve 196
Garden Route National Park 213
Kirstenbosch 10, 131, 138
Knysna area 214
Kogelberg Biosphere Reserve 194–5
Rhodes Memorial 131
safety 152
Stellenbosch area 187–8
Table Mountain 151–3
Tsitsikamma 216
history 26–49
HIV/AIDS 48–9, 245
Hoerikwaggo Trail 10, **152–3**
Holy Trinity Church (Knysna) 213
hotels 223–33
Atlantic Seaboard 229–30
best views 8
City Centre and the City Bowl 224–6
False Bay 230–1
Further Afield 231–3
Southern Suburbs 228
Victoria & Alfred Waterfront 226–7
Hottentots Holland Mountains 34, 121, 131, 147
Hottentots Holland Nature Reserve 188
Houses of Parliament 87–8
Hout Bay 165–7, 178–9, 230
Hout Bay Craft Market 177
Huguenot Memorial Museum (Franschhoek) 190
Huguenots 22, 190, 202
human rights 44, 46, 47, 48
hunter-gatherers 31
hyraxes 155

I

Ibrahim, Abdullah 66
Imizamo Yethu 125
independence movements 42–3
infrastructure projects 40
Inkatha Freedom Party 47, 48
International Slave Route Project 87
Internet access 246
Irma Stern Museum 8,

66, **129–30**
Isaacs, David 63
Islam 35, 114, 115, 171, 173
isolation 46
Iziko Bertram House 93
Iziko Bo-Kaap Museum 8, **117–18**
Iziko Groot Constantia 7, 11, **139–40**
Iziko Koopmans-De Wet House 83–4
Iziko Maritime Centre **105**, 169
Iziko Michaelis Collection 85
Iziko Rust en Vreugd 92, 92–3
Iziko Slave Lodge Museum 86–7
Iziko South African Museum 8, **89–91**
Iziko South African National Gallery 65, **91**

J

Jacobsz, Rijkhaart 25
Jansen, Robbie 66
jazz 66, 237–8
Jazzart Dance Theatre 64, 235
jewellery 94, 108
Jewish community 25, 91, 209
Jikeleza 64
João II of Portugal 31–2
Jonkershoek Nature Reserve 188
Joseph, Helen 45
Jubilee Square (Simon's Town) 171
Just Nuisance, Abel Seaman 171

K

Kadalie, Clements 40
Kalk Bay 160, **175–6**, 179, 230
Kalk Bay Theatre 237
Kani, John 63
Karoo 157, 193
Karoo Desert National Botanical Garden (Worcester) 193
Kau, David 64
Kentridge, William 65
Keurbooms River Nature Reserve 214–15
Keurboomstrand 214
Kgosana, Philip 45
Khayelitsha 121, **125**
Khayelitsha Craft Market 125
Khoi people 31, 32, 33–4, 36, 147, 148
Kimberley 37, 39
King's Blockhouse 131
Kipling, Rudyard 130
Kirstenbosch National Botanical Garden 7, 34, **135–8**, 147, 236
  hikes 10, 131, 138
  tours 138
kitesurfing 53
Kloof Nek 149, 151
Knysna **213–14**, 217, 233
Knysna Elephant Park 215
Knysna Lagoon 213
Kogel Bay 167
Kogelberg Biosphere Reserve 194–5
Kommetjie 160, **167**, 229
Koopmans-De Wet, Marie 79, 84
Koopmans-De Wet family 83–4
kramats 118
Kramer, David 63
Kruger, Jimmy 46
Kruithuis (Stellenbosch) 186
kwaito 66
KwaZulu Natal 37
kwela 66
KWV Cellars 191

L

La Rosa Spanish Dance Theatre 64
Laborie 11
Lambert's Bay **198**, 232
Landskroon 192
Langa 121, **123–4**, 125, 143
Langa-Sharpeville Massacre Memorial 124
Langebaan Lagoon **197–8**, 201
language, Afrikaans 192
Laserquest 241
Le Roux Townhouse (Oudtshoorn) 210
legislative capital 86
Leipoldt, Louis 57
Lewis, Jack 25
Lewis-Williams, David 90
lighthouses
  Agulhas 195
  Cape Point 168
  Green Point 109
  Slangkop 167
Lion's Head 10, 147, **151**
listings magazines 236
literature 62–3
  Afrikaans 21–2
Lithuli, Albert 104
Little Karoo 194, 208, 209, **211–12**
Llandudno 10, **164**
Long Street 6, **93–5**
Long Street Baths 95
Lookout Hill 125
lost property 246
Lottering, Marc 64
Lutheran Church 96
Lwandle 125
Lwandle Migrant Labour Museum 125

M

Maclear's Beacon 152
Macmillan, Harold 43
Malan, D.F. 42, 43, 186
Malema, Julius 49
Malmesbury 199
Mandela, Nelson 49, 82
  imprisonment 45, 112–13, 140, 191, 192
  presidency and retirement 48
  release 47
  statue 104
  transition to democracy 47–8, 86
Marcus, Gill 25
marine life 183
Mariner's Wharf (Hout Bay) 165
Market Square (V&A Waterfront) 9, **183**
markets
  Grand Parade 81
  Green Point Flea Market 109
  Greenmarket Square Flea Market 94
  Hout Bay Craft Market 177
  Khayelitsha Craft Market 125
  Pan-African Market 94, 95
  Trafalgar Place Flower Market 83
Marsh, John H. 105
Martello Tower (Simon's Town) 170, 171
Martin Melck House 96
Masekala, Hugh 66
Mashile, Colbert 65
Masjid al Borhan 119
Masjid al Jami 119
Masjid Boorhaanol Islam 119
Mass Democratic Movement 47
Mbeki, Govan 112
Mbeki, Thabo 48–9
Mda, Zakes 63
media 246
medical facilities 245
Meerlust vineyards 202
Melck, Martin 96
Mellon, Niall 125
Michael Stevenson Contemporary 65
Michaelis, Sir Max 85
Military Museum 80
Mineral World (Simon's Town) 174–5
Mineral World (V&A Waterfront) 107
miners' strike (1922) 41
minibus taxis 222
missionary schools 123
Mixed Marriages Act (1949) 43
Mlangeni, Sabelo 65
mobile phones 248
Moederkerk (George) 208
Moederkerk (Worcester) 193
money 244, 246–7
money-saving tips 11
Monkeybiz 118
Monkeyland 215
Montagu Pass 210
Montebello Design Centre 133
Moravians 195
mosques
  Auwal Mosque 118–19
  Masjid al Borhan 119
  Masjid al Jami 119
  Masjid Boorhaanol Islam 119
  Nurul Islam Mosque 119
  Palm Tree Mosque 95
Mossel Bay **206–7**, 217,

233
Mostert's Mill 129
Mother City 17, 19
motorbike hire 222
Mouille Point 109
Mount Nelson Hotel 92, 93
mountain biking 155
mountain climbing 240
Mountbatten, Lord 86
Mowbray 129
MTN ScienCentre 241
Muholi, Zanele 65
Muizenberg 10, 53, 131, 160, **176–7**, 179
Muizenberg, Battle of 177
museums and galleries
Bartolomeu Dias Museum Complex (Mossel Bay) 207
Bronze Age Art Foundry, Gallery and Sculpture Garden (Simon's Town) 171
Cape Town Holocaust Centre 91–2
Chavonnes Cannon Battery Museum 108–9
C.P. Nel Museum (Oudtshoorn) 210
District Six Museum 8, 44, 59, **81–3**
Fish Hoek Valley Museum 175
George Museum 208
Gold of Africa Museum 8, 59, **95–6**
Heart of Cape Town Museum 132
Heritage Museum (Simon's Town) 171
Huguenot Memorial Museum (Franschhoek) 190
Irma Stern Museum 8, 66, **129–30**
Iziko Bertram House 93
Iziko Bo-Kaap Museum 8, **117–18**
Iziko Groot Constantia 139–40
Iziko Koopmans-De Wet House 8, **83–4**
Iziko Maritime Centre **105**, 169
Iziko Michaelis Collection 85
Iziko Rust en Vreugd 92–3
Iziko Slave Lodge Museum 86–7
Iziko South African Museum 8, **89–91**
Iziko South African National Gallery 65, **91**
Kruithuis (Stellenbosch) 186
Lwandle Migrant Labour Museum 125
Michael Stevenson Contemporary 65
Military Museum 80
MTN ScienCentre 241
Natale Labia Museum (Muizenberg) 177
Old Harbour Museum (Hermanus) 194
Old Town House 84–5
Paarl Museum 191
Robben Island 107–8, **112–13**
Rugby Museum 134
SA Naval Museum (Simon's Town) 169, **171**
Sasol Art Museum (Stellenbosch) 186
Simon's Town Museum 172–4
South African Jewish Museum 91
Stellenbosch Village Museum 11, **186–7**
William Fehr Collection 80, 92
music 63–4, 66, 235–6
live venues 237–8
shops 94, 108

N

Namaqua Wines 198–9
Napier 195
Natal 39
Natale Labia, Count 177
Natale Labia Museum (Muizenberg) 177
national anthem 48
National Arts Council 62
National Library of South Africa 86
national parks
Agulhas 195
Bontebok **196**, 232
Cape Peninsula *see* Table Mountain
Garden Route (Tsitsikamma Section) 215–16
Garden Route (Wilderness Section) 212–13
Table Mountain 10, 131, **147–55**, 157, 159, **168–9**
West Coast 197–8
National Party 20, 48
Nationalist Party 42, 192
Natives Land Act (1913) 40, 41
nature reserves
Cape of Good Hope Nature Reserve *see* Table Mountain National Park
De Hoop Nature Reserve **196**, 232
Featherbed Nature Reserve 214
Fernkloof Nature Reserve 194
Helderberg Nature Reserve 190
Hottentots Holland Nature Reserve 188
Jonkershoek Nature Reserve 188
Keurbooms River Nature Reserve 214–15
Kogelberg Biosphere Reserve 194–5
Paarl Mountain Nature Reserve 191
Robberg Nature Reserve 214
Salmonsdam Nature Reserve **195**, 232
Nature's Valley 216
Nederburg Estate **191–2**, 202
Nelson Mandela Gateway 107–8
Newlands **133–4**
restaurants, cafés and bars 143
Newlands Cricket Ground **134**, 135
Newlands Forest 131, 152
Newlands Rugby Stadium 134–5
newspapers 246
Ngema, Mbongeni 63
nightlife 237–9
Nobel Square 104
Nongawuza, Golden 125
Noon Gun **119**, 129
Noordhoek 10, **167**
Noordhoek Peak 167
nudist beaches 165
Nurul Islam Mosque 119
Nyanga 121
Nyasaland 43

O

Observatory **129**, 143
Old Harbour Museum (Hermanus) 194
Old Mutual Building 81
Old Synagogue 91
Old Town House 84–5
Olifants River Valley **198–9**, 202
Oliver Tambo Hall 125
On Broadway 237
Oom Samie's se Winkel (Stellenbosch) 186, 199
opening hours 247
opera 63, 64, 235–6
Orange Free State 37, 39
Orange Kloof Protected Area 153, 154
Orange River Valley 202
Organisation of African Unity (OAU) 42
orientation 77–9, 221
Orlando 42
Ossawa Brandwag 42
ostrich industry 209, 210
Oude Drostdy (near Tulbagh) 192
Oudekraal 164
Oudtshoorn **209–11**, 217, 233
outdoor gear 108
Outeniqua Mountains 207, 208
Overberg 183, **193–6**, 201, 232

P

Paarl 183, **191**, 200, 201, 202, 232
Paarl Mountain Nature Reserve 191
Paarl Museum 191
Paarl Wine Route 191–2
packing 249
Palm Tree Mosque 95
Pan Africanist Congress (PAC) 42, 44, 112, 113
Pan-African Market 94, 95
parks and gardens

Abalimi Bezekhaya Peace Park and Community Garden 125
Botanical Garden (Stellenbosch) 186
Botanical Society Conservatory (Kirstenbsoch) 137–8
Company's Garden 32, 35, 59, **88–9**
Harold Porter National Botanical Gardens 194
Iziko Rust en Vreugd 92
Karoo Desert National Botanical Garden (Worcester) 193
Kirstenbosch National Botanical Garden 7, 10, 34, **135–8**
Peninsula Garden (Kirstenbosch) 138
Parow 21
Paternoster 198
Pearson, Professor 137
Peers Cave 175
Pemba, George 65
penguins 169–70
Peninsula Garden (Kirstenbosch) 138
people 19–25
Petersen, Oscar 63
pharmacies 245
Pipe Track 149, **151**
Plaatje, Sol 40
Planetarium 90–1, 241
Platteklip Gorge 10, 148, **151–2**
Plattekloof 21
Plettenberg Bay 214, 217, 233
police 244
brutality 46, 47
political prisoners 45, 107, 112
politics 19–20, 21, 48, 49, 86
Portuguese explorers 31–2
Post Office Tree (Mossel Bay) 207
postal services 247
Prince Albert 211
proteas 138, 153, 156–7
public holidays 247
public transport 221–2

R

racial integration 19
racial mix 20
racism *see* **apartheid**
radio 246
rafting 240
rail travel 11, 220, 222
Outeniqua Choo Tjoe 208
Rampolokeng, Lesego 63
Ras, Catharina 140
Red Shed Craft Workshop 103
religion
African Indigenous Churches (AIC) 23–4
Christianity in the townships 123, 124
religious services 247
Remix Dance Company 64
Republic of South Africa 45
restaurants, bars and cafés 56
see also separate listing
Bo-Kaap 119
Cape Peninsula 178–9
City Centre 97–9
Further Afield 200–1
Garden Route 217
Southern Suburbs 142–3
Rex, George 213
Rhebokskloof Winery 192
Rhodes, Cecil John 37, **130**
Company's Garden 89
Cottage (Muizenberg) 131, **177**
Groote Schuur 67, **132–3**
Kirstenbosch 136–7
Rhodes Memorial 67, **130–1**
Rhodes Cottage (Muizenberg) 131, **177**
Rhodes Memorial 67, **130–1**
Rhodesia 43, 45, 130
riots 45, 46
Rive, Richard 24
Riversdale 206
Rivonia trials 45
road travel 221, 222
Robben Island 6, 45, 107–8, **112–13**, 118
Robberg Nature Reserve 214
Robinson Pass 210
rock art, San 90, 199, 211
rock climbing 155
rock music 238
Rondebosch 132–3
Rosebank 129–31
Royal Navy 171, 172, 173
Royal Observatory 129
rugby 52, 134–5, 240–1
Rugby Museum 134
running 240
Rust-en-Vrede (Muizenberg) 177
Rust-en-Vrede winery 189
Rustenberg Estate 189

S

Sachs, Albie 25
Safari Ostrich Farm 210–11
safety 243–4
hiking 152
St George's Cathedral 67, **85–6**
St George's Mall 83
St James 10, 160, **176**
St Peter the Fisherman (Hout Bay) 166
St Saviour's Church 135
Saldanha Bay 198, 232
Salmonsdam Nature Reserve 195, 232
Salt River 128–9
San people 31, 90, 199, 211
Sandy Bay 164–5
Sasol Art Museum (Stellenbosch) 186
Scarborough 167–8
Scratch Patch 9, **105–7**, 174
Sea Point 109, 148, **160–1**, 178, 229–30
Sea Point Public Pool 161
sea travel 221
seafood 59
Seal Island 9, 207
seals, Cape fur 166, 207, 214
Searle, Berni 65
Second Beach 163
sedan taxis 222
Sekoto, Gerard 65
Sephuma, Judith 66
Serote, Wally 63
"Sestigers" movement 21–2
Seweweekspoort Pass 211–12
shanty towns, bulldozing of 43, 44, 82
sharks 175, 207
Sharpeville massacre 44–5, 124
shipwrecks 169, 174
shopping
Cape Peninsula 177
with children 241
City Centre 94
Southern Suburbs 134, 135
Stellenbosch and Franschhoek 199
V&A Waterfront 103–4, **108**
sightseeing tours 239–40
Signal Hill 8, 109, 118, 119, 147, 148
Simon's Town 160, **170–5**, 179, 230–1
Simon's Town Museum 172–4
Simonsberg 188
Simonsvlei 192
Sisulu, Walter 45, 112
Sivuyile Tourism Centre 124–5
Skeleton Gorge 152
Slangkop Lighthouse 167
slavery 20, 24, 33, 34–6
Slave Lodge 85, 86–7
Slovo, Joe 122
Small, Adam 24
Smith, Ian 45
Smuts, Jan 41, 42, 186
snakes 155
Sobopha, Mgcineni "Pro" 65
Sobukwe, Robert 42, 44, 45, 112, 113
Somerset, Lord Charles 88, 164, 192
Somerset West 189
South African Breweries 134
South African Jewish Museum 91
South African National Congress 41
South African Naval Museum (Simon's Town) 169, **171**
South African War *see* **Anglo-Boer War**
Southern Suburbs 127–41

accommodation 228
restaurants, bars and cafés 142–3
Soweto 23, 42, 44, 46, 192
Spier Estate 11, **189**
sports 52–3, 155, **240–1**
Sports Science Institute 134
Stanford 195
Steenberg Wine Estate 140–1
Stellenbosch 7, 183, **185–8**, 202
accommodation 231
nightlife 187
restaurants, bars and cafés 200
shopping 199
Stellenbosch Mountains 188
Stellenbosch Village Museum 11, **186–7**
Stern, Irma 66, 129–30
Stevin, Simon 79
Stone Age 31
Storms River 216, 233
Strooidakkerk (Paarl) 191
student travellers 247–8
surfing 53, 164, 240
Suzman, Helen 25, 91
Swartberg Pass 211
Swartland 199
Swellendam 196, 201, 206, 232

T

Table Bay 160
Table Bay Hotel 103
Table Mountain 7, **148–52**
Table Mountain Cableway 9, **149**, 151
Table Mountain National Park 10, 131, **147–55**, 159
Cape of Good Hope Section 157, **168–9**
conservation 150
Tana Baru Karamat 119
tax 248
taxis 11, 222
telephones 248
television 246
theatre 63, 236–7
Theatre on the Bay 237
Thesen House (Knysna) 213
Theuniskraal Estate 192
Thibault, Louis Michel 86, 89, 192
Third Beach 162–3
Thwaites, Edmund 64
tickets and passes 11, 235
Tillim, Guy 65
time zone 248
tipping 56, 247
toilets 248
tour operators and travel agents 248–9
tourist information 82, 107, **249**
Touws River 212, 213
The Townships 22–4, 42, **121–5**
accommodation 224
Trafalgar Place Flower Market 83
Transkei 121
transport 11, **220–2**
Transvaal 37, 39
Truth and Reconciliation Commission 48
Tsafendas, Demetri 45–6
Tsitsikamma 206, 212, **215–16**, 233
Tsoga Environmental Centre 124
Tuan Guru 118–19
Tuan Sayed Alawie 119
Tulbagh 192, 201
Tutu, Archbishop Desmond 22, 47, 48, 49, 85, 86
statue 104
Tuynhuys 88
Twelve Apostles 149, 153, **163**
Two Oceans Aquarium 7, 9, 103, **104–5**, 241
Tygervalley 21

U

Union of South Africa 39, 86
United Democratic Front 47
United Nations 42
University of Cape Town 46, 130, **132**
University of Stellenbosch 186
University of the Western Cape 46
Uys, Pieter Dirk 64, 197

V

van der Merwe Mysewski (architects) 67
van der Stel, Simon 22, 89, 139, 141, 170, 185, 202
van der Stel, Willem Adriaan 87, 189
van Riebeeck, Jan 32, 33, 34, 79, 89, 148, 202
Vergelegen 11, **189**, 202
Vergenoegd Estate 189
Verwoerd, Hendrik 21, 45
Verwoerd, Melanie 21
Victor Verster Prison (near Paarl) 192
Victoria and Alfred Hotel 104
Victoria and Alfred Waterfront 6, 9, **101–9**
accommodation 226–7
restaurants and bars 110–11
shopping 108
Victoria, Queen 37, 88, 102
Victoria Wharf 103
Victorian architecture 37
Villion, François 22
Vineyard Trail 188
visas and passports 249
vital statistics 20
VOC *see* **Dutch East India Company**
Voortrekkers 36–7
Vredendal 198

W

Waalburg Building 81
Walker Bay 194
walking *see* **hiking and trekking**
walking tours 240
Watts, George Frederick 130
Welgemoed 21
Wellington 192
West Coast 196–9, 201, 232
West Coast National Park 197–8
Western Cape Province 183
whale-watching 9, 170, **194**
Wilderness 212–13, 233
wildlife 9
see also **national parks; nature reserves**
Aquila Private Game Reserve 9, **194**
Birds of Eden 215
Cango Wildlife Ranch 211
Cape Fur Seals 166, 207, 214
Cape Point Ostrich Farm **169**, 241
Knysna Elephant Park 215
marine life 183
Monkeyland 215
penguins 169–70
Safari Ostrich Farm 210–11
sharks 175, 207
Table Mountain National Park 154–5
Two Oceans Aquarium 7, 9, 103, **104–5**, 241
whale-watching 9, 170, **194**
World of Birds 9, 166–7, **166–7**, 241
William Fehr Collection 80, 92
William of Orange, Prince 79
wine 202–3
best wine estates 11
Cape Winelands **185–93**
Constantia Valley 139–41
shops 94, 108, 199
women travellers 249
Woodstock 128
restaurants, cafés and bars 143
Woolworths 83
Worcester 192–3
World of Birds 9, 166–7, **166–7**, 241
World War I 40, 42, 173–4
World War II 42, 92
Wynberg 138

X, Y, Z

Xhosa people 36, 44
Yusuf, Sheik 35
Zille, Helen 20, 49
Zimbabwe 46, 130
Zuma, Jacob 49